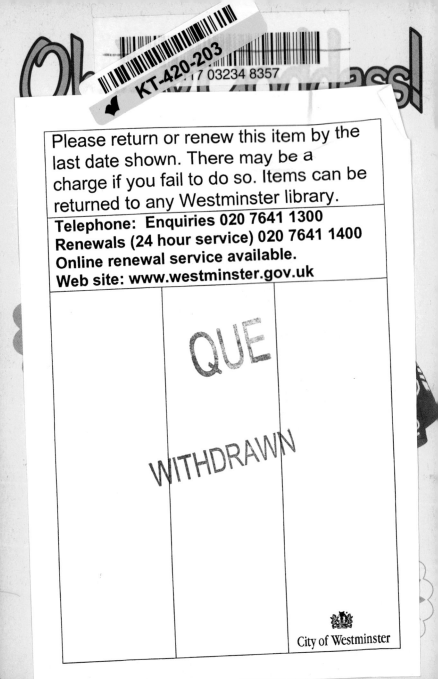

KT-420-203

7 03234 8357

Please return or renew this item by the last date shown. There may be a charge if you fail to do so. Items can be returned to any Westminster library.

**Telephone: Enquiries 020 7641 1300**
**Renewals (24 hour service) 020 7641 1400**
**Online renewal service available.**
**Web site: www.westminster.gov.uk**

QUE

WITHDRAWN

City of Westminster

# WHO'S WHO
## IN OH MY GODDESS!

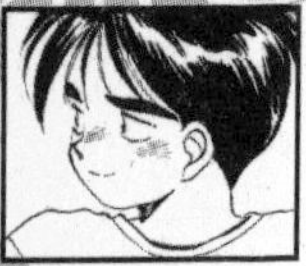

**KEIICHI MORISATO** — Student. Doofus. He was quite content to enjoy a quiet life before the sudden arrival of a magical being named Belldandy... now all he wants is some time alone with her... and away from her pesky sisters!

**BELLDANDY** — Goddess. Beauty. Granter of wishes. When Keiichi accidentally dials the Goddess Technical Hotline, he inadvertently summons Belldandy into his dorm room. Her only goal in life is to make everybody happy now she's a part of humanity.

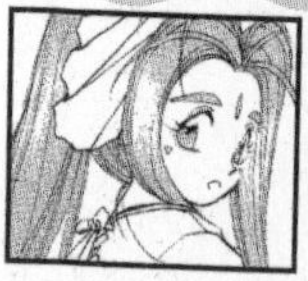

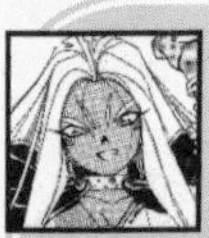

**URD** — Bell's mischievous sister. Her frequent efforts to bring Keichii and Bell together often cause more trouble than it's worth! Hasn't shown any signs of megalomaniacal tendencies. Yet.

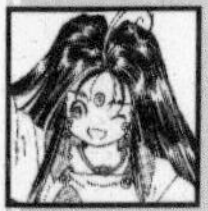

**SKULD** — Belldandy's not-so-mischevious sister. Actually has a pretty smart brain between her pretty ears. Her off-the-cuff inventions are often patent pending.

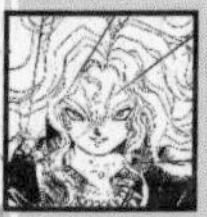

**MARA** — Trouble comes in many different sizes... and this Demon has plenty of differently sized terrors in her bag of tricks to inflict upon our happy couple!

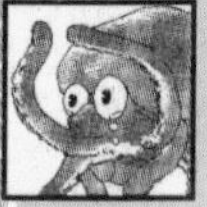

**THE BOOSTERS** — Acephalic Cephalapods love chocolate. Any chocolate. Even if it's evil.

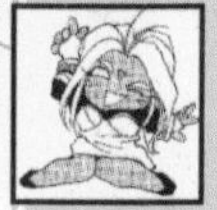

**MINI-URD** — She's cute isn't she. No, really!

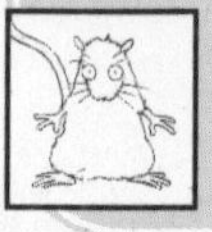

**MR. RAT** — ...has absolutely no reason to be on this list. Sheesh!

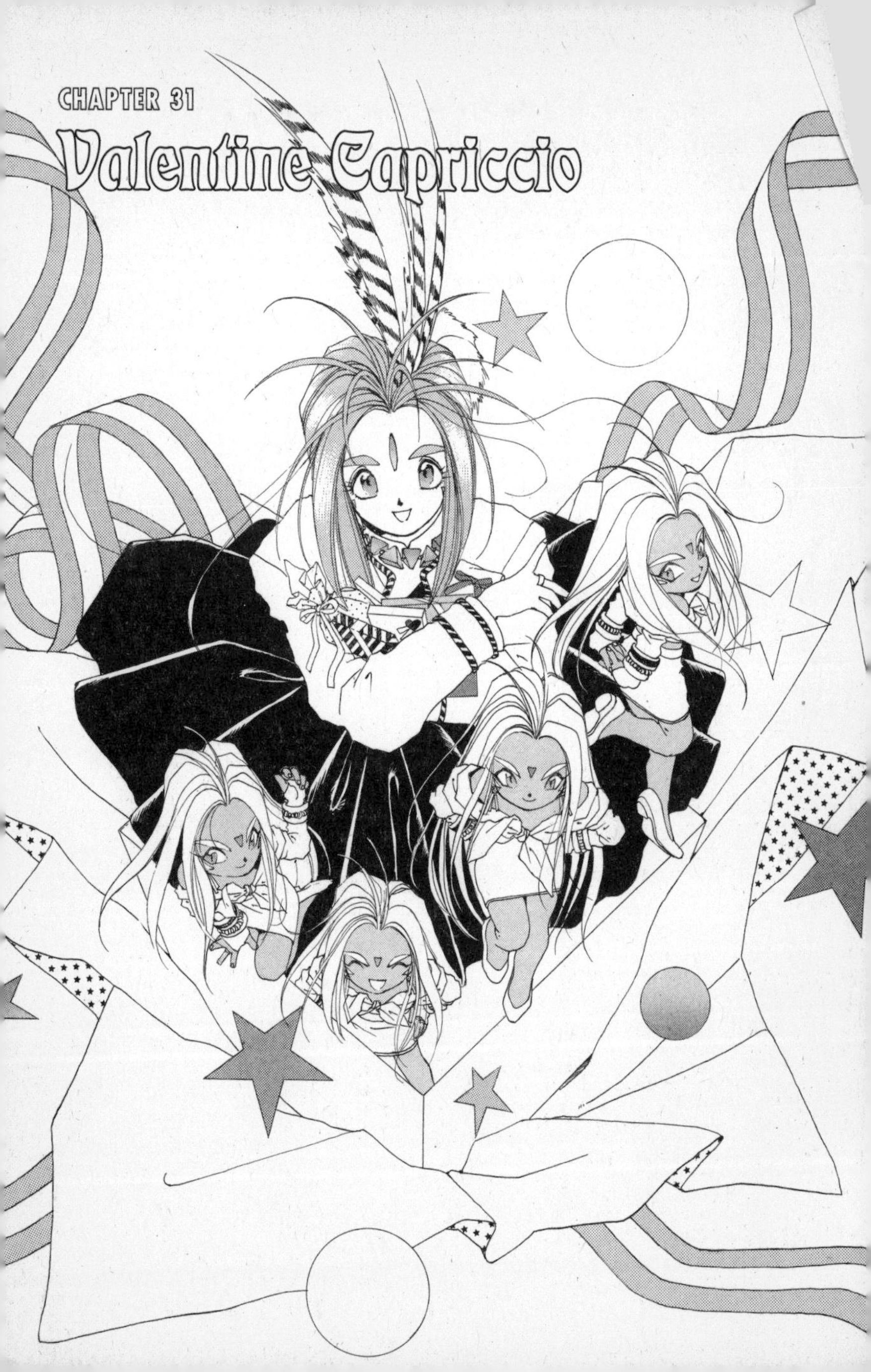
CHAPTER 31
Valentine Capriccio

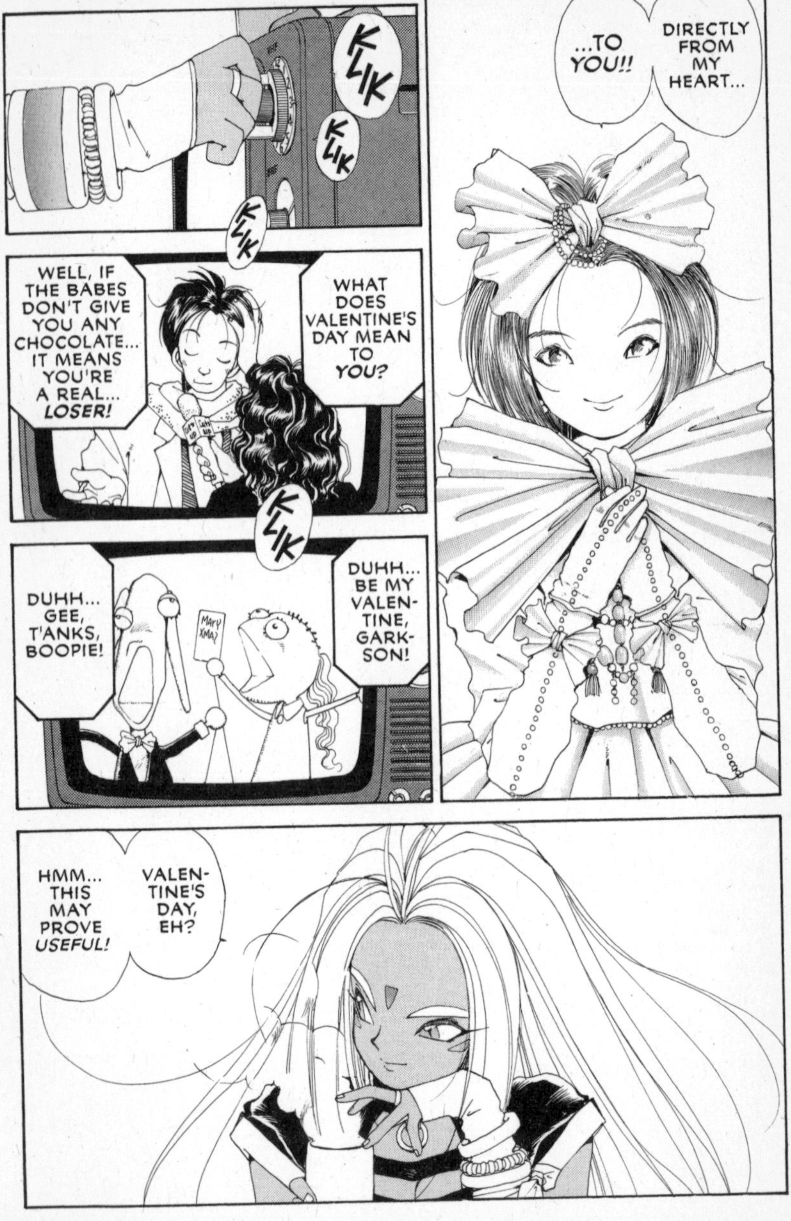
DIRECTLY FROM MY HEART...
...TO *YOU!!*
KLIK
KLIK
KLIK
WHAT DOES VALENTINE'S DAY MEAN TO *YOU?*
WELL, IF THE BABES DON'T GIVE YOU ANY CHOCOLATE... IT MEANS YOU'RE A REAL... ***LOSER!***
KLIK
DUHH... BE MY VALENTINE, GARKSON!
DUHH... GEE, T'ANKS, BOOPIE!
VALENTINE'S DAY, EH?
HMM... THIS MAY PROVE *USEFUL!*

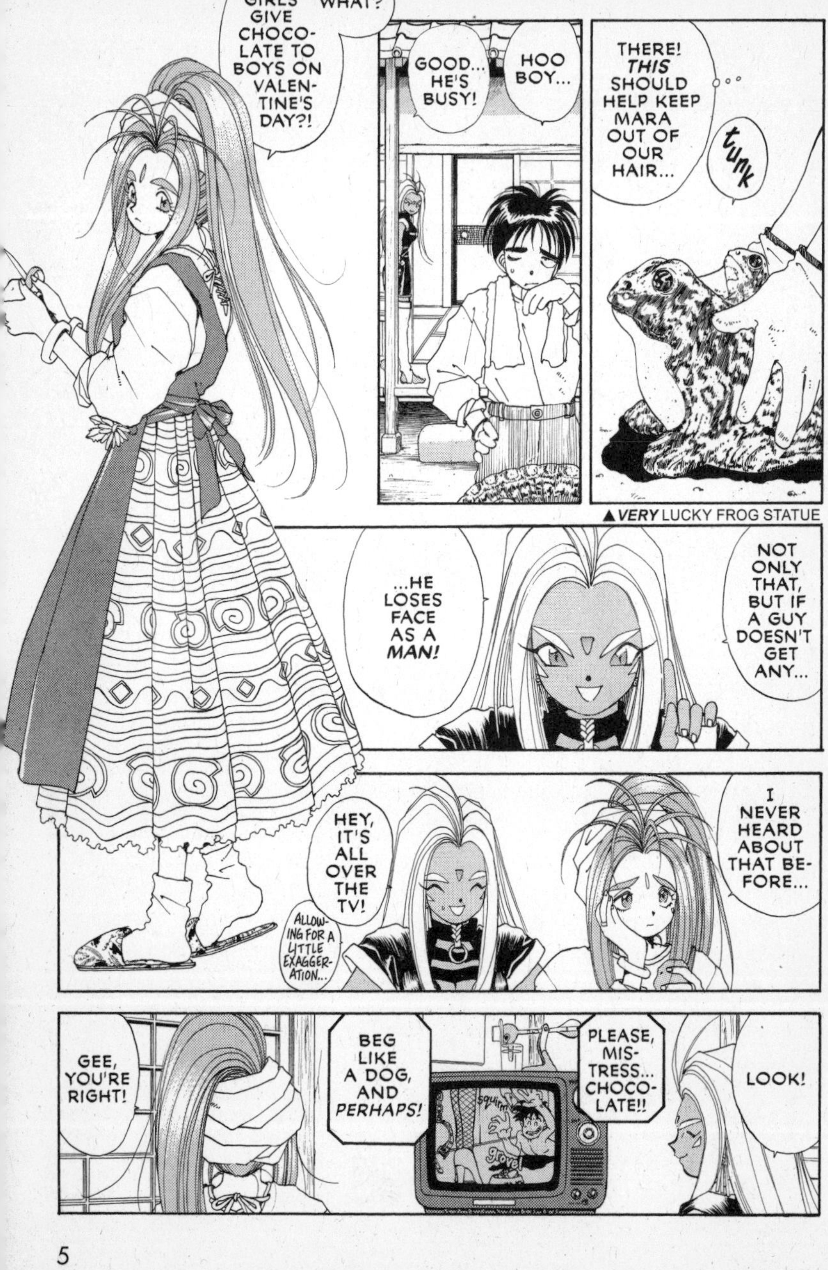
THERE! *THIS* SHOULD HELP KEEP MARA OUT OF OUR HAIR...
tunk
▲*VERY* LUCKY FROG STATUE
HOO BOY...
GOOD... HE'S BUSY!
WHAT?
GIRLS GIVE CHOCOLATE TO BOYS ON VALENTINE'S DAY?!
NOT ONLY THAT, BUT IF A GUY DOESN'T GET ANY...
...HE LOSES FACE AS A *MAN!*
I NEVER HEARD ABOUT THAT BEFORE...
HEY, IT'S ALL OVER THE TV!
ALLOWING FOR A LITTLE EXAGGERATION...
LOOK!
PLEASE, MISTRESS... CHOCOLATE!!
squirm
grovel
BEG LIKE A DOG, AND *PERHAPS!*
GEE, YOU'RE RIGHT!

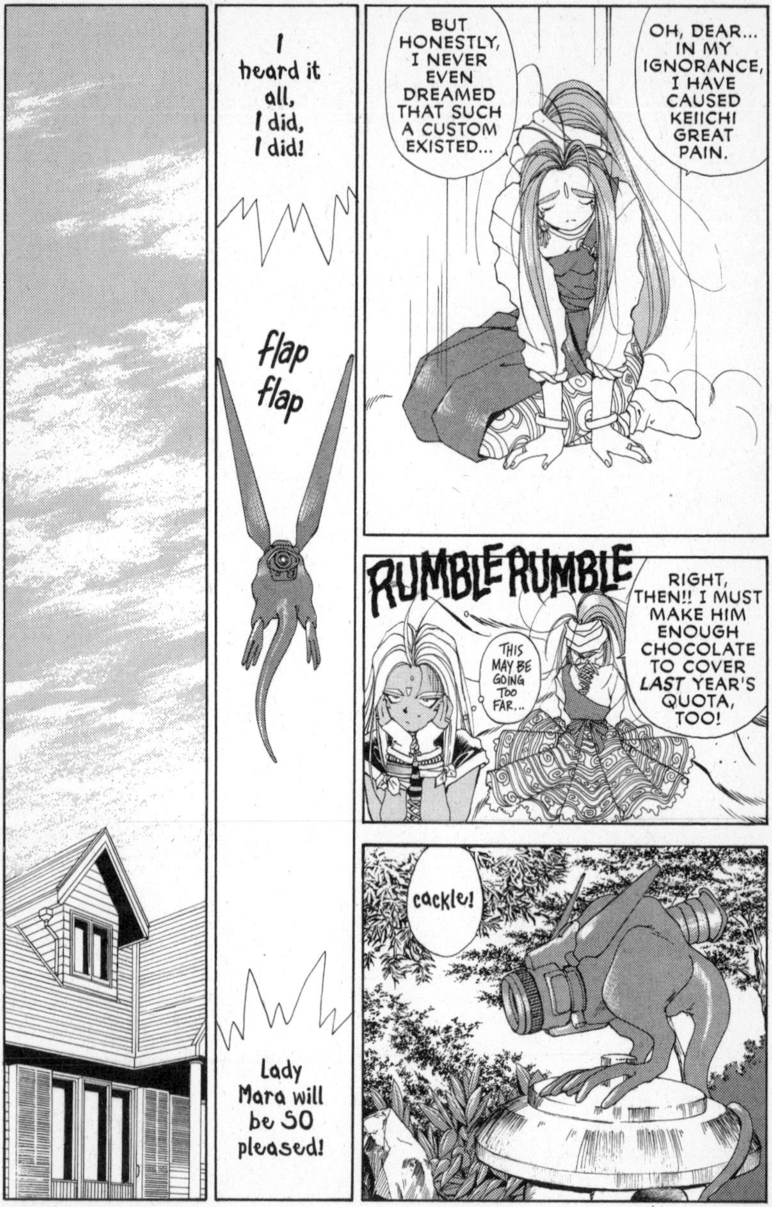
OH, DEAR... IN MY IGNORANCE, I HAVE CAUSED KEIICHI GREAT PAIN.
BUT HONESTLY, I NEVER EVEN DREAMED THAT SUCH A CUSTOM EXISTED...
RUMBLE RUMBLE
RIGHT, THEN!! I MUST MAKE HIM ENOUGH CHOCOLATE TO COVER *LAST* YEAR'S QUOTA, TOO!
THIS MAY BE GOING TOO FAR...
cackle!
I heard it all, I did, I did!
flap flap
Lady Mara will be SO pleased!

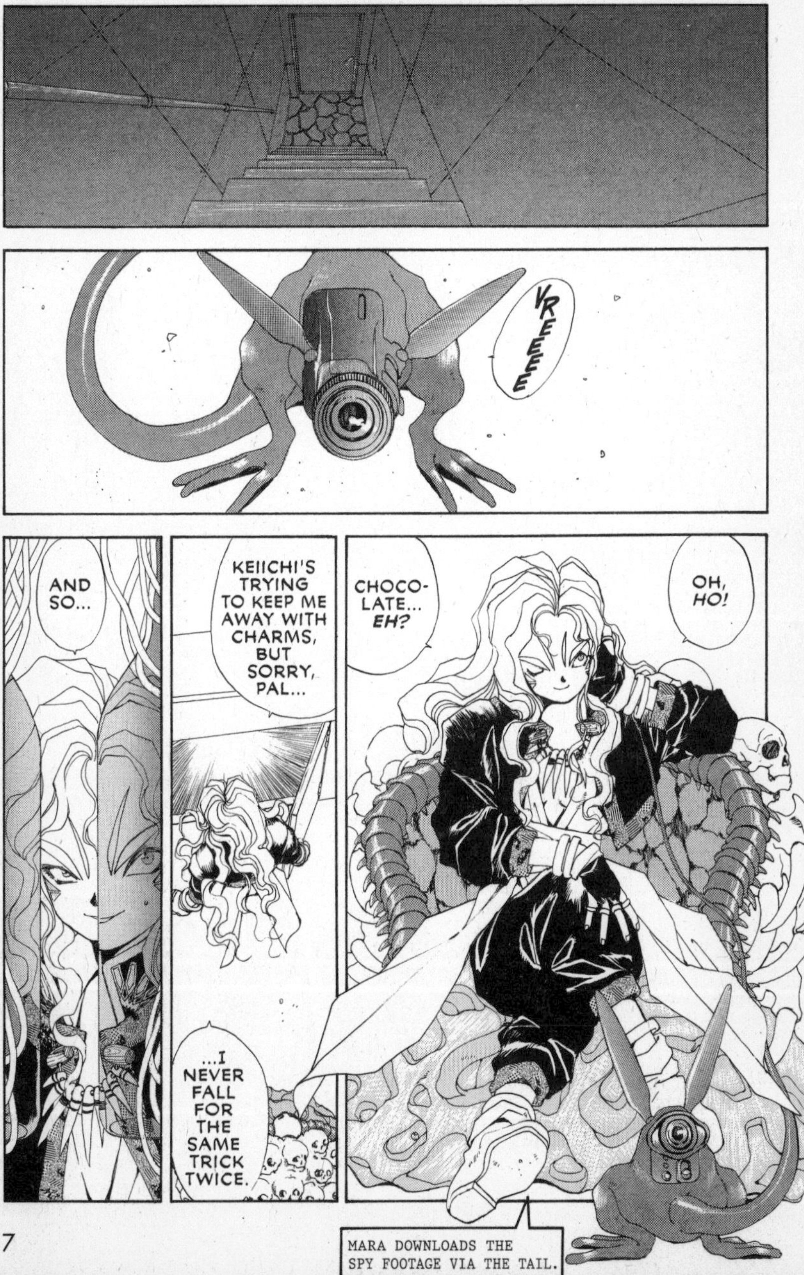
VREEEE
OH, HO!
CHOCOLATE... EH?
KEIICHI'S TRYING TO KEEP ME AWAY WITH CHARMS, BUT SORRY, PAL...
...I NEVER FALL FOR THE SAME TRICK TWICE.
AND SO...
MARA DOWNLOADS THE SPY FOOTAGE VIA THE TAIL.

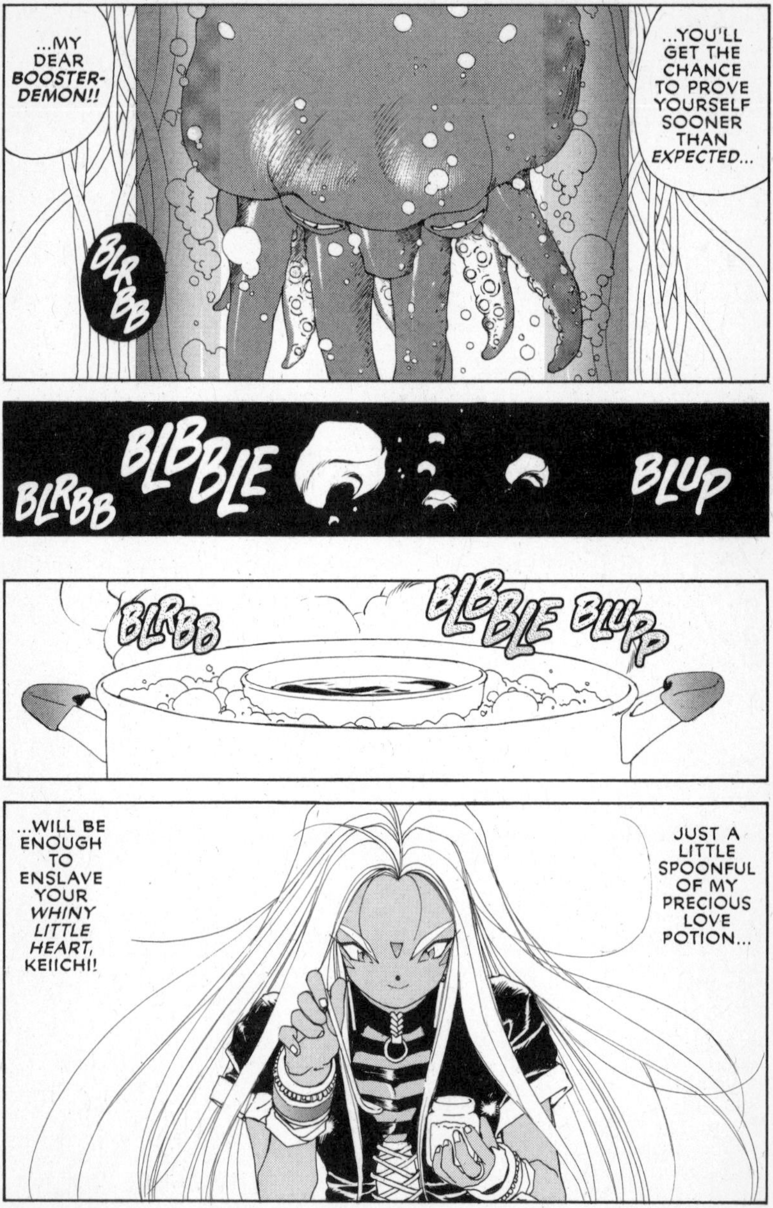
...YOU'LL GET THE CHANCE TO PROVE YOURSELF SOONER THAN *EXPECTED*...
...MY DEAR *BOOSTER-DEMON!!*
BLRBB
BLUP
BLBBLE
BLRBB
BLBBLE BLUPP
BLRBB
JUST A LITTLE SPOONFUL OF MY PRECIOUS LOVE POTION...
...WILL BE ENOUGH TO ENSLAVE YOUR *WHINY LITTLE HEART,* KEIICHI!

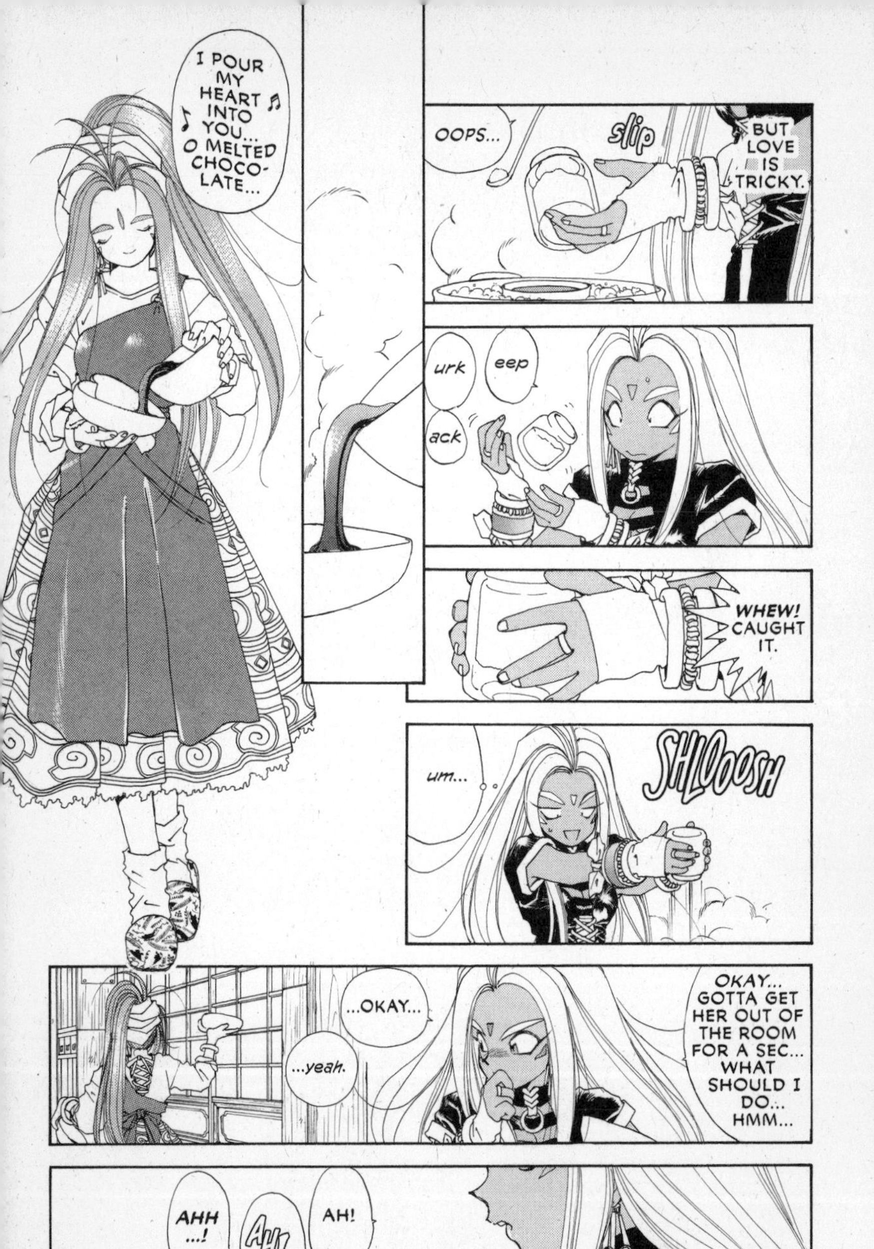
BUT LOVE IS TRICKY.
slip
OOPS...
eep
urk
ack
WHEW! CAUGHT IT.
SHLOOOSH
um...
I POUR MY HEART INTO YOU... O MELTED CHOCOLATE...
OKAY... GOTTA GET HER OUT OF THE ROOM FOR A SEC... WHAT SHOULD I DO... HMM...
...OKAY...
...yeah.
AH!
AHH ...!
AH!

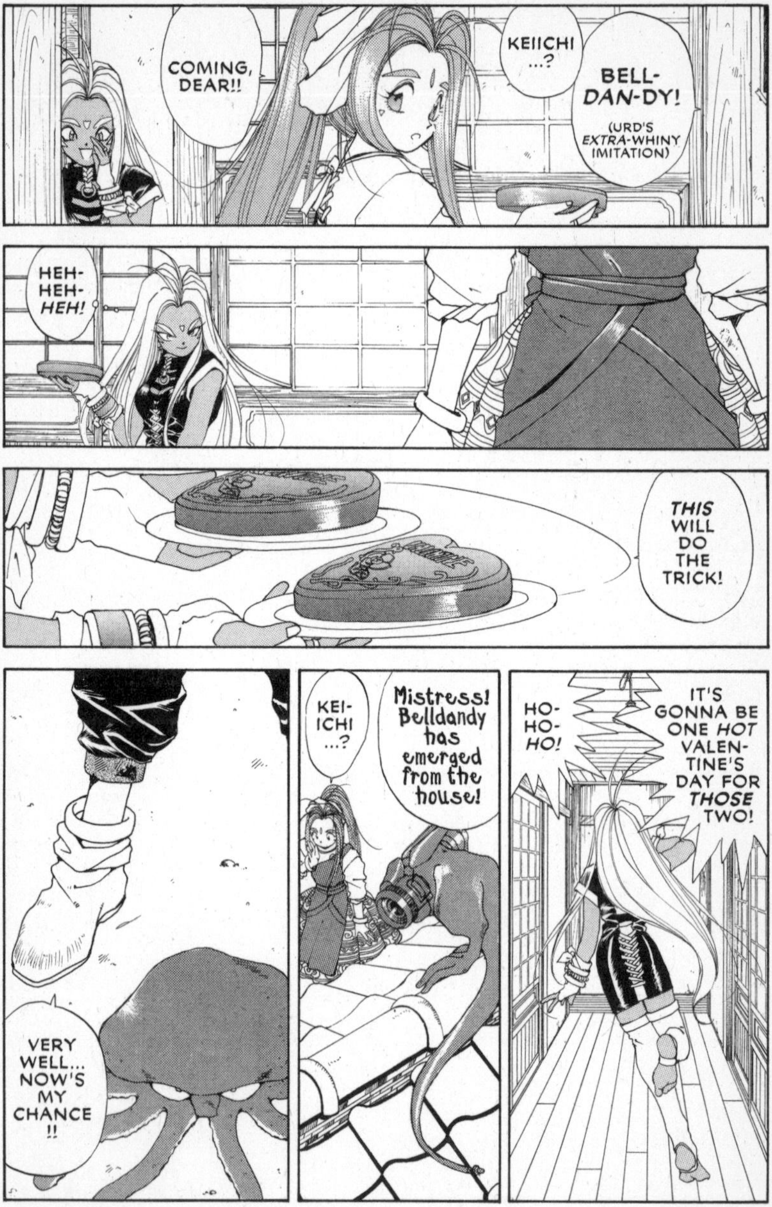
BELL-DAN-DY!
(URD'S EXTRA-WHINY IMITATION)
KEIICHI ...?
COMING, DEAR!!
HEH-HEH-HEH!
THIS WILL DO THE TRICK!
IT'S GONNA BE ONE HOT VALENTINE'S DAY FOR THOSE TWO!
HO-HO-HO!
Mistress! Belldandy has emerged from the house!
KEI-ICHI ...?
VERY WELL... NOW'S MY CHANCE !!

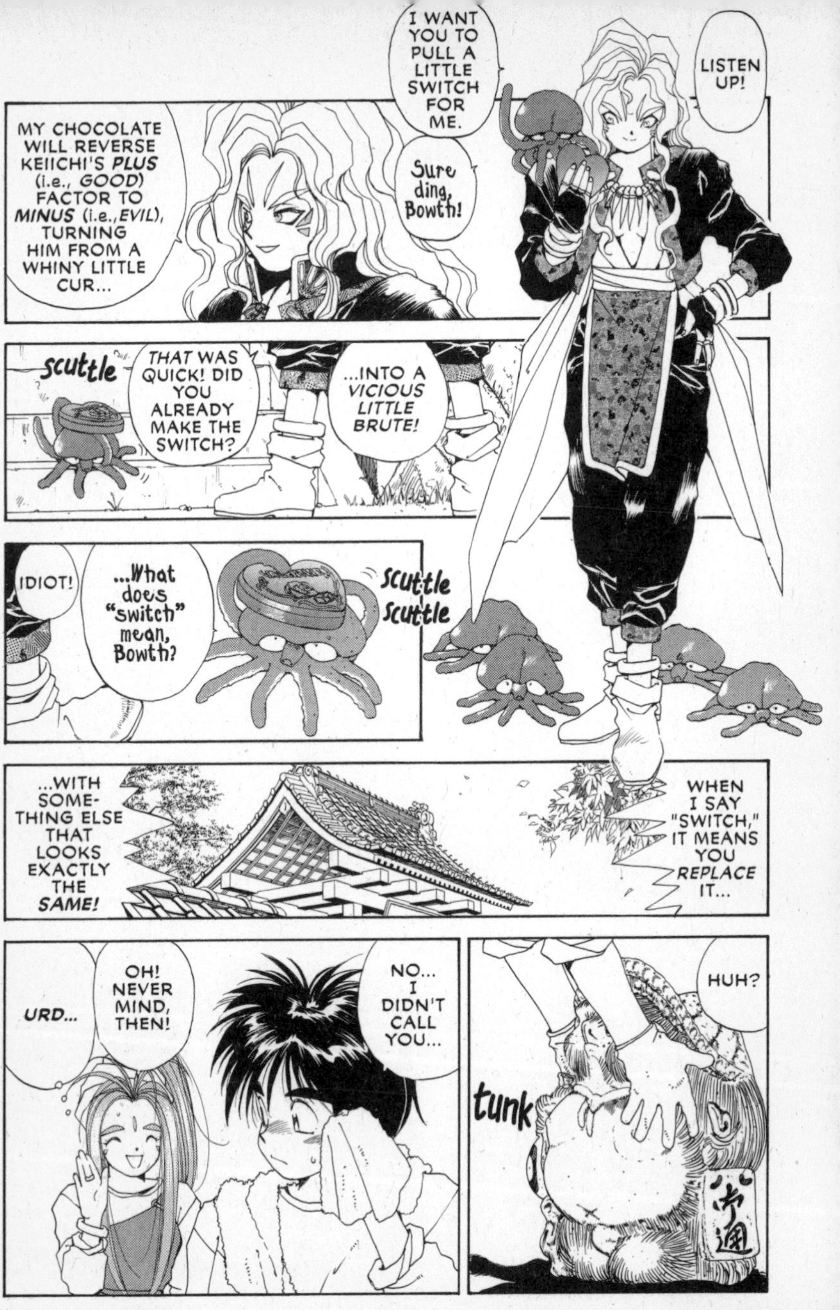

LISTEN UP!
I WANT YOU TO PULL A LITTLE SWITCH FOR ME.
Sure ding, Bowth!
MY CHOCOLATE WILL REVERSE KEIICHI'S *PLUS* (i.e., *GOOD*) FACTOR TO *MINUS* (i.e., *EVIL*), TURNING HIM FROM A WHINY LITTLE CUR...
...INTO A *VICIOUS LITTLE BRUTE!*
*THAT* WAS QUICK! DID YOU ALREADY MAKE THE SWITCH?
scuttle
scuttle scuttle
...What does "switch" mean, Bowth?
IDIOT!
WHEN I SAY "SWITCH," IT MEANS YOU *REPLACE* IT...
...WITH SOMETHING ELSE THAT LOOKS EXACTLY THE *SAME!*
HUH?
tunk
NO... I DIDN'T CALL YOU...
OH! NEVER MIND, THEN!
*URD...*

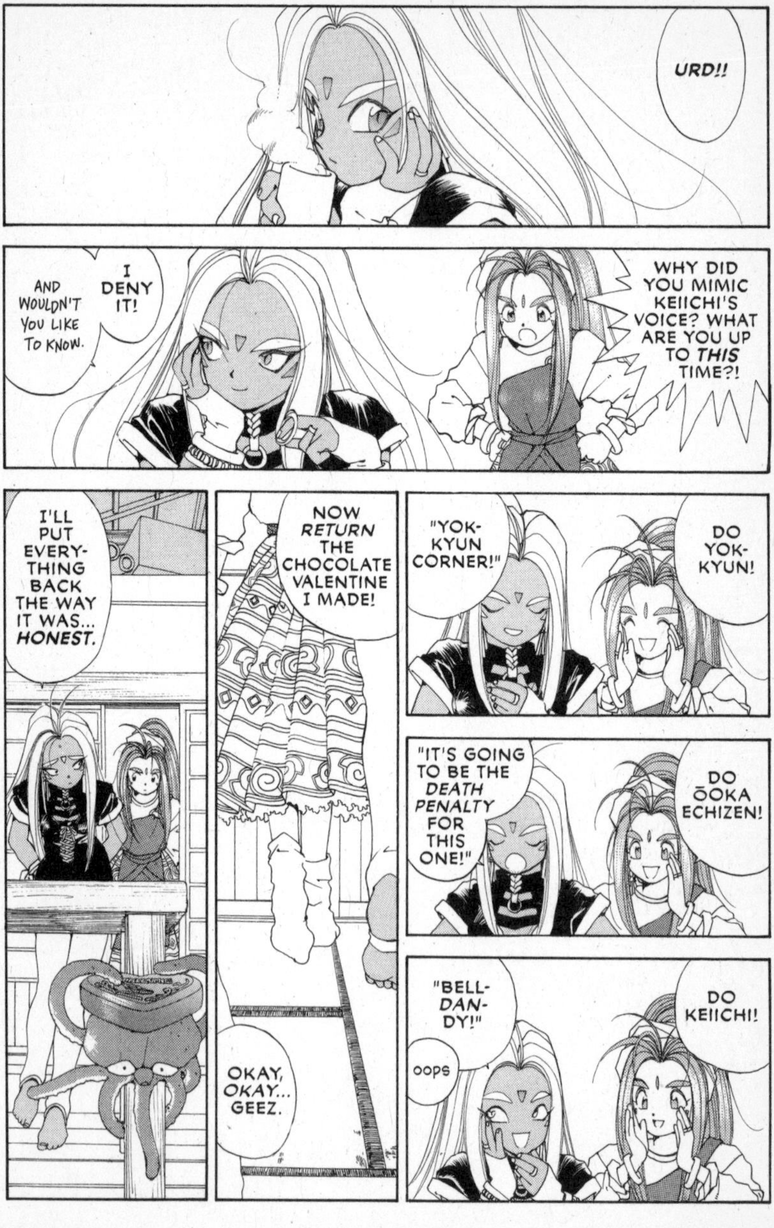
URD!!
WHY DID YOU MIMIC KEIICHI'S VOICE? WHAT ARE YOU UP TO THIS TIME?!
I DENY IT!
AND WOULDN'T YOU LIKE TO KNOW.
DO YOK-KYUN!
"YOK-KYUN CORNER!"
DO ŌOKA ECHIZEN!
"IT'S GOING TO BE THE DEATH PENALTY FOR THIS ONE!"
DO KEIICHI!
"BELL-DAN-DY!"
oops
NOW RETURN THE CHOCOLATE VALENTINE I MADE!
OKAY, OKAY... GEEZ.
I'LL PUT EVERY-THING BACK THE WAY IT WAS... HONEST.

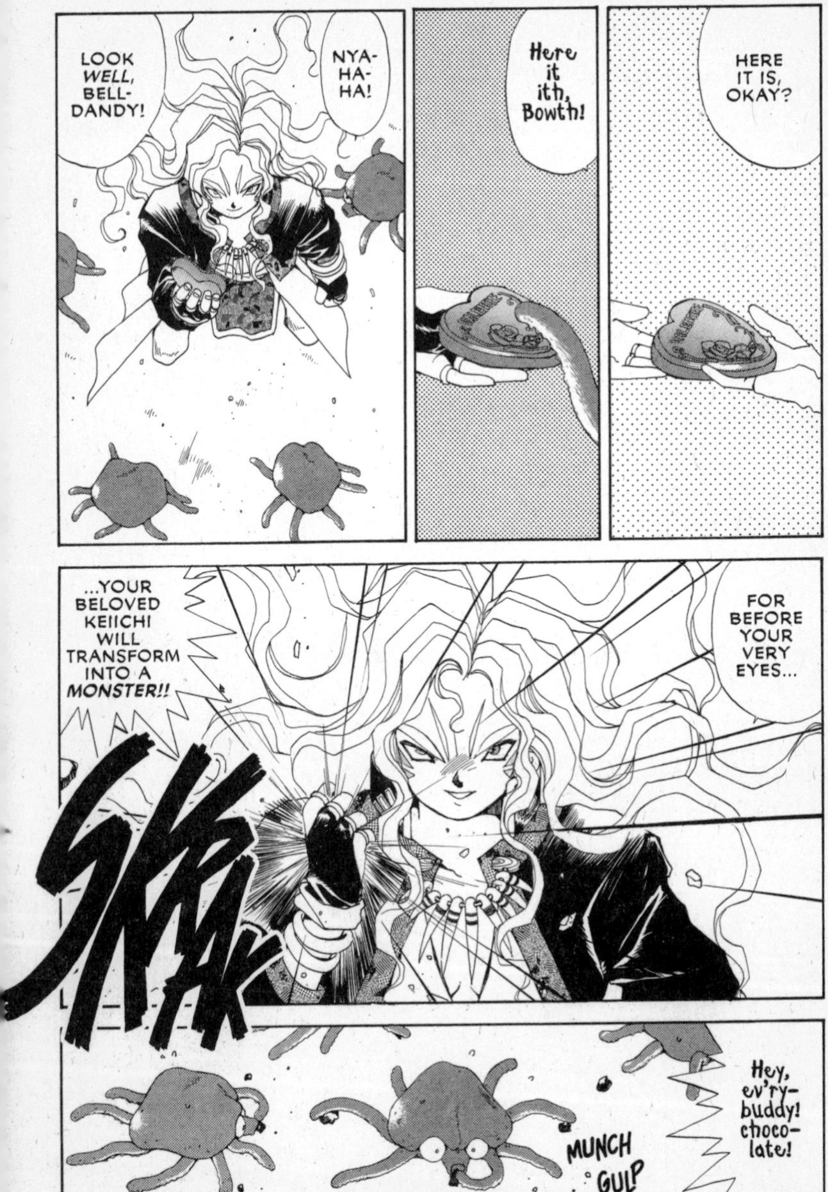

HERE IT IS, OKAY?
Here it ith, Bowth!
NYA-HA-HA!
LOOK WELL, BELL-DANDY!
FOR BEFORE YOUR VERY EYES...
...YOUR BELOVED KEIICHI WILL TRANSFORM INTO A MONSTER!!
Hey, ev'ry-buddy! chocolate!
MUNCH GULP

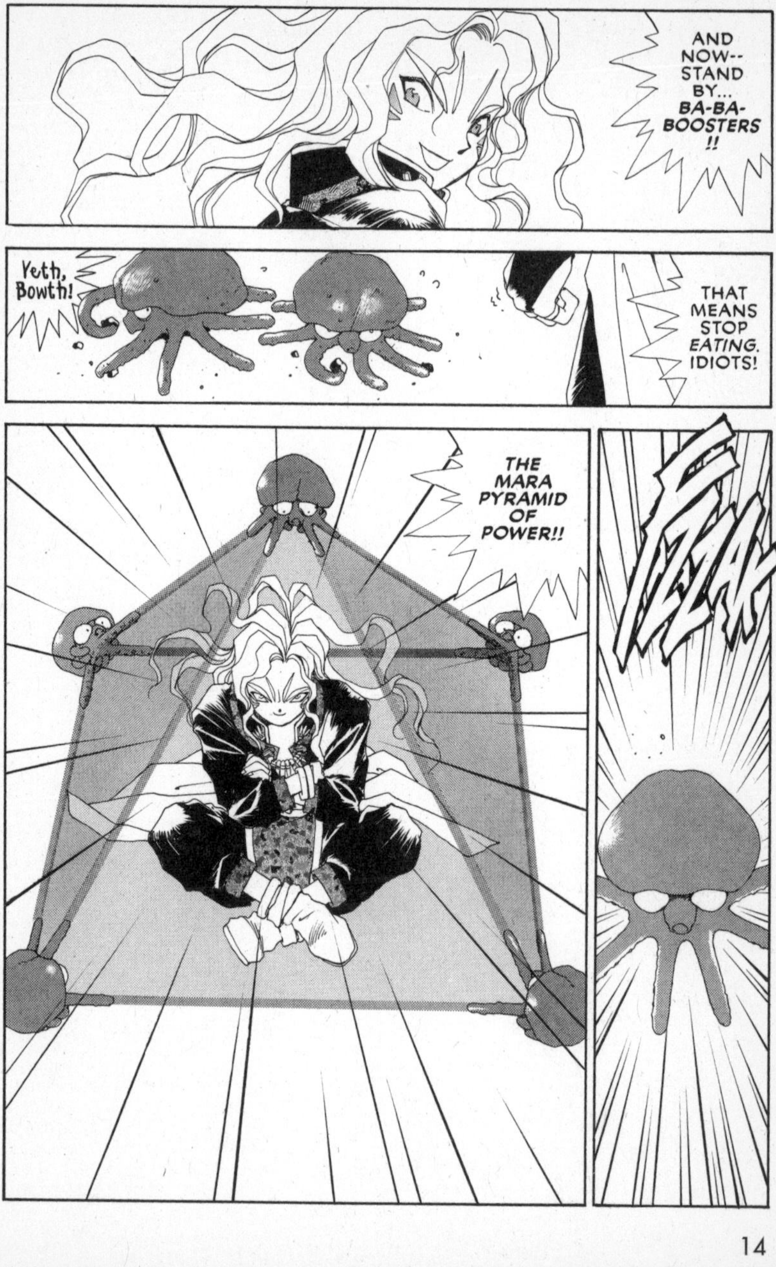
AND NOW-- STAND BY... BA-BA-BOOSTERS !!
THAT MEANS STOP EATING. IDIOTS!
Yeth, Bowth!
ZZAK
THE MARA PYRAMID OF POWER!!

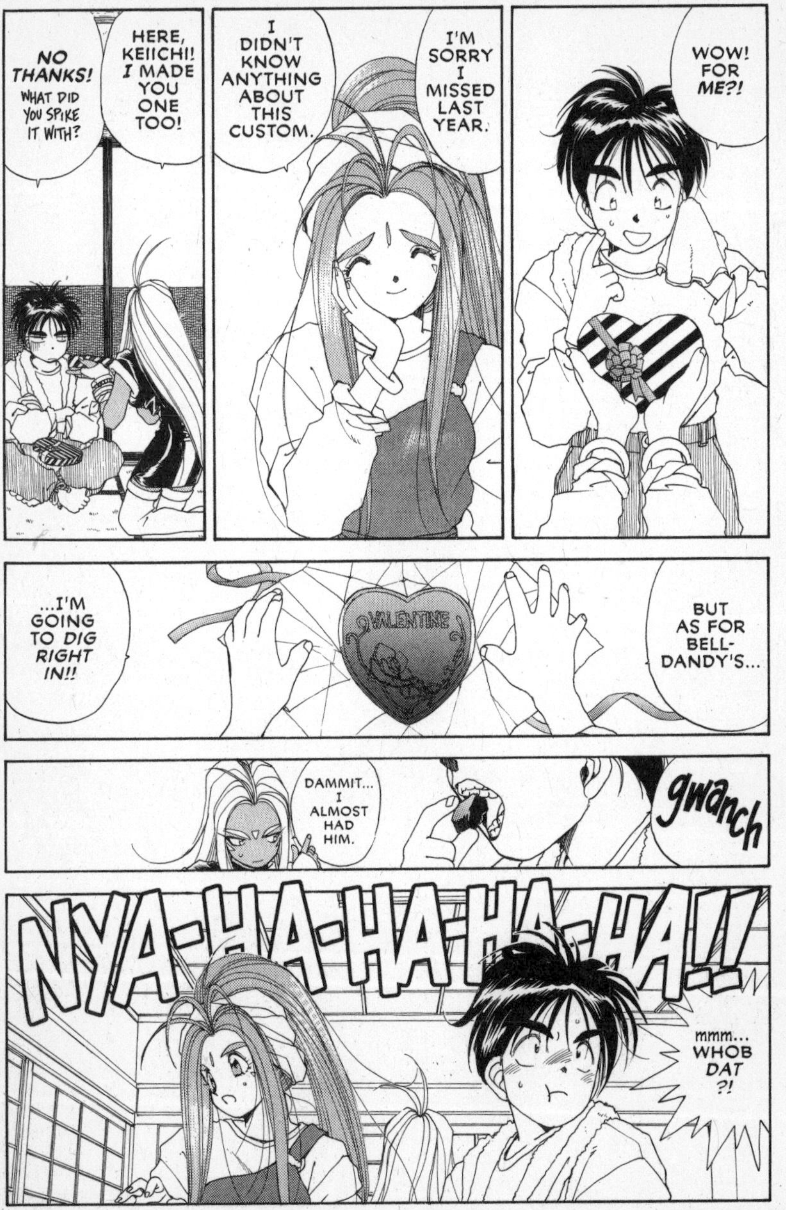
WOW! FOR ME?!
I'M SORRY I MISSED LAST YEAR.
I DIDN'T KNOW ANYTHING ABOUT THIS CUSTOM.
HERE, KEIICHI! I MADE YOU ONE TOO!
NO THANKS! WHAT DID YOU SPIKE IT WITH?
BUT AS FOR BELL-DANDY'S...
VALENTINE
...I'M GOING TO DIG RIGHT IN!!
gwanch
DAMMIT... I ALMOST HAD HIM.
NYA-HA-HA-HA-HA-HA!!
mmm... WHOB DAT ?!

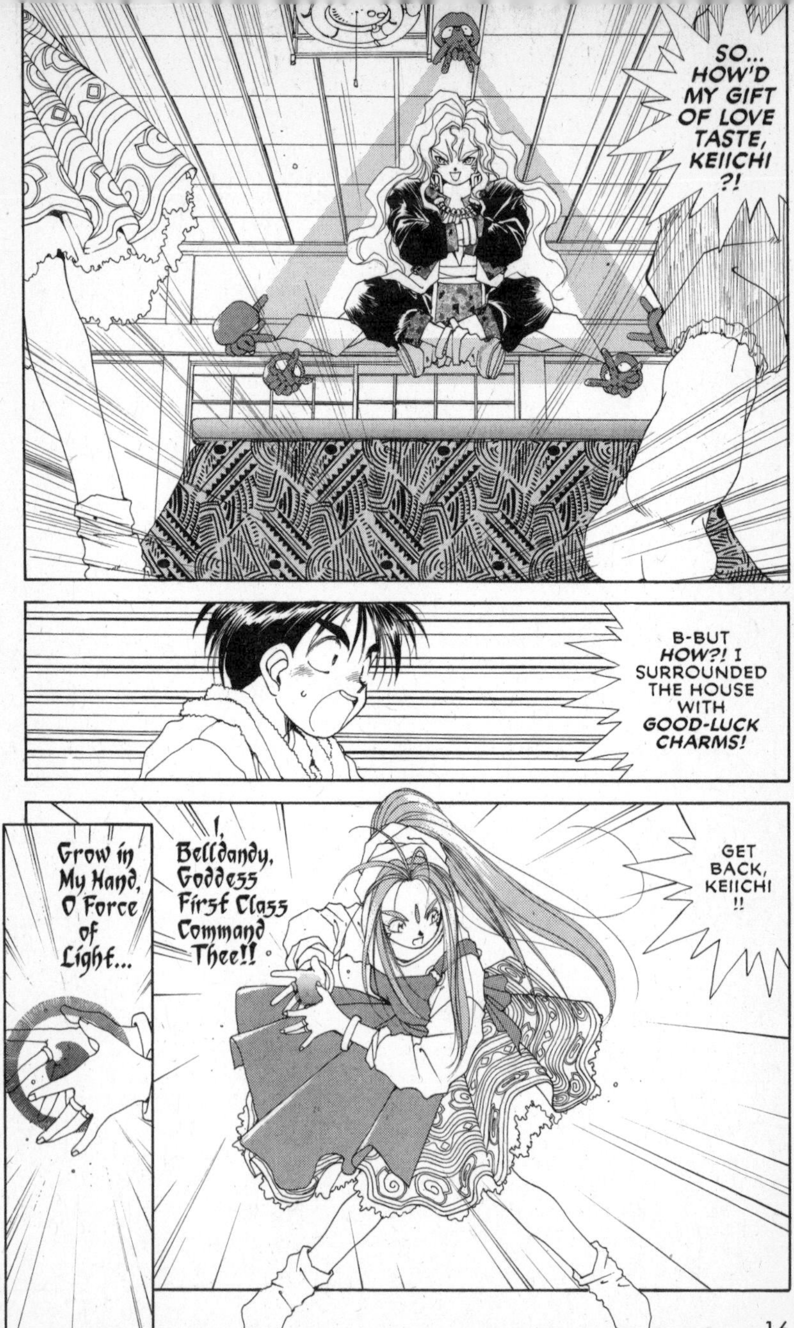
SO... HOW'D MY GIFT OF LOVE TASTE, KEIICHI ?!
B-BUT *HOW?!* I SURROUNDED THE HOUSE WITH *GOOD-LUCK* CHARMS!
GET BACK, KEIICHI !!
I, Belldandy, Goddess First Class Command Thee!!
Grow in My Hand, O Force of Light...

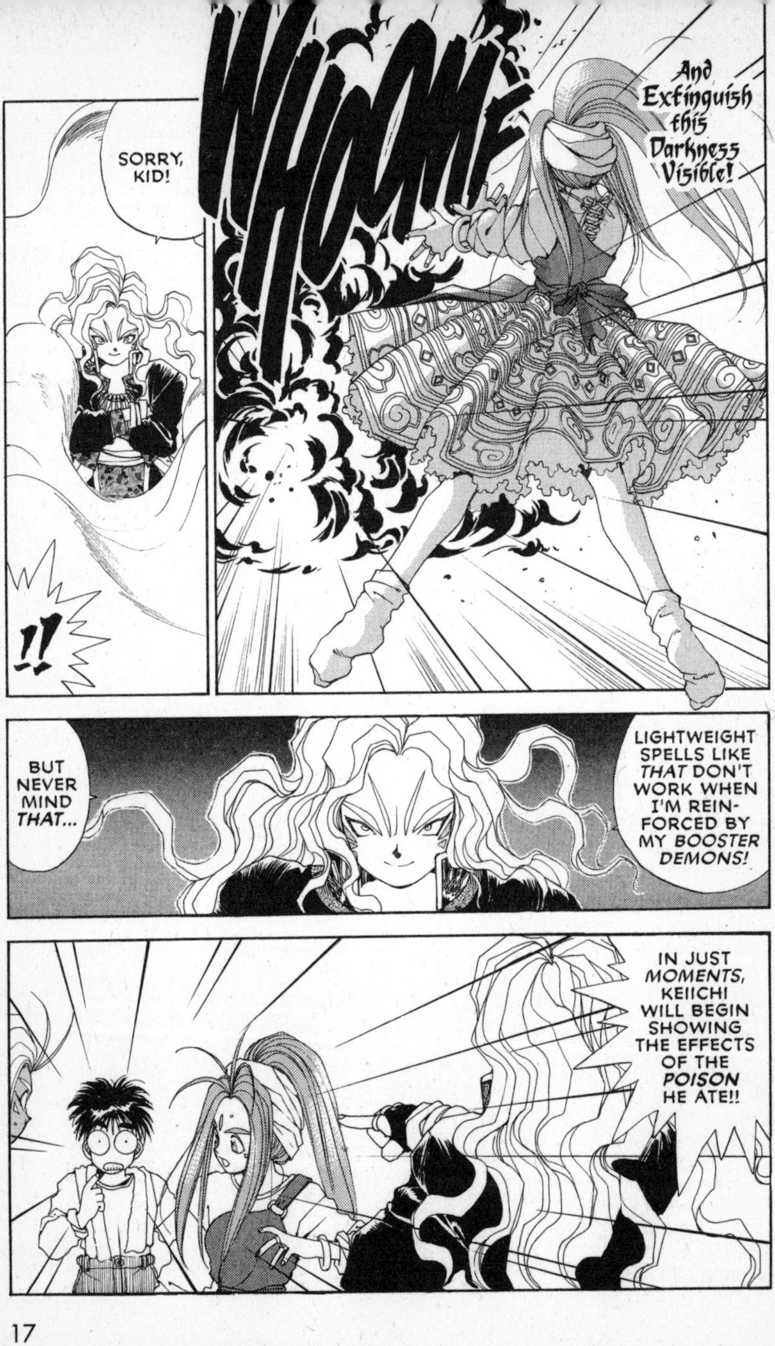
And Extinguish this Darkness Visible!
WHOOM
SORRY, KID!
!!
LIGHTWEIGHT SPELLS LIKE THAT DON'T WORK WHEN I'M REINFORCED BY MY BOOSTER DEMONS!
BUT NEVER MIND THAT...
IN JUST MOMENTS, KEIICHI WILL BEGIN SHOWING THE EFFECTS OF THE POISON HE ATE!!

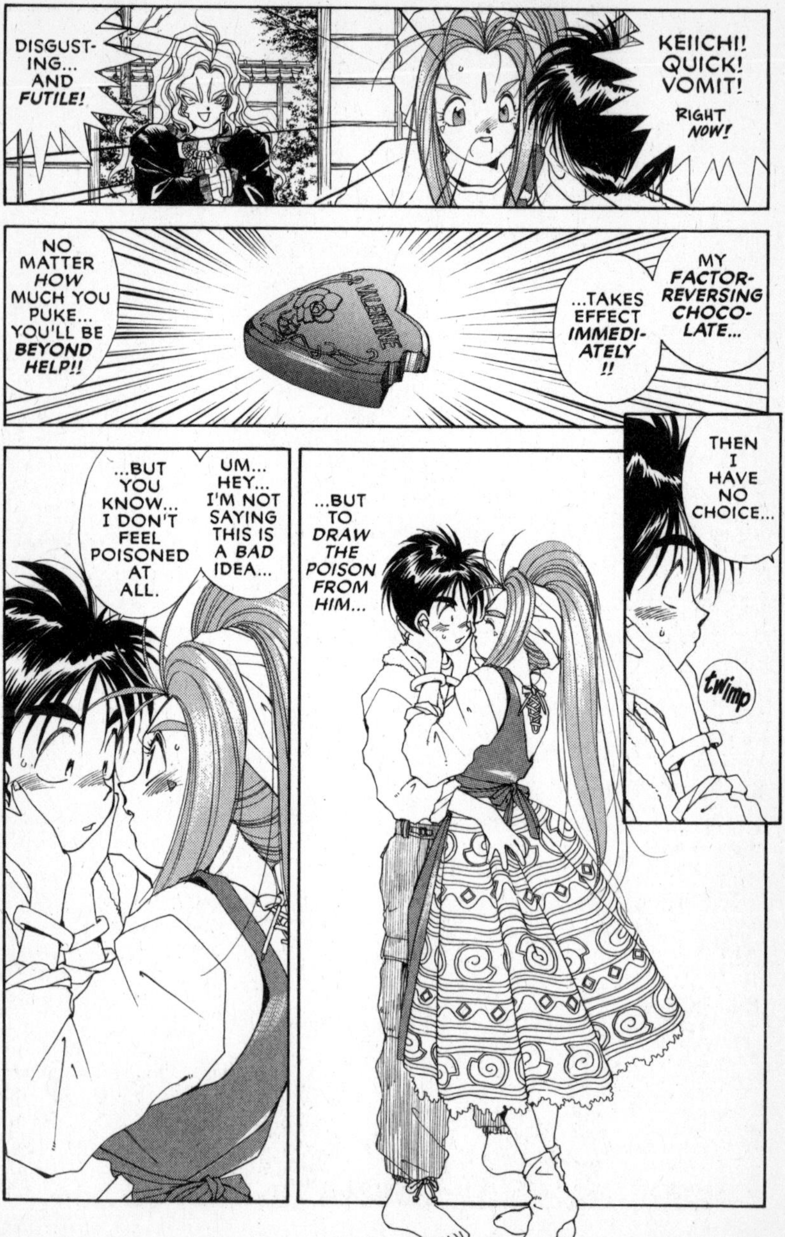
KEIICHI! QUICK! VOMIT!
RIGHT NOW!
DISGUST-ING... AND FUTILE!
MY FACTOR-REVERSING CHOCO-LATE...
...TAKES EFFECT IMMEDI-ATELY!!
VALENTINE
NO MATTER HOW MUCH YOU PUKE... YOU'LL BE BEYOND HELP!!
THEN I HAVE NO CHOICE...
twimp
...BUT TO DRAW THE POISON FROM HIM...
UM... HEY... I'M NOT SAYING THIS IS A BAD IDEA...
...BUT YOU KNOW... I DON'T FEEL POISONED AT ALL.

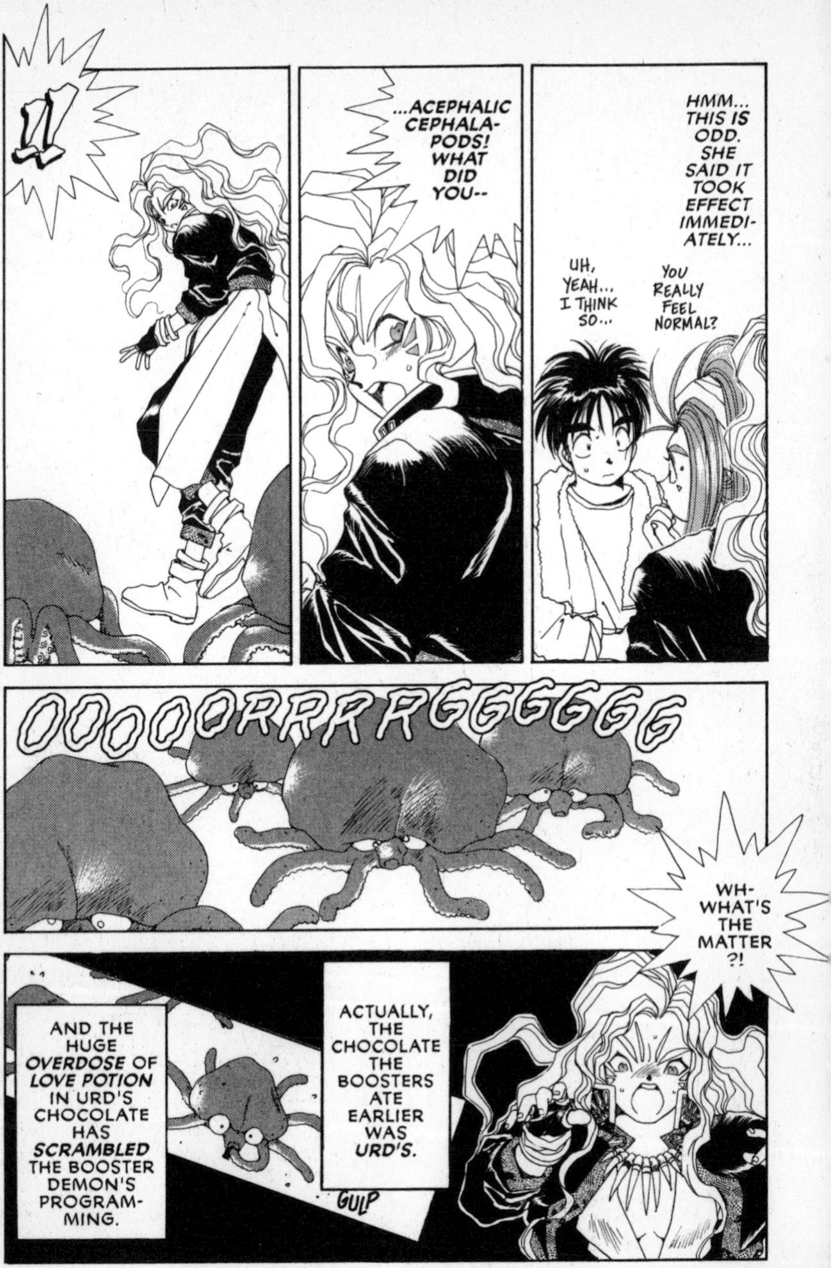
HMM... THIS IS ODD. SHE SAID IT TOOK EFFECT IMMEDIATELY...
YOU REALLY FEEL NORMAL?
UH, YEAH... I THINK SO...
...ACEPHALIC CEPHALAPODS! WHAT DID YOU--
OOOOORRRRGGGGGG
WH-WHAT'S THE MATTER?!
ACTUALLY, THE CHOCOLATE THE BOOSTERS ATE EARLIER WAS *URD'S.*
GULP
AND THE HUGE *OVERDOSE* OF *LOVE POTION* IN URD'S CHOCOLATE HAS *SCRAMBLED* THE BOOSTER DEMON'S PROGRAMMING.

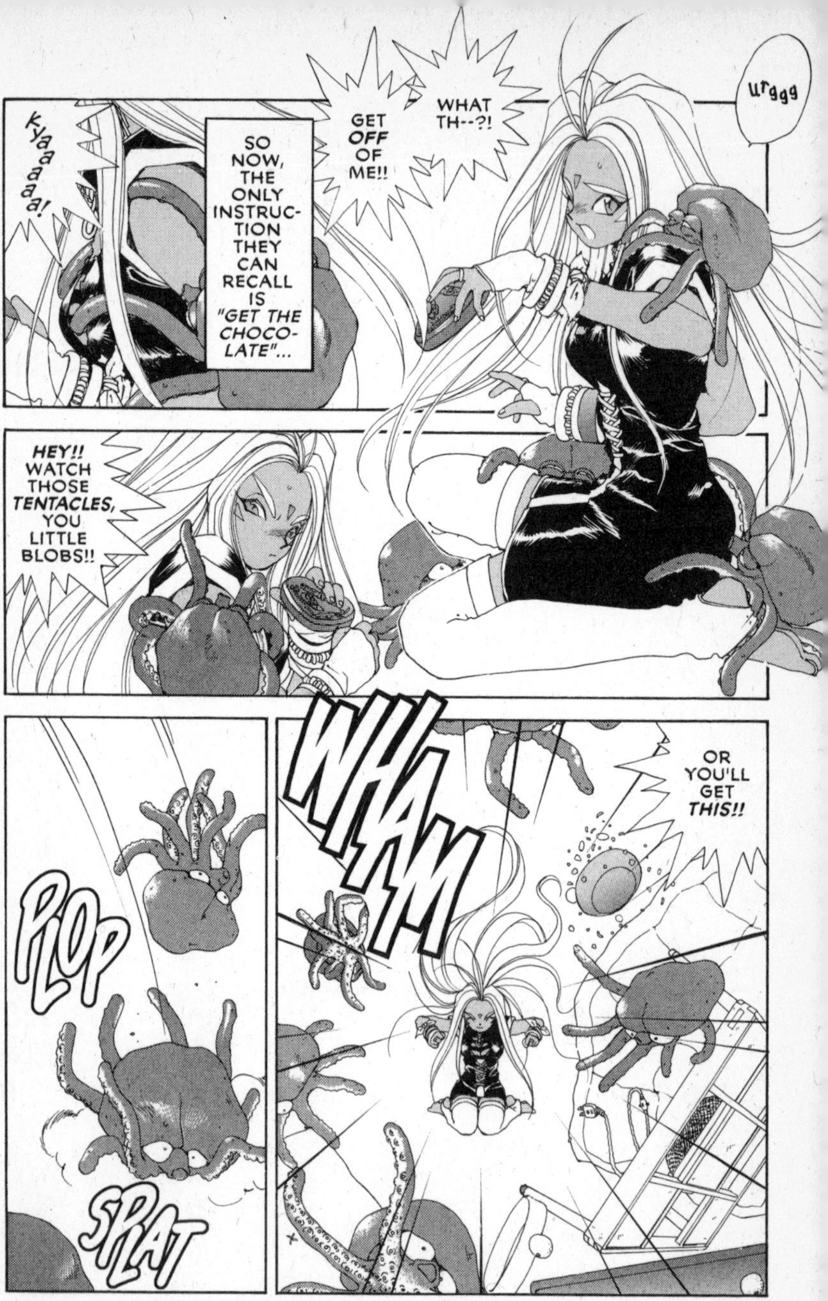
Urggg
WHAT TH--?!
GET OFF OF ME!!
SO NOW, THE ONLY INSTRUCTION THEY CAN RECALL IS "GET THE CHOCOLATE"...
Kyaaaaaa!
HEY!! WATCH THOSE TENTACLES, YOU LITTLE BLOBS!!
OR YOU'LL GET THIS!!
WHAM
PLOP
SPLAT

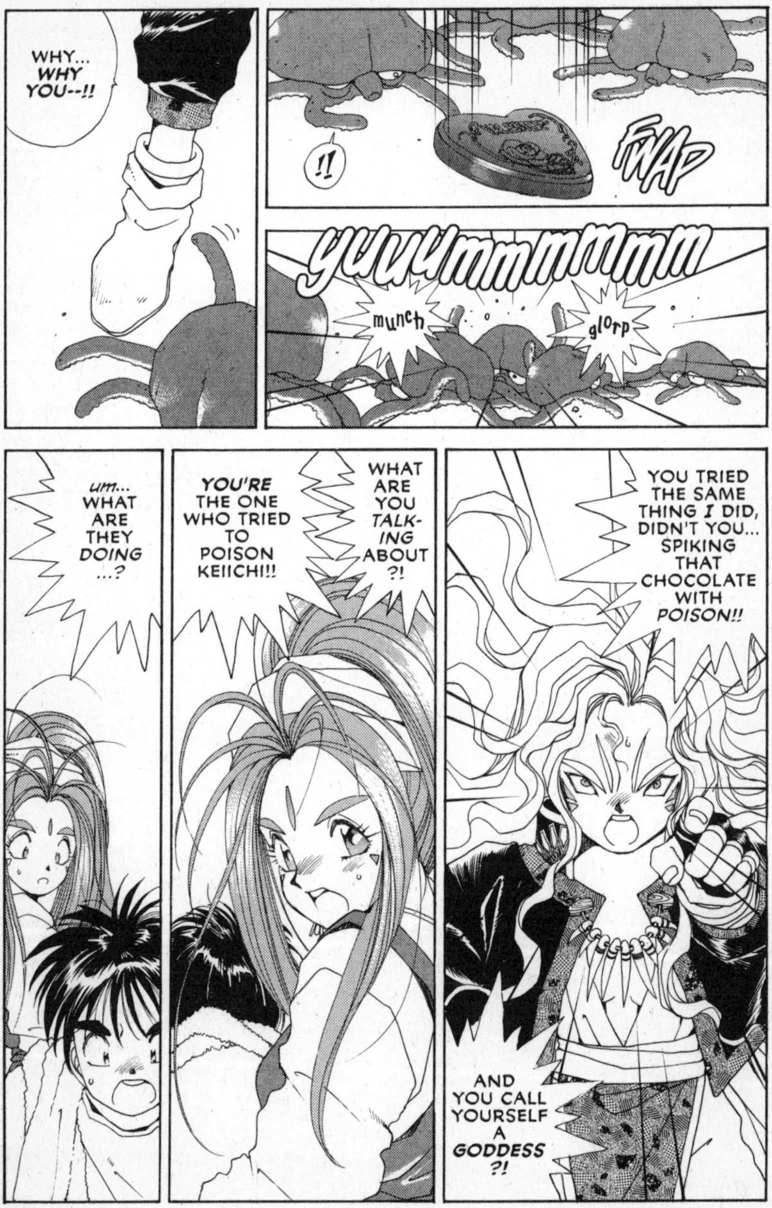
FWAP
!!
yuuummmmmmm
glorp
munch
WHY... WHY YOU--!!
YOU TRIED THE SAME THING I DID, DIDN'T YOU... SPIKING THAT CHOCOLATE WITH POISON!!
AND YOU CALL YOURSELF A GODDESS?!
WHAT ARE YOU TALKING ABOUT?!
YOU'RE THE ONE WHO TRIED TO POISON KEIICHI!!
um... WHAT ARE THEY DOING...?

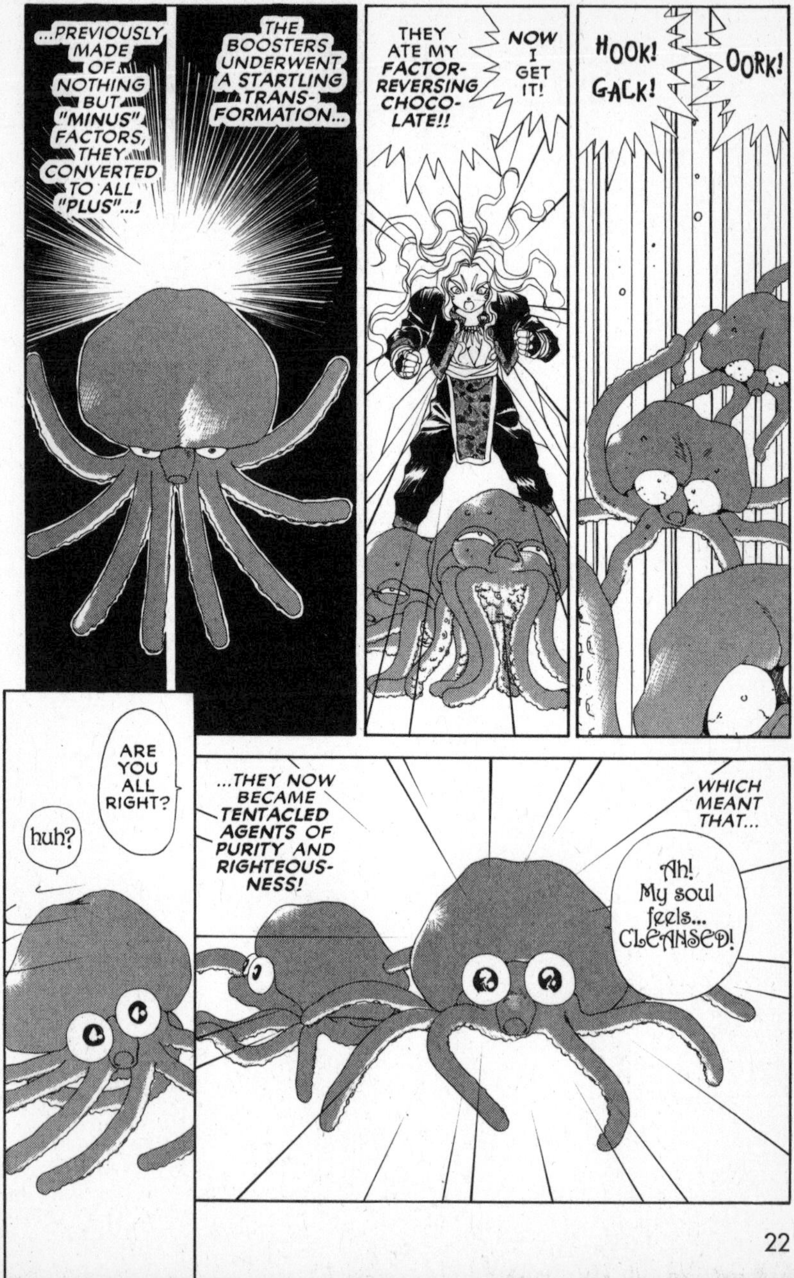
OORK!
HOOK!
GACK!
NOW I GET IT!
THEY ATE MY FACTOR-REVERSING CHOCOLATE!!
THE BOOSTERS UNDERWENT A STARTLING TRANSFORMATION...
...PREVIOUSLY MADE OF NOTHING BUT "MINUS" FACTORS, THEY CONVERTED TO ALL "PLUS"...!
WHICH MEANT THAT...
Ah! My soul feels... CLEANSED!
...THEY NOW BECAME TENTACLED AGENTS OF PURITY AND RIGHTEOUSNESS!
ARE YOU ALL RIGHT?
huh?

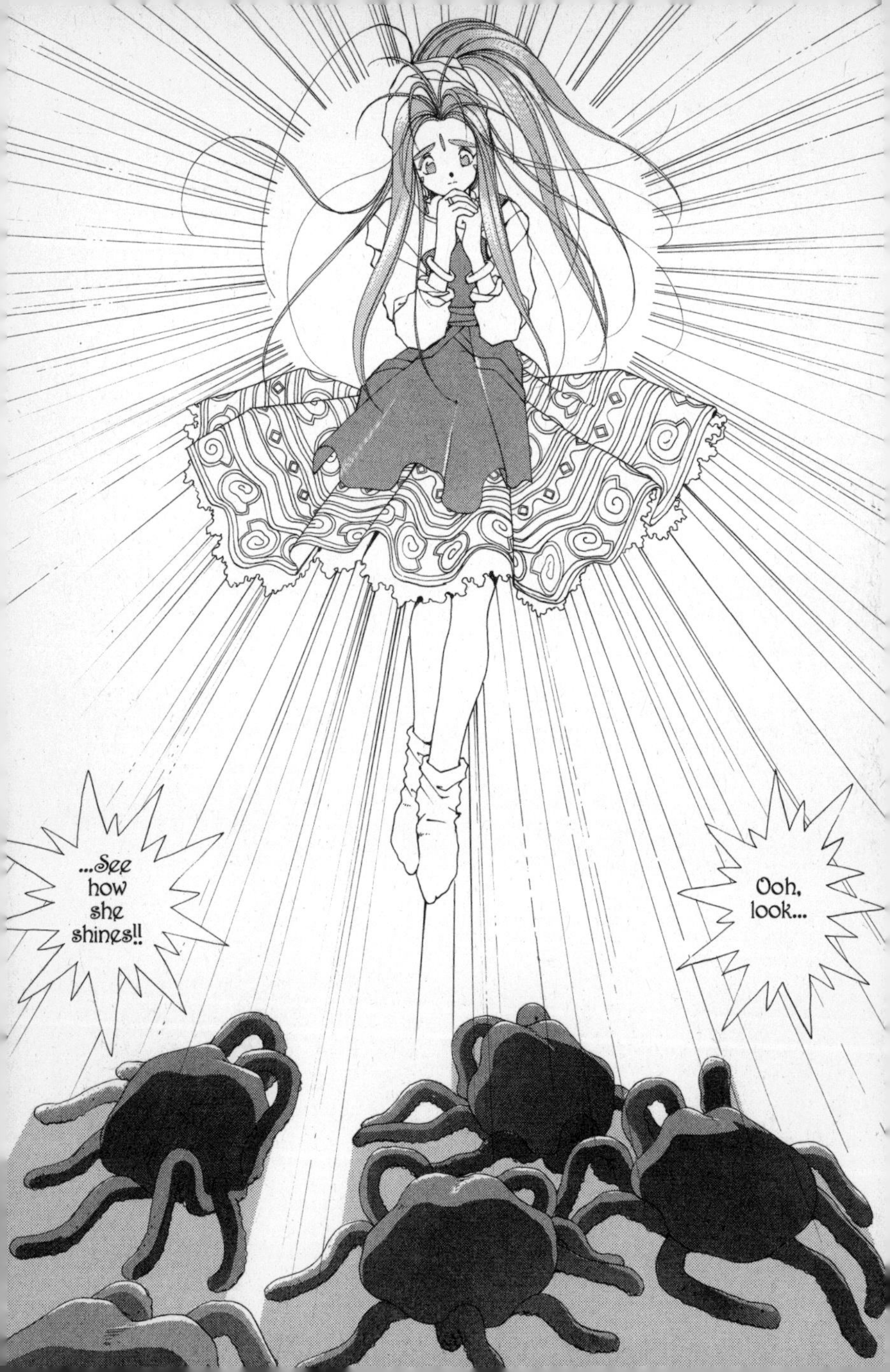
Ooh, look...
...See how she shines!!

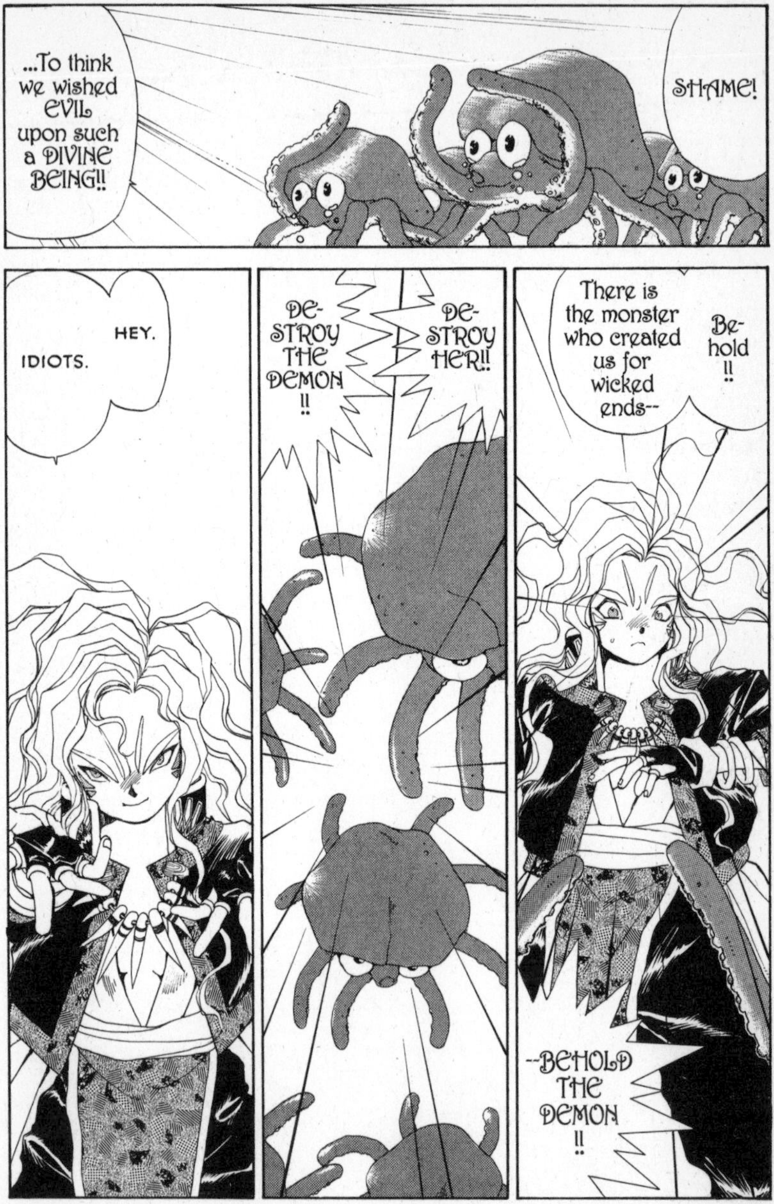
SHAME!
...To think we wished EVIL upon such a DIVINE BEING!!
Be-hold!!
There is the monster who created us for wicked ends--
--BEHOLD THE DEMON!!
DE-STROY HER!!
DE-STROY THE DEMON!!
HEY. IDIOTS.

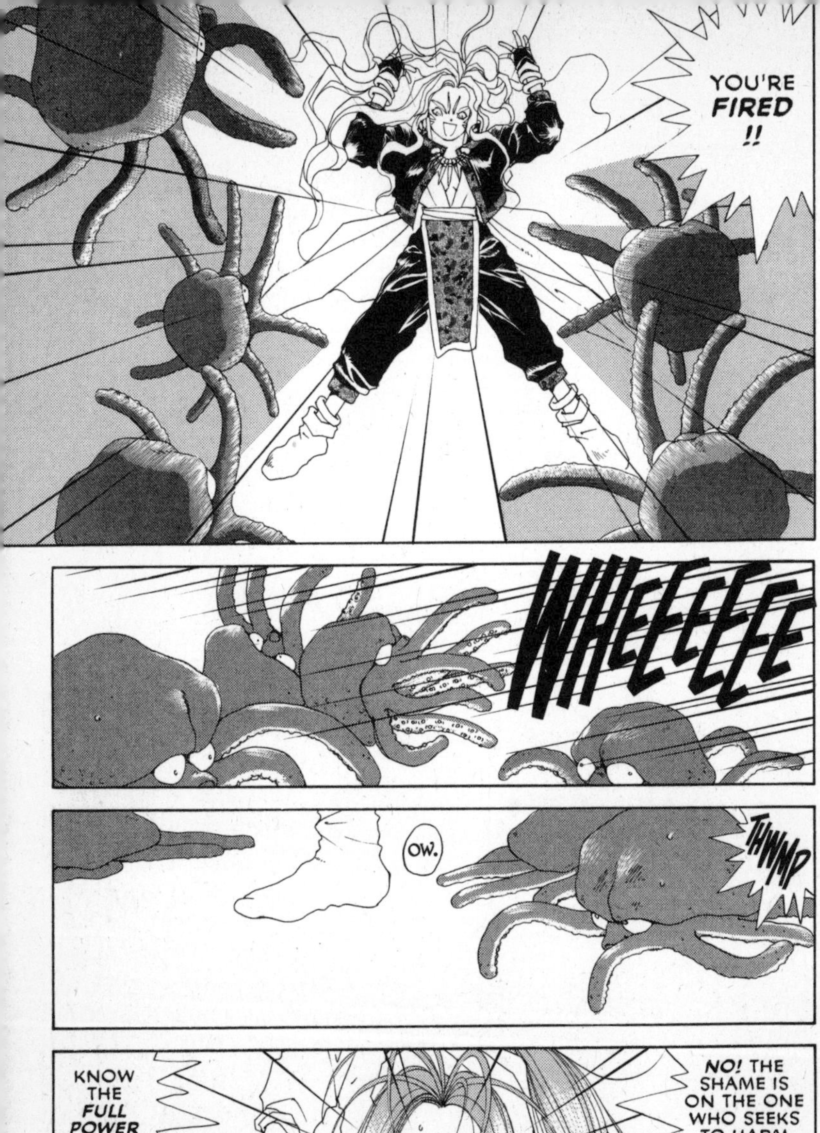
YOU'RE FIRED !!
WHEEEEEE
THWMP
OW.
NO! THE SHAME IS ON THE ONE WHO SEEKS TO HARM HER OWN POOR CREATIONS !!
KNOW THE FULL POWER OF GOOD, MARA!!

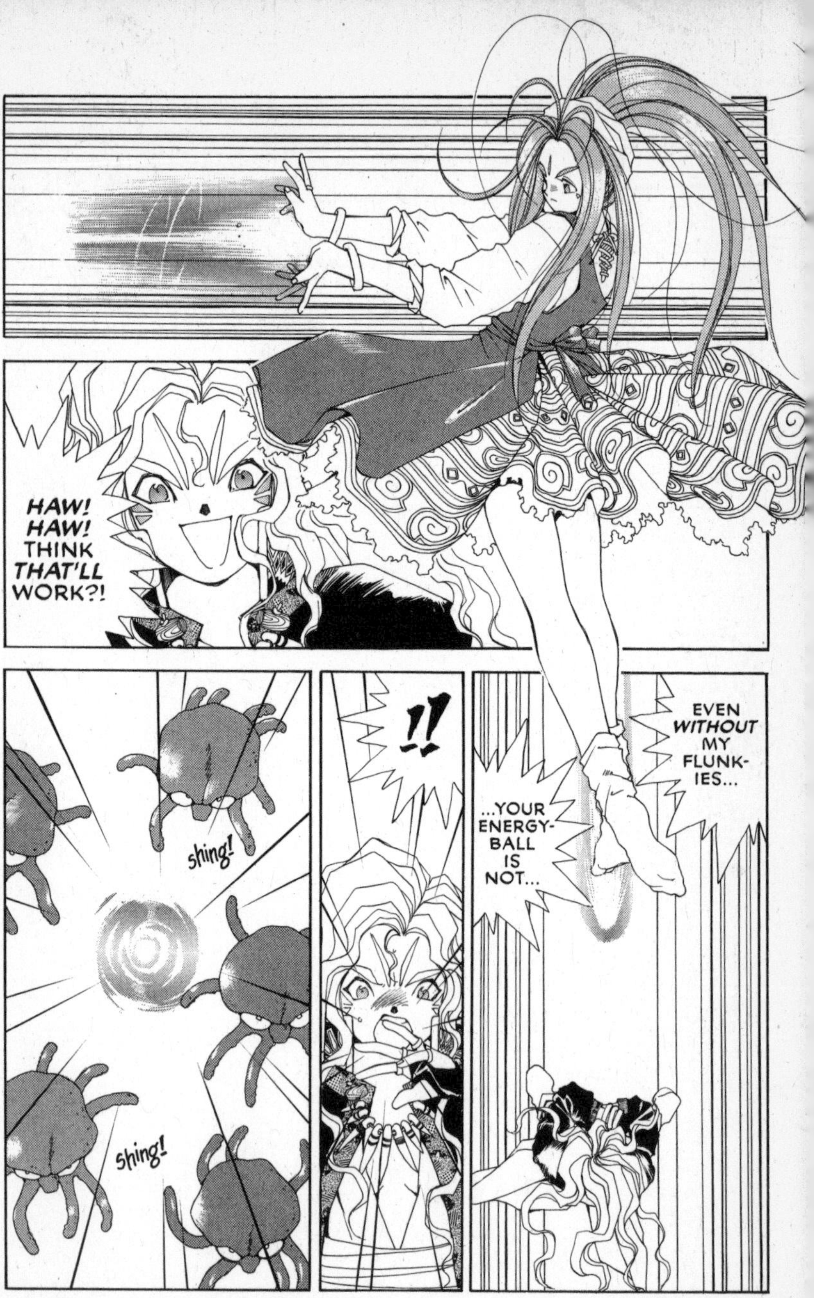
HAW! HAW! THINK THAT'LL WORK?!
EVEN WITHOUT MY FLUNK-IES...
...YOUR ENERGY-BALL IS NOT...
!!
shing!
shing!

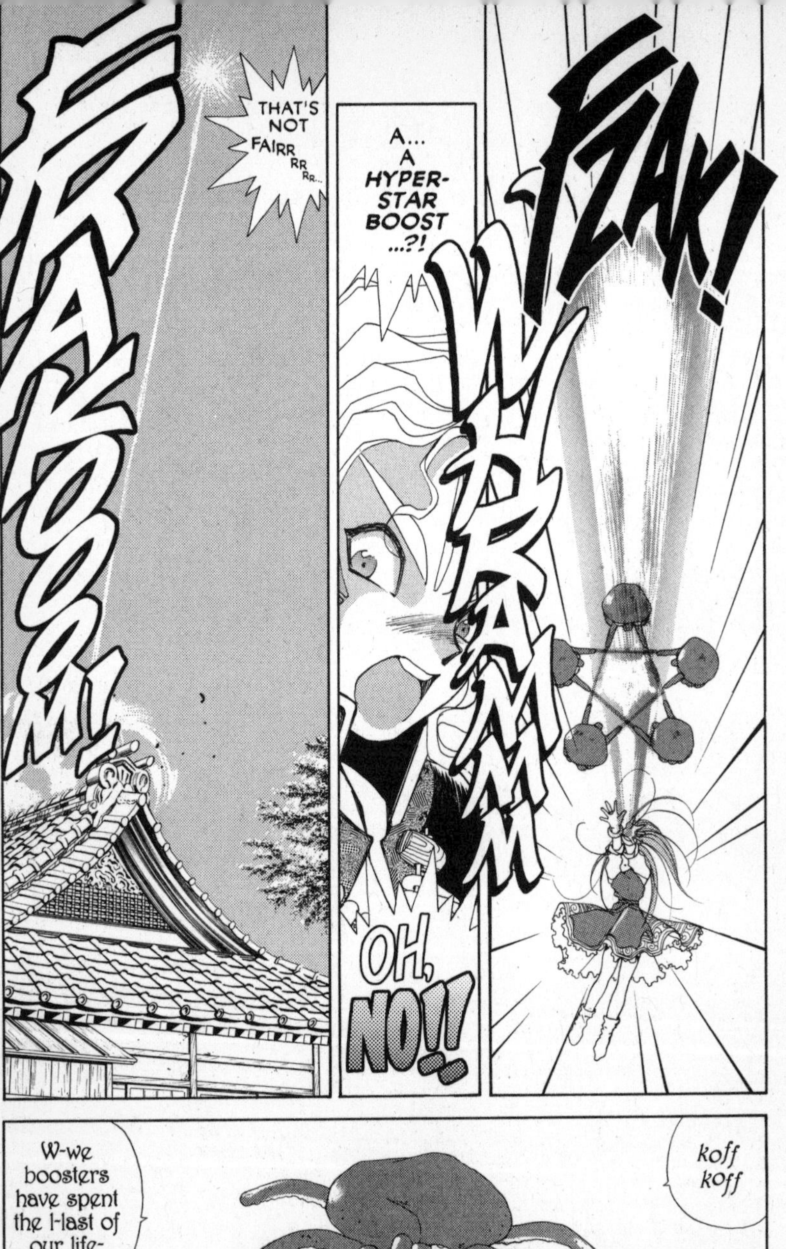
FZAK!
WHRAMMMM
A... A HYPER-STAR BOOST ...?!
OH, NO!!
KRAKOOOM!
THAT'S NOT FAIRRRRRR...
koff koff
W-we boosters have spent the l-last of our life-force...

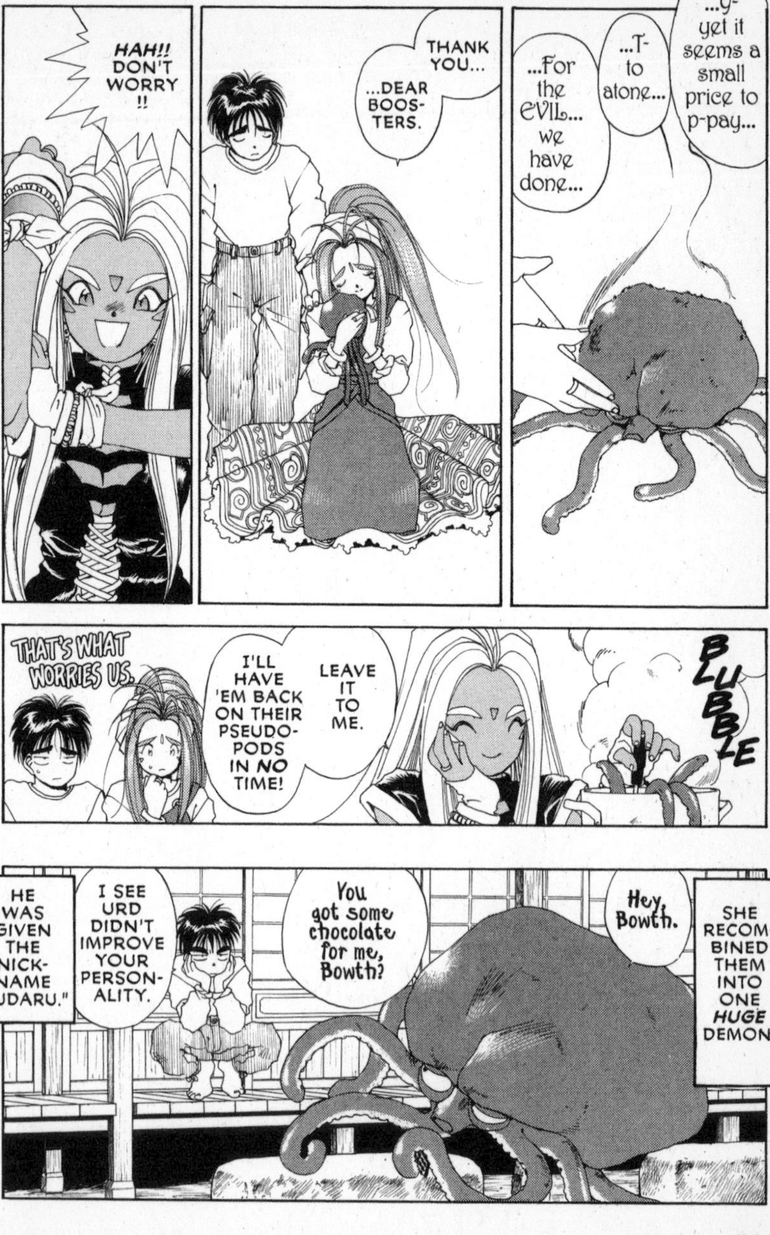

...For the EVIL... we have done...
...T-to atone...
...Y-yet it seems a small price to p-pay...
THANK YOU...
...DEAR BOOSTERS.
HAH!! DON'T WORRY !!
BLUBBLE
LEAVE IT TO ME.
I'LL HAVE 'EM BACK ON THEIR PSEUDOPODS IN NO TIME!
THAT'S WHAT WORRIES US.
SHE RECOMBINED THEM INTO ONE HUGE DEMON.
Hey, Bowth.
You got some chocolate for me, Bowth?
I SEE URD DIDN'T IMPROVE YOUR PERSONALITY.
HE WAS GIVEN THE NICKNAME "SUDARU."

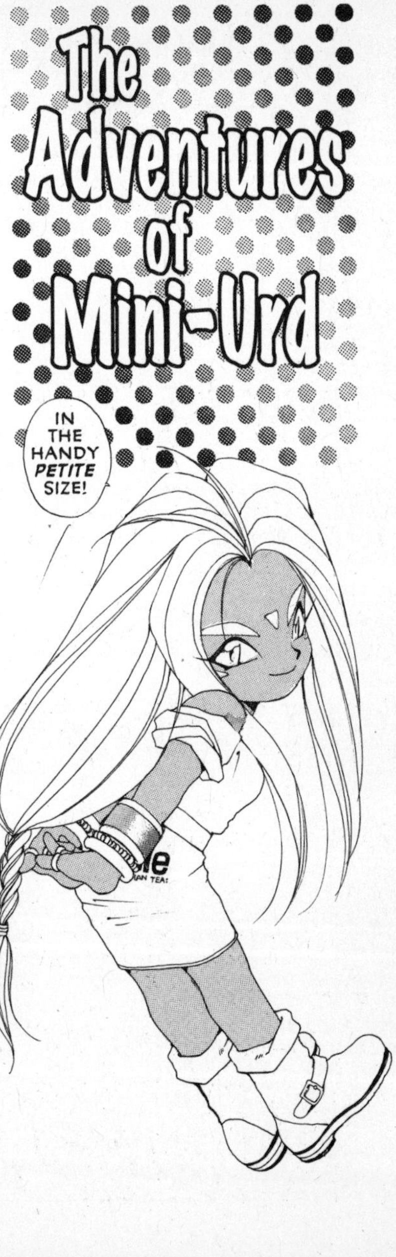
The Adventures of Mini-Urd
IN THE HANDY *PETITE* SIZE!

## ◆CUP O' URD◆

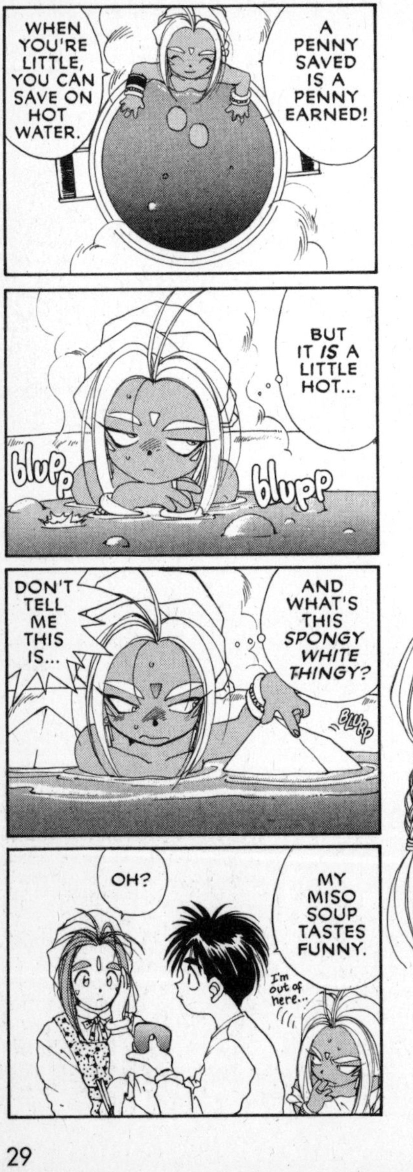
A PENNY SAVED IS A PENNY EARNED!
WHEN YOU'RE LITTLE, YOU CAN SAVE ON HOT WATER.
BUT IT *IS* A LITTLE HOT...
blupp
blupp
AND WHAT'S THIS *SPONGY WHITE THINGY?*
DON'T TELL ME THIS IS...
BLURP
MY MISO SOUP TASTES FUNNY.
OH?
I'm out of here...

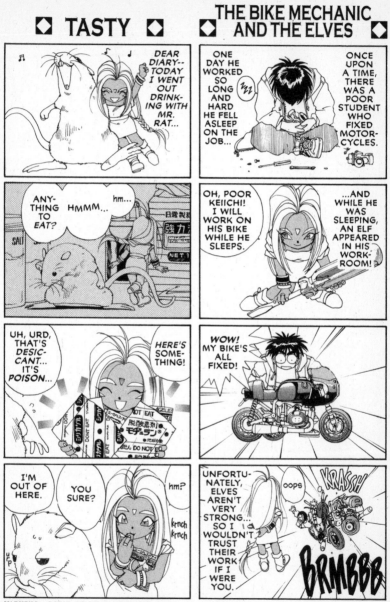

## THE BIKE MECHANIC AND THE ELVES

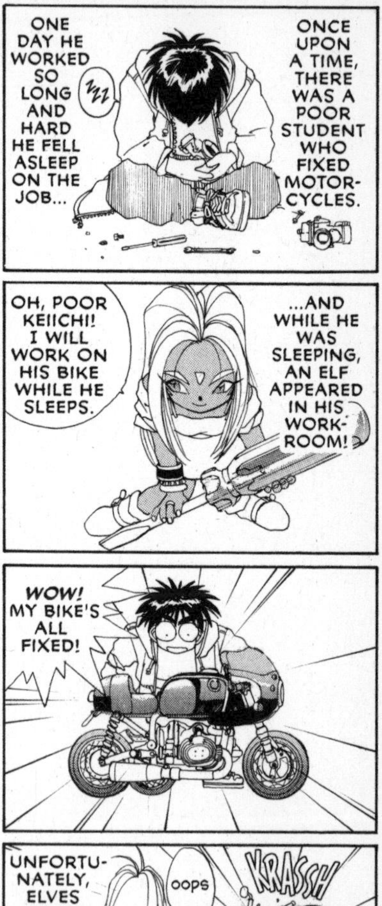
ONCE UPON A TIME, THERE WAS A POOR STUDENT WHO FIXED MOTORCYCLES.
ONE DAY HE WORKED SO LONG AND HARD HE FELL ASLEEP ON THE JOB...
ZZZ
...AND WHILE HE WAS SLEEPING, AN ELF APPEARED IN HIS WORK-ROOM!
OH, POOR KEIICHI! I WILL WORK ON HIS BIKE WHILE HE SLEEPS.
WOW! MY BIKE'S ALL FIXED!
KRASSH
oops
UNFORTU-NATELY, ELVES AREN'T VERY STRONG... SO I WOULDN'T TRUST THEIR WORK IF I WERE YOU.
BRMBBB

## TASTY

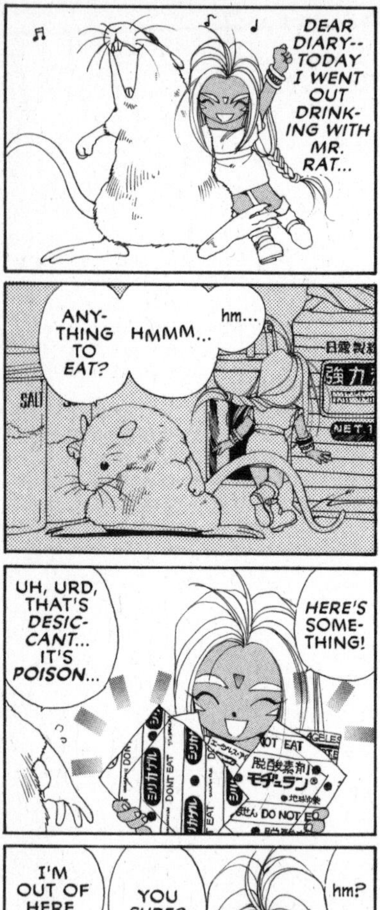
DEAR DIARY-- TODAY I WENT OUT DRINK-ING WITH MR. RAT...
hm...
ANY-THING TO EAT? HMMM...
HERE'S SOME-THING!
UH, URD, THAT'S DESIC-CANT... IT'S POISON...
DON'T EAT
脱酸素剤
モヂュラン
hm?
YOU SURE?
I'M OUT OF HERE.
krnch krnch
urp

WARNING: ***DON'T DO*** WHAT MINI-URD ***DOES.***

## ◆ CELL DIVISION ◆

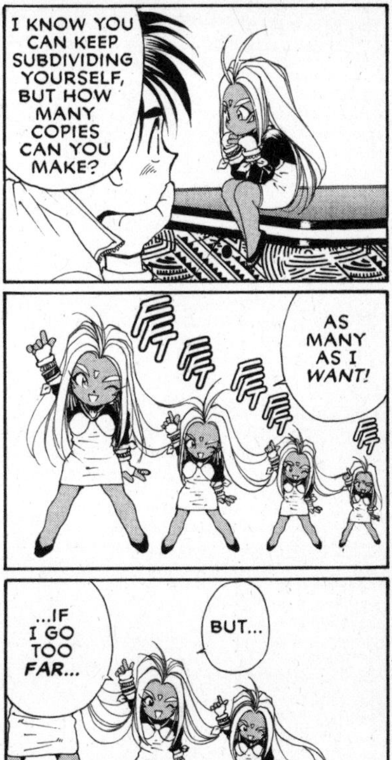
I KNOW YOU CAN KEEP SUBDIVIDING YOURSELF, BUT HOW MANY COPIES CAN YOU MAKE?
AS MANY AS I WANT!
FFT FFT FFT FFT FFT
BUT...
...IF I GO TOO FAR...
...THEY START GETTING KINDA FUNNY-LOOKING...
STOP! STOP !!

## ◆ LOST AND FOUND ◆

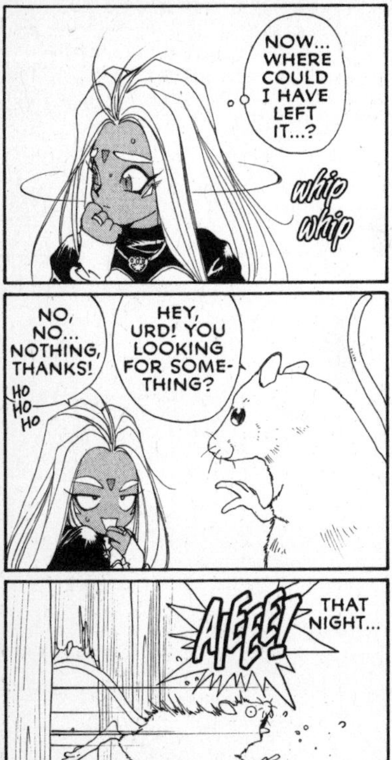
NOW... WHERE COULD I HAVE LEFT IT...?
whip whip
HEY, URD! YOU LOOKING FOR SOME-THING?
NO, NO... NOTHING, THANKS!
HO HO HO
THAT NIGHT...
AIEEE!
YOO-HOO! RATTY DEAR!
I KNEW I WAS MISSING ONE OF THE DARN THINGS!

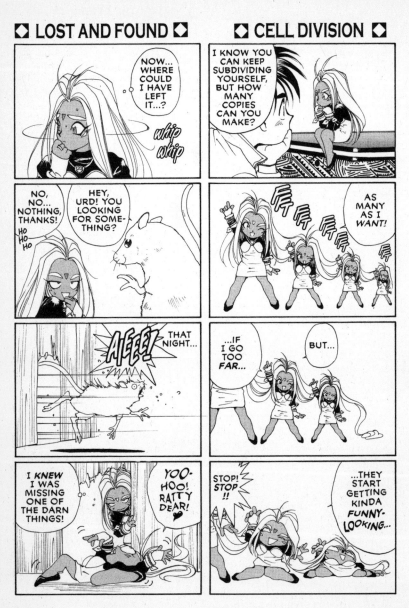

## IT'S THE THOUGHT THAT COUNTS

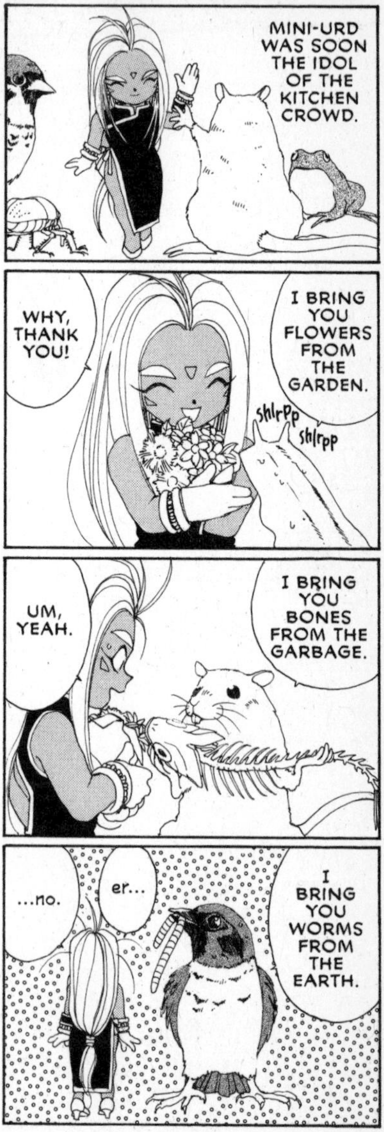
MINI-URD WAS SOON THE IDOL OF THE KITCHEN CROWD.
I BRING YOU FLOWERS FROM THE GARDEN.
shlrpp shlrpp
WHY, THANK YOU!
I BRING YOU BONES FROM THE GARBAGE.
UM, YEAH.
I BRING YOU WORMS FROM THE EARTH.
er...
...no.

## FAMILY

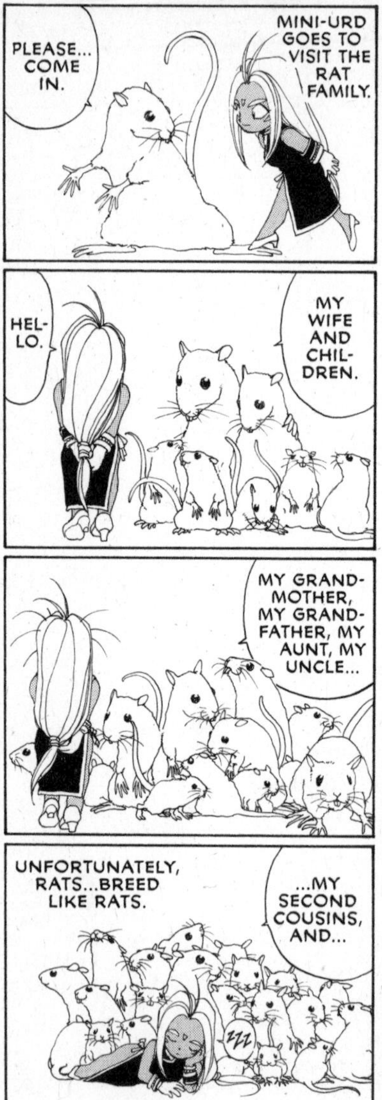
MINI-URD GOES TO VISIT THE RAT FAMILY.
PLEASE... COME IN.
MY WIFE AND CHIL-DREN.
HEL-LO.
MY GRAND-MOTHER, MY GRAND-FATHER, MY AUNT, MY UNCLE...
...MY SECOND COUSINS, AND...
UNFORTUNATELY, RATS...BREED LIKE RATS.
zzz

## TRUST ME!

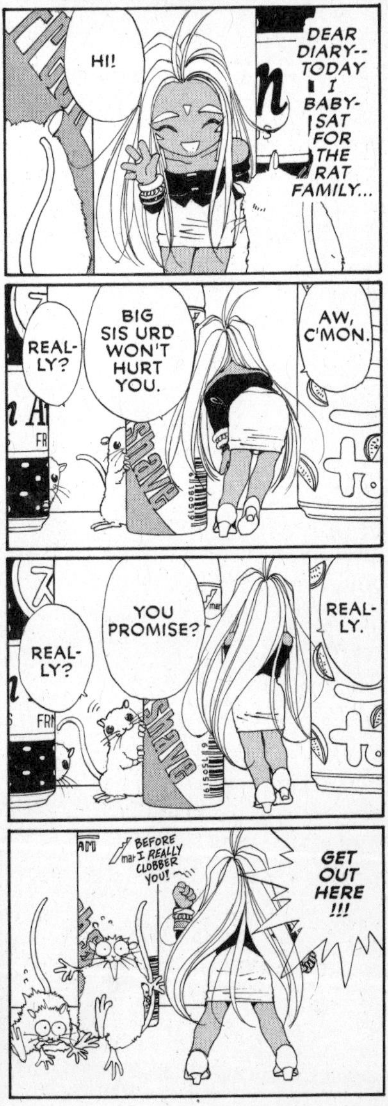
DEAR DIARY-- TODAY I BABY-SAT FOR THE RAT FAMILY...
HI!
AW, C'MON.
BIG SIS URD WON'T HURT YOU.
REAL-LY?
REAL-LY.
YOU PROMISE?
REAL-LY?
GET OUT HERE !!!
BEFORE I REALLY CLOBBER YOU!

## GOD OF GAMBLERS

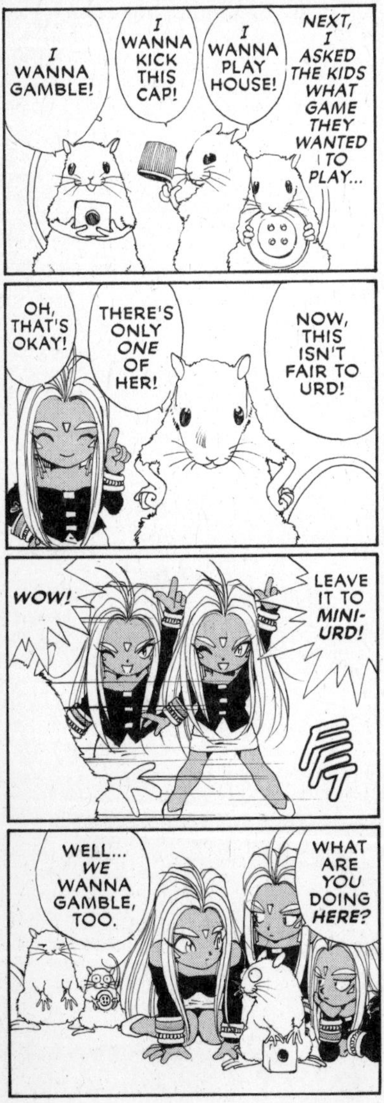
NEXT, I ASKED THE KIDS WHAT GAME THEY WANTED TO PLAY...
I WANNA PLAY HOUSE!
I WANNA KICK THIS CAP!
I WANNA GAMBLE!
NOW, THIS ISN'T FAIR TO URD!
THERE'S ONLY ONE OF HER!
OH, THAT'S OKAY!
LEAVE IT TO MINI-URD!
WOW!
FFT
WHAT ARE YOU DOING HERE?
WELL... WE WANNA GAMBLE, TOO.

## AMAZING! ◆ THE CARDS NEVER LIE! ◆

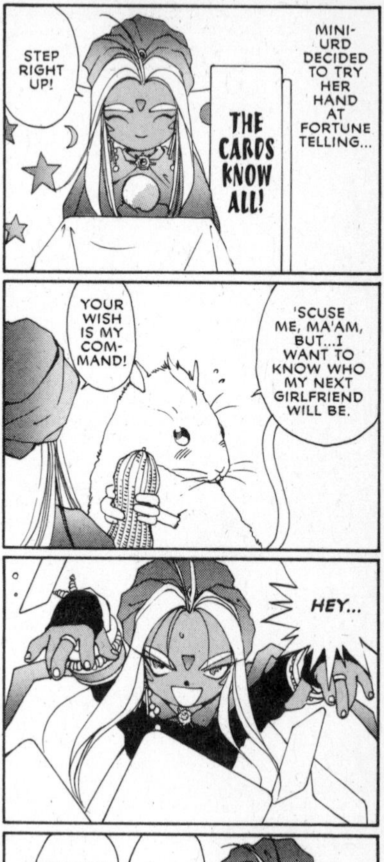
MINI-URD DECIDED TO TRY HER HAND AT FORTUNE TELLING...
THE CARDS KNOW ALL!
STEP RIGHT UP!
'SCUSE ME, MA'AM, BUT...I WANT TO KNOW WHO MY NEXT GIRLFRIEND WILL BE.
YOUR WISH IS MY COMMAND!
HEY...
...PRESTO.
"PRESTO"?
A
TEA
POT

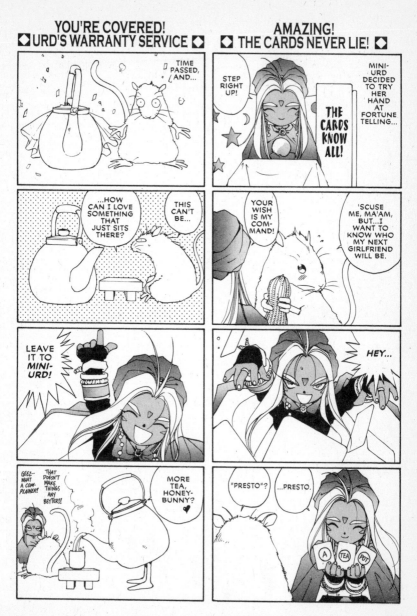

## YOU'RE COVERED! ◆ URD'S WARRANTY SERVICE ◆

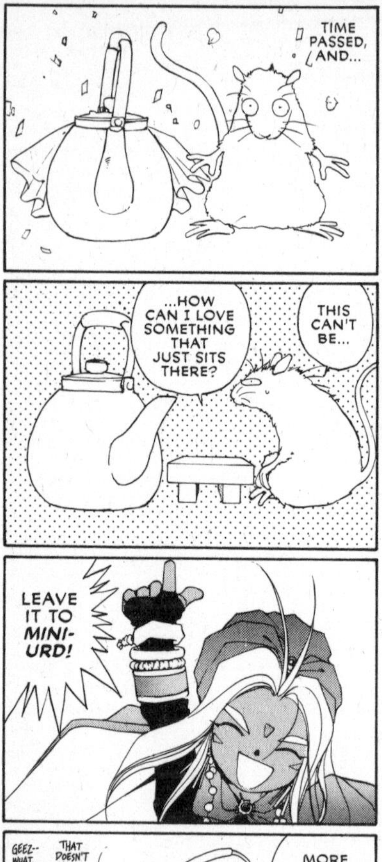
TIME PASSED, AND...
THIS CAN'T BE...
...HOW CAN I LOVE SOMETHING THAT JUST SITS THERE?
LEAVE IT TO MINI-URD!
MORE TEA, HONEY-BUNNY? ♥
THAT DOESN'T MAKE THINGS ANY BETTER!!
GEEZ--WHAT A COMPLAINER!

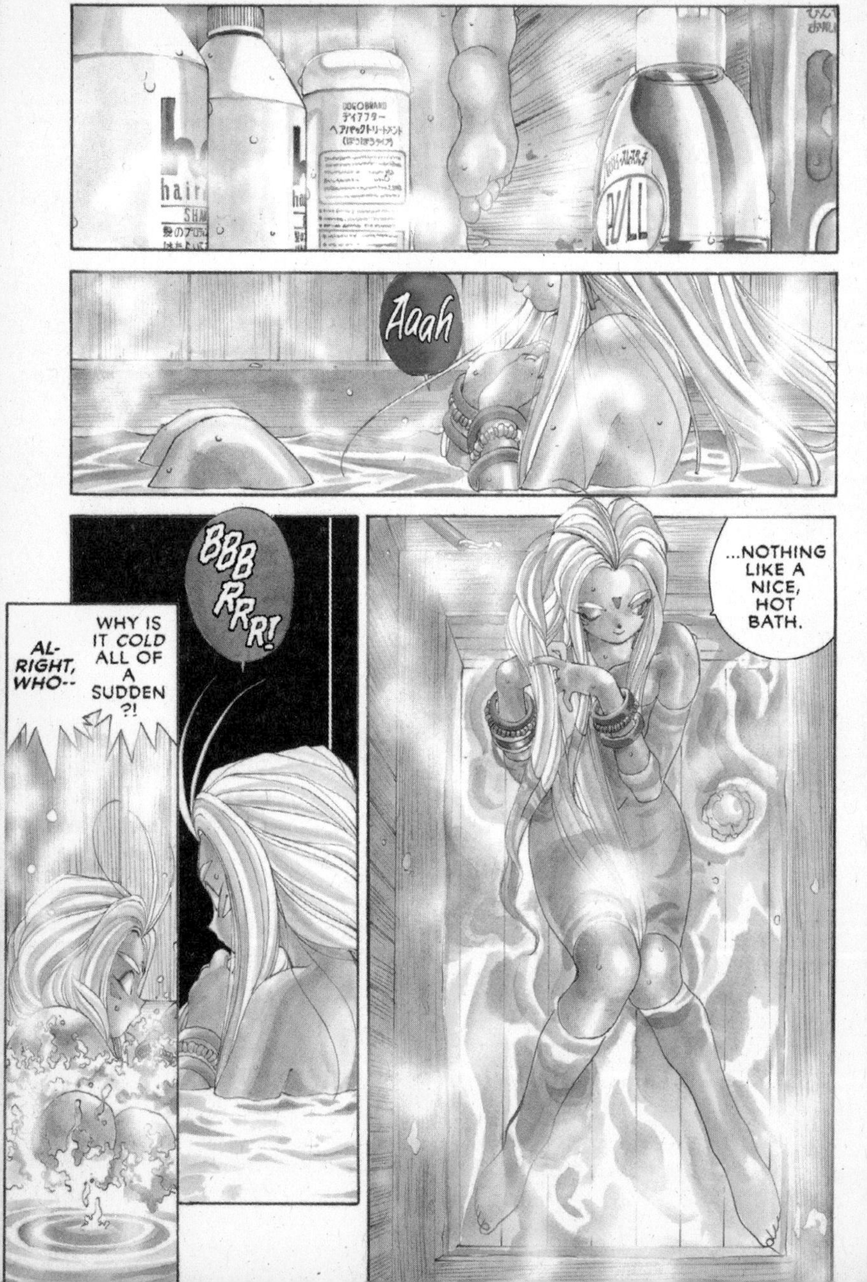
Aaah
...NOTHING LIKE A NICE, HOT BATH.
BBBRRR!
WHY IS IT COLD ALL OF A SUDDEN ?!
AL-RIGHT, WHO--

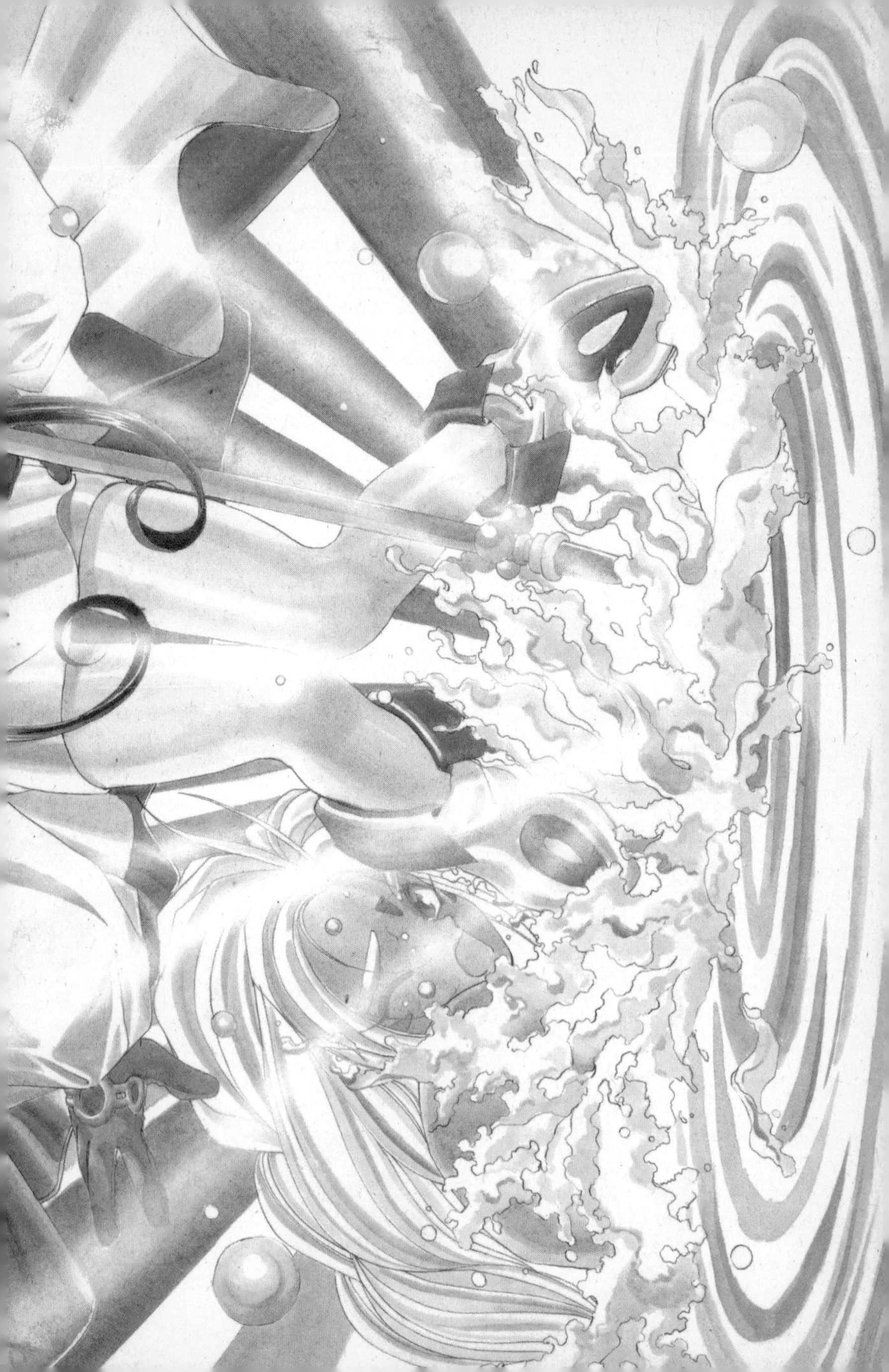

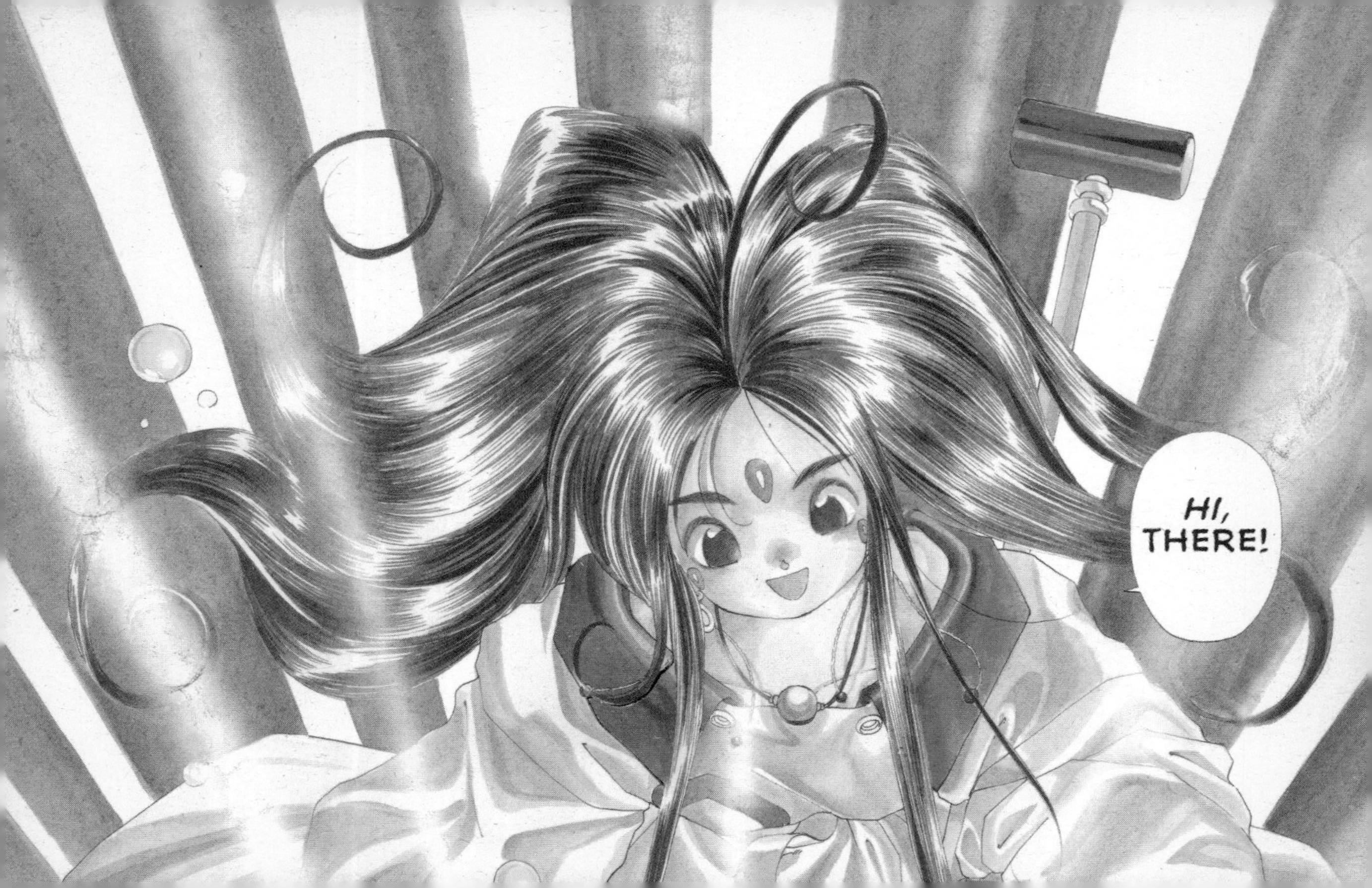
HI, THERE!

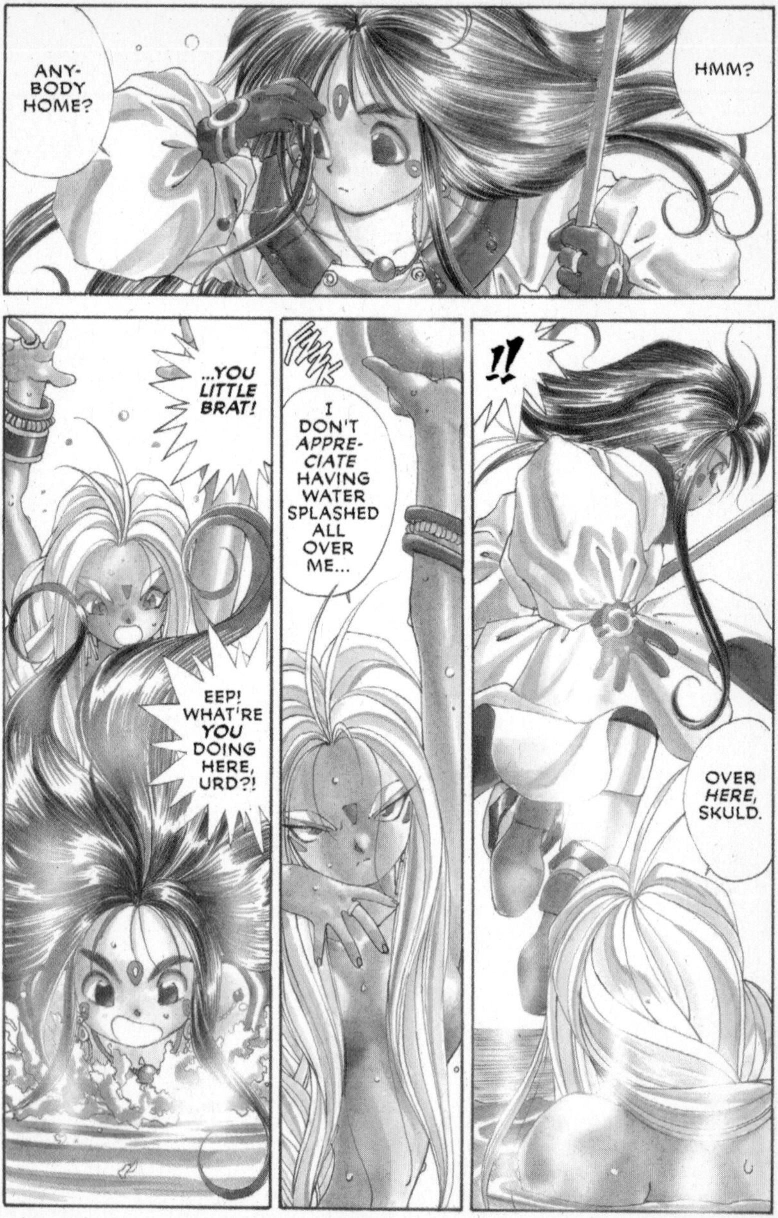
HMM?
ANY-BODY HOME?
!!
OVER HERE, SKULD.
I DON'T APPRECIATE HAVING WATER SPLASHED ALL OVER ME...
...YOU LITTLE BRAT!
EEP! WHAT'RE YOU DOING HERE, URD?!

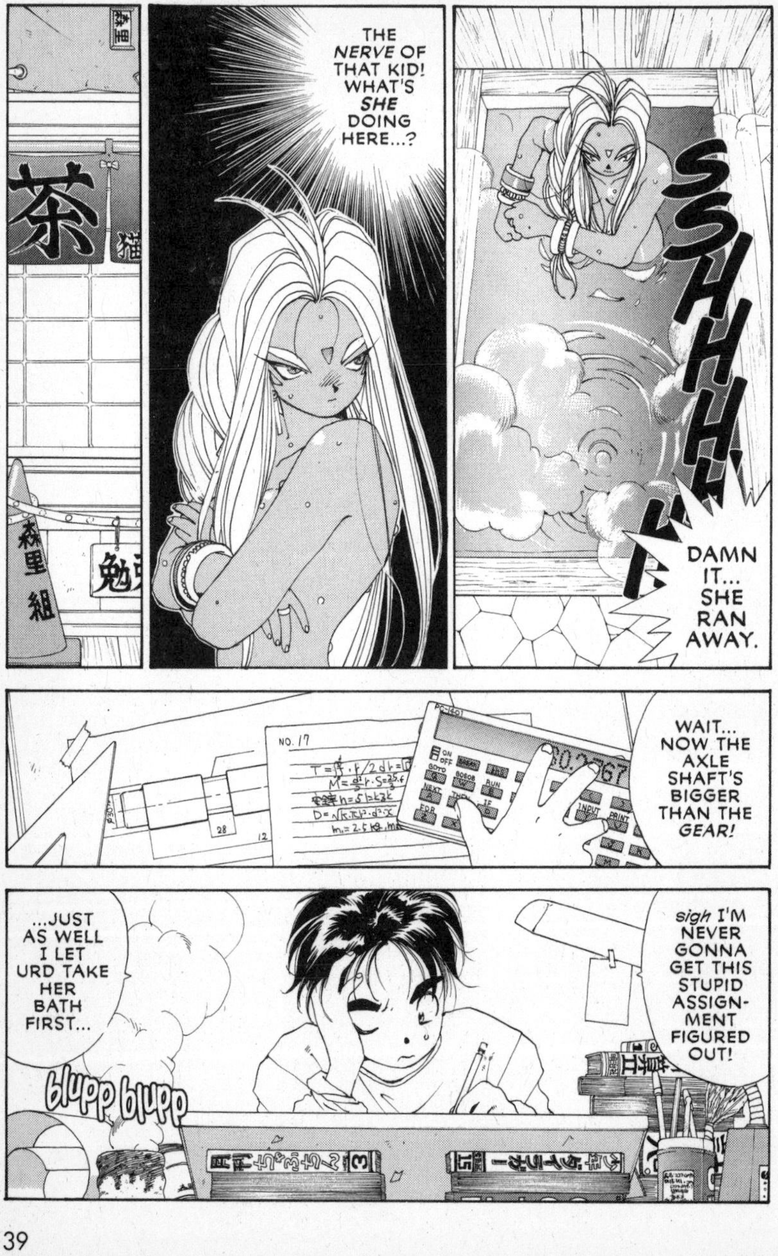
SHHHHH
DAMN IT... SHE RAN AWAY.
THE *NERVE* OF THAT KID! WHAT'S *SHE* DOING HERE...?
茶
森里組
WAIT... NOW THE AXLE SHAFT'S BIGGER THAN THE *GEAR!*
*sigh* I'M NEVER GONNA GET THIS STUPID ASSIGNMENT FIGURED OUT!
...JUST AS WELL I LET URD TAKE HER BATH FIRST...
blupp blupp

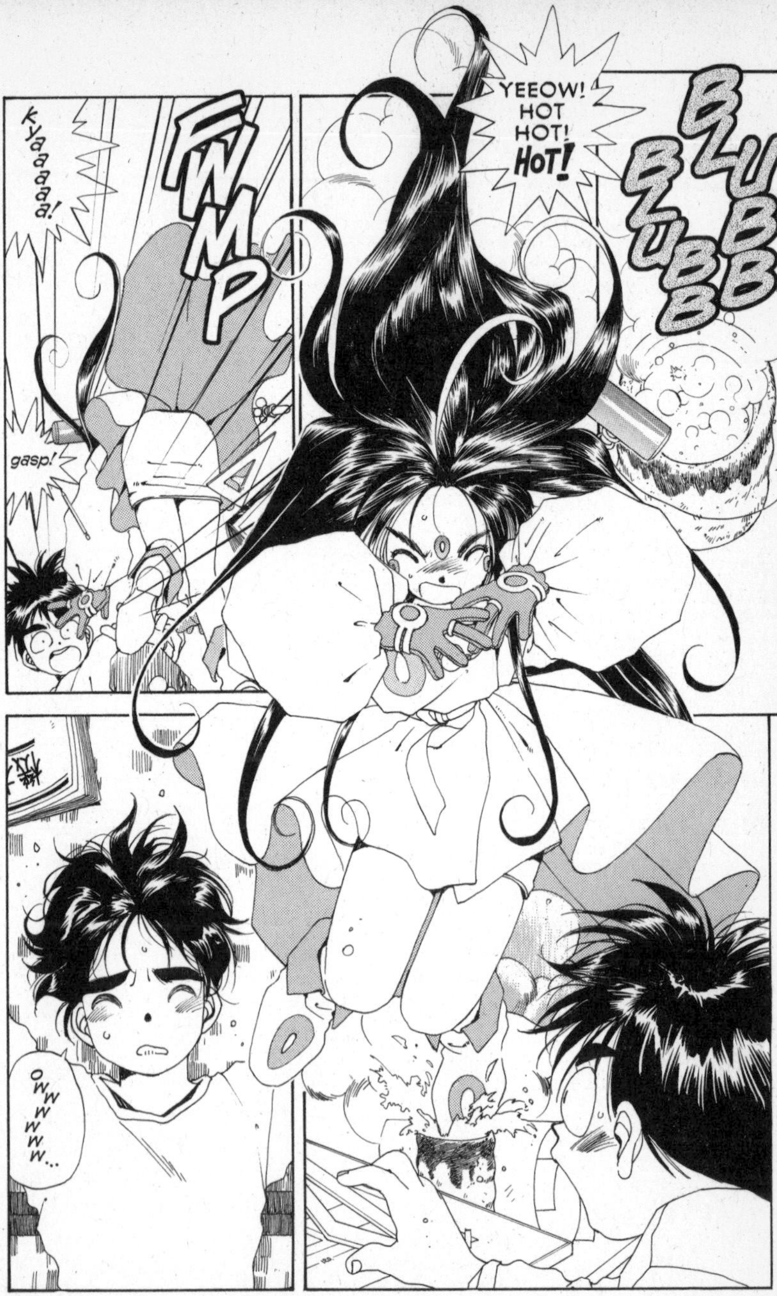
YEEOW! HOT HOT! HOT!
BLUBB BLUBB
FWMP
kyaaaaa!
gasp!
owwwwww...

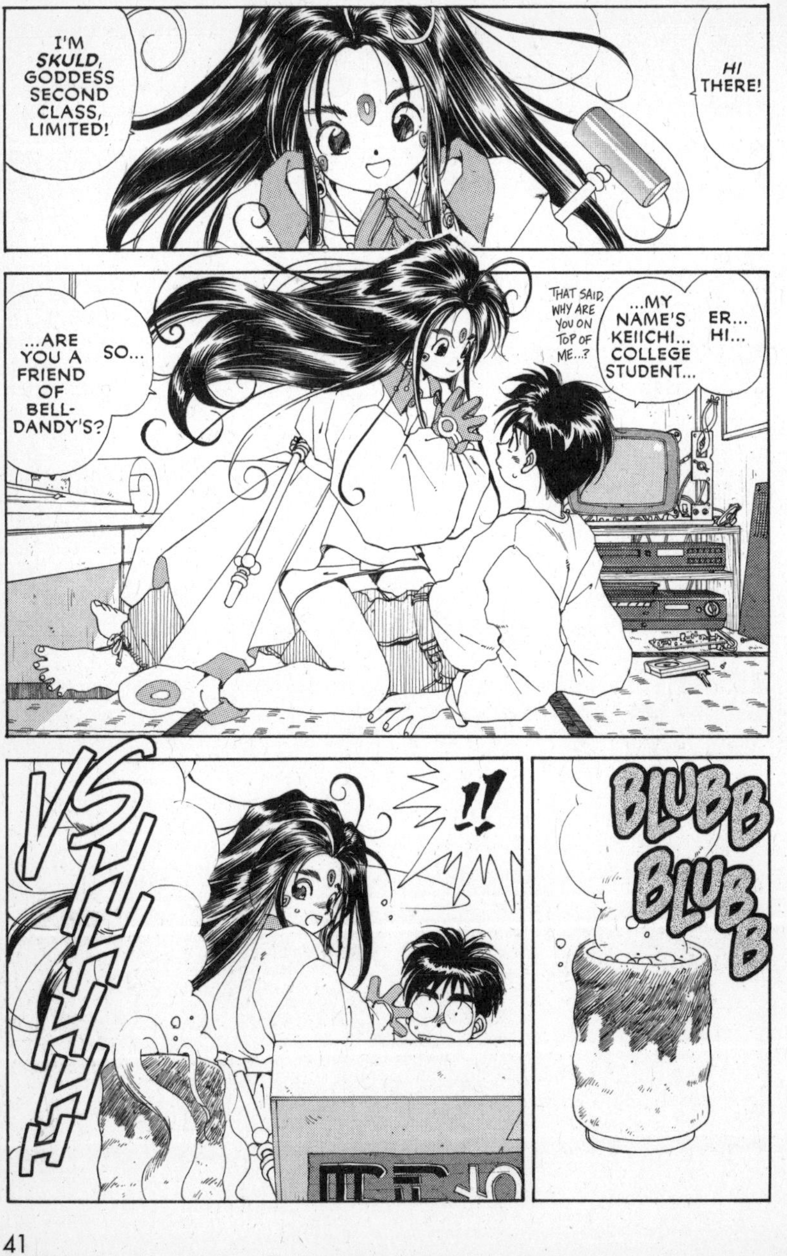
HI THERE!
I'M SKULD, GODDESS SECOND CLASS, LIMITED!
ER... HI...
...MY NAME'S KEIICHI... COLLEGE STUDENT...
THAT SAID, WHY ARE YOU ON TOP OF ME...?
SO...
...ARE YOU A FRIEND OF BELL-DANDY'S?
BLUBB BLUBB
!!
VSHHHHHH

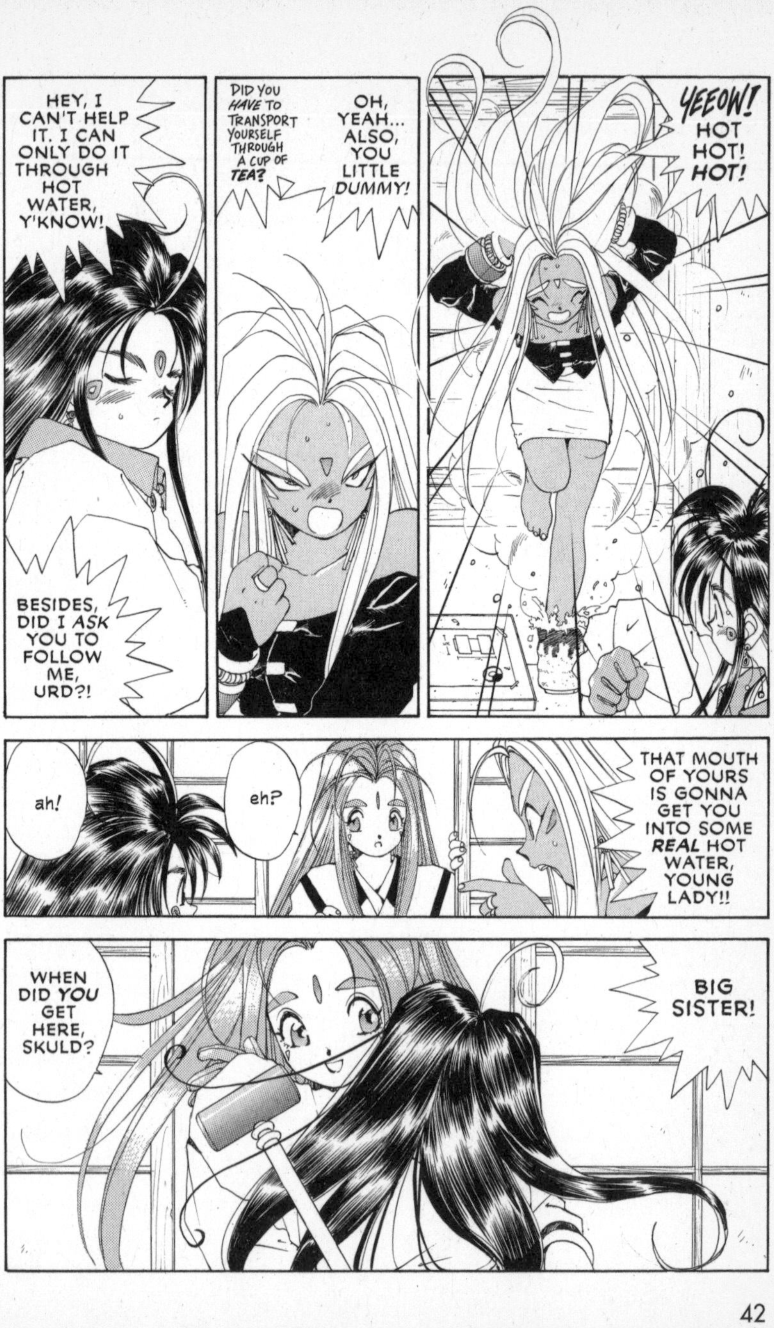
YEEOW!
HOT HOT! HOT!
OH, YEAH... ALSO, YOU LITTLE DUMMY!
DID YOU HAVE TO TRANSPORT YOURSELF THROUGH A CUP OF TEA?
HEY, I CAN'T HELP IT. I CAN ONLY DO IT THROUGH HOT WATER, Y'KNOW!
BESIDES, DID I ASK YOU TO FOLLOW ME, URD?!
THAT MOUTH OF YOURS IS GONNA GET YOU INTO SOME REAL HOT WATER, YOUNG LADY!!
eh?
ah!
BIG SISTER!
WHEN DID YOU GET HERE, SKULD?

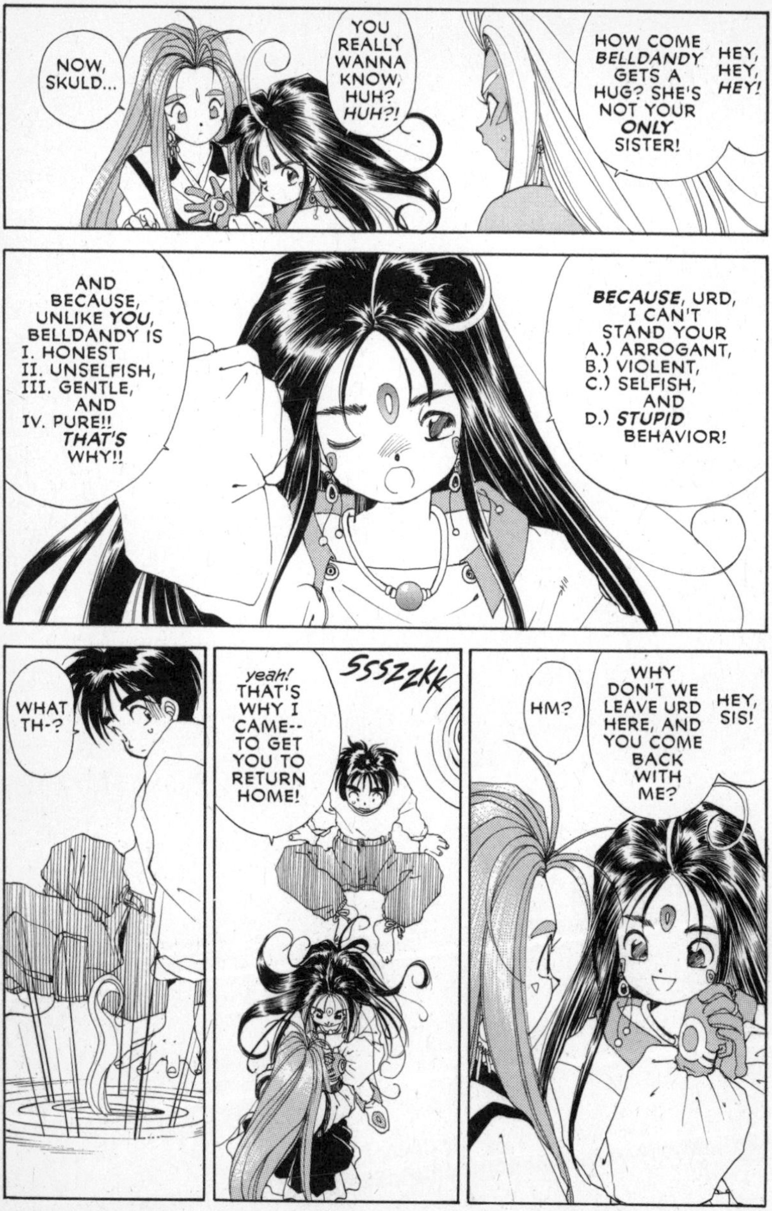
HEY, HEY, HEY!
HOW COME BELLDANDY GETS A HUG? SHE'S NOT YOUR ONLY SISTER!
YOU REALLY WANNA KNOW, HUH? HUH?!
NOW, SKULD...
BECAUSE, URD, I CAN'T STAND YOUR A.) ARROGANT, B.) VIOLENT, C.) SELFISH, AND D.) STUPID BEHAVIOR!
AND BECAUSE, UNLIKE YOU, BELLDANDY IS I. HONEST II. UNSELFISH, III. GENTLE, AND IV. PURE!! THAT'S WHY!!
HEY, SIS!
WHY DON'T WE LEAVE URD HERE, AND YOU COME BACK WITH ME?
HM?
SSSZZKK
yeah! THAT'S WHY I CAME-- TO GET YOU TO RETURN HOME!
WHAT TH-?

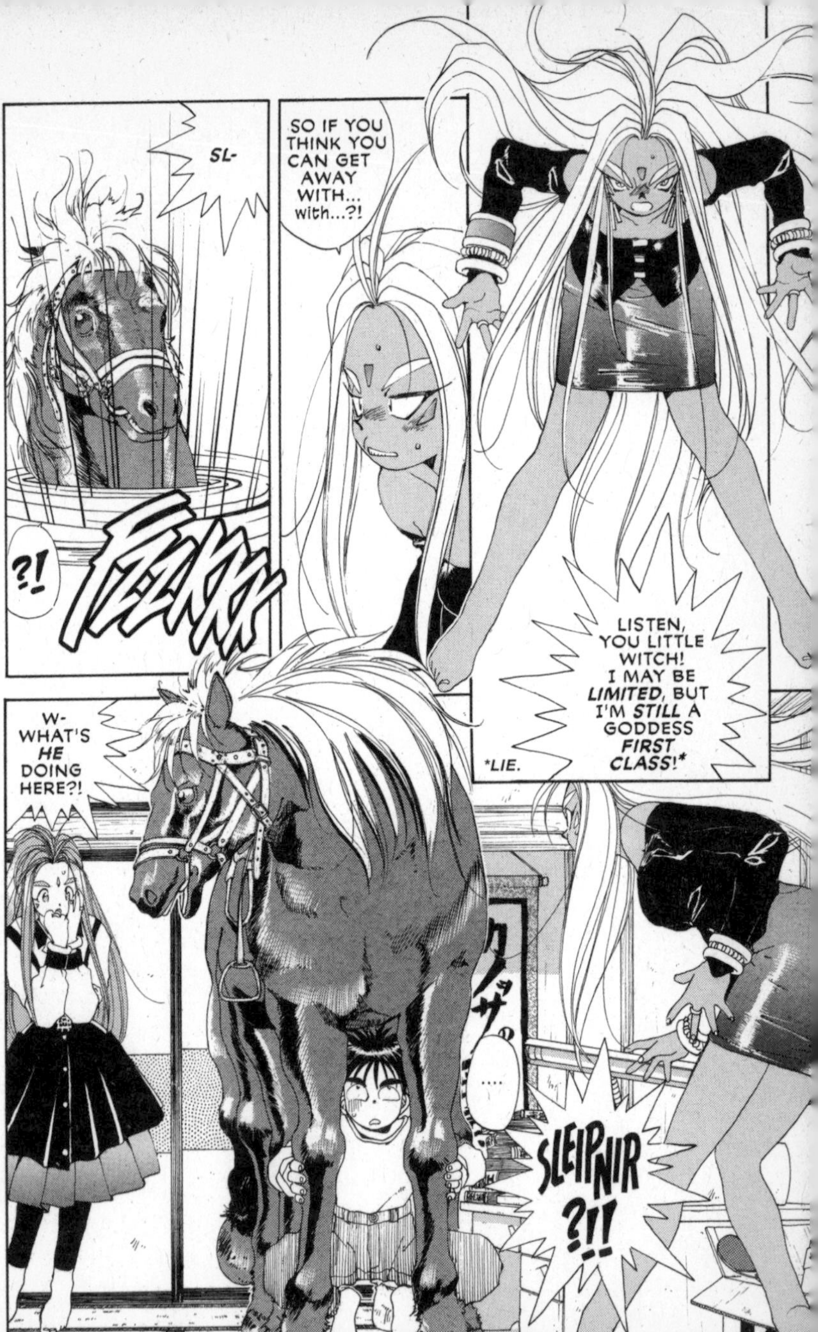
LISTEN, YOU LITTLE WITCH! I MAY BE *LIMITED*, BUT I'M *STILL* A GODDESS *FIRST CLASS*!*
*LIE.
SO IF YOU THINK YOU CAN GET AWAY WITH... with...?!
SL-
FZZKKK
?!
SLEIPNIR ?!!
....
W- WHAT'S *HE* DOING HERE?!

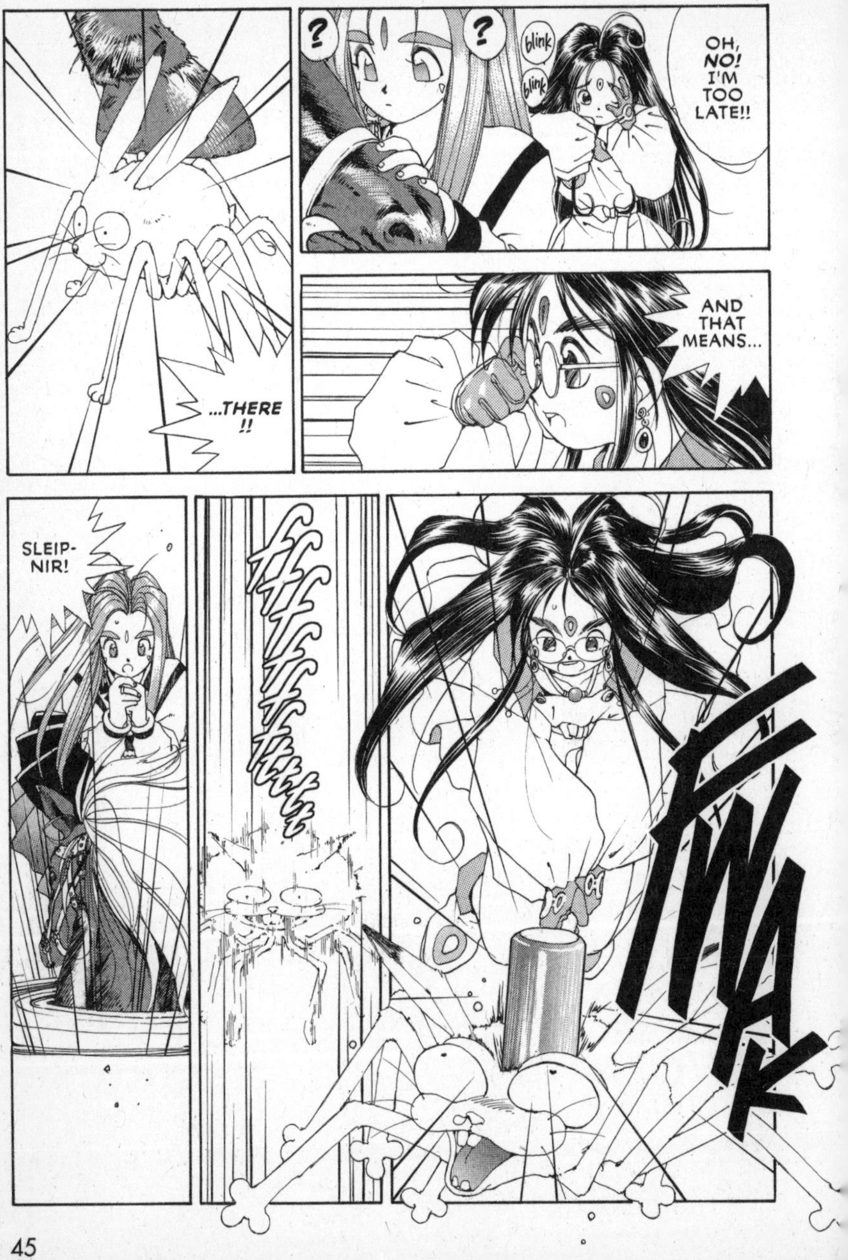
?
?
blink
blink
OH, NO! I'M TOO LATE!!
AND THAT MEANS...
...THERE !!
FWAK
SLEIP-NIR!

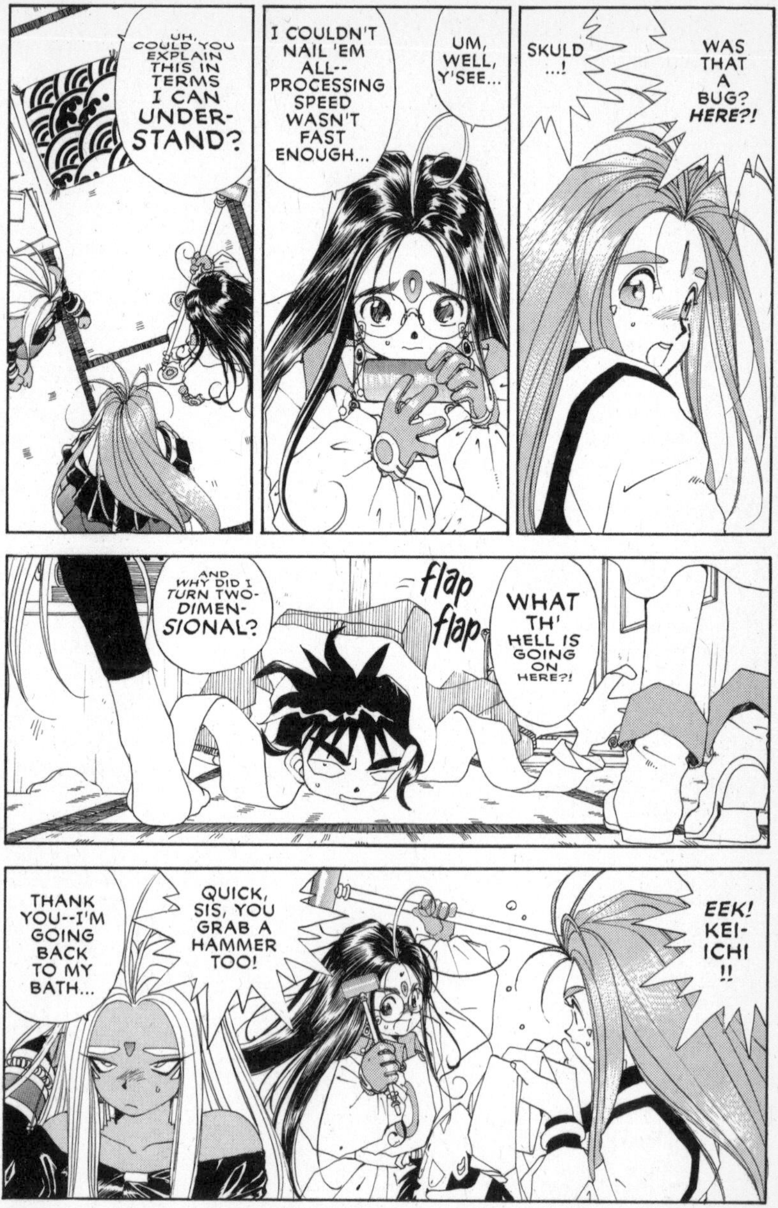
WAS THAT A BUG? HERE?!
SKULD ...!
UM, WELL, Y'SEE...
I COULDN'T NAIL 'EM ALL--PROCESSING SPEED WASN'T FAST ENOUGH...
UH, COULD YOU EXPLAIN THIS IN TERMS I CAN UNDER-STAND?
WHAT TH' HELL IS GOING ON HERE?!
flap flap
AND WHY DID I TURN TWO-DIMEN-SIONAL?
EEK! KEI-ICHI !!
QUICK, SIS, YOU GRAB A HAMMER TOO!
THANK YOU--I'M GOING BACK TO MY BATH...

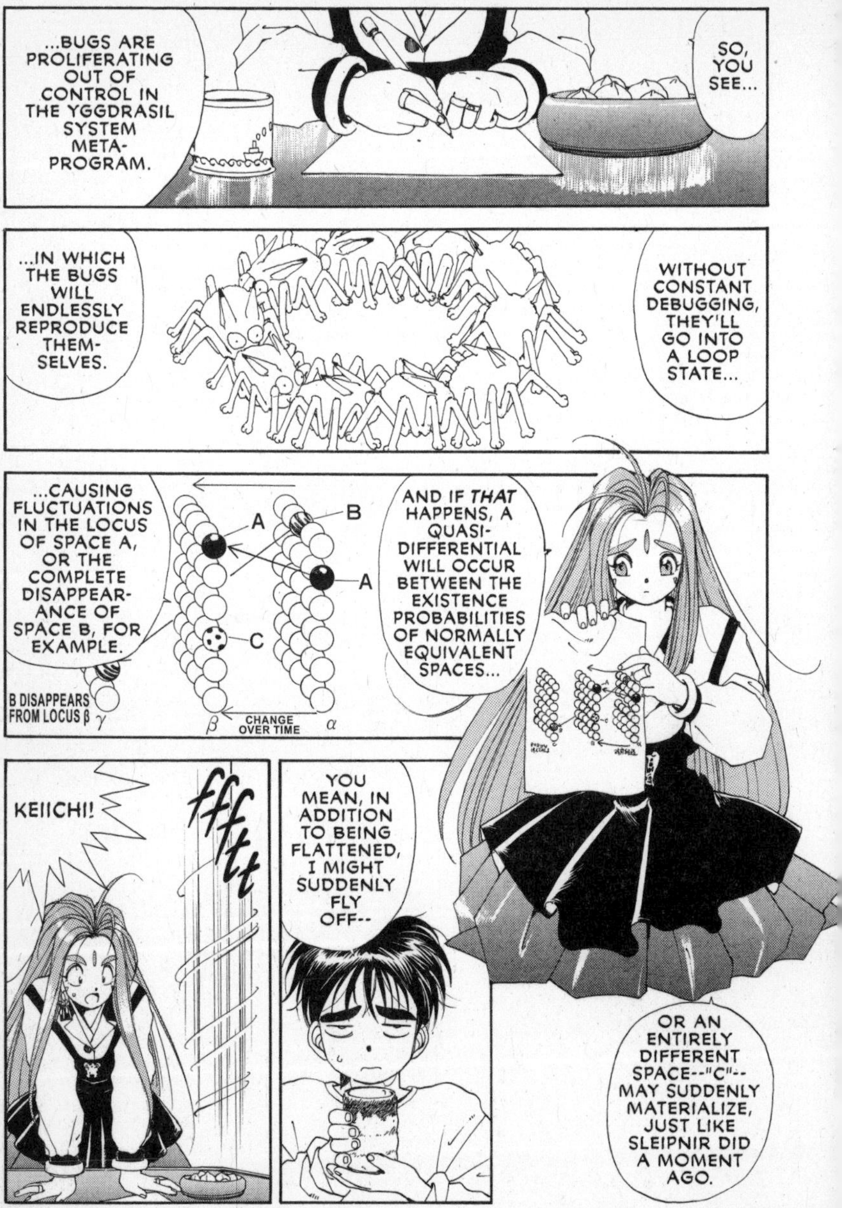
SO, YOU SEE...
...BUGS ARE PROLIFERATING OUT OF CONTROL IN THE YGGDRASIL SYSTEM META-PROGRAM.
WITHOUT CONSTANT DEBUGGING, THEY'LL GO INTO A LOOP STATE...
...IN WHICH THE BUGS WILL ENDLESSLY REPRODUCE THEM-SELVES.
AND IF *THAT* HAPPENS, A QUASI-DIFFERENTIAL WILL OCCUR BETWEEN THE EXISTENCE PROBABILITIES OF NORMALLY EQUIVALENT SPACES...
...CAUSING FLUCTUATIONS IN THE LOCUS OF SPACE A, OR THE COMPLETE DISAPPEAR-ANCE OF SPACE B, FOR EXAMPLE.
A
B
A
C
B DISAPPEARS FROM LOCUS β
γ
β
CHANGE OVER TIME
α
OR AN ENTIRELY DIFFERENT SPACE--"C"--MAY SUDDENLY MATERIALIZE, JUST LIKE SLEIPNIR DID A MOMENT AGO.
YOU MEAN, IN ADDITION TO BEING FLATTENED, I MIGHT SUDDENLY FLY OFF--
fffftt
KEIICHI!

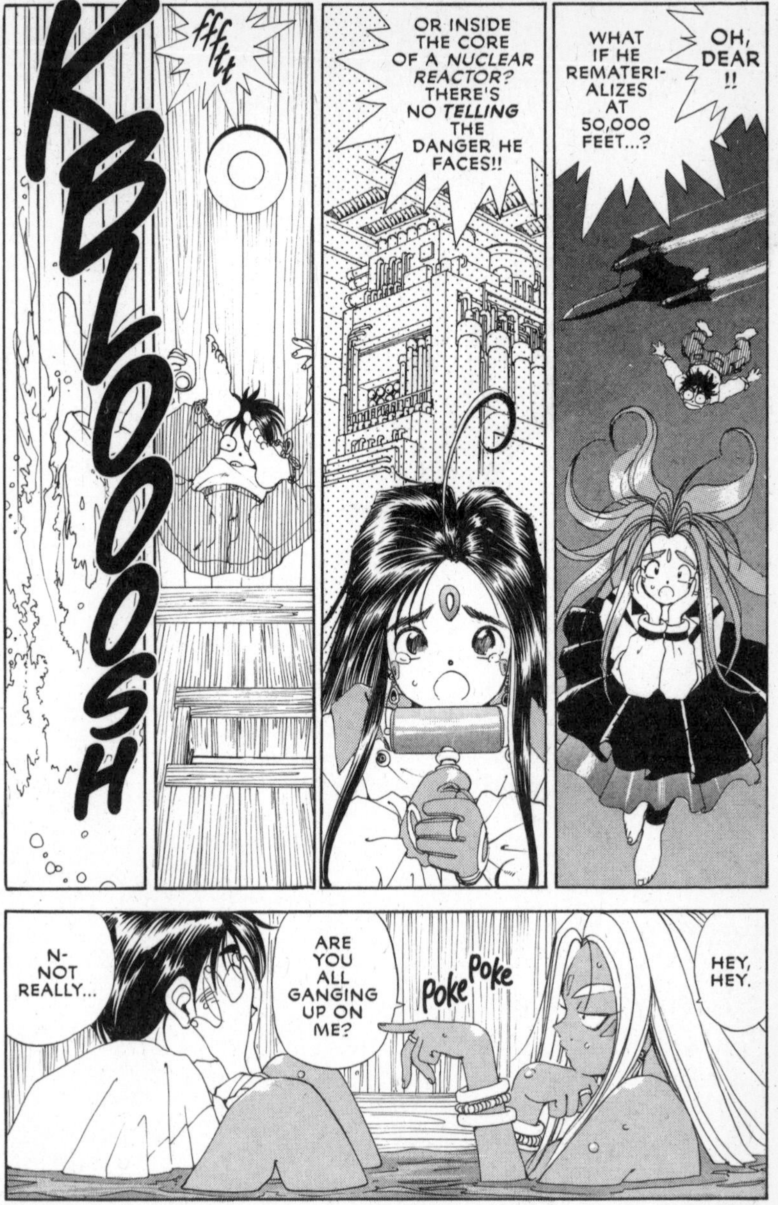
OH, DEAR !!
WHAT IF HE REMATERI-ALIZES AT 50,000 FEET...?
OR INSIDE THE CORE OF A NUCLEAR REACTOR? THERE'S NO TELLING THE DANGER HE FACES!!
ffftt
KBLOOSH
HEY, HEY.
Poke Poke
ARE YOU ALL GANGING UP ON ME?
N-NOT REALLY...

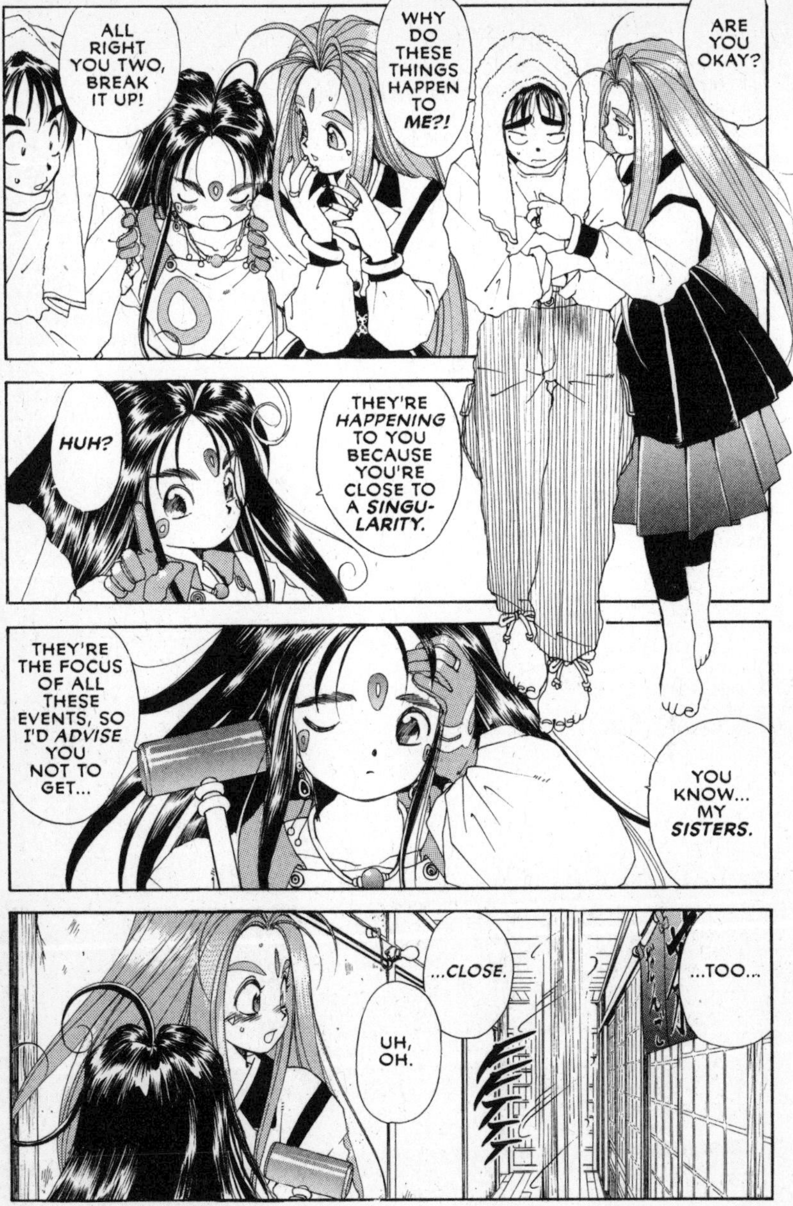
ARE YOU OKAY?
WHY DO THESE THINGS HAPPEN TO *ME?!*
ALL RIGHT YOU TWO, BREAK IT UP!
THEY'RE *HAPPENING* TO YOU BECAUSE YOU'RE CLOSE TO A *SINGU-LARITY.*
*HUH?*
YOU KNOW... MY *SISTERS.*
THEY'RE THE FOCUS OF ALL THESE EVENTS, SO I'D *ADVISE* YOU NOT TO GET...
...TOO...
...*CLOSE.*
UH, OH.

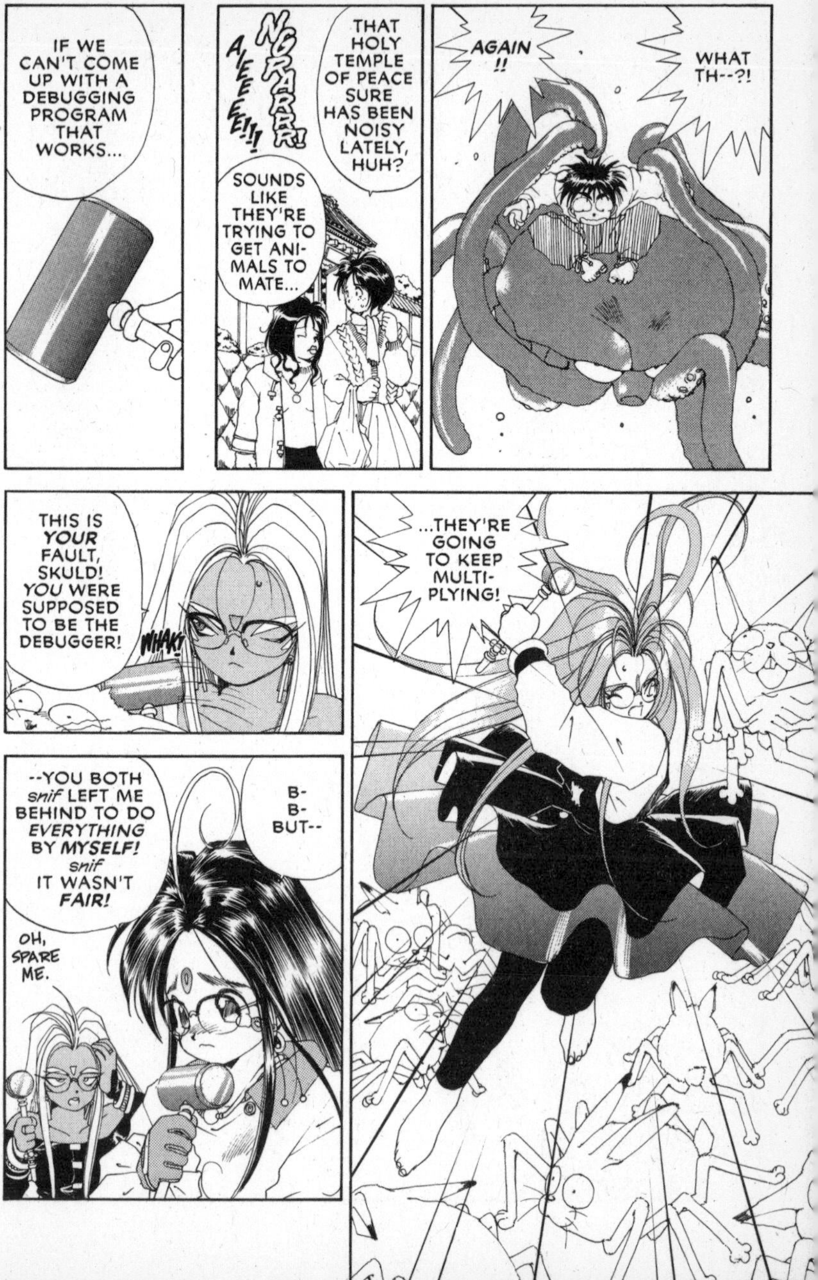
WHAT TH--?!
AGAIN !!
NGRARRR!
AIEEEEE!!!
THAT HOLY TEMPLE OF PEACE SURE HAS BEEN NOISY LATELY, HUH?
SOUNDS LIKE THEY'RE TRYING TO GET ANI-MALS TO MATE...
IF WE CAN'T COME UP WITH A DEBUGGING PROGRAM THAT WORKS...
...THEY'RE GOING TO KEEP MULTI-PLYING!
THIS IS *YOUR* FAULT, SKULD! *YOU* WERE SUPPOSED TO BE THE DEBUGGER!
WHAK!
B- B- BUT--
--YOU BOTH *snif* LEFT ME BEHIND TO DO *EVERYTHING* BY ***MYSELF!*** *snif* IT WASN'T ***FAIR!***
OH, SPARE ME.

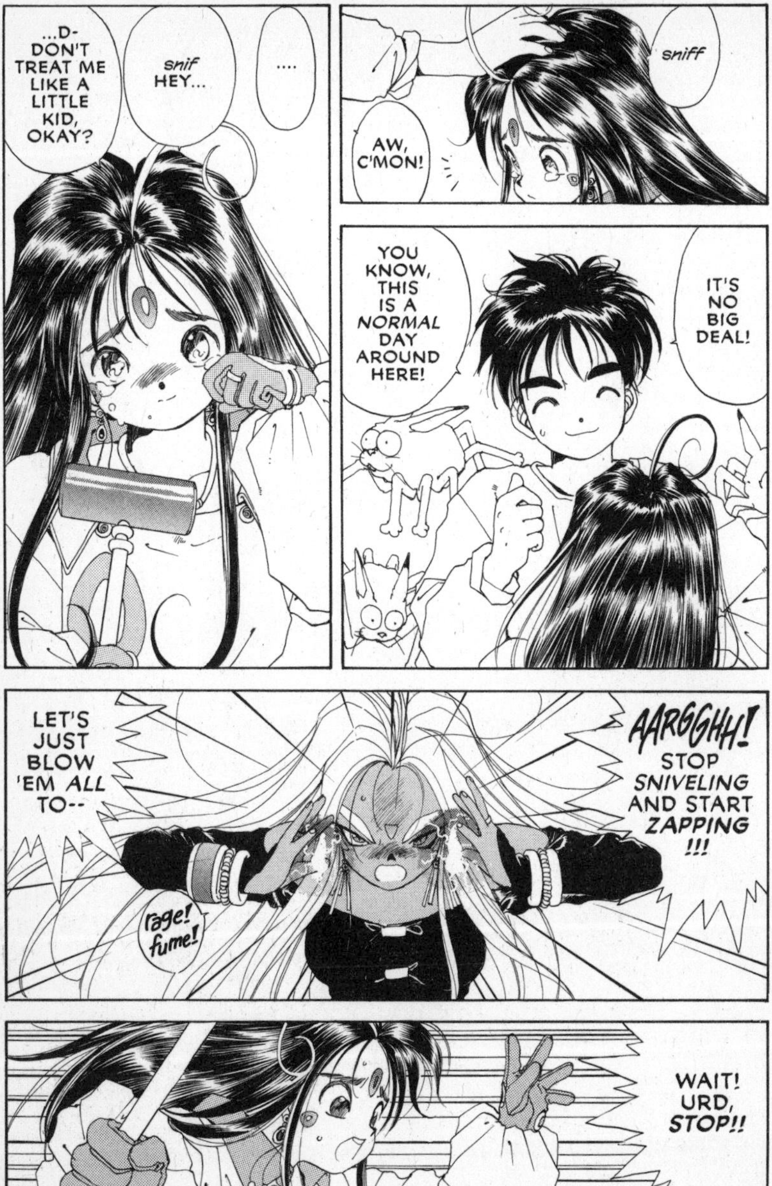
sniff
AW, C'MON!
IT'S NO BIG DEAL!
YOU KNOW, THIS IS A NORMAL DAY AROUND HERE!
....
snif HEY...
...D-DON'T TREAT ME LIKE A LITTLE KID, OKAY?
AARGGHH! STOP SNIVELING AND START ZAPPING!!!
rage! fume!
LET'S JUST BLOW 'EM ALL TO--
WAIT! URD, STOP!!

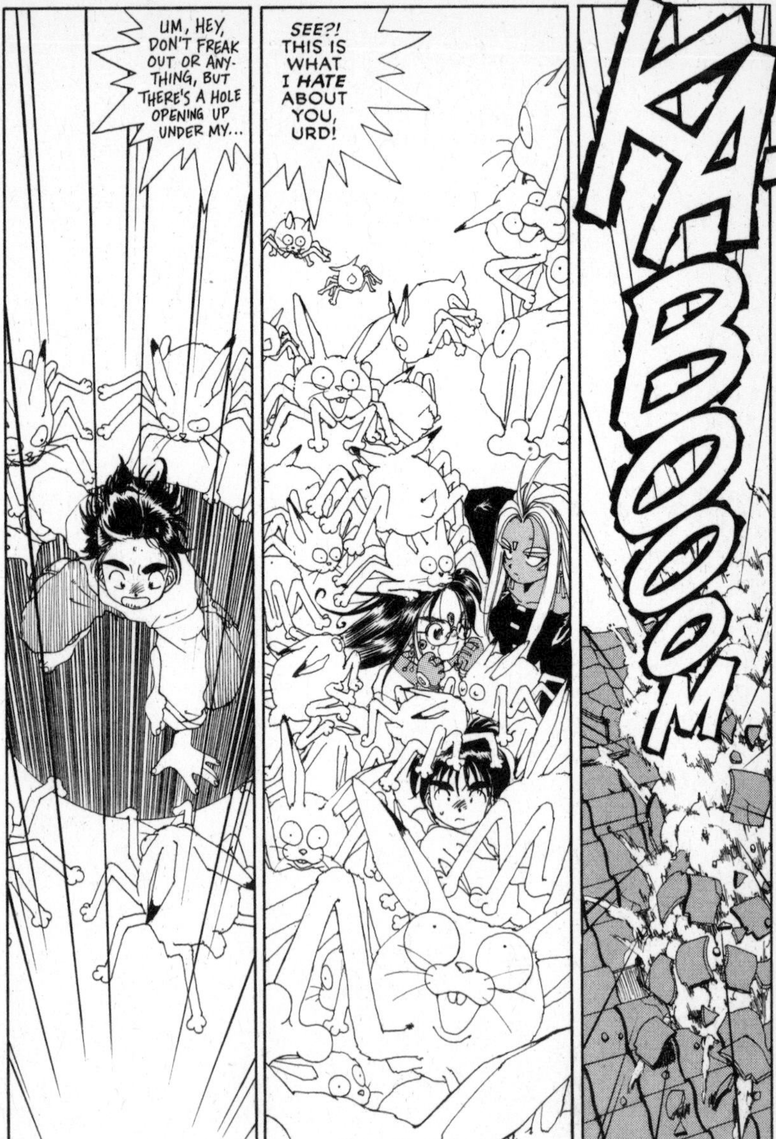
UM, HEY, DON'T FREAK OUT OR ANY-THING, BUT THERE'S A HOLE OPENING UP UNDER MY...
SEE?! THIS IS WHAT I *HATE* ABOUT YOU, URD!
KA-BOOOM.

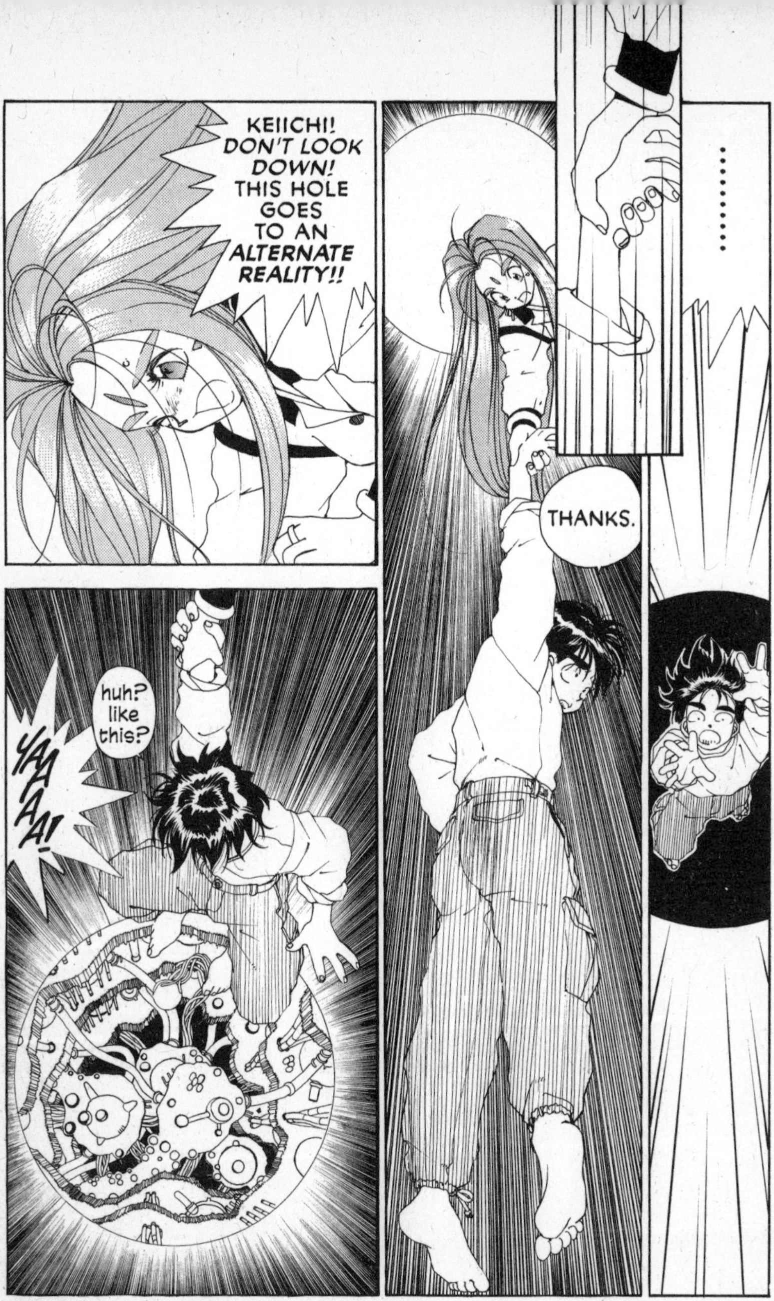
......
THANKS.
KEIICHI! DON'T LOOK DOWN! THIS HOLE GOES TO AN ALTERNATE REALITY!!
huh? like this?
YAAAAA!

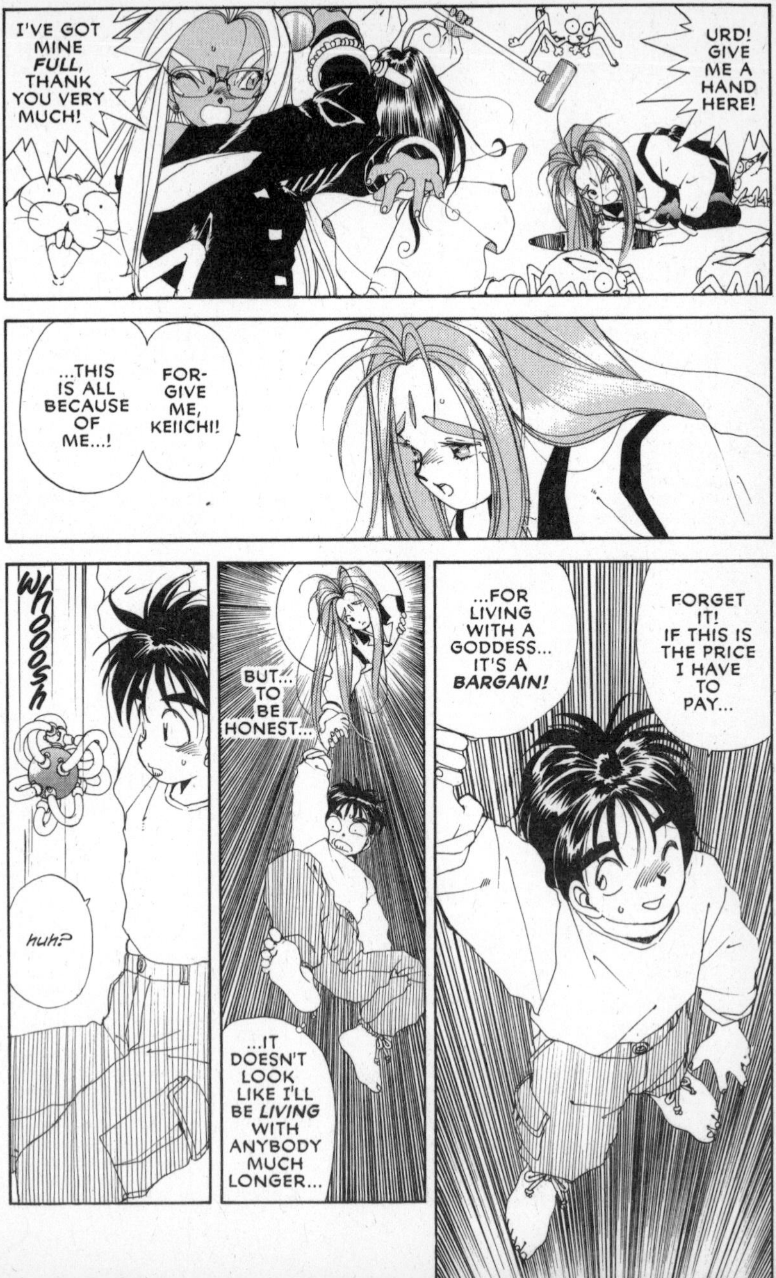
URD! GIVE ME A HAND HERE!
I'VE GOT MINE FULL, THANK YOU VERY MUCH!
FOR-GIVE ME, KEIICHI!
...THIS IS ALL BECAUSE OF ME...!
FORGET IT! IF THIS IS THE PRICE I HAVE TO PAY...
...FOR LIVING WITH A GODDESS... IT'S A BARGAIN!
BUT... TO BE HONEST...
...IT DOESN'T LOOK LIKE I'LL BE LIVING WITH ANYBODY MUCH LONGER...
whoooosh
huh?

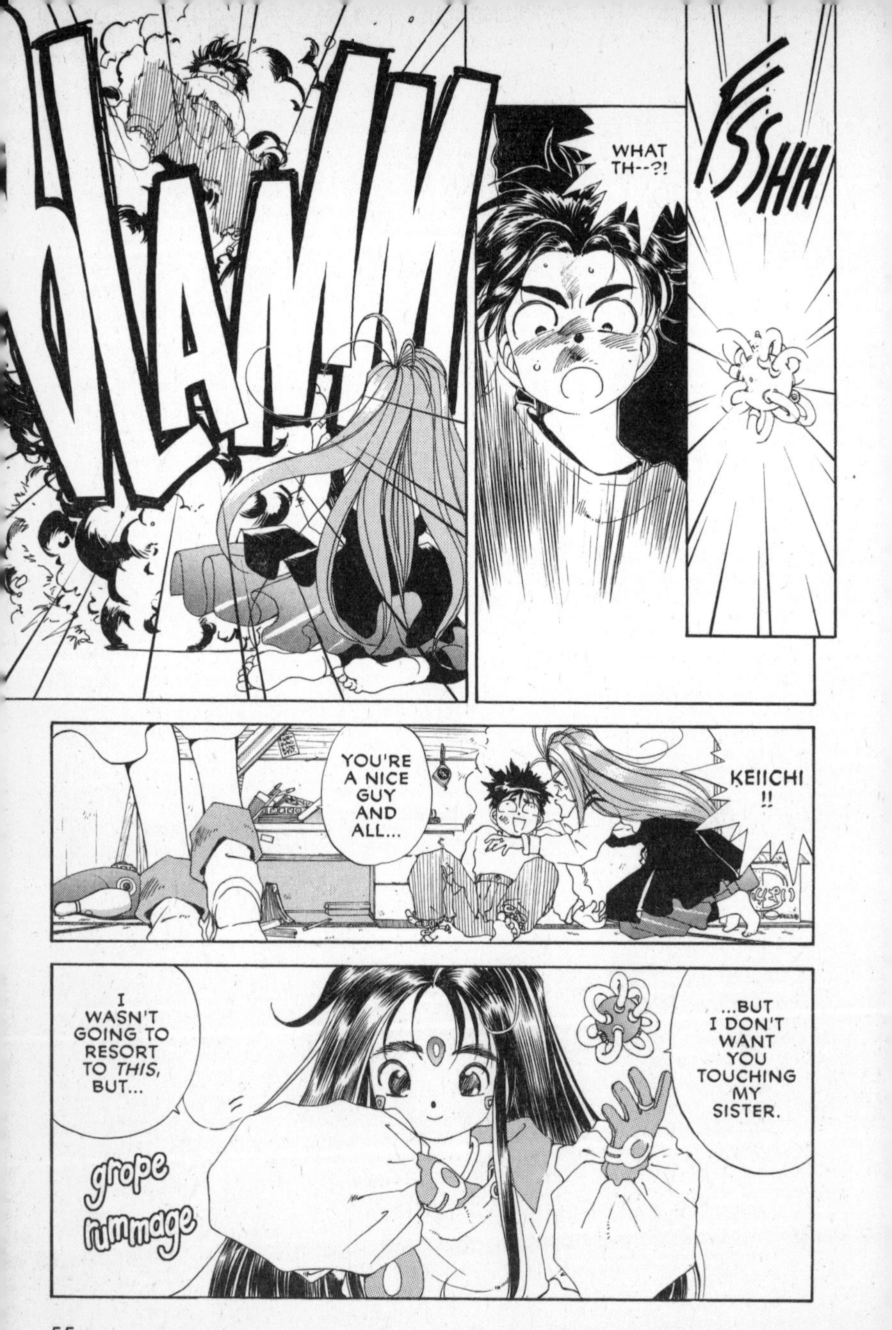
FSSHH
WHAT TH--?!
SLAMM
KEIICHI !!
YOU'RE A NICE GUY AND ALL...
...BUT I DON'T WANT YOU TOUCHING MY SISTER.
I WASN'T GOING TO RESORT TO *THIS*, BUT...
grope rummage

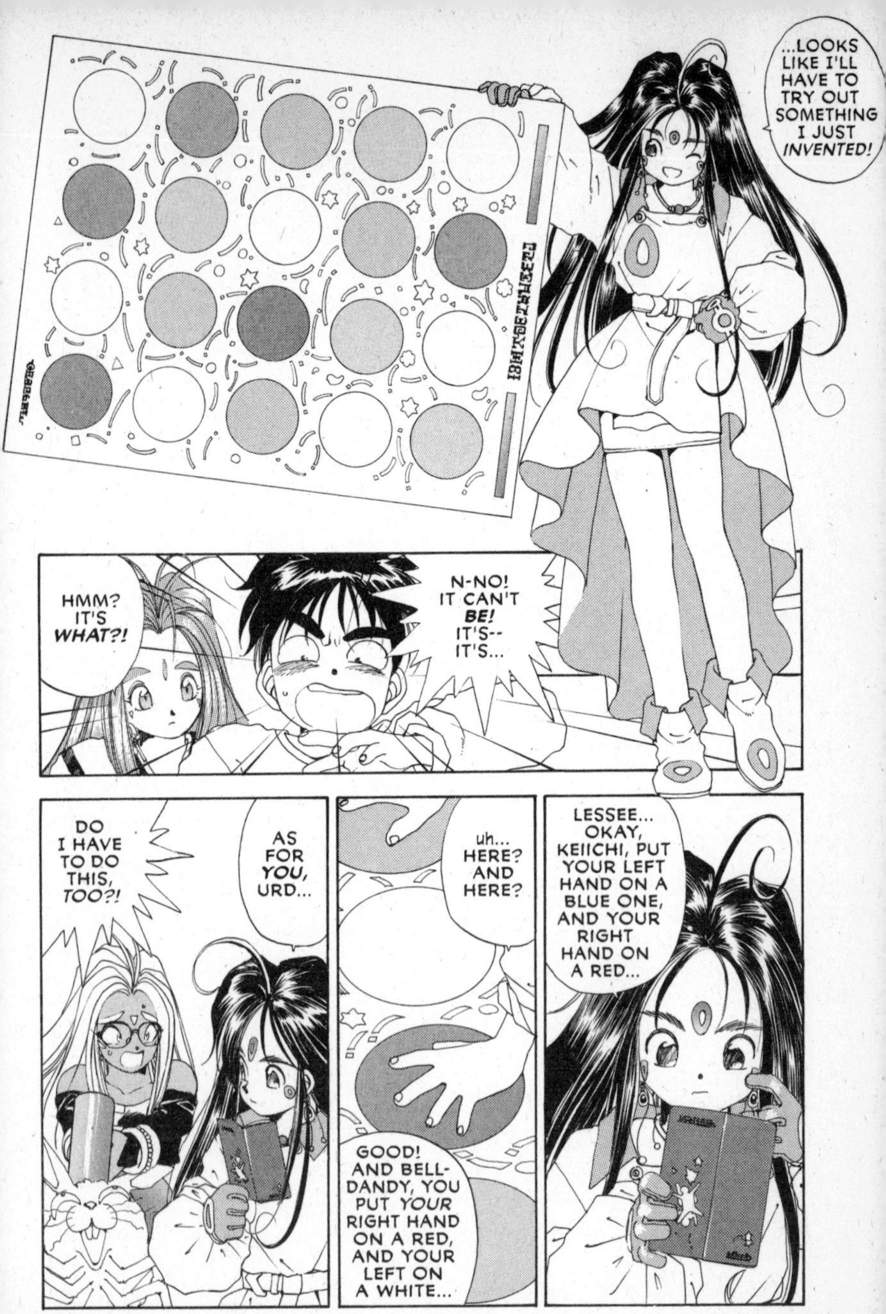
...LOOKS LIKE I'LL HAVE TO TRY OUT SOMETHING I JUST *INVENTED!*
N-NO! IT CAN'T *BE!* IT'S-- IT'S...
HMM? IT'S *WHAT?!*
LESSEE... OKAY, KEIICHI, PUT YOUR LEFT HAND ON A BLUE ONE, AND YOUR RIGHT HAND ON A RED...
uh... HERE? AND HERE?
GOOD! AND BELL-DANDY, YOU PUT *YOUR* RIGHT HAND ON A RED, AND YOUR LEFT ON A WHITE...
AS FOR *YOU,* URD...
DO I HAVE TO DO THIS, *TOO?!*

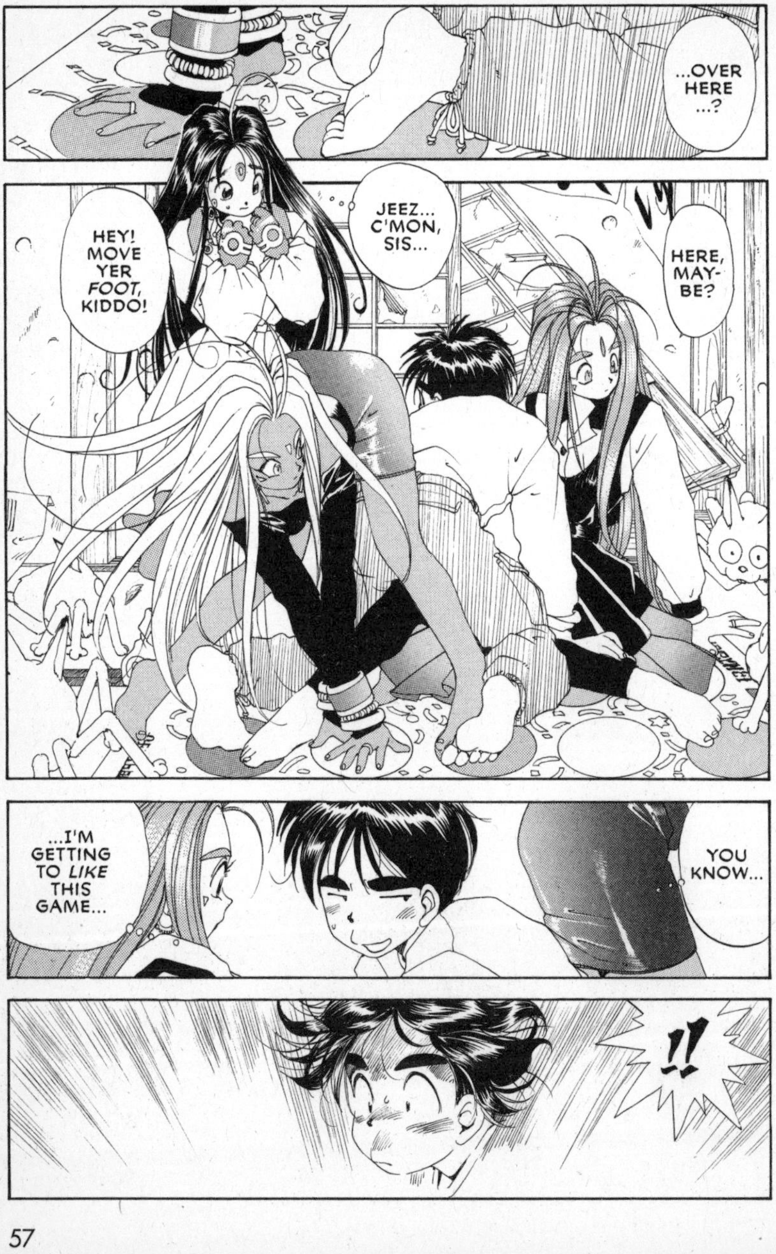
...OVER HERE ...?
HERE, MAY-BE?
JEEZ... C'MON, SIS...
HEY! MOVE YER *FOOT*, KIDDO!
YOU KNOW...
...I'M GETTING TO *LIKE* THIS GAME...
!!

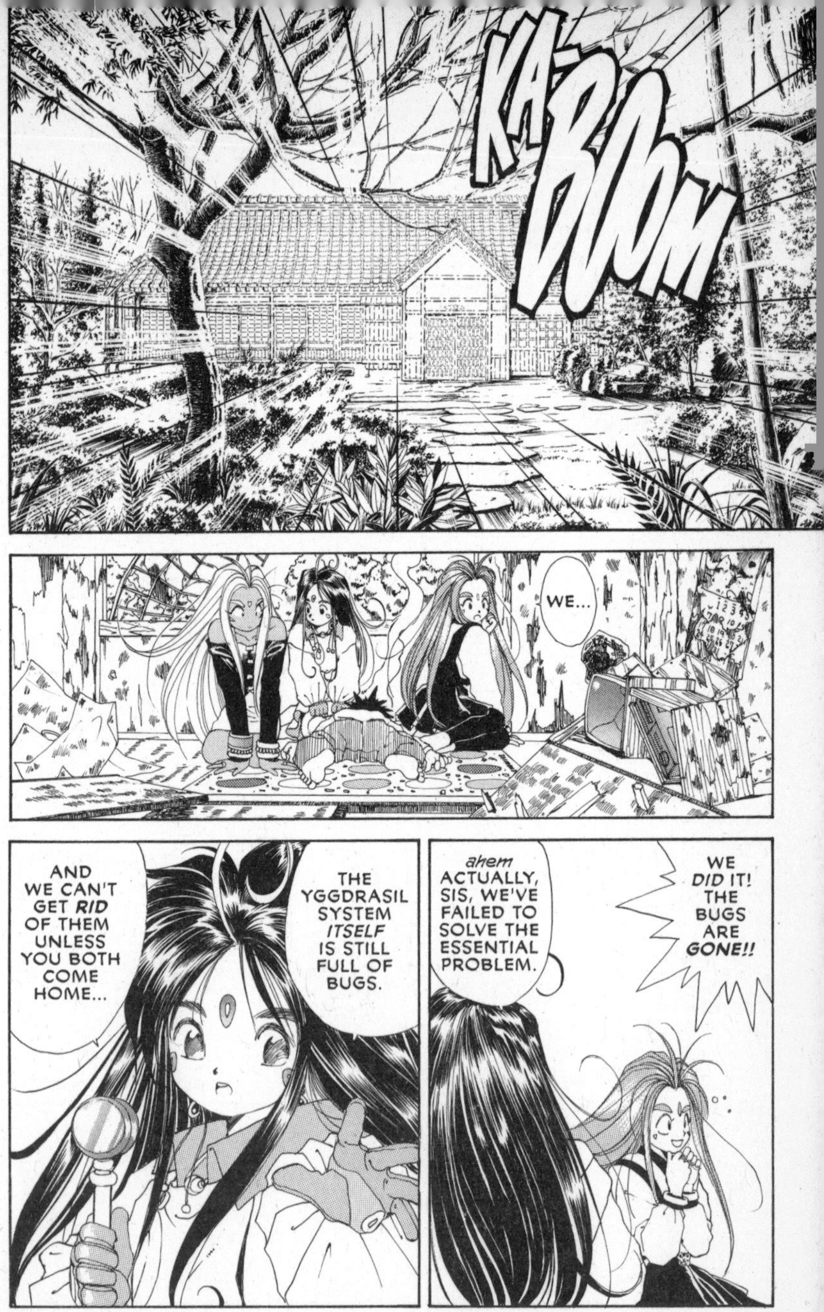
KA-BOOM
WE...
WE *DID* IT! THE BUGS ARE *GONE!!*
*ahem* ACTUALLY, SIS, WE'VE FAILED TO SOLVE THE ESSENTIAL PROBLEM.
THE YGGDRASIL SYSTEM *ITSELF* IS STILL FULL OF BUGS.
AND WE CAN'T GET *RID* OF THEM UNLESS YOU BOTH COME HOME...

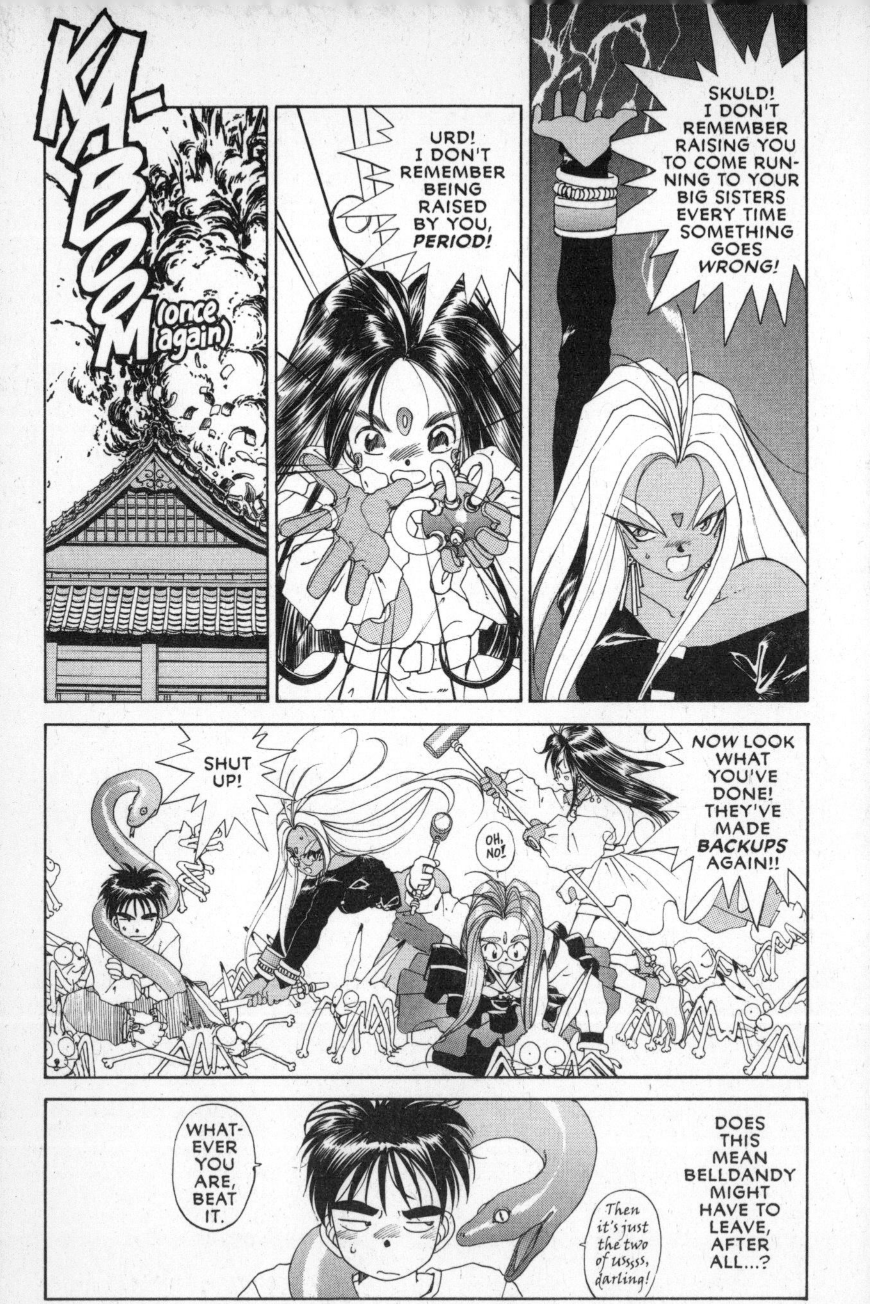
SKULD! I DON'T REMEMBER RAISING YOU TO COME RUNNING TO YOUR BIG SISTERS EVERY TIME SOMETHING GOES *WRONG!*
URD! I DON'T REMEMBER BEING RAISED BY YOU, *PERIOD!*
KA-BOOOM (once again)
*NOW* LOOK WHAT YOU'VE DONE! THEY'VE MADE **BACKUPS** AGAIN!!
OH, NO!
SHUT UP!
DOES THIS MEAN BELLDANDY MIGHT HAVE TO LEAVE, AFTER ALL...?
Then it's just the two of ussss, darling!
WHAT-EVER YOU ARE, BEAT IT.

# THE ADVENTURES OF MINI-URD

introducing MINI-SKULD!!

## ◆ A CASUAL BET ◆

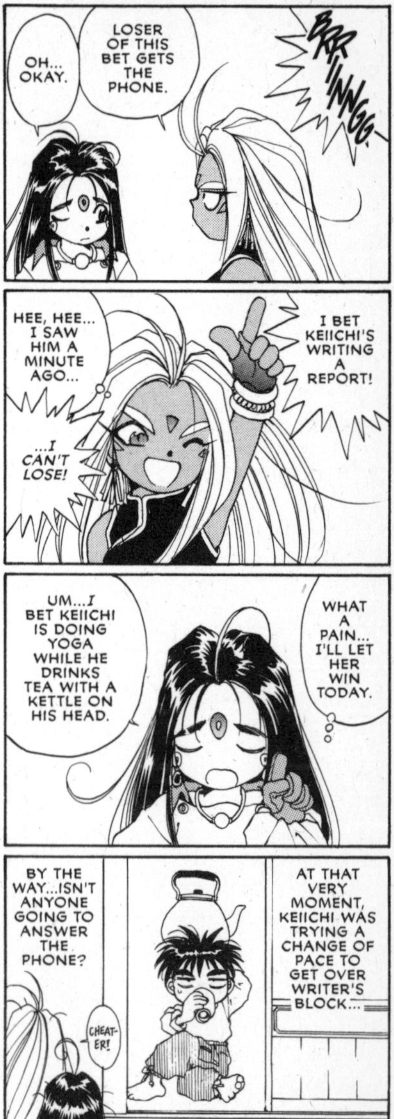
BRRIIINNGG
LOSER OF THIS BET GETS THE PHONE.
OH... OKAY.
I BET KEIICHI'S WRITING A REPORT!
HEE, HEE... I SAW HIM A MINUTE AGO...
...I CAN'T LOSE!
WHAT A PAIN... I'LL LET HER WIN TODAY.
UM...I BET KEIICHI IS DOING YOGA WHILE HE DRINKS TEA WITH A KETTLE ON HIS HEAD.
AT THAT VERY MOMENT, KEIICHI WAS TRYING A CHANGE OF PACE TO GET OVER WRITER'S BLOCK...
BY THE WAY...ISN'T ANYONE GOING TO ANSWER THE PHONE?
CHEAT-ER!

## CAN YOU EAT THIS?! ◆THE ULTIMATE GOURMAND!◆

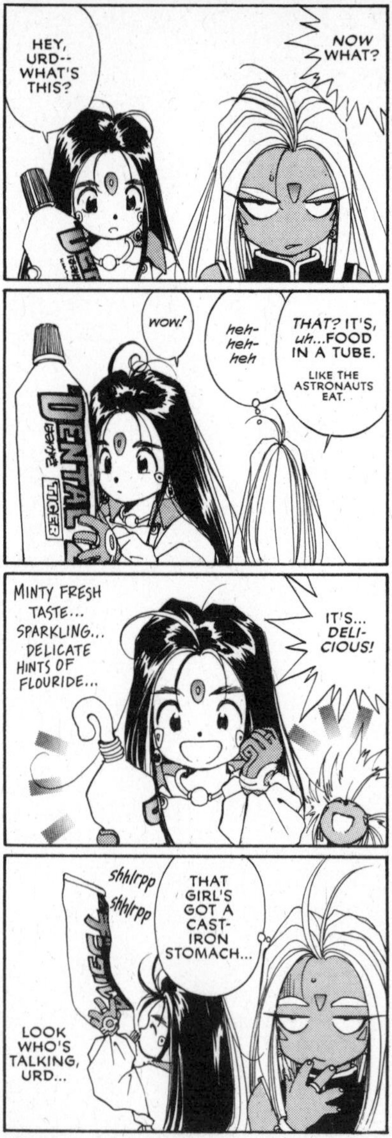
NOW WHAT?
HEY, URD-- WHAT'S THIS?
THAT? IT'S, uh...FOOD IN A TUBE.
LIKE THE ASTRONAUTS EAT.
heh-heh-heh
WOW!
DENTAL
TIGER
IT'S... DELICIOUS!
MINTY FRESH TASTE... SPARKLING... DELICATE HINTS OF FLOURIDE...
THAT GIRL'S GOT A CAST-IRON STOMACH...
shhlrpp
shhlrpp
LOOK WHO'S TALKING, URD...

## CHAPTER 33

# The Goddesses' Greatest Danger

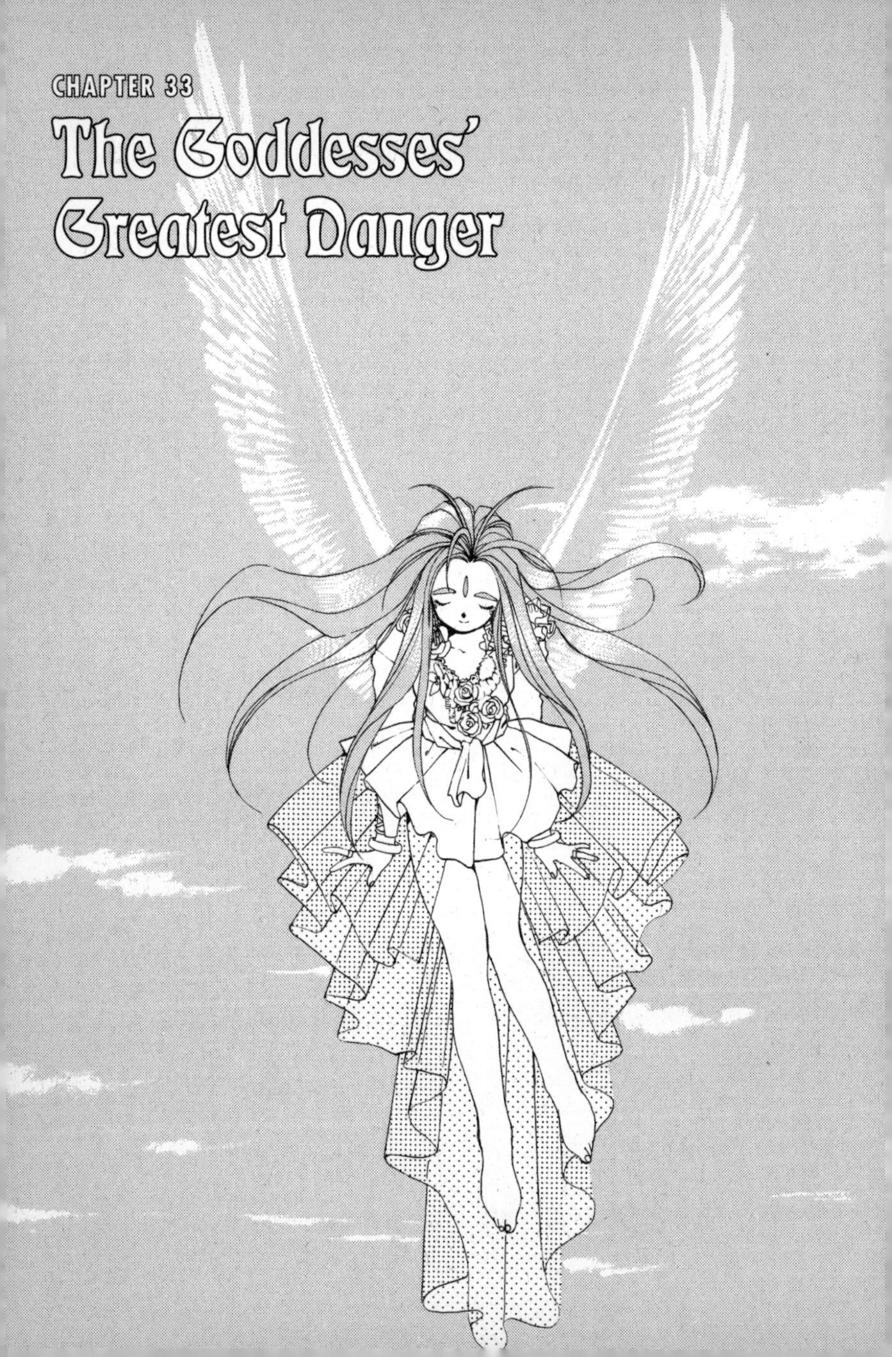

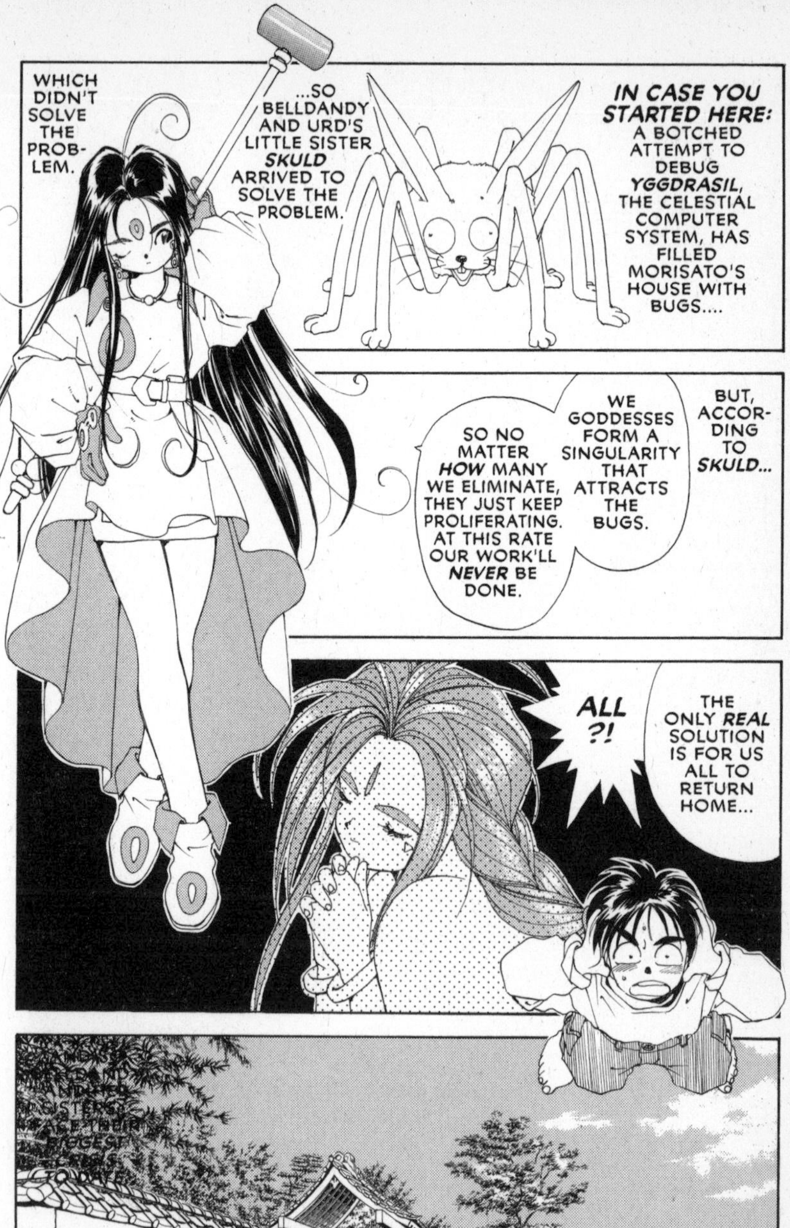
IN CASE YOU STARTED HERE: A BOTCHED ATTEMPT TO DEBUG YGGDRASIL, THE CELESTIAL COMPUTER SYSTEM, HAS FILLED MORISATO'S HOUSE WITH BUGS....
...SO BELLDANDY AND URD'S LITTLE SISTER SKULD ARRIVED TO SOLVE THE PROBLEM.
WHICH DIDN'T SOLVE THE PROB-LEM.
BUT, ACCORD-DING TO SKULD...
WE GODDESSES FORM A SINGULARITY THAT ATTRACTS THE BUGS.
SO NO MATTER HOW MANY WE ELIMINATE, THEY JUST KEEP PROLIFERATING. AT THIS RATE OUR WORK'LL NEVER BE DONE.
THE ONLY REAL SOLUTION IS FOR US ALL TO RETURN HOME...
ALL ?!

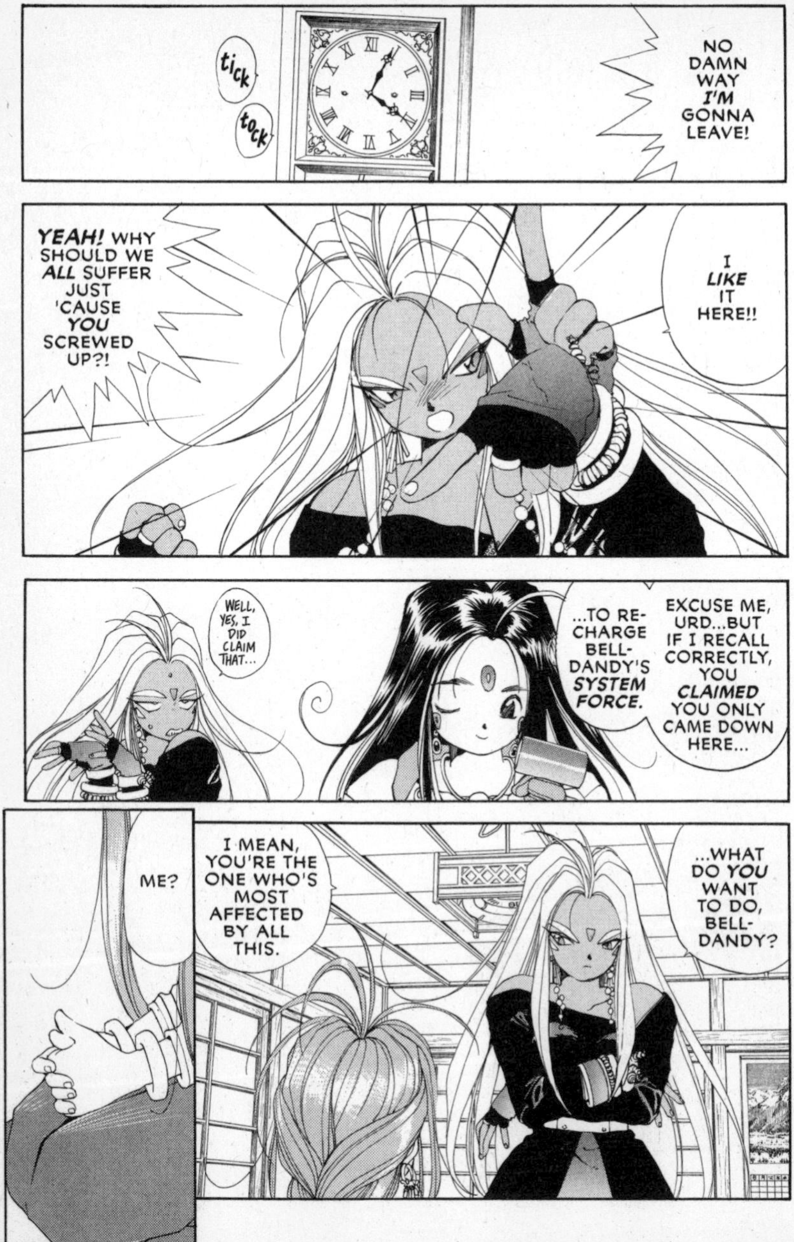
NO DAMN WAY I'M GONNA LEAVE!
tick
tock
I LIKE IT HERE!!
YEAH! WHY SHOULD WE ALL SUFFER JUST 'CAUSE YOU SCREWED UP?!
EXCUSE ME, URD...BUT IF I RECALL CORRECTLY, YOU CLAIMED YOU ONLY CAME DOWN HERE...
...TO RE-CHARGE BELL-DANDY'S SYSTEM FORCE.
WELL, YES, I DID CLAIM THAT...
...WHAT DO YOU WANT TO DO, BELL-DANDY?
I MEAN, YOU'RE THE ONE WHO'S MOST AFFECTED BY ALL THIS.
ME?

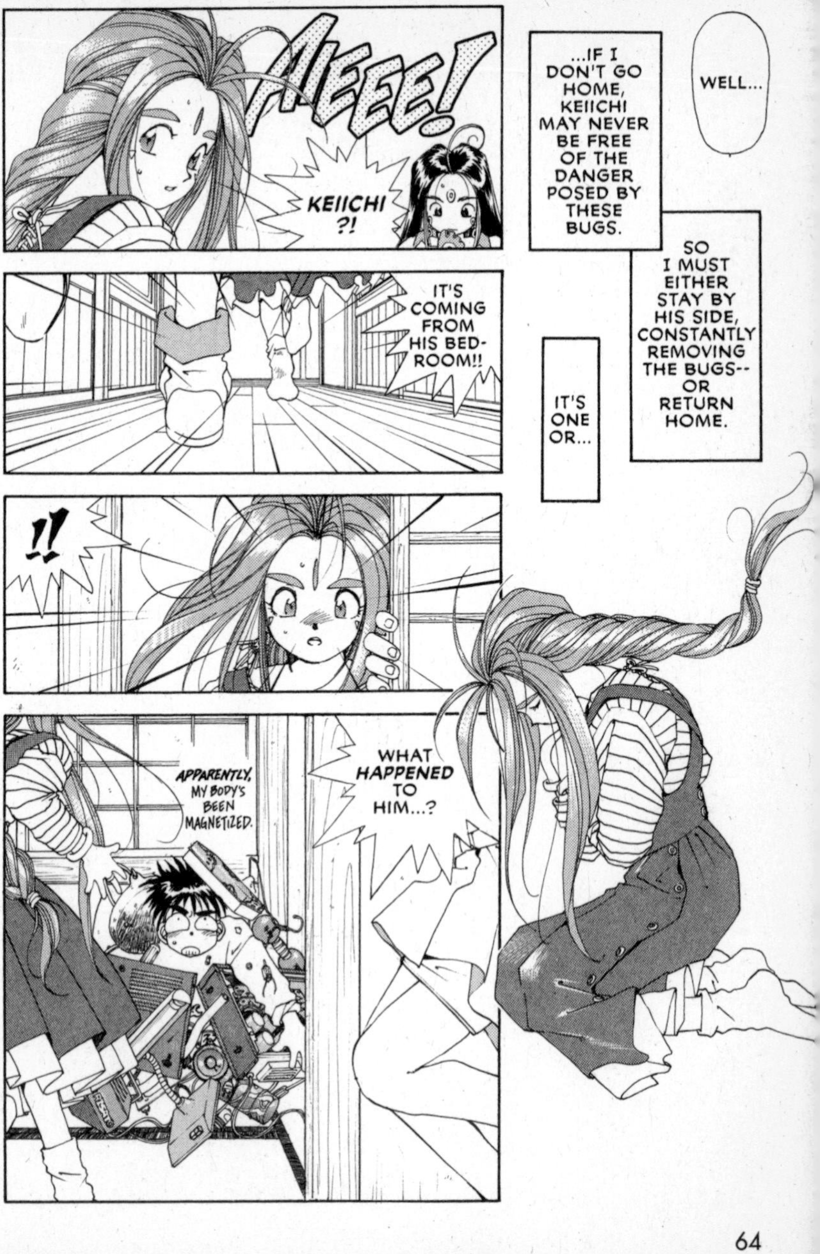
WELL...
...IF I DON'T GO HOME, KEIICHI MAY NEVER BE FREE OF THE DANGER POSED BY THESE BUGS.
SO I MUST EITHER STAY BY HIS SIDE, CONSTANTLY REMOVING THE BUGS--OR RETURN HOME.
IT'S ONE OR...
AIEEE!
KEIICHI ?!
IT'S COMING FROM HIS BED-ROOM!!
!!
WHAT HAPPENED TO HIM...?
APPARENTLY, MY BODY'S BEEN MAGNETIZED.

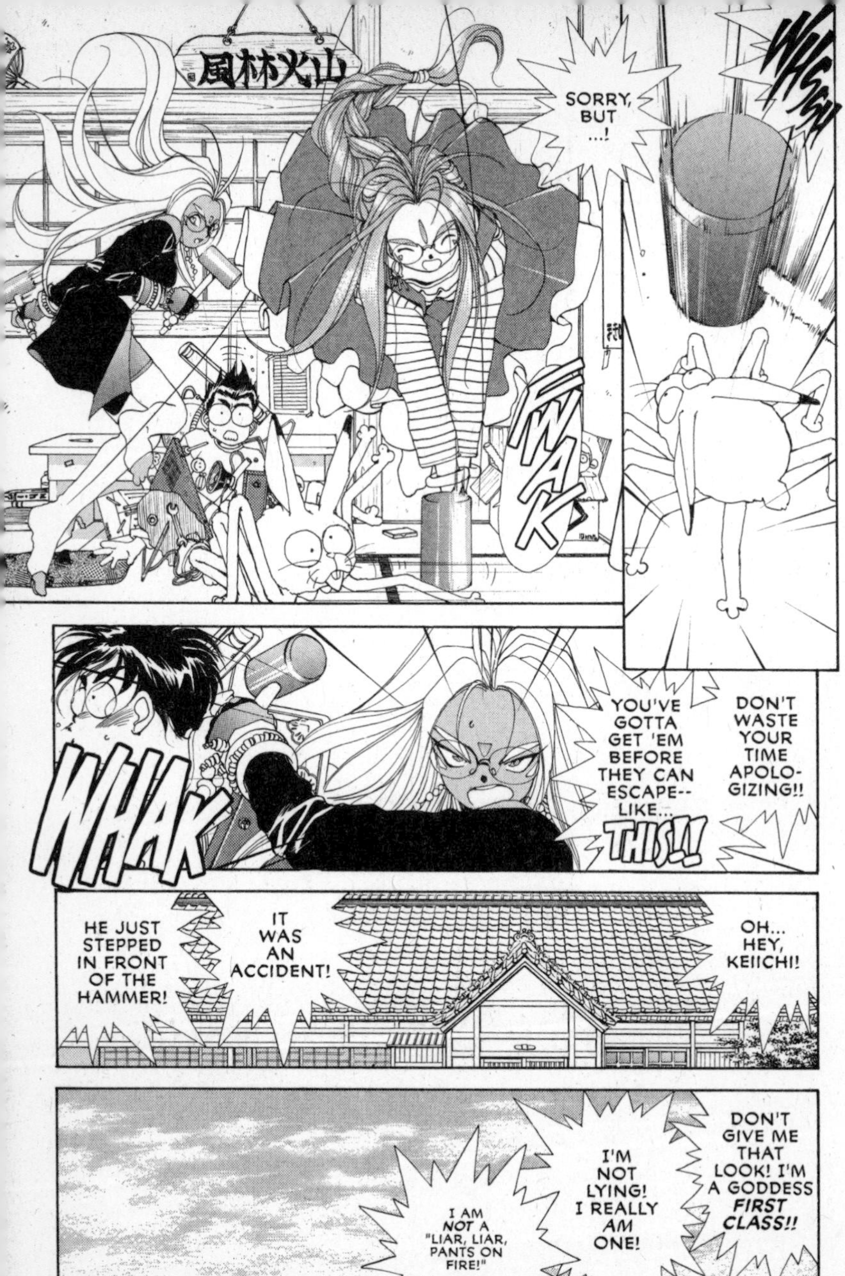
WHSSH
風林火山
SORRY, BUT ...!
FWAK
DON'T WASTE YOUR TIME APOLO-GIZING!!
YOU'VE GOTTA GET 'EM BEFORE THEY CAN ESCAPE-- LIKE...
THIS!!
WHAK
OH... HEY, KEIICHI!
IT WAS AN ACCIDENT!
HE JUST STEPPED IN FRONT OF THE HAMMER!
DON'T GIVE ME THAT LOOK! I'M A GODDESS *FIRST CLASS!!*
I'M NOT LYING! I REALLY *AM* ONE!
I AM *NOT* A "LIAR, LIAR, PANTS ON FIRE!"

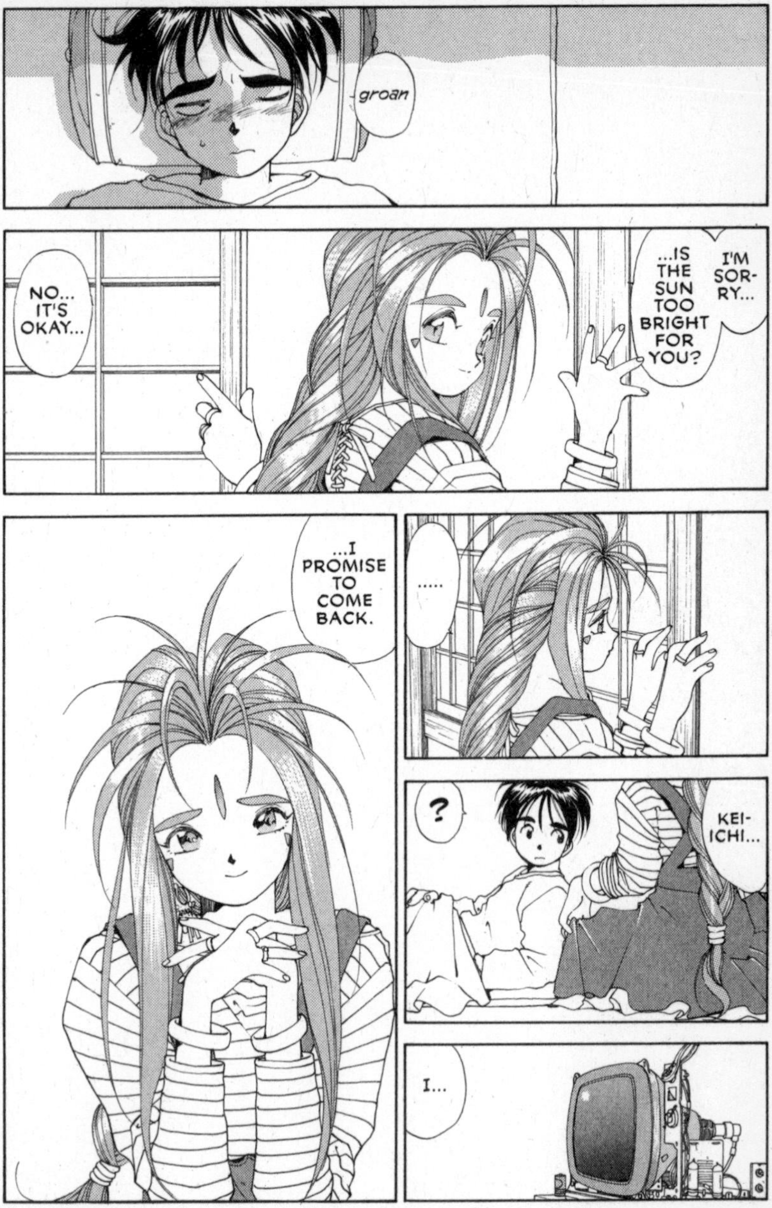
groan
I'M SORRY...
...IS THE SUN TOO BRIGHT FOR YOU?
NO... IT'S OKAY...
.....
KEI-ICHI...
?
I...
...I PROMISE TO COME BACK.

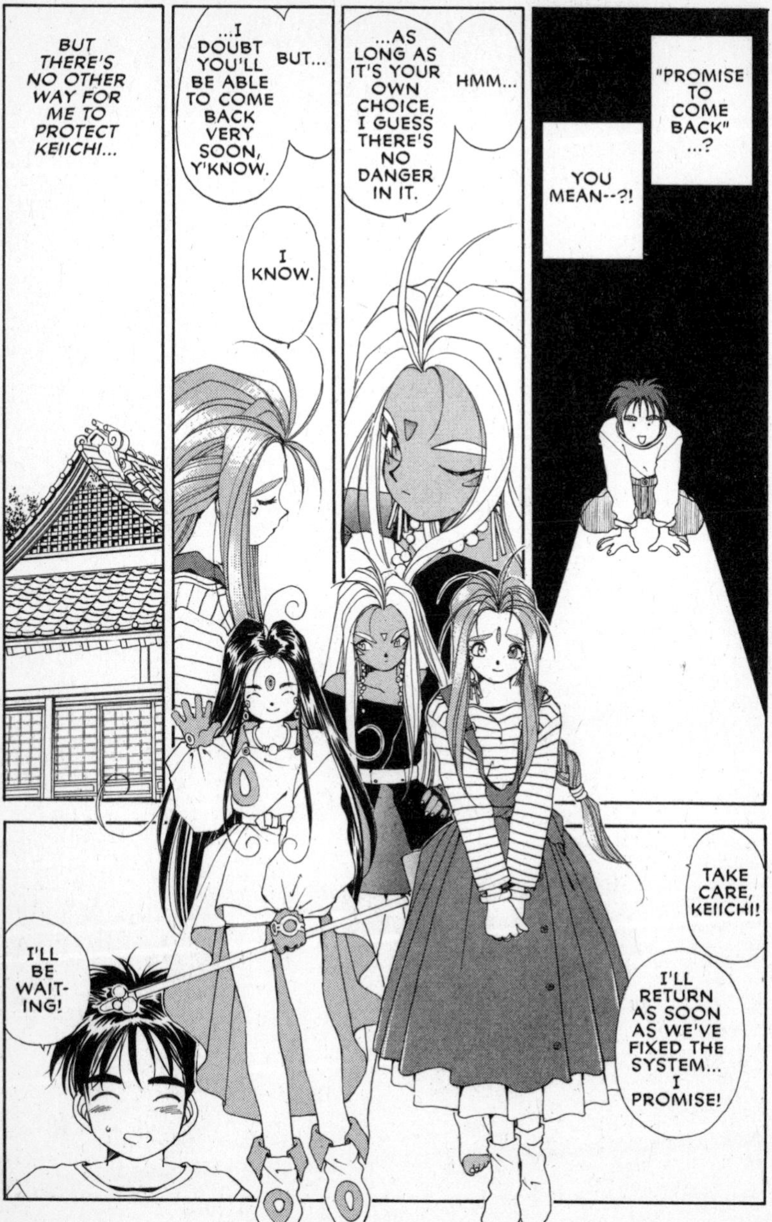
"PROMISE TO COME BACK" ...?
YOU MEAN--?!
HMM...
...AS LONG AS IT'S YOUR OWN CHOICE, I GUESS THERE'S NO DANGER IN IT.
BUT...
...I DOUBT YOU'LL BE ABLE TO COME BACK VERY SOON, Y'KNOW.
I KNOW.
BUT THERE'S NO OTHER WAY FOR ME TO PROTECT KEIICHI...
TAKE CARE, KEIICHI!
I'LL RETURN AS SOON AS WE'VE FIXED THE SYSTEM... I PROMISE!
I'LL BE WAIT-ING!

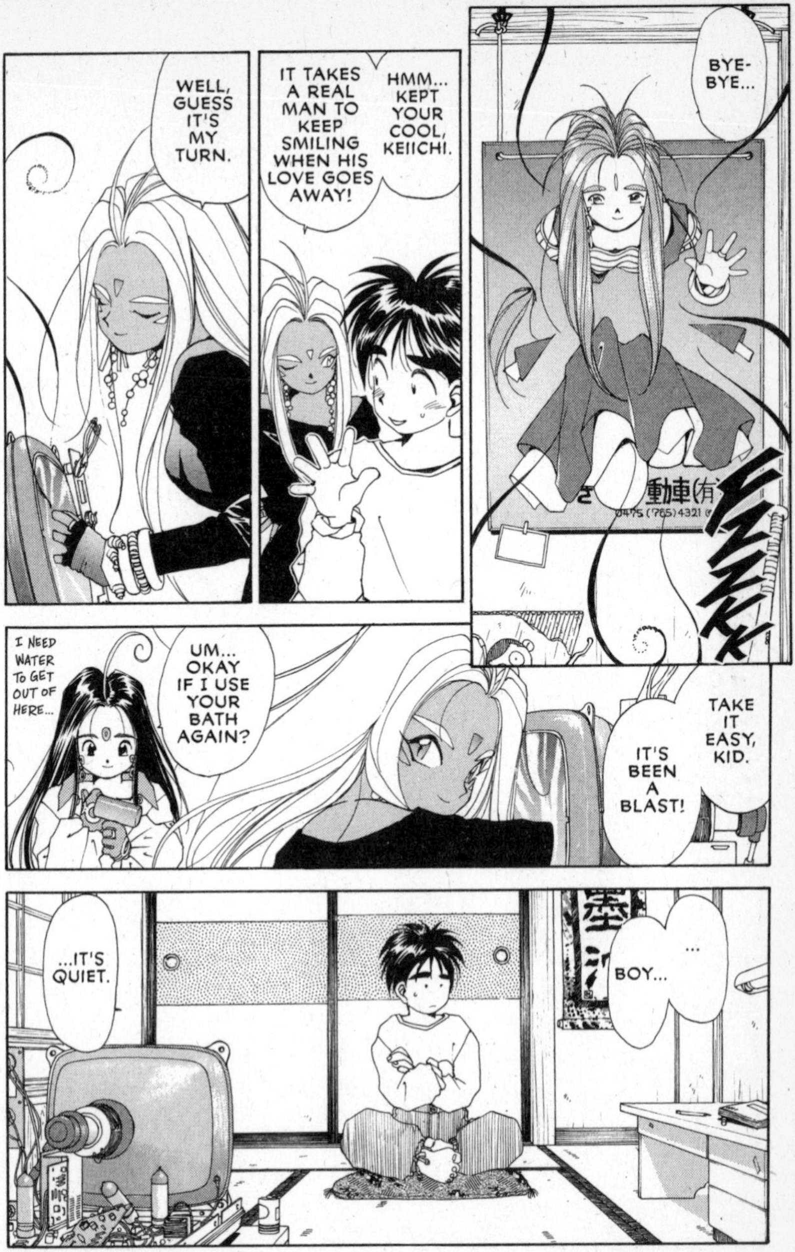
BYE-BYE...
ZZZZKK
HMM... KEPT YOUR COOL, KEIICHI.
IT TAKES A REAL MAN TO KEEP SMILING WHEN HIS LOVE GOES AWAY!
WELL, GUESS IT'S MY TURN.
TAKE IT EASY, KID.
IT'S BEEN A BLAST!
UM... OKAY IF I USE YOUR BATH AGAIN?
I NEED WATER TO GET OUT OF HERE...
... BOY...
...IT'S QUIET.

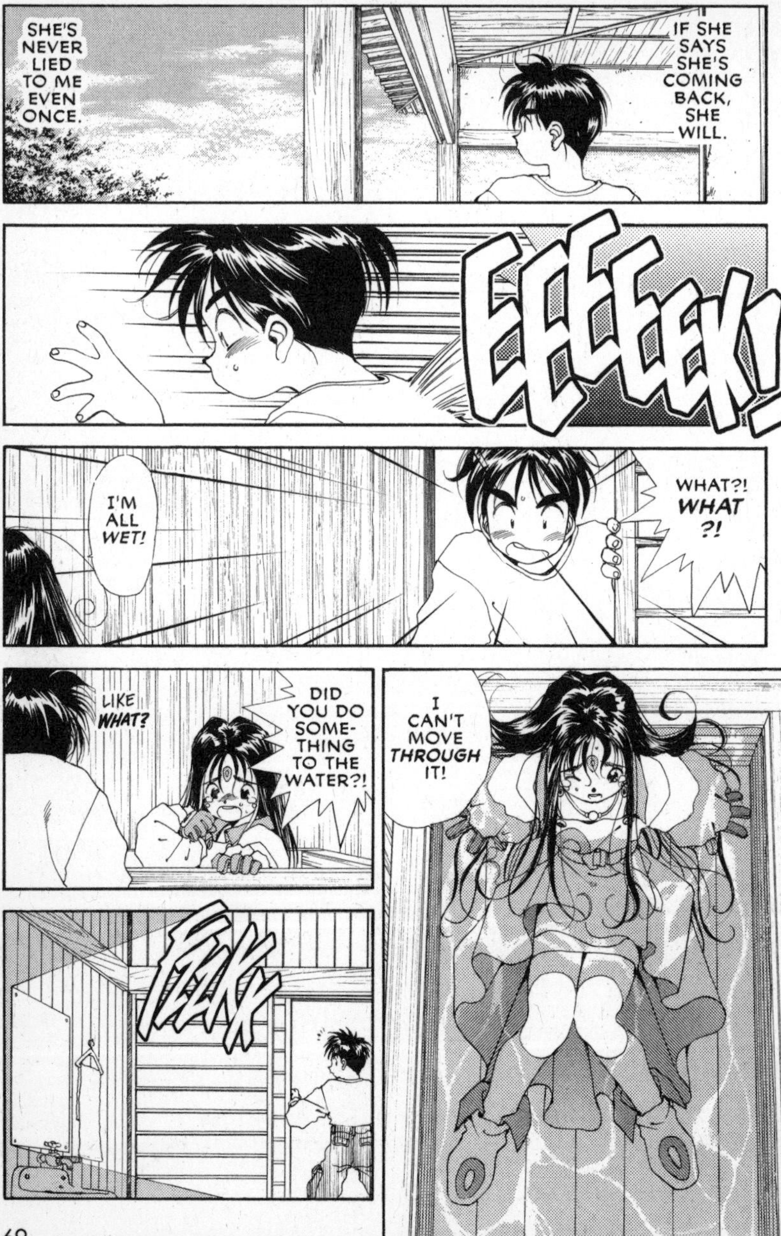

IF SHE SAYS SHE'S COMING BACK, SHE WILL.
SHE'S NEVER LIED TO ME EVEN ONCE.
EEEEEK!
WHAT?! WHAT?!
I'M ALL WET!
I CAN'T MOVE THROUGH IT!
DID YOU DO SOME-THING TO THE WATER?!
LIKE WHAT?
FZKK

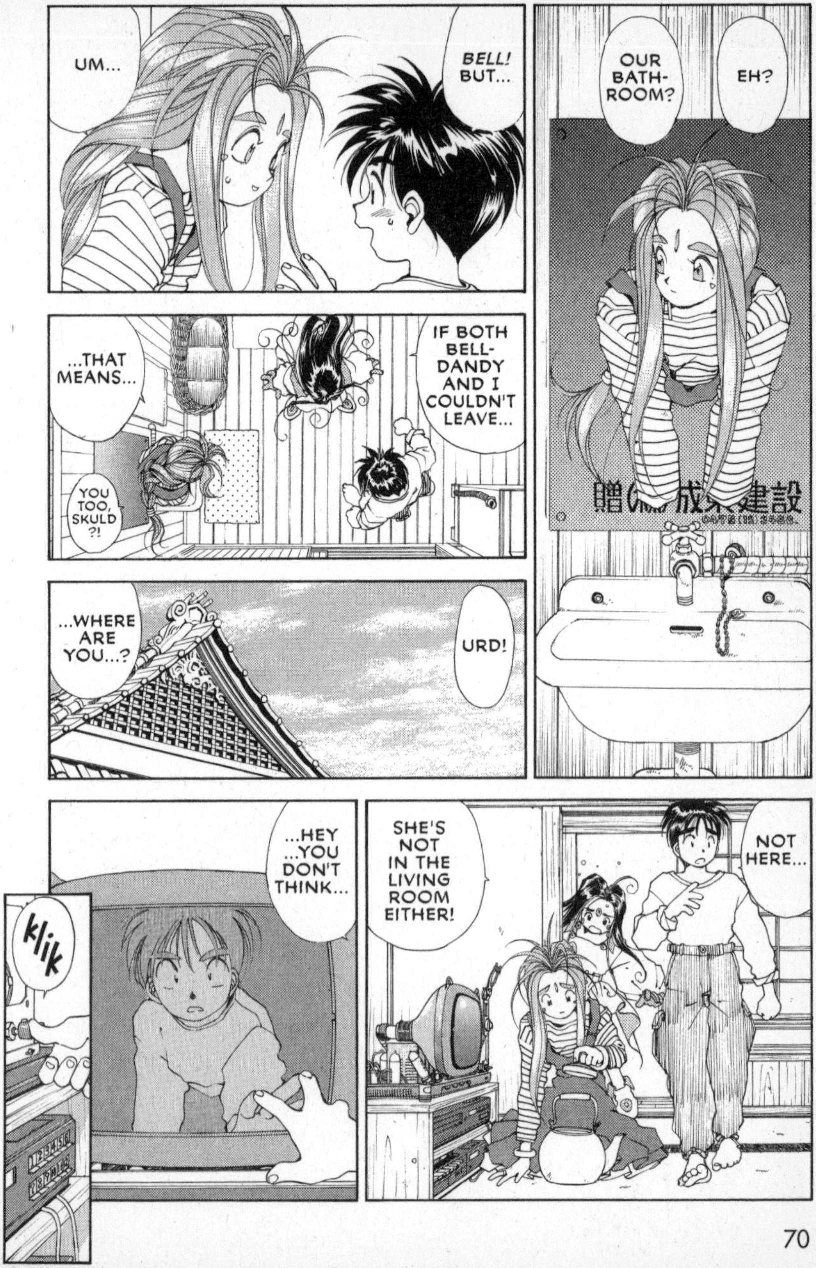
EH?
OUR BATHROOM?
BELL! BUT...
UM...
IF BOTH BELL-DANDY AND I COULDN'T LEAVE...
...THAT MEANS...
YOU TOO, SKULD?!
URD!
...WHERE ARE YOU...?
NOT HERE...
SHE'S NOT IN THE LIVING ROOM EITHER!
...HEY ...YOU DON'T THINK...
klik

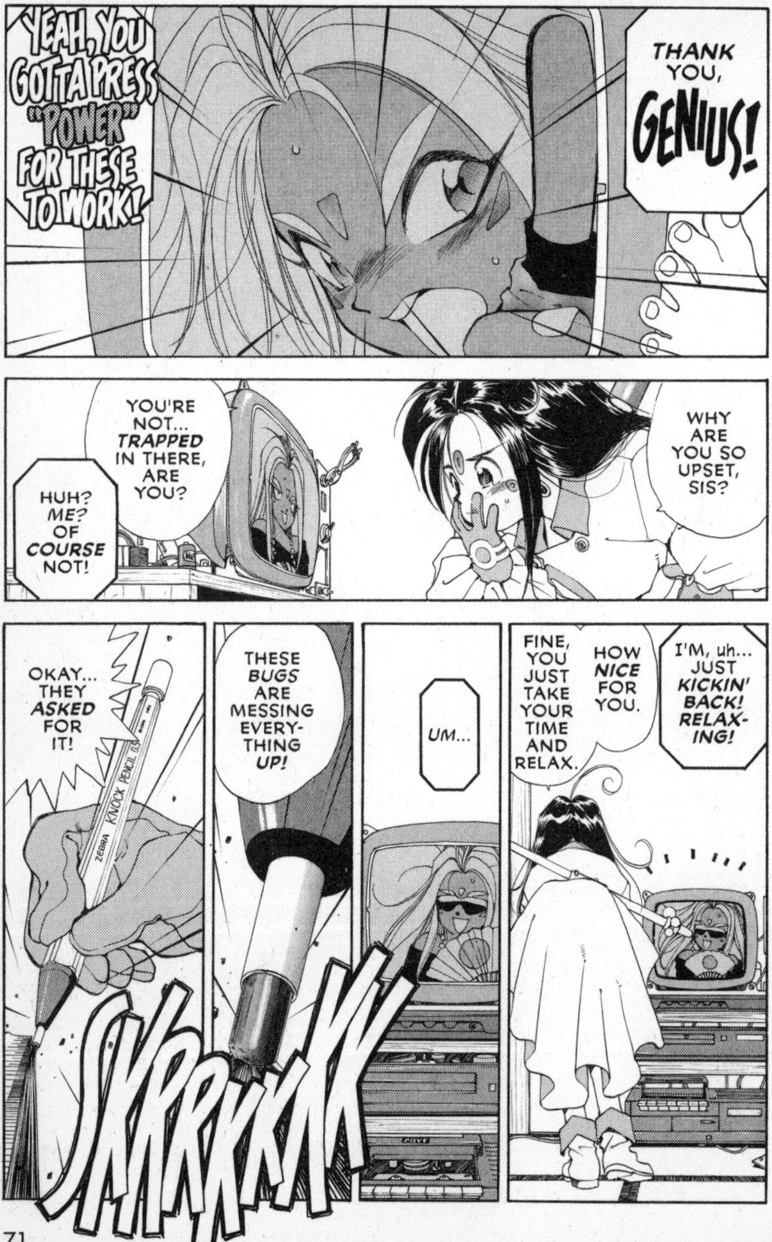
THANK YOU, GENIUS!
YEAH, YOU GOTTA PRESS "POWER" FOR THESE TO WORK!
WHY ARE YOU SO UPSET, SIS?
YOU'RE NOT... TRAPPED IN THERE, ARE YOU?
HUH? ME? OF COURSE NOT!
I'M, uh... JUST KICKIN' BACK! RELAXING!
HOW NICE FOR YOU.
FINE, YOU JUST TAKE YOUR TIME AND RELAX.
UM...
THESE BUGS ARE MESSING EVERYTHING UP!
OKAY... THEY ASKED FOR IT!
ZEBRA KNOCK PENCIL 0.5
SKRRKKKK

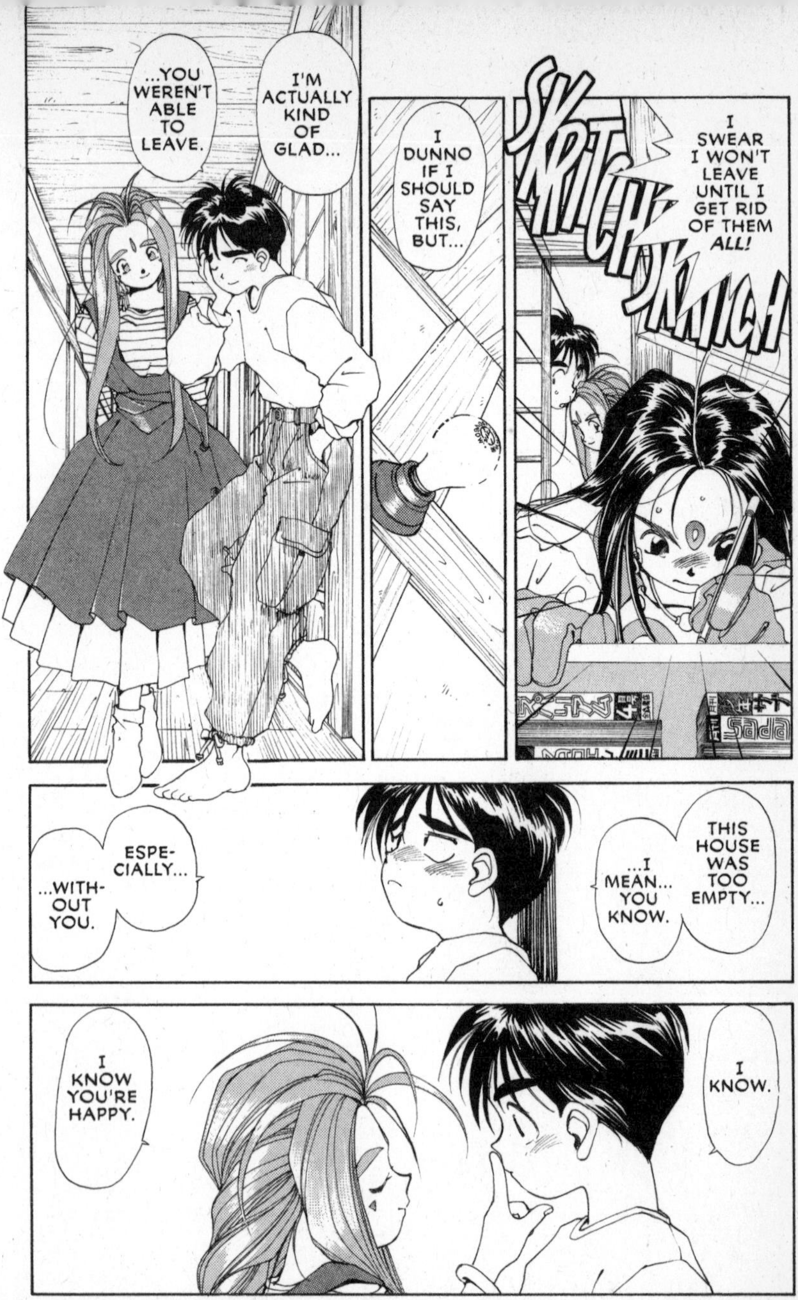
SKRITCH
SKRITCH
I SWEAR I WON'T LEAVE UNTIL I GET RID OF THEM *ALL!*
I DUNNO IF I SHOULD SAY THIS, BUT...
I'M ACTUALLY KIND OF GLAD...
...YOU WEREN'T ABLE TO LEAVE.
THIS HOUSE WAS TOO EMPTY...
...I MEAN... YOU KNOW.
ESPE-CIALLY...
...WITH-OUT YOU.
I KNOW.
I KNOW YOU'RE HAPPY.

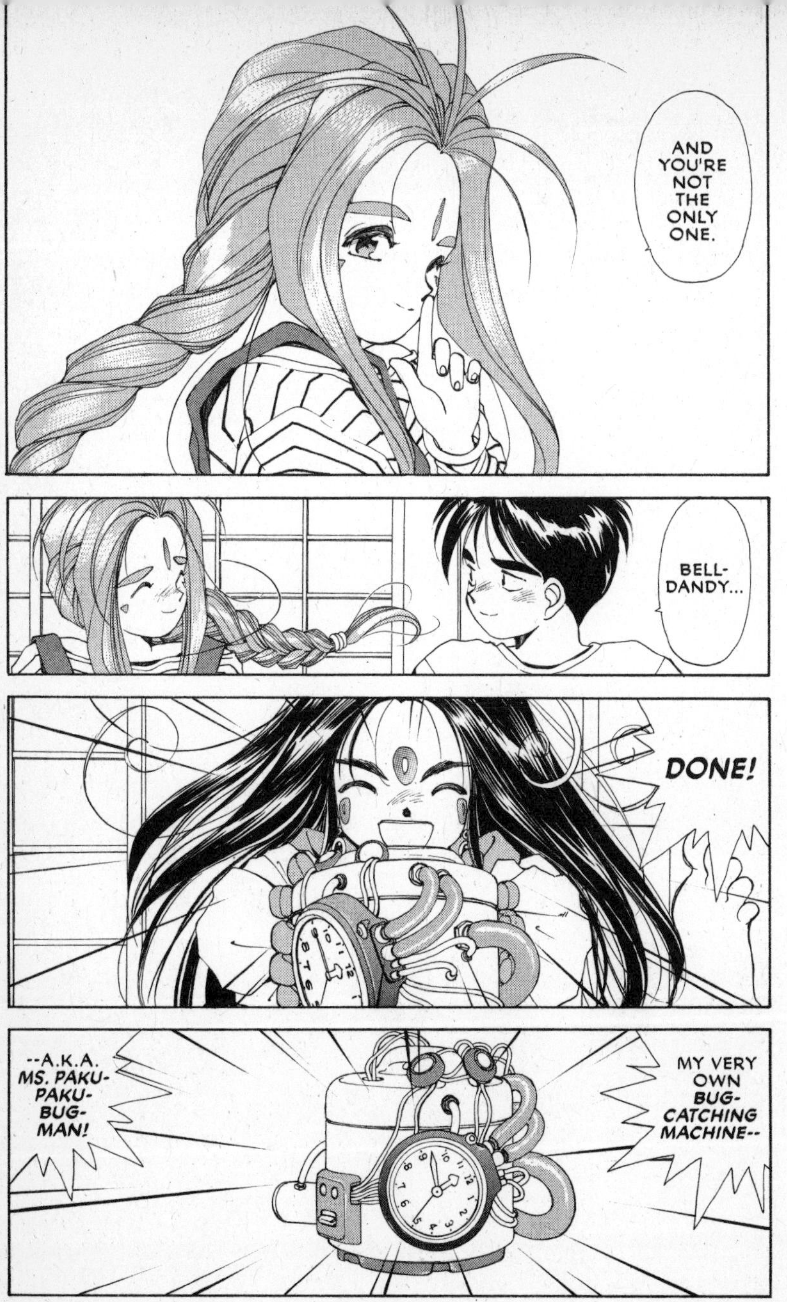
AND YOU'RE NOT THE ONLY ONE.
BELL-DANDY...
DONE!
MY VERY OWN BUG-CATCHING MACHINE--
--A.K.A. MS. PAKU-PAKU-BUG-MAN!

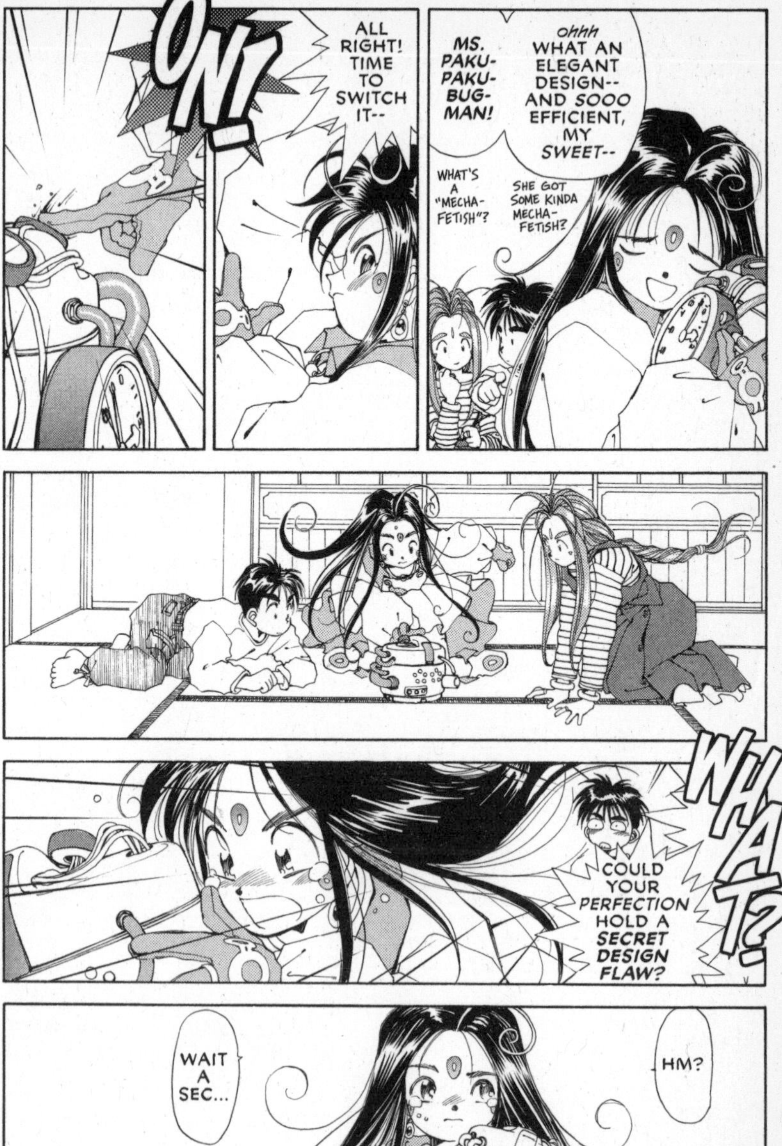
ohhh WHAT AN ELEGANT DESIGN-- AND SOOO EFFICIENT, MY SWEET--
MS. PAKU-PAKU-BUG-MAN!
SHE GOT SOME KINDA MECHA-FETISH?
WHAT'S A "MECHA-FETISH"?
ALL RIGHT! TIME TO SWITCH IT--
ON!
WHAT?!
COULD YOUR PERFECTION HOLD A SECRET DESIGN FLAW?
HM?
WAIT A SEC...

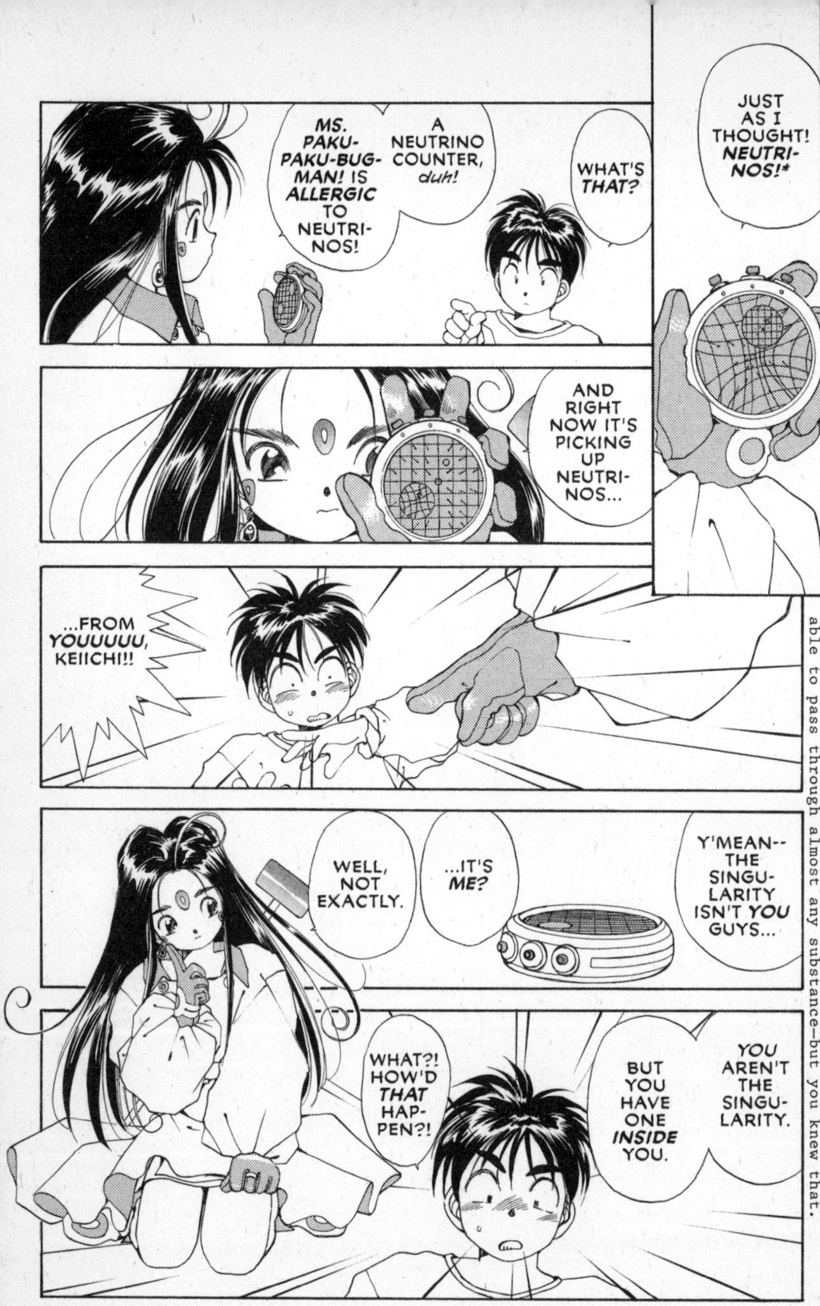
JUST AS I THOUGHT! NEUTRINOS!*
WHAT'S THAT?
A NEUTRINO COUNTER, duh!
MS. PAKU-PAKU-BUG-MAN! IS ALLERGIC TO NEUTRINOS!
AND RIGHT NOW IT'S PICKING UP NEUTRINOS...
...FROM YOUUUUU, KEIICHI!!
Y'MEAN-- THE SINGULARITY ISN'T YOU GUYS...
...IT'S ME?
WELL, NOT EXACTLY.
YOU AREN'T THE SINGULARITY.
BUT YOU HAVE ONE INSIDE YOU.
WHAT?! HOW'D THAT HAPPEN?!

*nearly massless elementary particles without electric charge, able to pass through almost any substance—but you knew that.

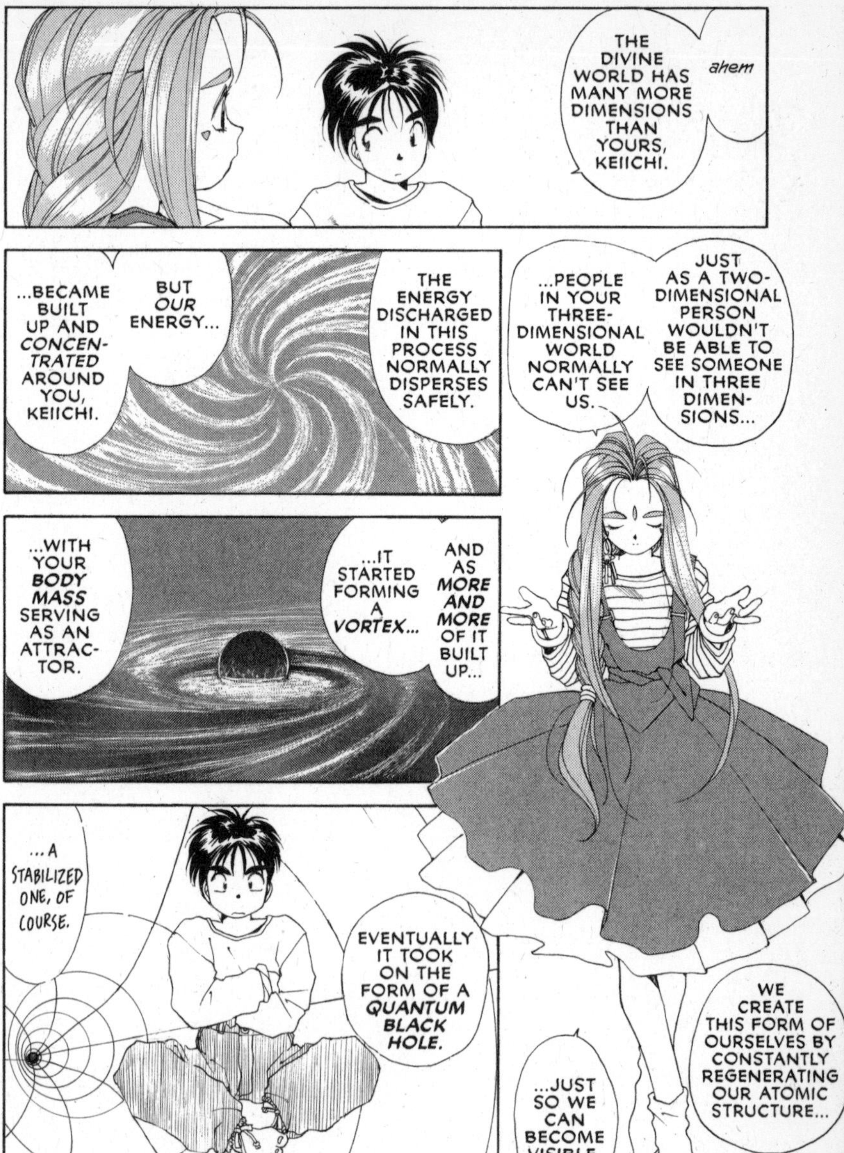
ahem
THE DIVINE WORLD HAS MANY MORE DIMENSIONS THAN YOURS, KEIICHI.
JUST AS A TWO-DIMENSIONAL PERSON WOULDN'T BE ABLE TO SEE SOMEONE IN THREE DIMENSIONS...
...PEOPLE IN YOUR THREE-DIMENSIONAL WORLD NORMALLY CAN'T SEE US.
WE CREATE THIS FORM OF OURSELVES BY CONSTANTLY REGENERATING OUR ATOMIC STRUCTURE...
...JUST SO WE CAN BECOME VISIBLE.
THE ENERGY DISCHARGED IN THIS PROCESS NORMALLY DISPERSES SAFELY.
BUT *OUR* ENERGY...
...BECAME BUILT UP AND *CONCENTRATED* AROUND YOU, KEIICHI.
AND AS *MORE AND MORE* OF IT BUILT UP...
...IT STARTED FORMING A *VORTEX*...
...WITH YOUR *BODY MASS* SERVING AS AN ATTRACTOR.
EVENTUALLY IT TOOK ON THE FORM OF A *QUANTUM BLACK HOLE.*
...A STABILIZED ONE, OF COURSE.

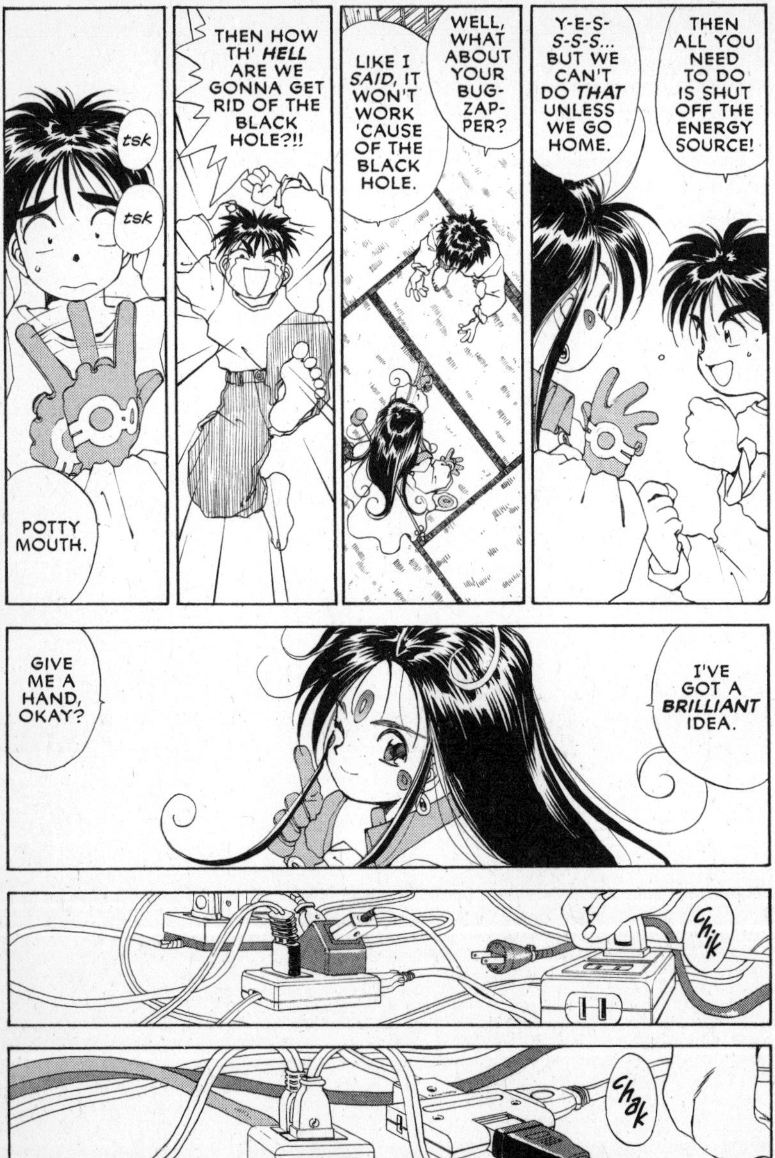
THEN ALL YOU NEED TO DO IS SHUT OFF THE ENERGY SOURCE!
Y-E-S-S-S-S... BUT WE CAN'T DO *THAT* UNLESS WE GO HOME.
WELL, WHAT ABOUT YOUR BUG-ZAPPER?
LIKE I *SAID*, IT WON'T WORK 'CAUSE OF THE BLACK HOLE.
THEN HOW TH' ***HELL*** ARE WE GONNA GET RID OF THE BLACK HOLE?!!
*tsk*
*tsk*
POTTY MOUTH.
I'VE GOT A ***BRILLIANT*** IDEA.
GIVE ME A HAND, OKAY?
chik
chak

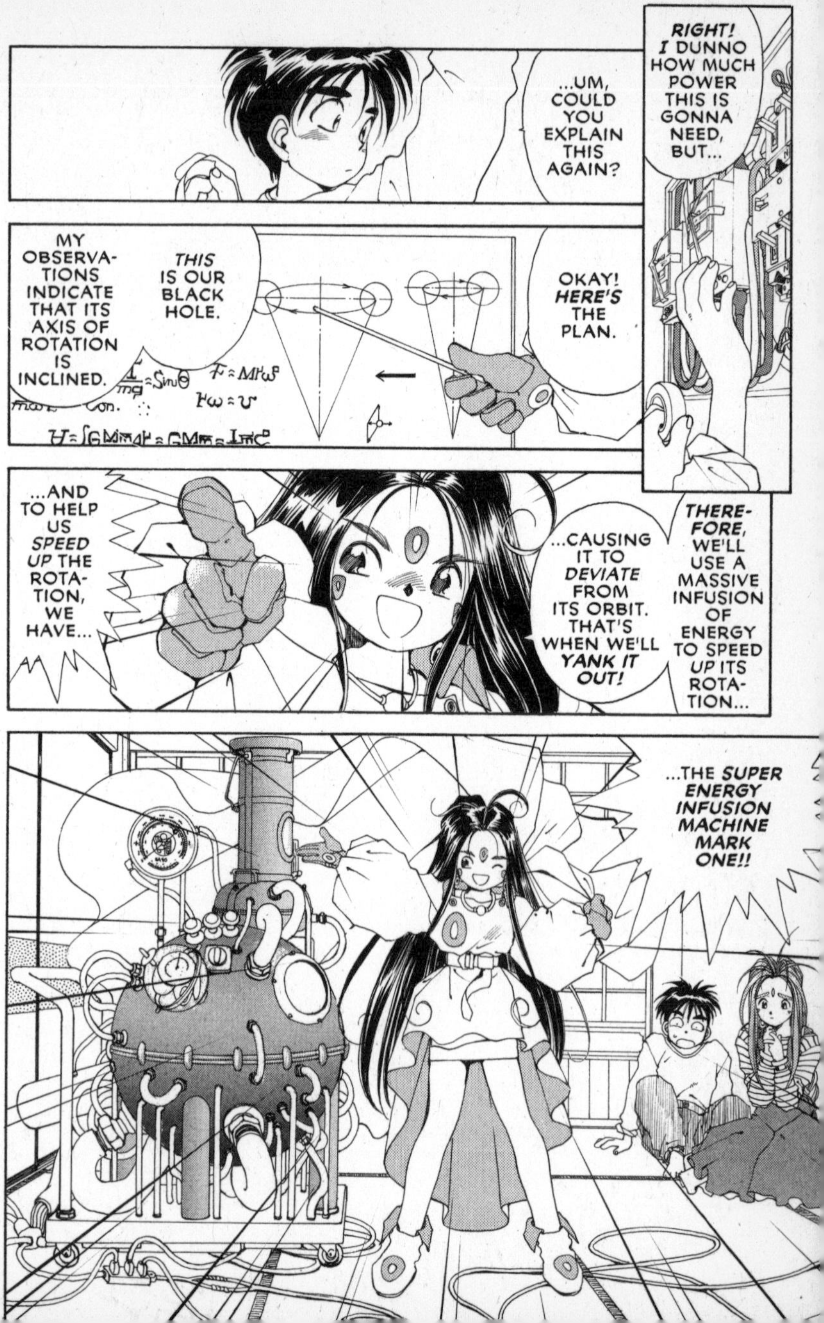
RIGHT! I DUNNO HOW MUCH POWER THIS IS GONNA NEED, BUT...
...UM, COULD YOU EXPLAIN THIS AGAIN?
OKAY! HERE'S THE PLAN.
THIS IS OUR BLACK HOLE.
MY OBSERVATIONS INDICATE THAT ITS AXIS OF ROTATION IS INCLINED.
THEREFORE, WE'LL USE A MASSIVE INFUSION OF ENERGY TO SPEED UP ITS ROTATION...
...CAUSING IT TO DEVIATE FROM ITS ORBIT. THAT'S WHEN WE'LL YANK IT OUT!
...AND TO HELP US SPEED UP THE ROTATION, WE HAVE...
...THE SUPER ENERGY INFUSION MACHINE MARK ONE!!

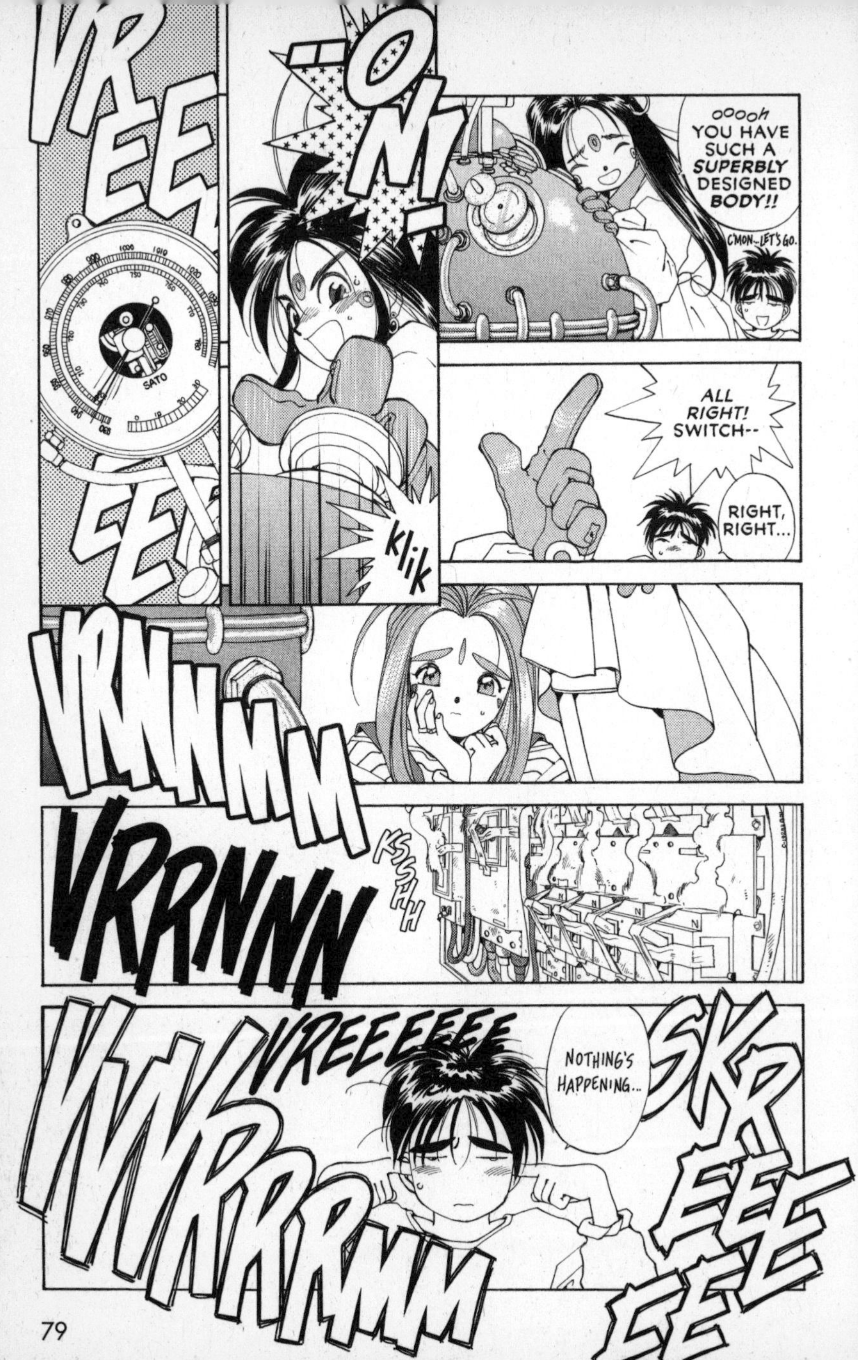
oooh YOU HAVE SUCH A SUPERBLY DESIGNED BODY!!
C'MON... LET'S GO.
ALL RIGHT! SWITCH--
RIGHT, RIGHT...
ON-
klik
VREEEE
EEE
VRNNMMM
KSSHH
VRRNNNN
SKREEEEE
NOTHING'S HAPPENING...
VREEEEEE
VVRRRRMM

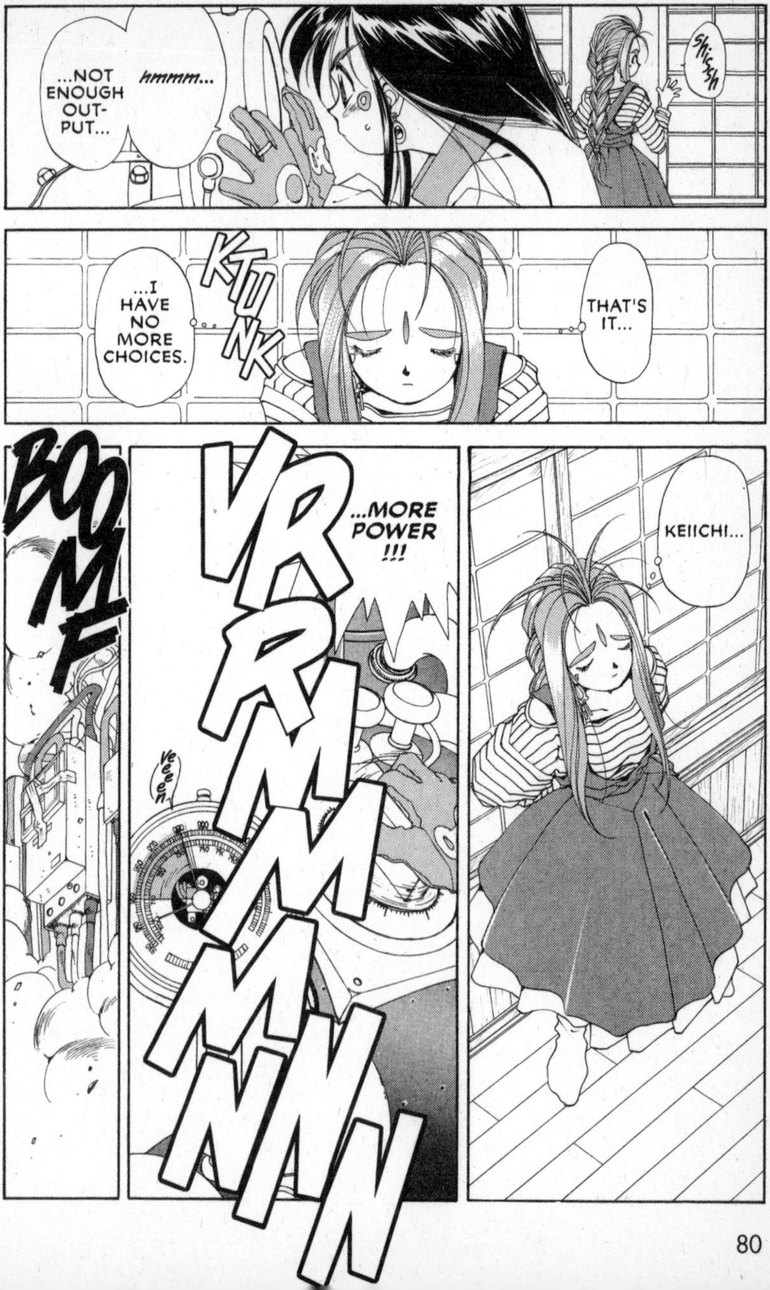
Shissh
hmmm...
...NOT ENOUGH OUT-PUT...
THAT'S IT...
KTUNK
...I HAVE NO MORE CHOICES.
KEIICHI...
...MORE POWER!!!
VRRMMMMNNN
Veeeen
BOOMF

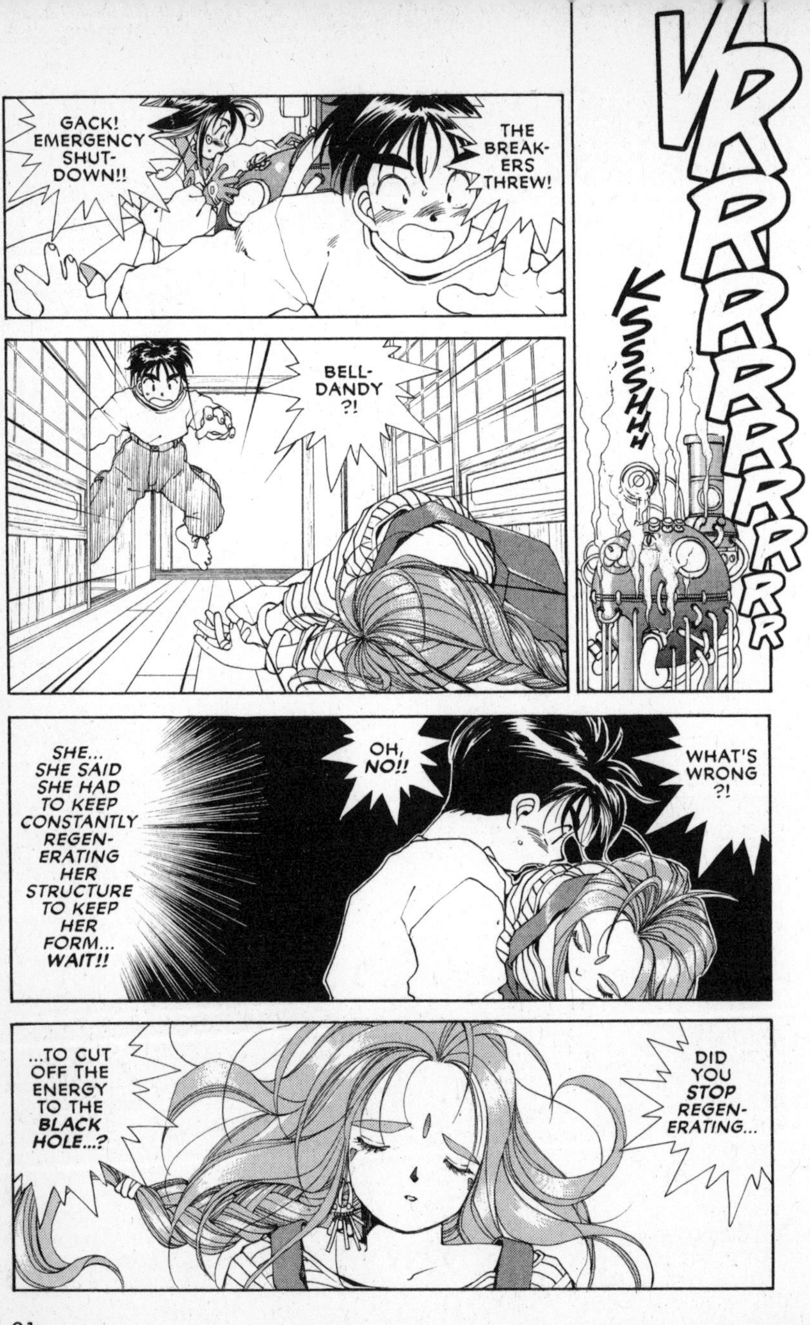
VRRRRRRRRRRR
KSSSHHH
THE BREAK-ERS THREW!
GACK! EMERGENCY SHUT-DOWN!!
BELL-DANDY ?!
WHAT'S WRONG ?!
OH, NO!!
SHE... SHE SAID SHE HAD TO KEEP CONSTANTLY REGEN-ERATING HER STRUCTURE TO KEEP HER FORM... WAIT!!
DID YOU STOP REGEN-ERATING...
...TO CUT OFF THE ENERGY TO THE BLACK HOLE...?

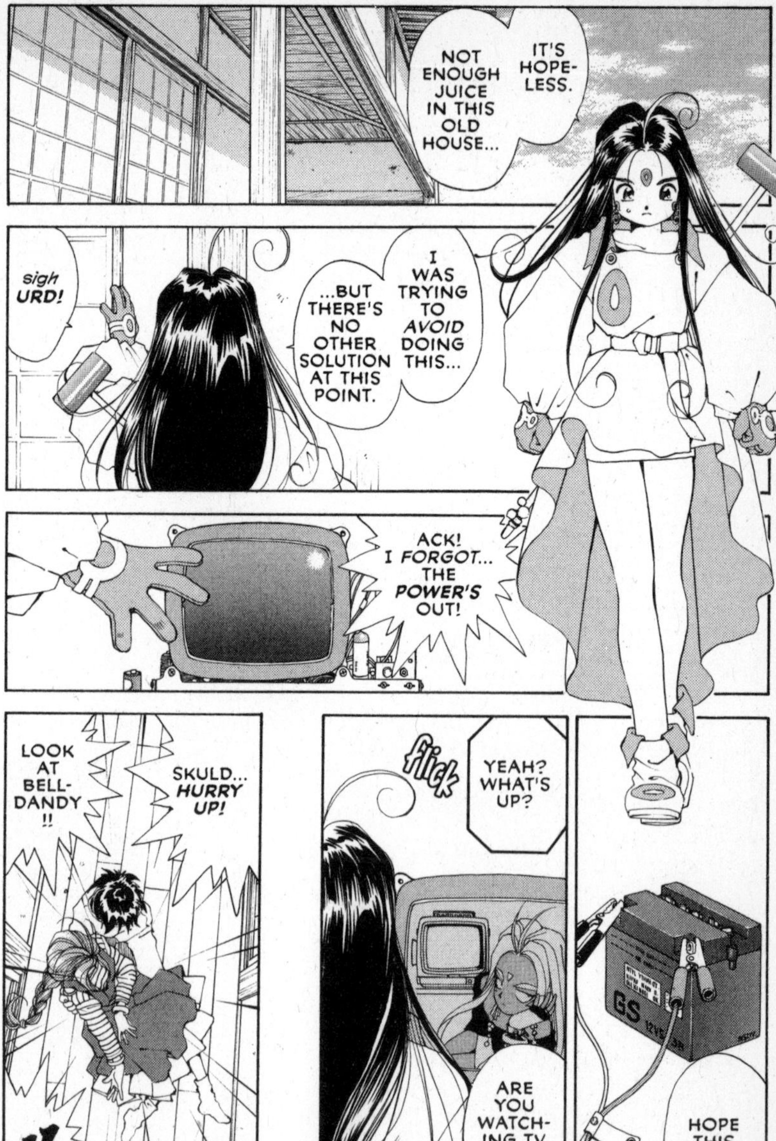
IT'S HOPE-LESS.
NOT ENOUGH JUICE IN THIS OLD HOUSE...
I WAS TRYING TO *AVOID* DOING THIS...
...BUT THERE'S NO OTHER SOLUTION AT THIS POINT.
*sigh* **URD!**
ACK! I *FORGOT*... THE ***POWER'S*** OUT!
HOPE THIS WORKS...
flick
YEAH? WHAT'S UP?
ARE YOU WATCHING TV *INSIDE* A TV?
SKULD... ***HURRY UP!***
LOOK AT BELL-DANDY !!
!!

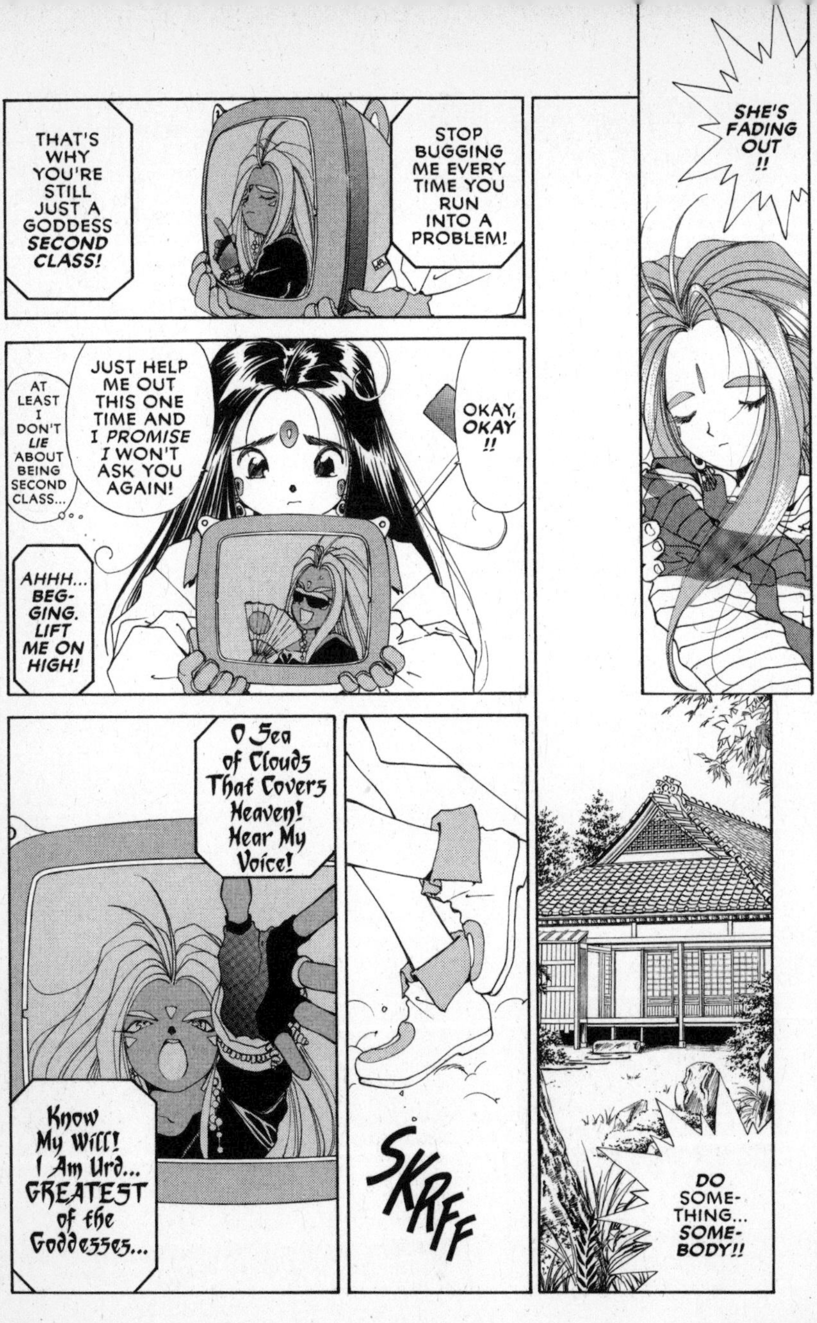
SHE'S FADING OUT !!
STOP BUGGING ME EVERY TIME YOU RUN INTO A PROBLEM!
THAT'S WHY YOU'RE STILL JUST A GODDESS *SECOND CLASS!*
JUST HELP ME OUT THIS ONE TIME AND I *PROMISE* *I* WON'T ASK YOU AGAIN!
AT LEAST I DON'T *LIE* ABOUT BEING SECOND CLASS...
*AHHH... BEGGING. LIFT ME ON HIGH!*
OKAY, *OKAY* !!
DO SOME-THING... SOMEBODY!!
SKRFF
O Sea of Clouds That Covers Heaven! Hear My Voice!
Know My Will! I Am Urd... GREATEST of the Goddesses...

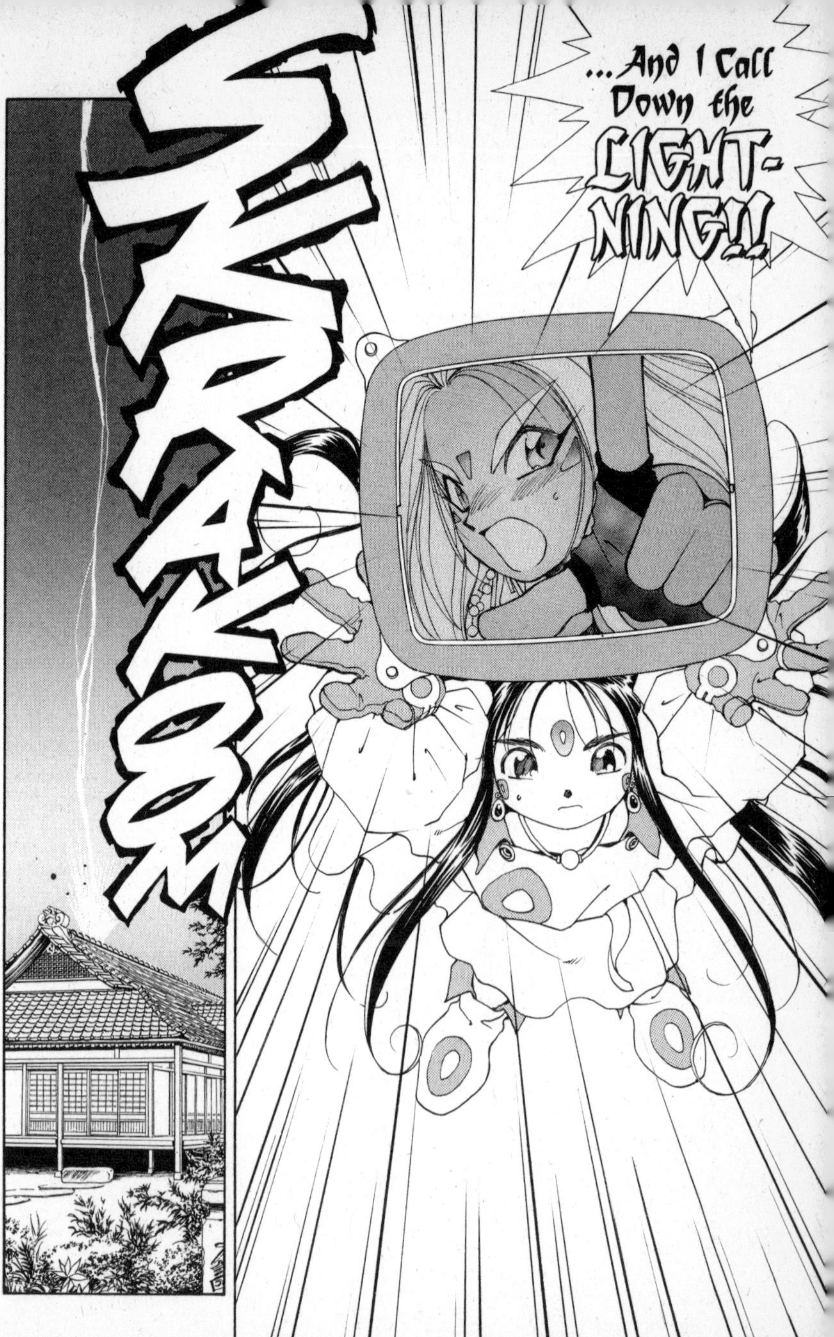
...And I Call Down the LIGHT-NING!!

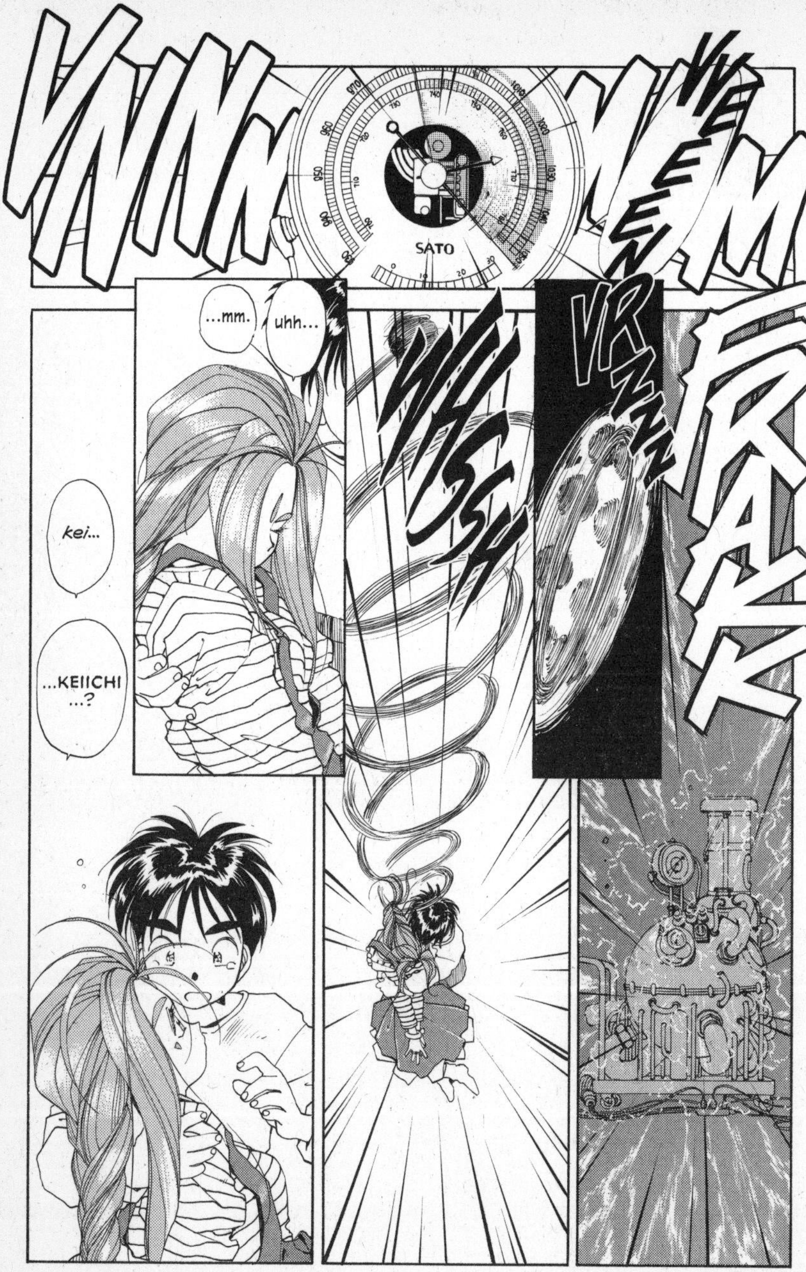
VVEEEEN
VNINNNNM
SATO
FRAK
VRZZZZ
WHSSH
uhh...
...mm.
kei...
...KEIICHI ...?

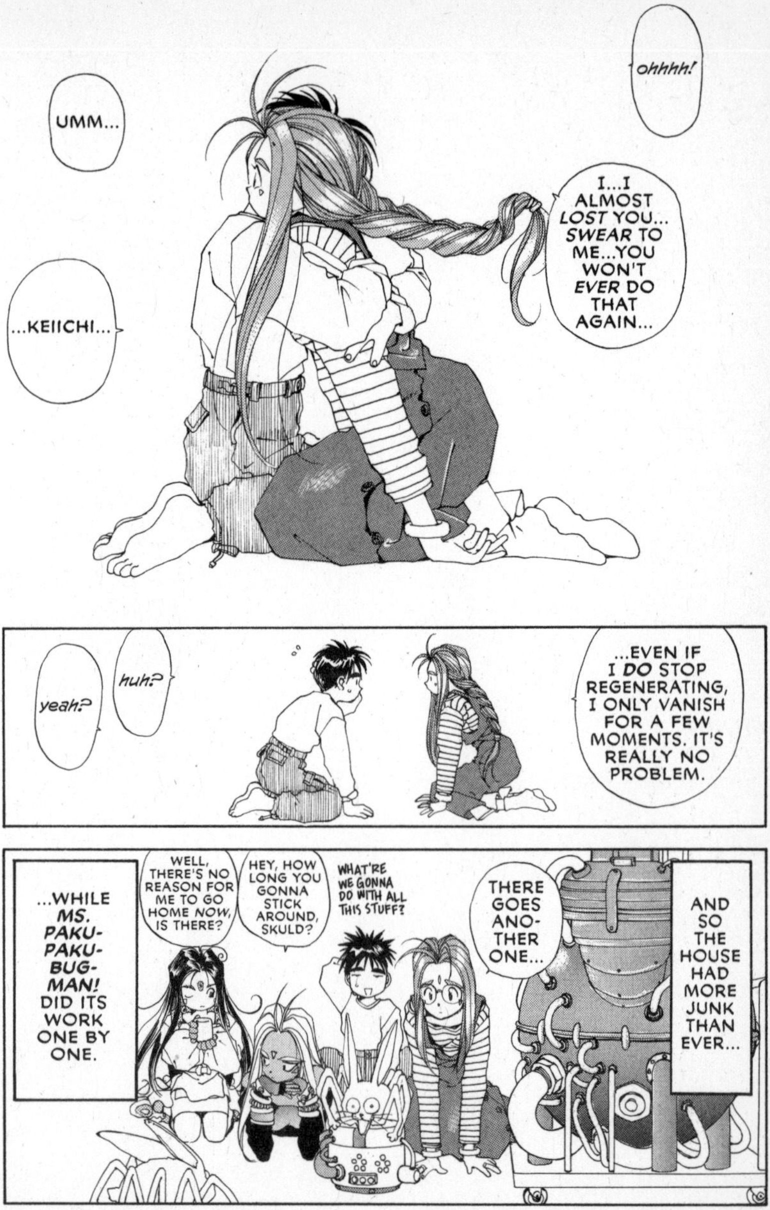
ohhhh!
I...I ALMOST LOST YOU... SWEAR TO ME...YOU WON'T EVER DO THAT AGAIN...
UMM...
...KEIICHI...
...EVEN IF I DO STOP REGENERATING, I ONLY VANISH FOR A FEW MOMENTS. IT'S REALLY NO PROBLEM.
huh?
yeah?
AND SO THE HOUSE HAD MORE JUNK THAN EVER...
THERE GOES ANO-THER ONE...
WHAT'RE WE GONNA DO WITH ALL THIS STUFF?
HEY, HOW LONG YOU GONNA STICK AROUND, SKULD?
WELL, THERE'S NO REASON FOR ME TO GO HOME NOW, IS THERE?
...WHILE MS. PAKU-PAKU-BUG-MAN! DID ITS WORK ONE BY ONE.

CHAPTER 34

# Urd Goes Wild

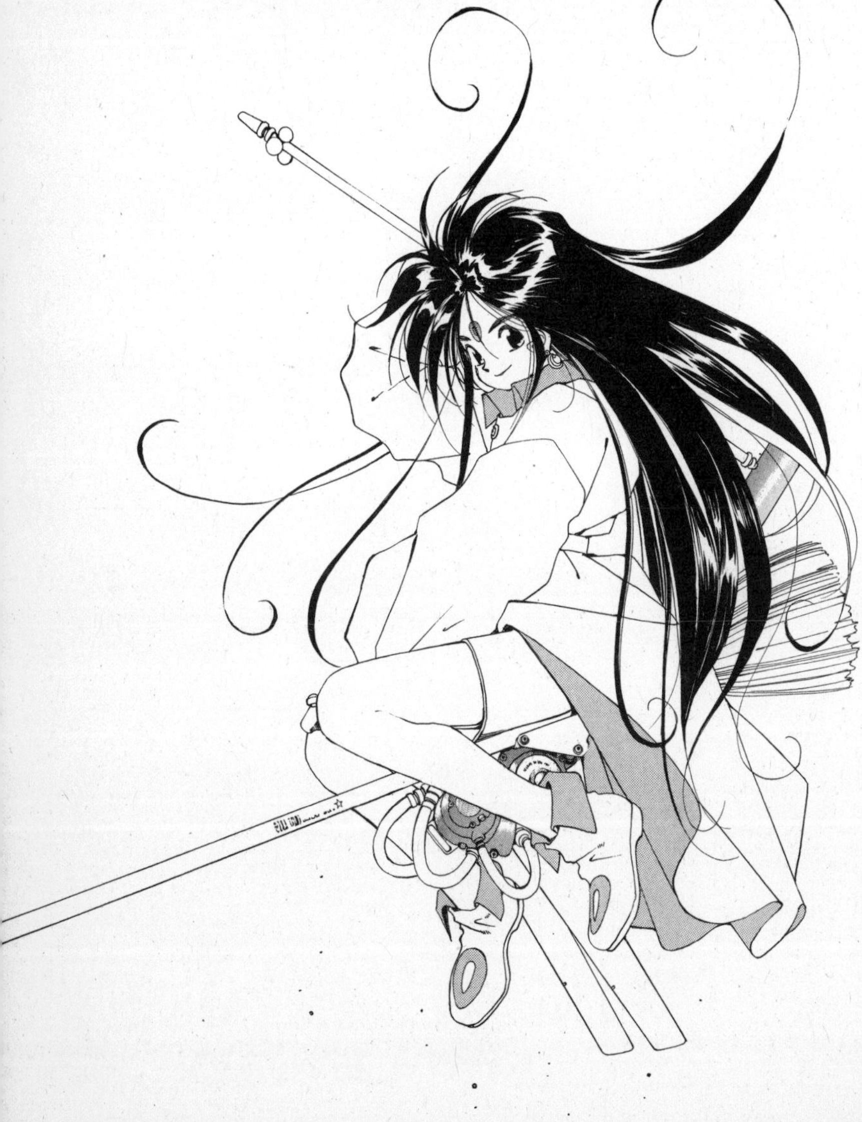

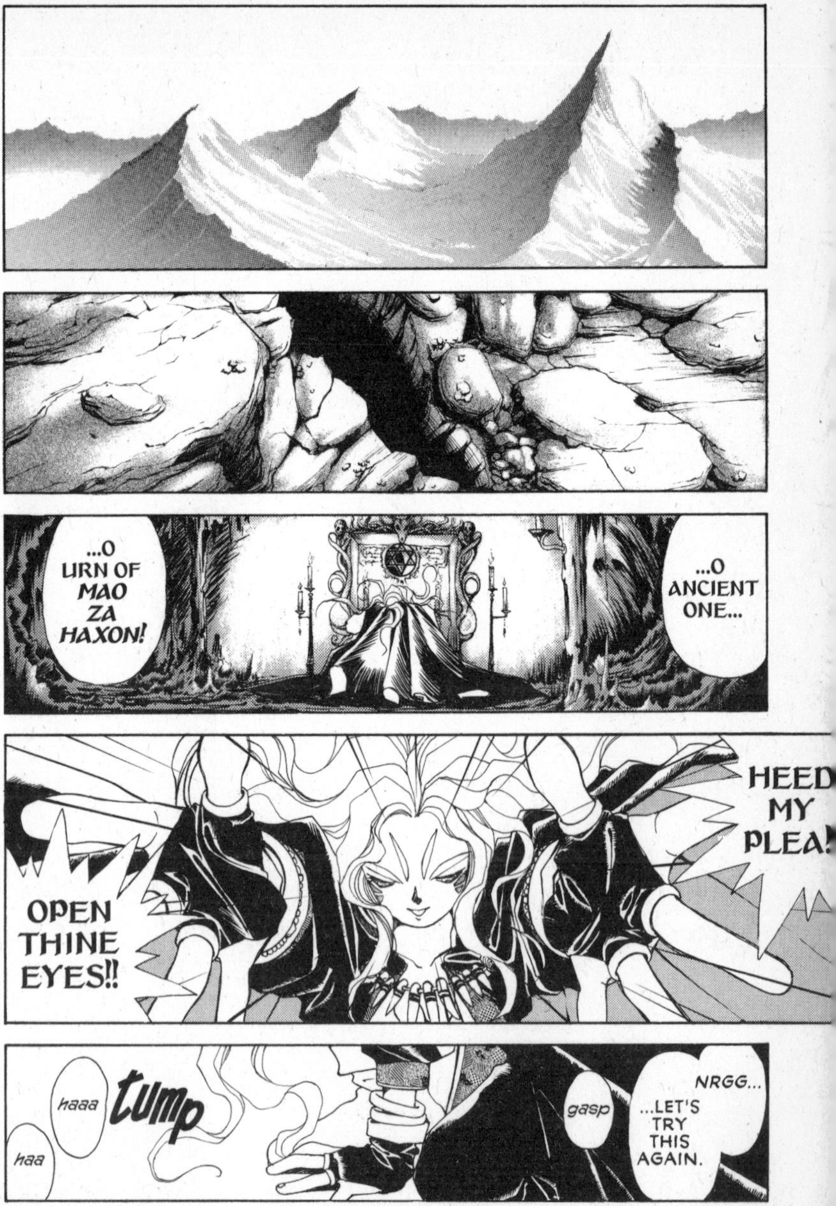
...O ANCIENT ONE...
...O URN OF MAO ZA HAXON!
HEED MY PLEA!
OPEN THINE EYES!!
NRGG... ...LET'S TRY THIS AGAIN.
gasp
tump
haaa
haa

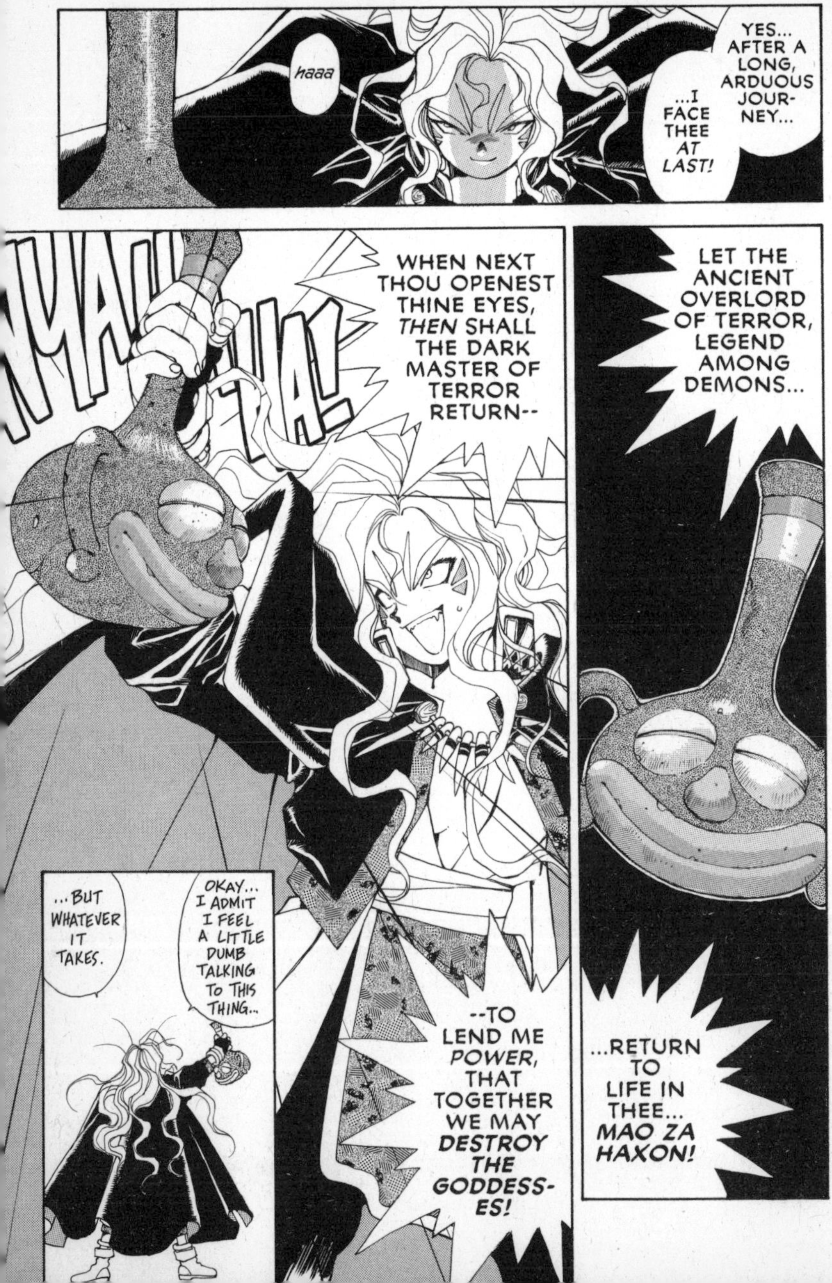
YES... AFTER A LONG, ARDUOUS JOURNEY...
...I FACE THEE *AT LAST!*
*haaa*
LET THE ANCIENT OVERLORD OF TERROR, LEGEND AMONG DEMONS...
...RETURN TO LIFE IN THEE... ***MAO ZA HAXON!***
WHEN NEXT THOU OPENEST THINE EYES, *THEN* SHALL THE DARK MASTER OF TERROR RETURN--
--TO LEND ME *POWER,* THAT TOGETHER WE MAY ***DESTROY THE GODDESS-ES!***
OKAY... I ADMIT I FEEL A LITTLE DUMB TALKING TO THIS THING...
...BUT WHATEVER IT TAKES.

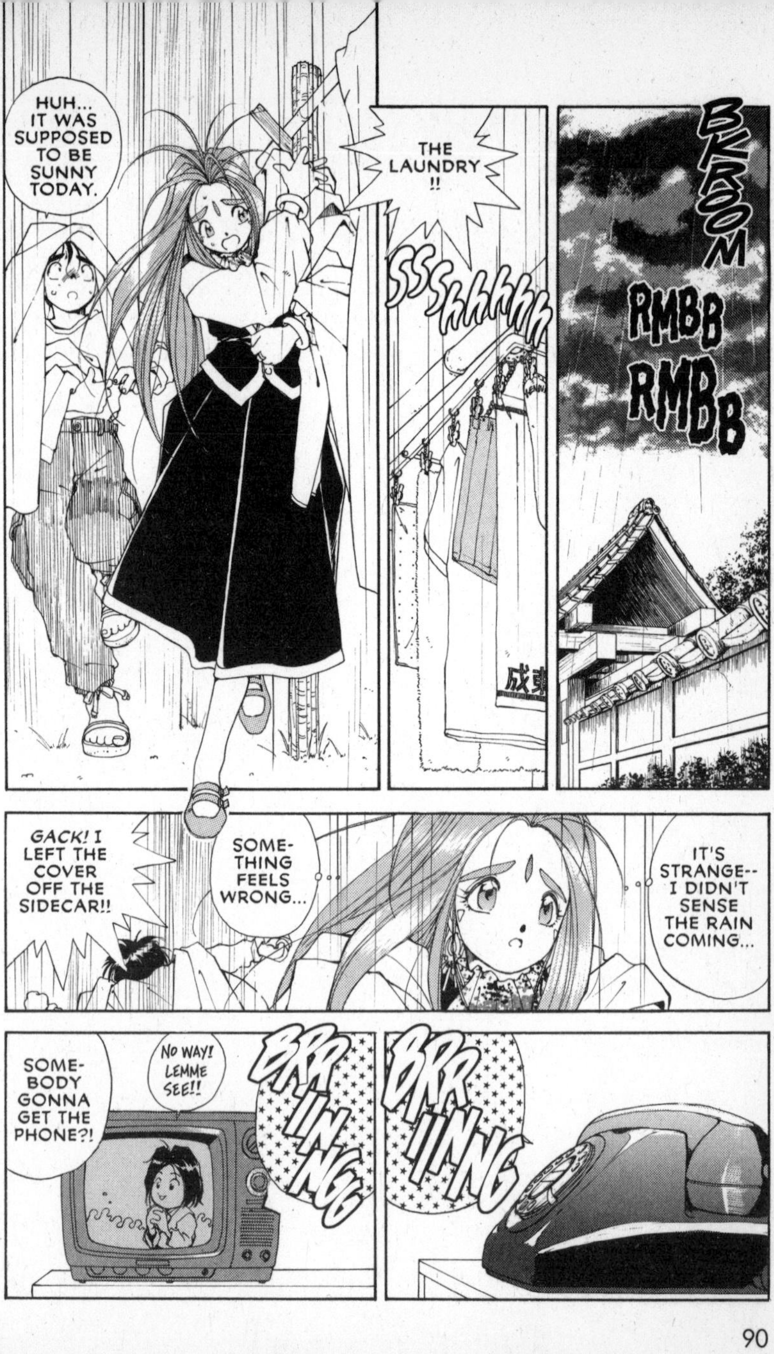
BKROOM
RMBB RMBB
THE LAUNDRY !!
SSSHHHHHHH
HUH... IT WAS SUPPOSED TO BE SUNNY TODAY.
IT'S STRANGE-- I DIDN'T SENSE THE RAIN COMING...
SOME-THING FEELS WRONG...
GACK! I LEFT THE COVER OFF THE SIDECAR!!
BRRIING
BRRIINGG
NO WAY! LEMME SEE!!
SOME-BODY GONNA GET THE PHONE?!

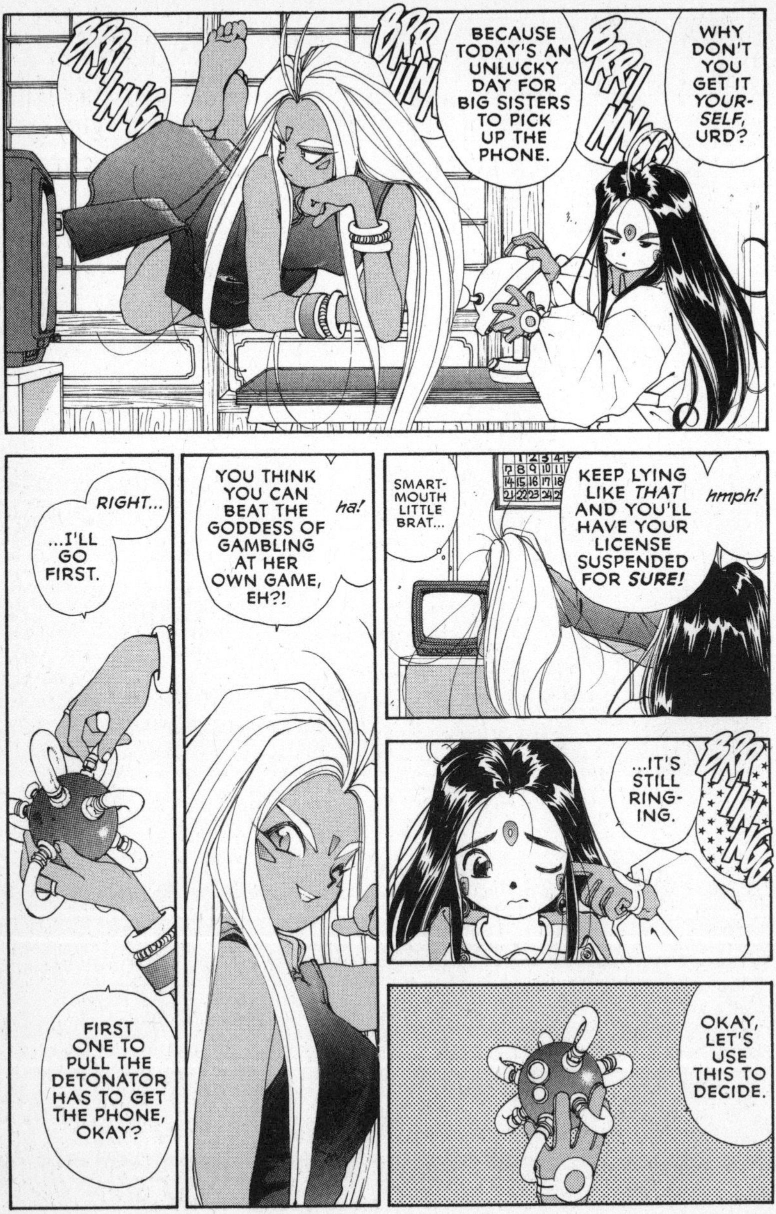
WHY DON'T YOU GET IT YOURSELF, URD?
BRRIINNG
BECAUSE TODAY'S AN UNLUCKY DAY FOR BIG SISTERS TO PICK UP THE PHONE.
BRRIINNG
BRRIINNG
hmph!
KEEP LYING LIKE THAT AND YOU'LL HAVE YOUR LICENSE SUSPENDED FOR SURE!
SMART-MOUTH LITTLE BRAT...
BRRIINNG
...IT'S STILL RINGING.
OKAY, LET'S USE THIS TO DECIDE.
ha!
YOU THINK YOU CAN BEAT THE GODDESS OF GAMBLING AT HER OWN GAME, EH?!
FIRST ONE TO PULL THE DETONATOR HAS TO GET THE PHONE, OKAY?
RIGHT...
...I'LL GO FIRST.

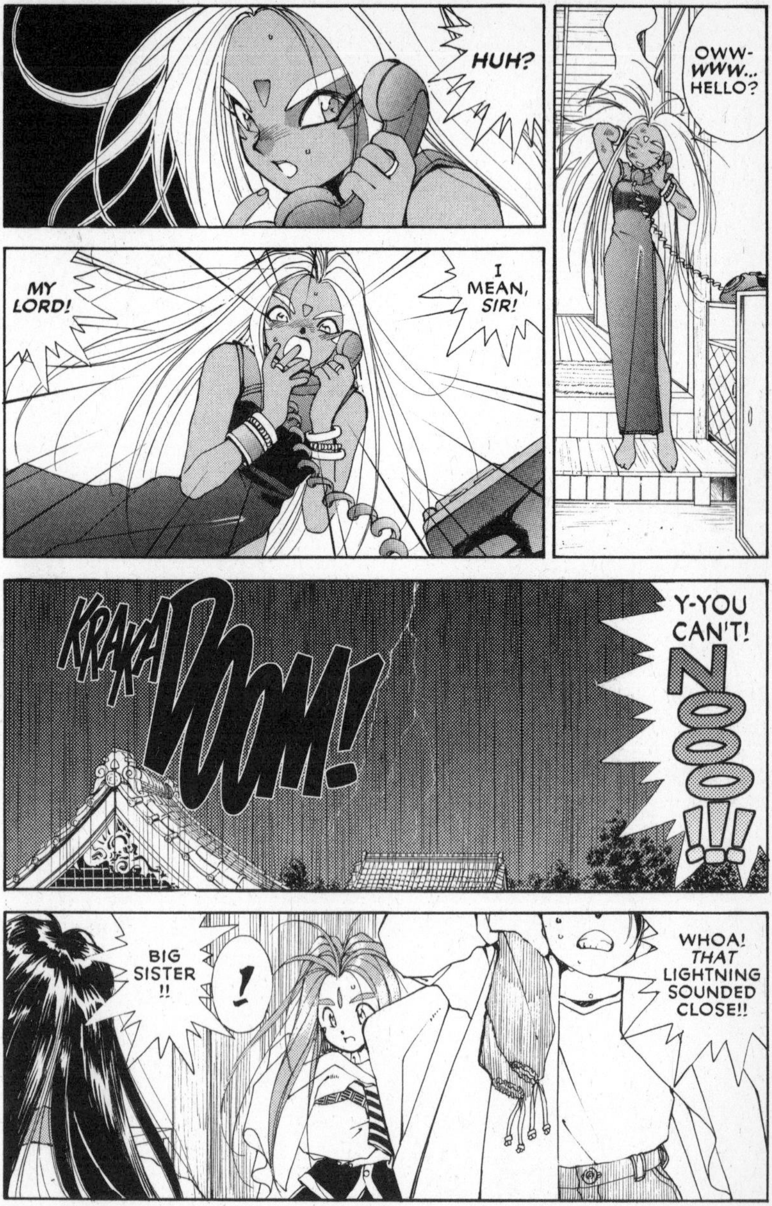
OWW-WWW... HELLO?
HUH?
I MEAN, SIR!
MY LORD!
Y-YOU CAN'T!
NOOO!!!
KRAKADOOM!
WHOA! THAT LIGHTNING SOUNDED CLOSE!!
!
BIG SISTER !!

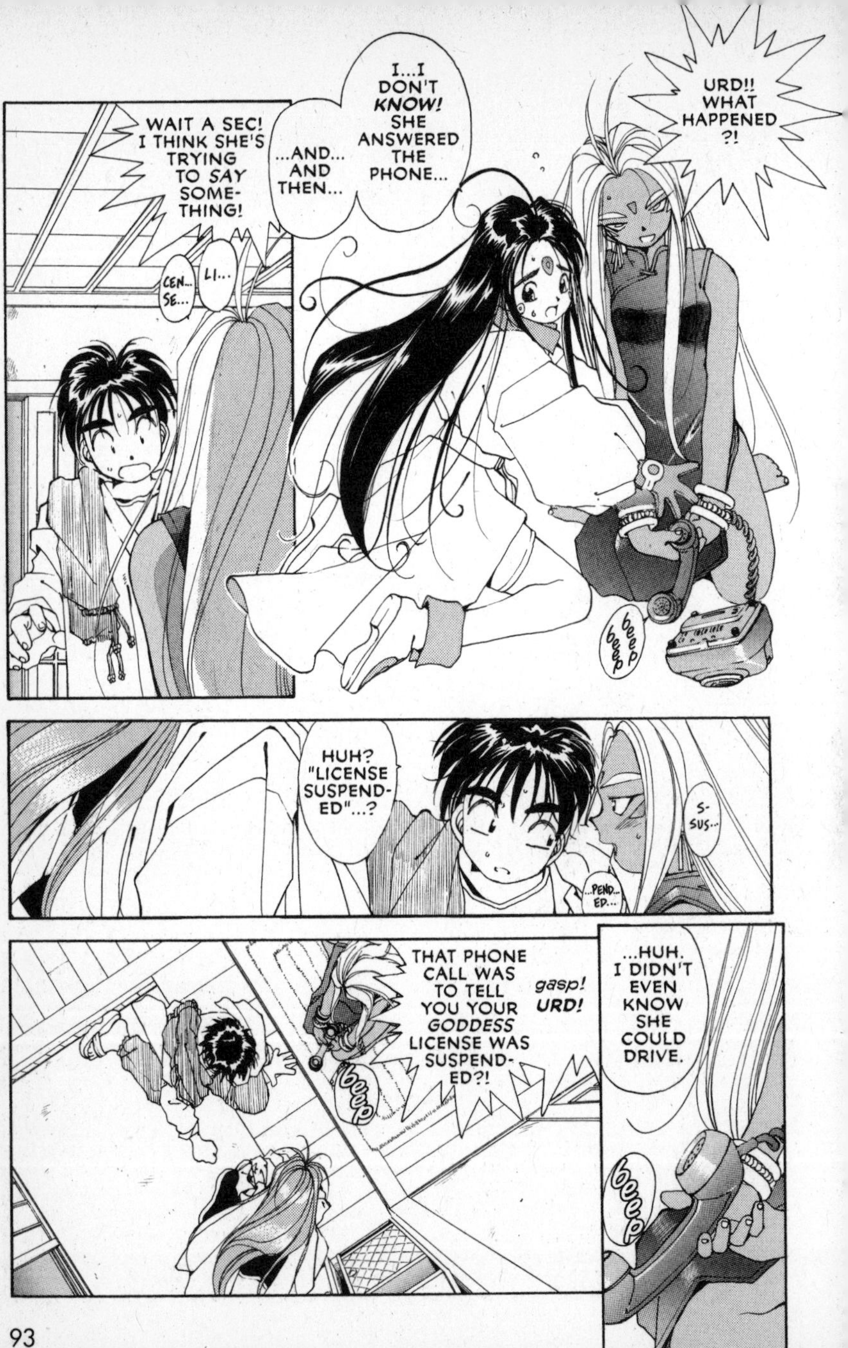
URD!! WHAT HAPPENED ?!
I...I DON'T *KNOW!* SHE ANSWERED THE PHONE...
...AND... AND THEN...
beep beep
WAIT A SEC! I THINK SHE'S TRYING TO *SAY* SOME-THING!
LI...
CEN... SE...
S-SUS...
...PEND... ED...
HUH? "LICENSE SUSPEND-ED"...?
...HUH. I DIDN'T EVEN KNOW SHE COULD DRIVE.
beep
gasp! URD!
THAT PHONE CALL WAS TO TELL YOU YOUR *GODDESS* LICENSE WAS SUSPEND-ED?!
beep

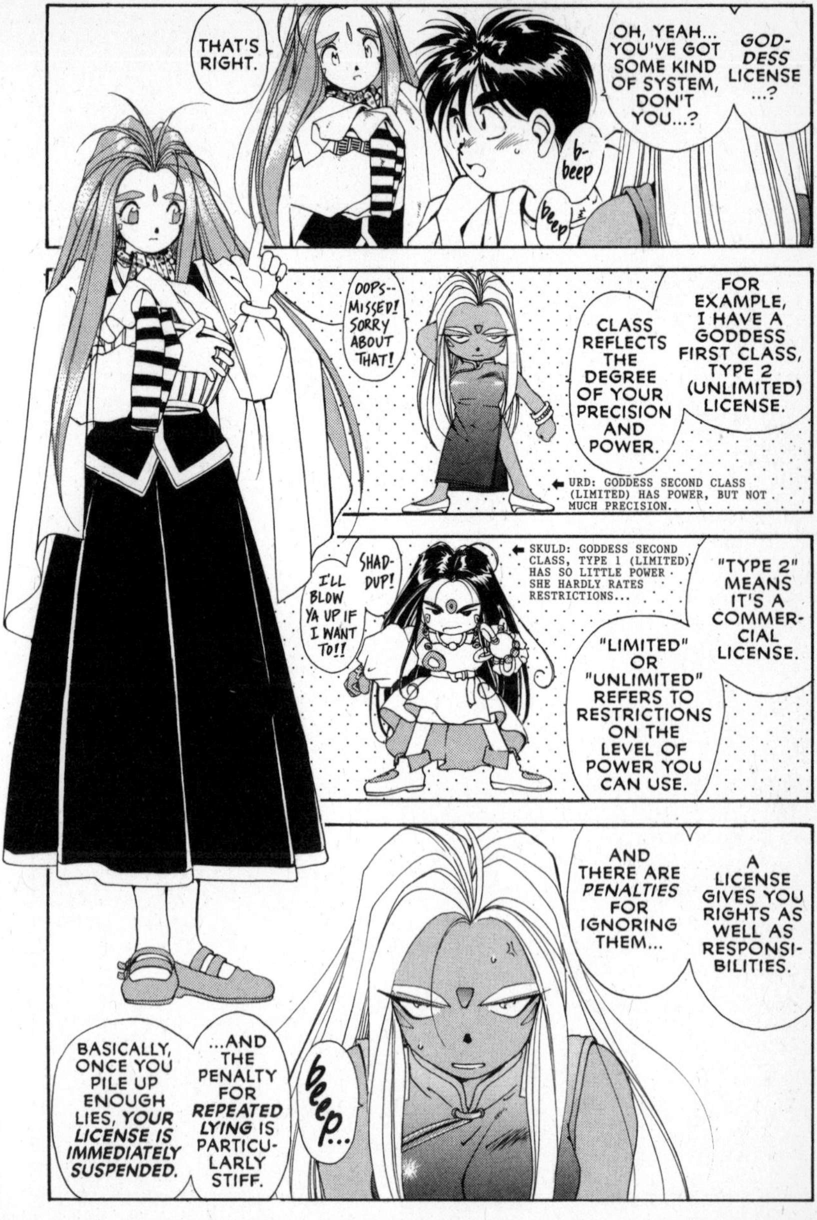

GOD-DESS LICENSE ...?
OH, YEAH... YOU'VE GOT SOME KIND OF SYSTEM, DON'T YOU...?
b-beep
beep
THAT'S RIGHT.
FOR EXAMPLE, I HAVE A GODDESS FIRST CLASS, TYPE 2 (UNLIMITED) LICENSE.
CLASS REFLECTS THE DEGREE OF YOUR PRECISION AND POWER.
URD: GODDESS SECOND CLASS (LIMITED) HAS POWER, BUT NOT MUCH PRECISION.
OOPS-- MISSED! SORRY ABOUT THAT!
"TYPE 2" MEANS IT'S A COMMERCIAL LICENSE.
"LIMITED" OR "UNLIMITED" REFERS TO RESTRICTIONS ON THE LEVEL OF POWER YOU CAN USE.
SKULD: GODDESS SECOND CLASS, TYPE 1 (LIMITED) HAS SO LITTLE POWER SHE HARDLY RATES RESTRICTIONS...
SHAD-DUP!
I'LL BLOW YA UP IF I WANT TO!!
A LICENSE GIVES YOU RIGHTS AS WELL AS RESPONSIBILITIES.
AND THERE ARE PENALTIES FOR IGNORING THEM...
beep...
...AND THE PENALTY FOR REPEATED LYING IS PARTICULARLY STIFF.
BASICALLY, ONCE YOU PILE UP ENOUGH LIES, YOUR LICENSE IS IMMEDIATELY SUSPENDED.

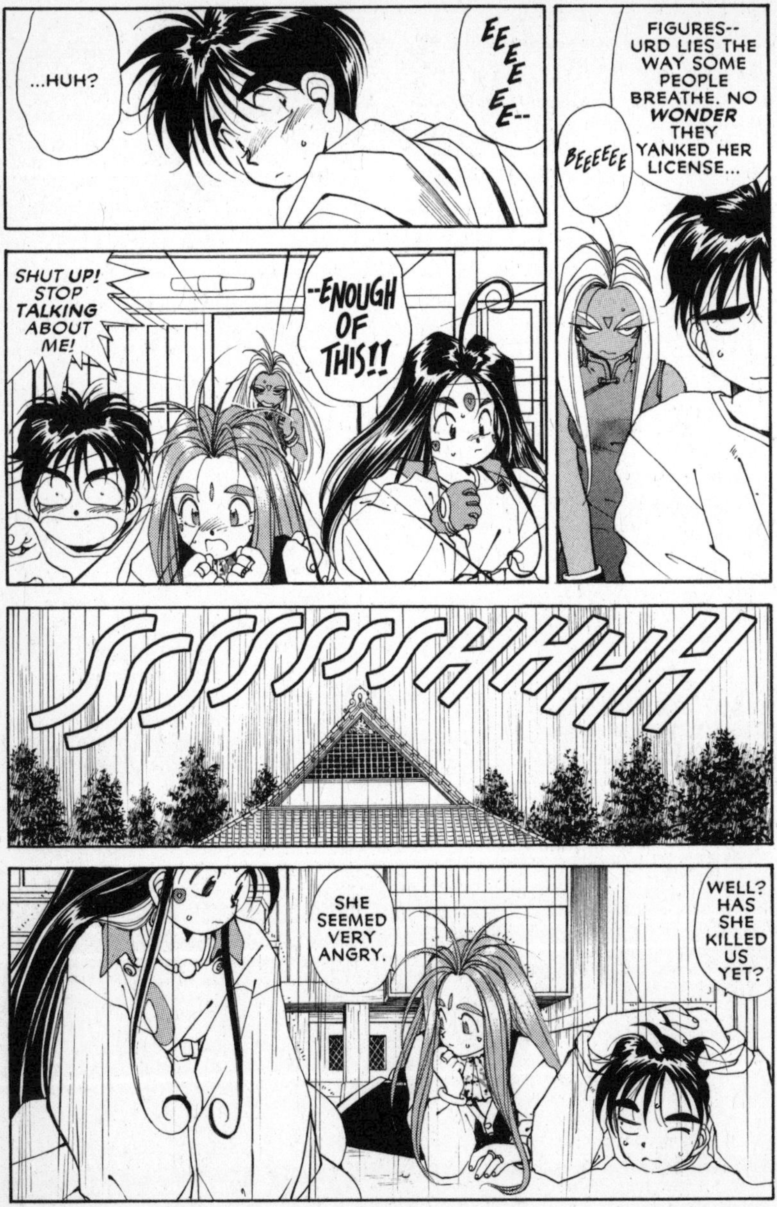
FIGURES-- URD LIES THE WAY SOME PEOPLE BREATHE. NO WONDER THEY YANKED HER LICENSE...
BEEEEEE
EEEEEE--
...HUH?
--ENOUGH OF THIS!!
SHUT UP! STOP TALKING ABOUT ME!
SSSSSSHHHHH
WELL? HAS SHE KILLED US YET?
SHE SEEMED VERY ANGRY.

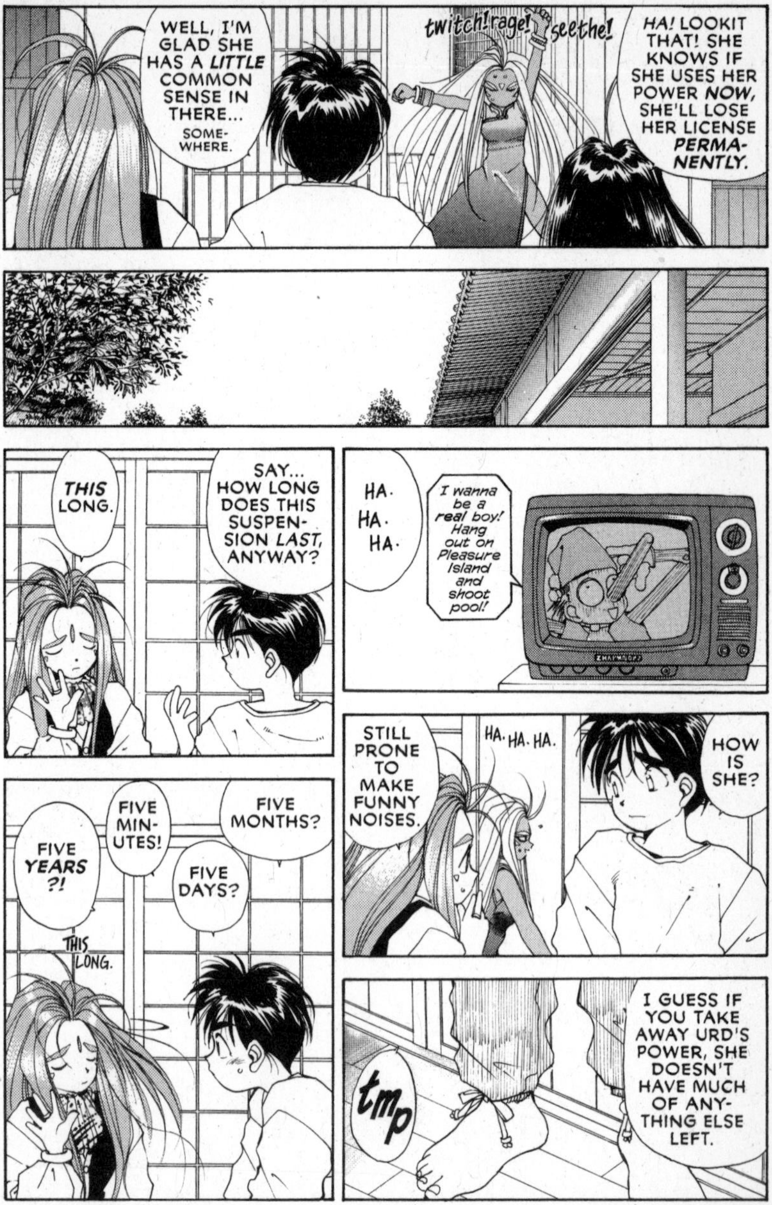

HA! LOOKIT THAT! SHE KNOWS IF SHE USES HER POWER NOW, SHE'LL LOSE HER LICENSE PERMA-NENTLY.
twitch! rage! seethe!
WELL, I'M GLAD SHE HAS A LITTLE COMMON SENSE IN THERE... SOME-WHERE.
I wanna be a real boy! Hang out on Pleasure Island and shoot pool!
HA. HA. HA.
SAY... HOW LONG DOES THIS SUSPEN-SION LAST, ANYWAY?
THIS LONG.
HOW IS SHE?
HA. HA. HA.
STILL PRONE TO MAKE FUNNY NOISES.
I GUESS IF YOU TAKE AWAY URD'S POWER, SHE DOESN'T HAVE MUCH OF ANY-THING ELSE LEFT.
tmp
FIVE MONTHS?
FIVE MIN-UTES!
FIVE DAYS?
FIVE YEARS ?!
THIS LONG.

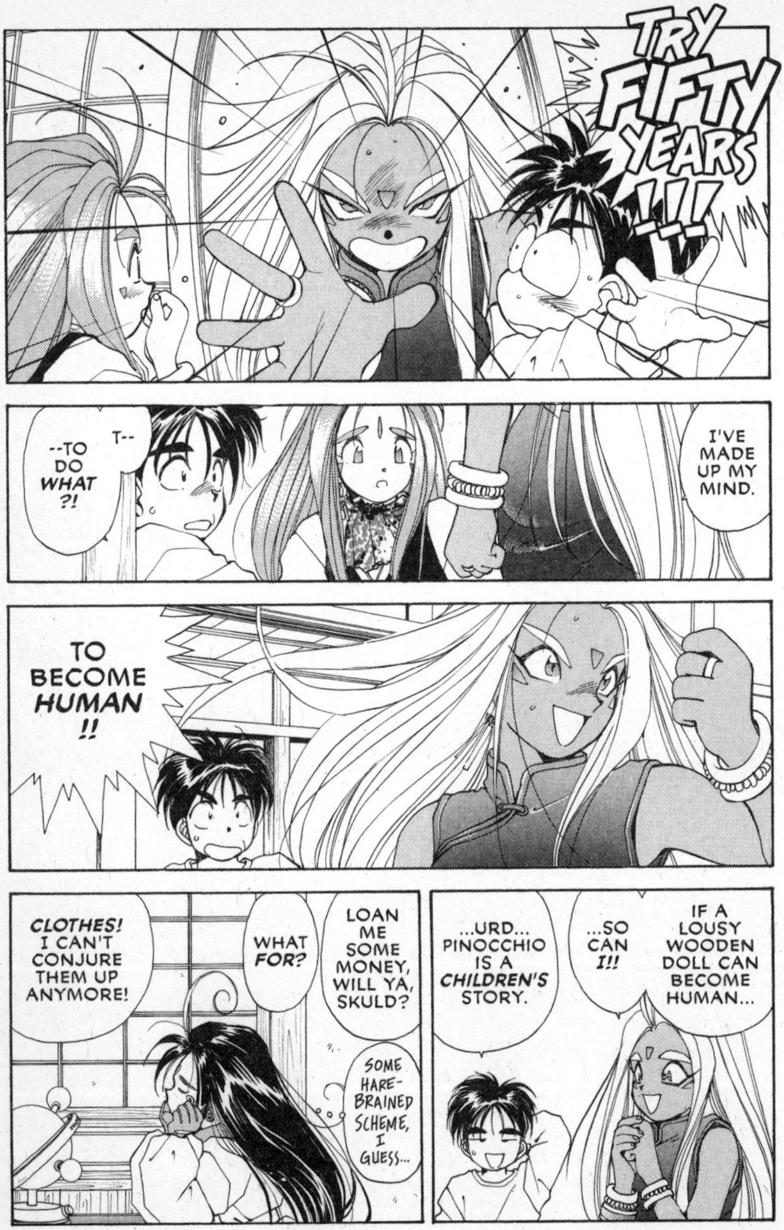
TRY FIFTY YEARS!!!
I'VE MADE UP MY MIND.
T--
--TO DO WHAT?!
TO BECOME HUMAN!!
IF A LOUSY WOODEN DOLL CAN BECOME HUMAN...
...SO CAN I!!
...URD... PINOCCHIO IS A CHILDREN'S STORY.
LOAN ME SOME MONEY, WILL YA, SKULD?
WHAT FOR?
CLOTHES! I CAN'T CONJURE THEM UP ANYMORE!
SOME HARE-BRAINED SCHEME, I GUESS...

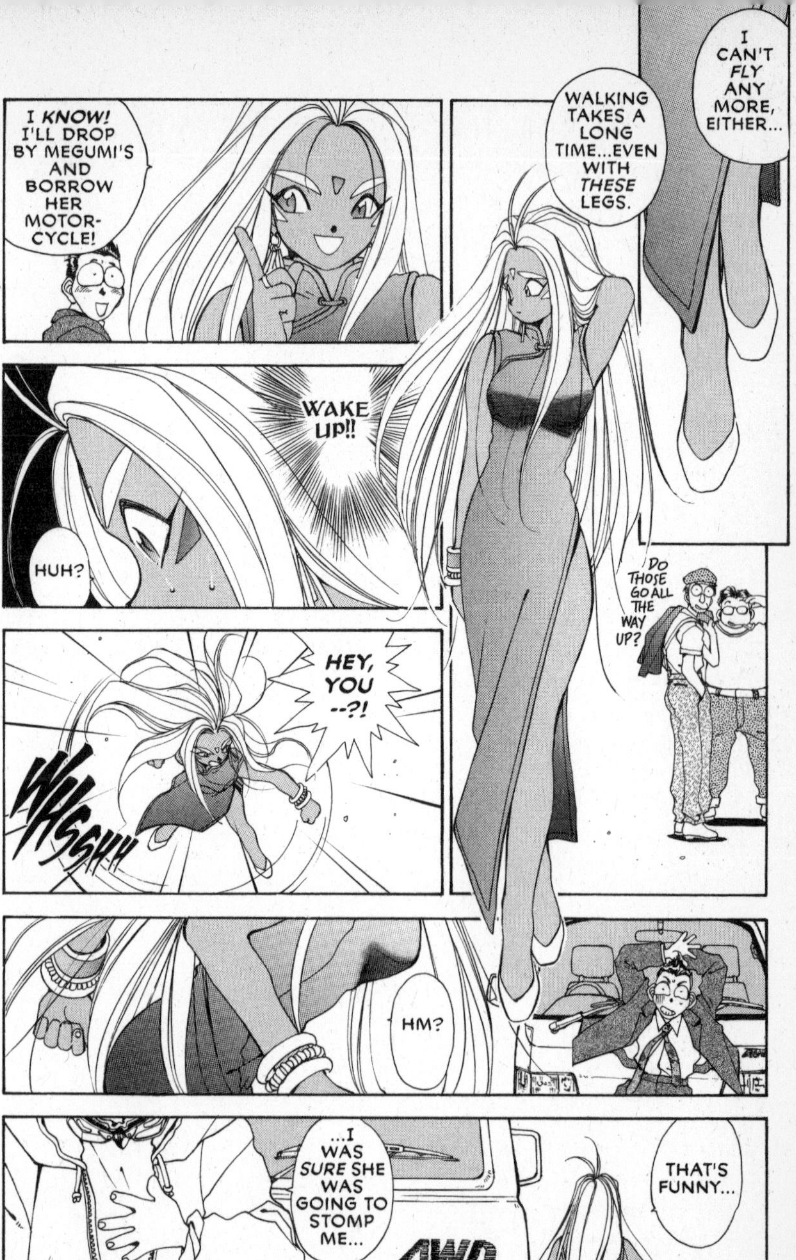
I CAN'T *FLY* ANY MORE, EITHER...
WALKING TAKES A LONG TIME...EVEN WITH *THESE* LEGS.
DO THOSE GO ALL THE WAY UP?
I *KNOW!* I'LL DROP BY MEGUMI'S AND BORROW HER MOTOR-CYCLE!
WAKE UP!!
HUH?
HEY, YOU --?!
WHSSHH
HM?
THAT'S FUNNY...
...I WAS *SURE* SHE WAS GOING TO STOMP ME...
4WD

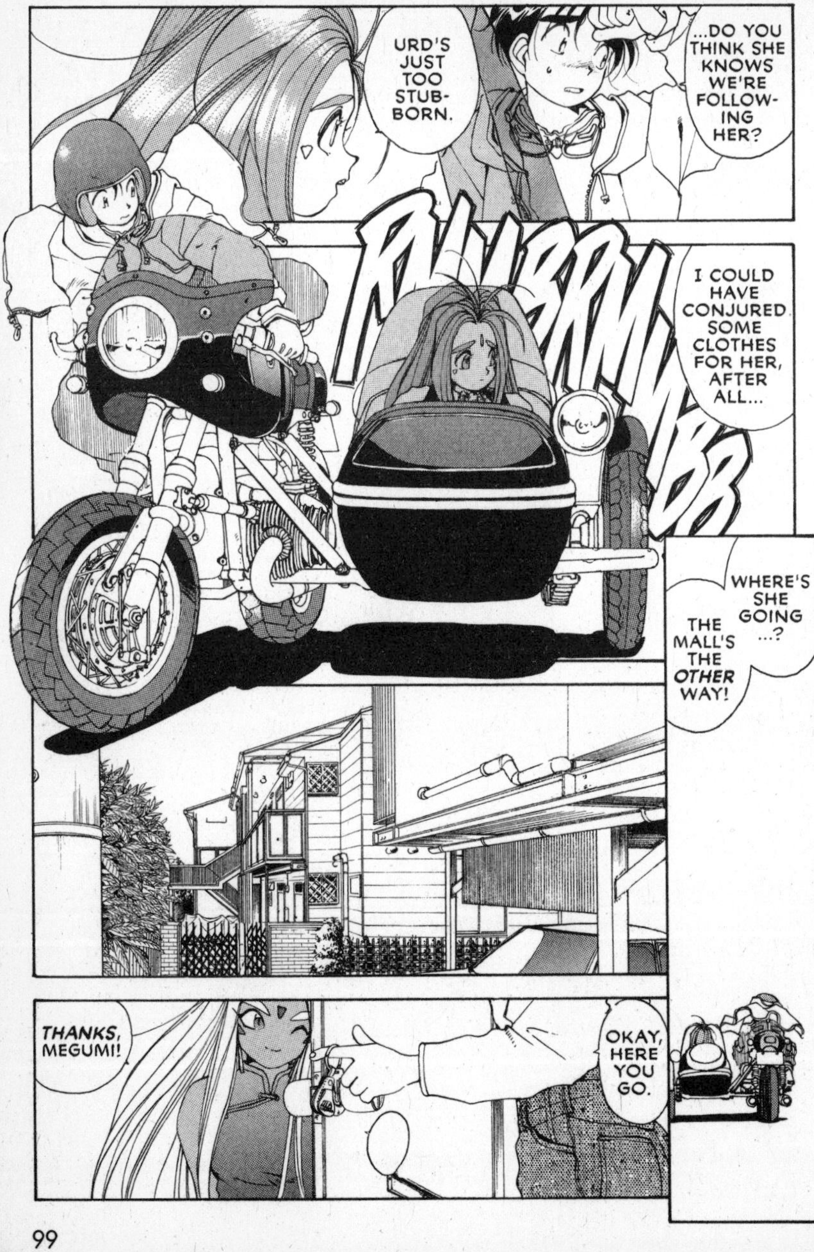
...DO YOU THINK SHE KNOWS WE'RE FOLLOWING HER?
URD'S JUST TOO STUBBORN.
I COULD HAVE CONJURED SOME CLOTHES FOR HER, AFTER ALL...
WHERE'S SHE GOING ...?
THE MALL'S THE *OTHER* WAY!
OKAY, HERE YOU GO.
*THANKS,* MEGUMI!

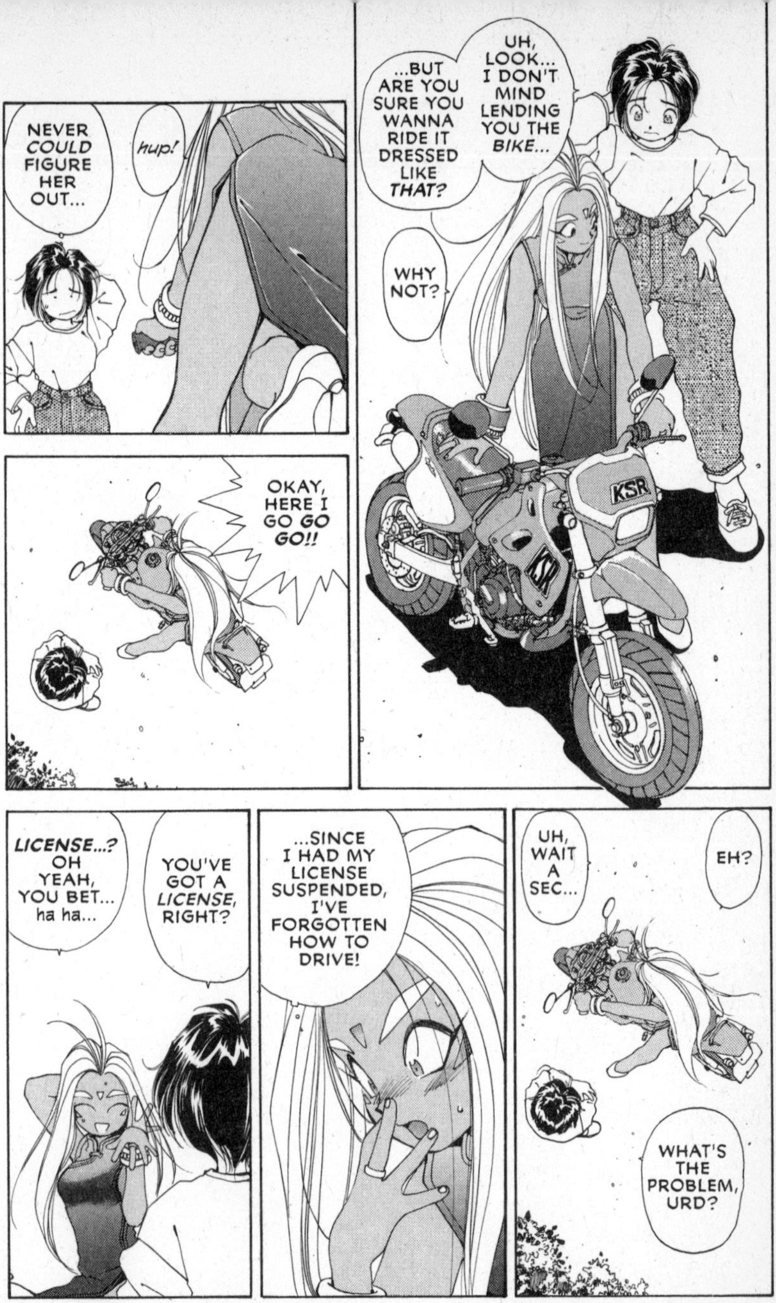
UH, LOOK... I DON'T MIND LENDING YOU THE *BIKE*...
...BUT ARE YOU SURE YOU WANNA RIDE IT DRESSED LIKE *THAT?*
WHY NOT?
*hup!*
NEVER *COULD* FIGURE HER OUT...
OKAY, HERE I GO *GO GO!!*
EH?
UH, WAIT A SEC...
WHAT'S THE PROBLEM, URD?
...SINCE I HAD MY LICENSE SUSPENDED, I'VE FORGOTTEN HOW TO DRIVE!
YOU'VE GOT A *LICENSE*, RIGHT?
*LICENSE...?* OH YEAH, YOU BET... ha ha...

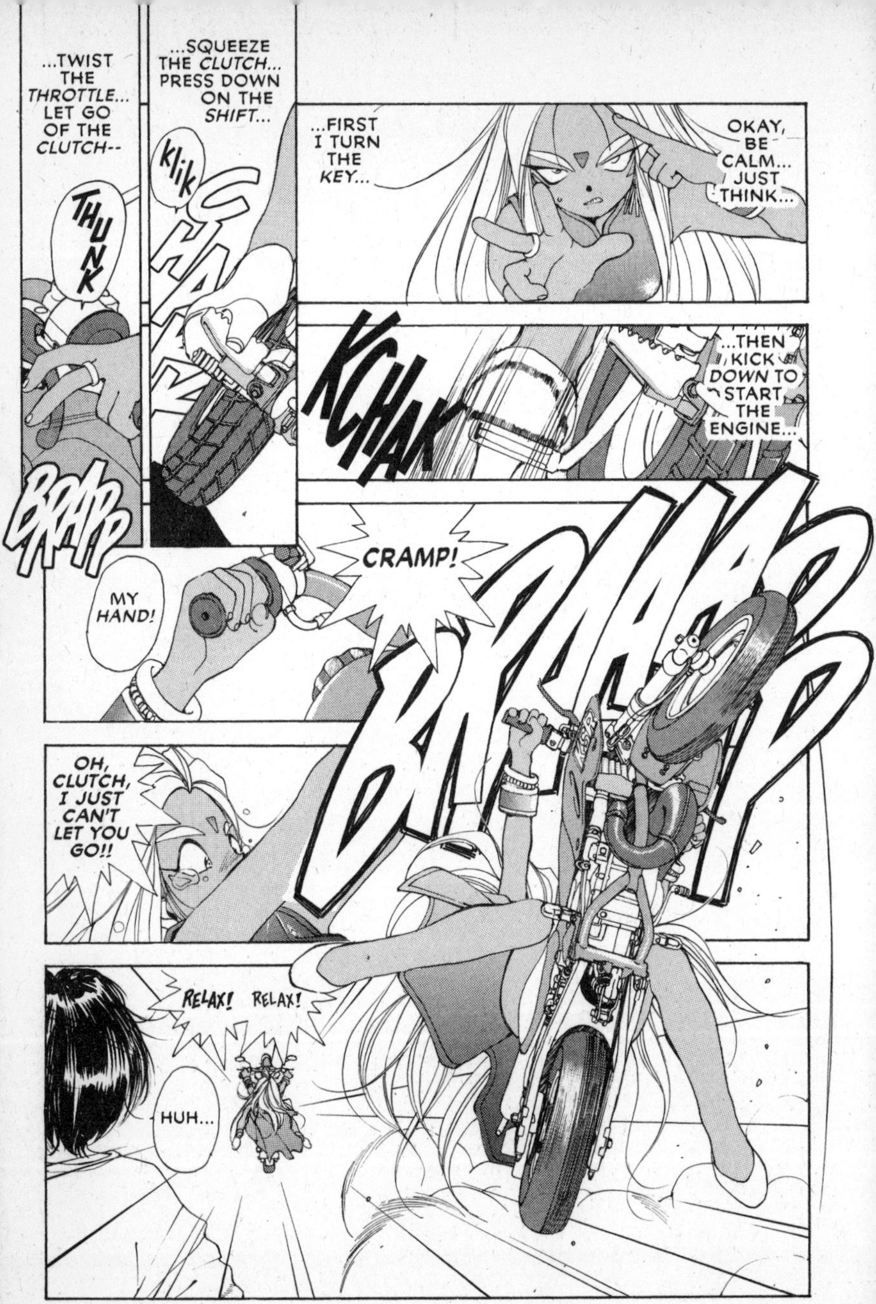
OKAY, BE CALM... JUST THINK...
...FIRST I TURN THE KEY...
...THEN KICK DOWN TO START THE ENGINE...
KCHAK
...SQUEEZE THE *CLUTCH*... PRESS DOWN ON THE *SHIFT*...
KLIK
...TWIST THE *THROTTLE*... LET GO OF THE *CLUTCH*--
THUNK
BRAPP
CRAMP!
MY HAND!
OH, CLUTCH, I JUST CAN'T LET YOU GO!!
RELAX! RELAX!
HUH...

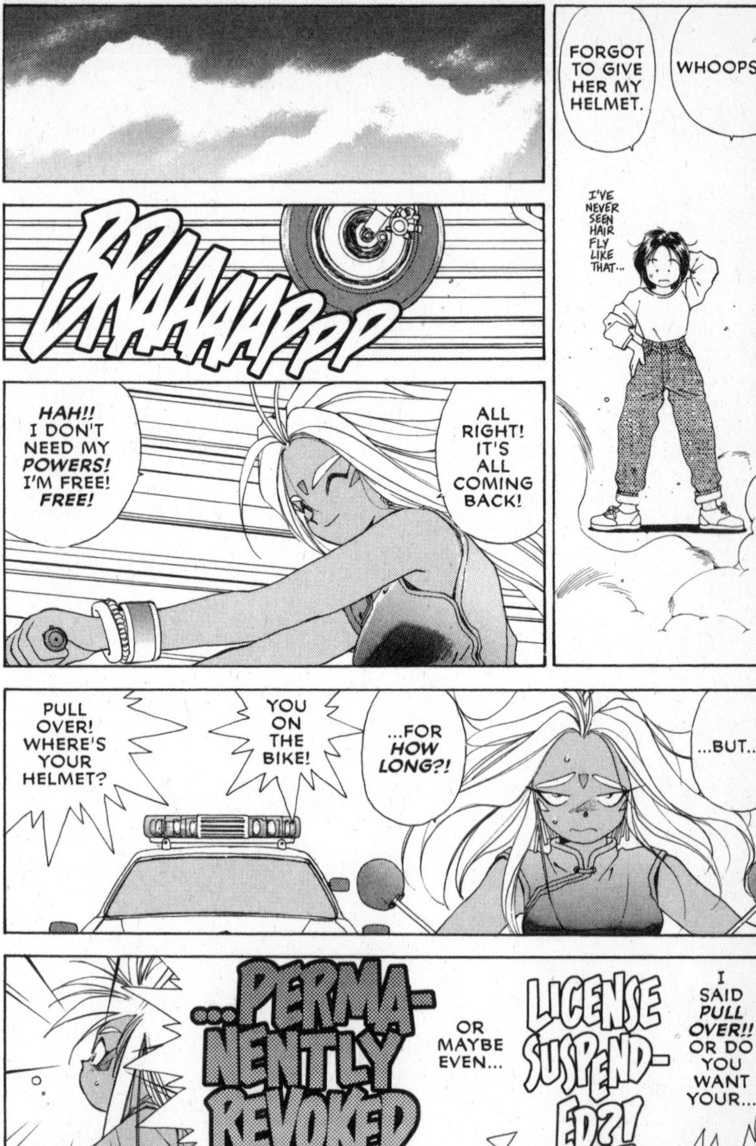
WHOOPS.
FORGOT TO GIVE HER MY HELMET.
I'VE NEVER SEEN HAIR FLY LIKE THAT...
BRAAAAAPPPP
ALL RIGHT! IT'S ALL COMING BACK!
HAH!! I DON'T NEED MY *POWERS!* I'M FREE! *FREE!*
...BUT...
...FOR *HOW LONG?!*
YOU ON THE BIKE!
PULL OVER! WHERE'S YOUR HELMET?
I SAID *PULL OVER!!* OR DO YOU WANT YOUR...
LICENSE SUSPEND-ED?!
OR MAYBE EVEN...
...PERMA-NENTLY REVOKED?!!

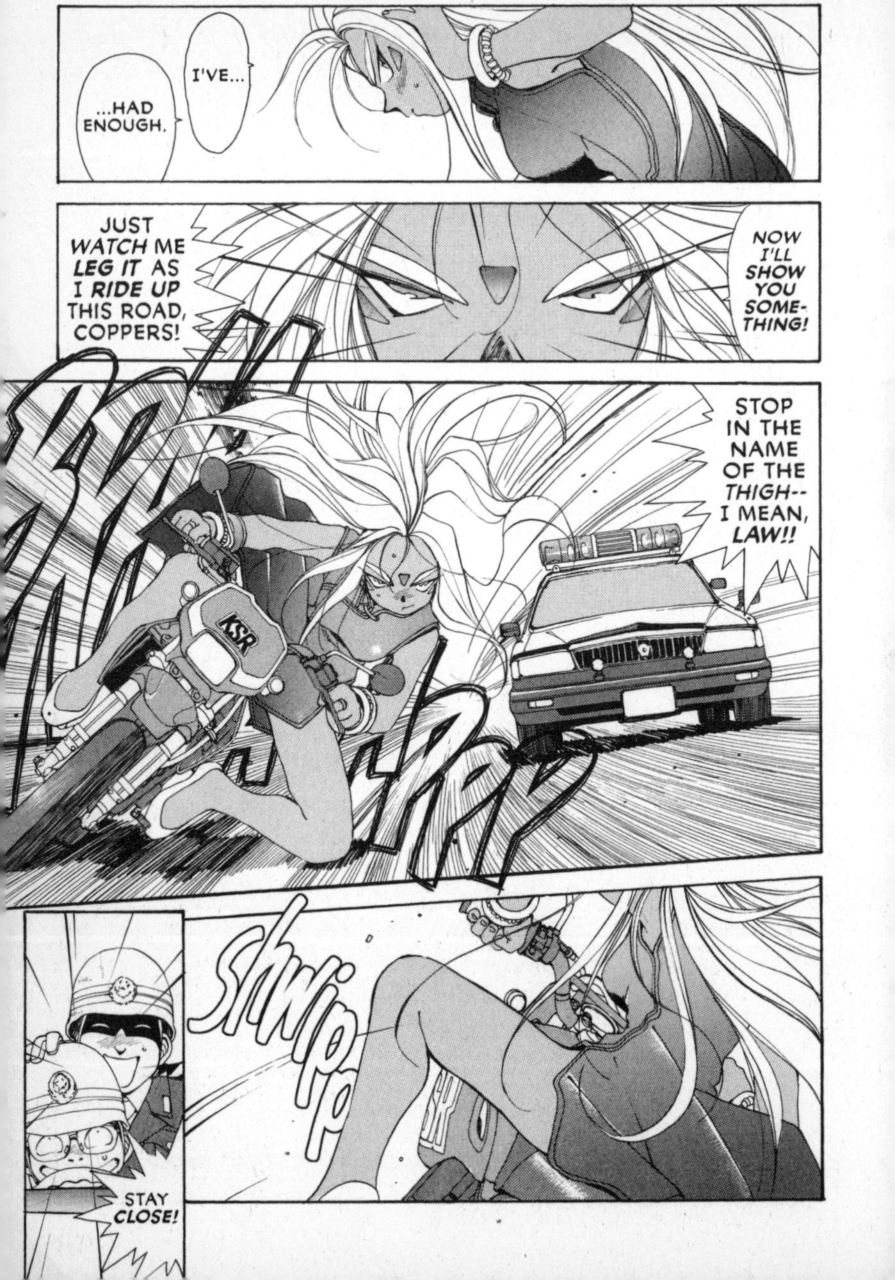
I'VE...
...HAD ENOUGH.
NOW I'LL SHOW YOU SOME-THING!
JUST WATCH ME LEG IT AS I RIDE UP THIS ROAD, COPPERS!
STOP IN THE NAME OF THE THIGH-- I MEAN, LAW!!
SHWIPP
STAY CLOSE!

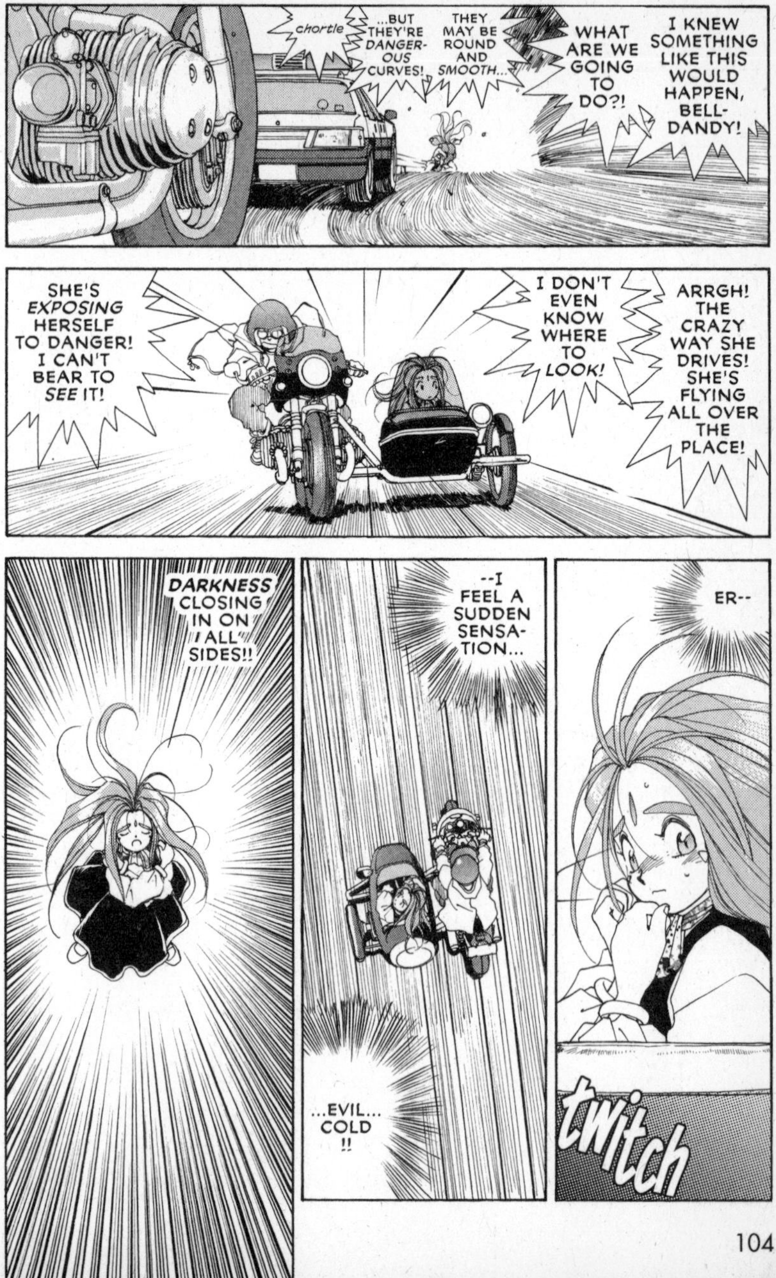
I KNEW SOMETHING LIKE THIS WOULD HAPPEN, BELL-DANDY!
WHAT ARE WE GOING TO DO?!
THEY MAY BE ROUND AND *SMOOTH*...
...BUT THEY'RE *DANGEROUS* CURVES!
*chortle*
ARRGH! THE CRAZY WAY SHE DRIVES! SHE'S FLYING ALL OVER THE PLACE!
I DON'T EVEN KNOW WHERE TO *LOOK!*
SHE'S *EXPOSING* HERSELF TO DANGER! I CAN'T BEAR TO *SEE* IT!
ER--
twitch
--I FEEL A SUDDEN SENSATION...
...EVIL... COLD !!
*DARKNESS* CLOSING IN ON ALL SIDES!!

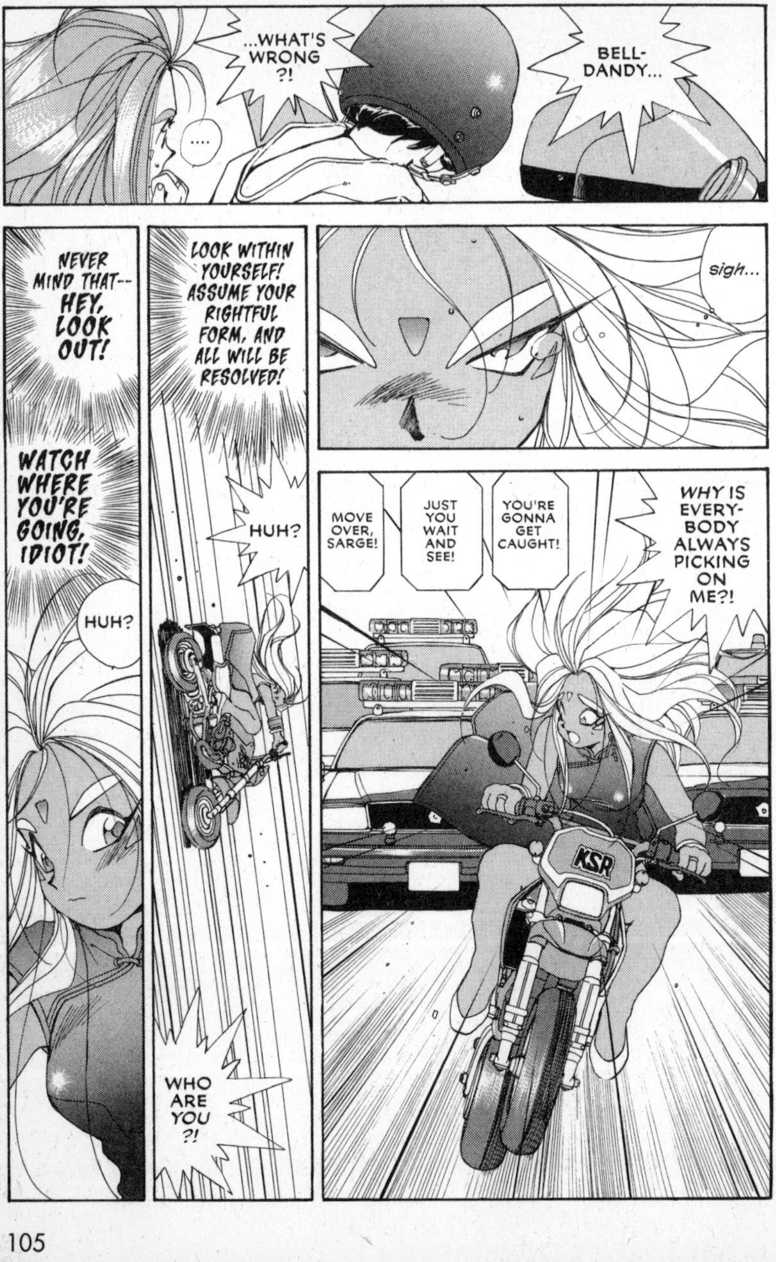
BELL-DANDY...
...WHAT'S WRONG?!
....
sigh...
*WHY* IS EVERYBODY ALWAYS PICKING ON ME?!
YOU'RE GONNA GET CAUGHT!
JUST YOU WAIT AND SEE!
MOVE OVER, SARGE!
LOOK WITHIN YOURSELF! ASSUME YOUR RIGHTFUL FORM, AND ALL WILL BE RESOLVED!
HUH?
WHO ARE YOU?!
NEVER MIND THAT-- HEY, LOOK OUT!
WATCH WHERE YOU'RE GOING, IDIOT!
HUH?

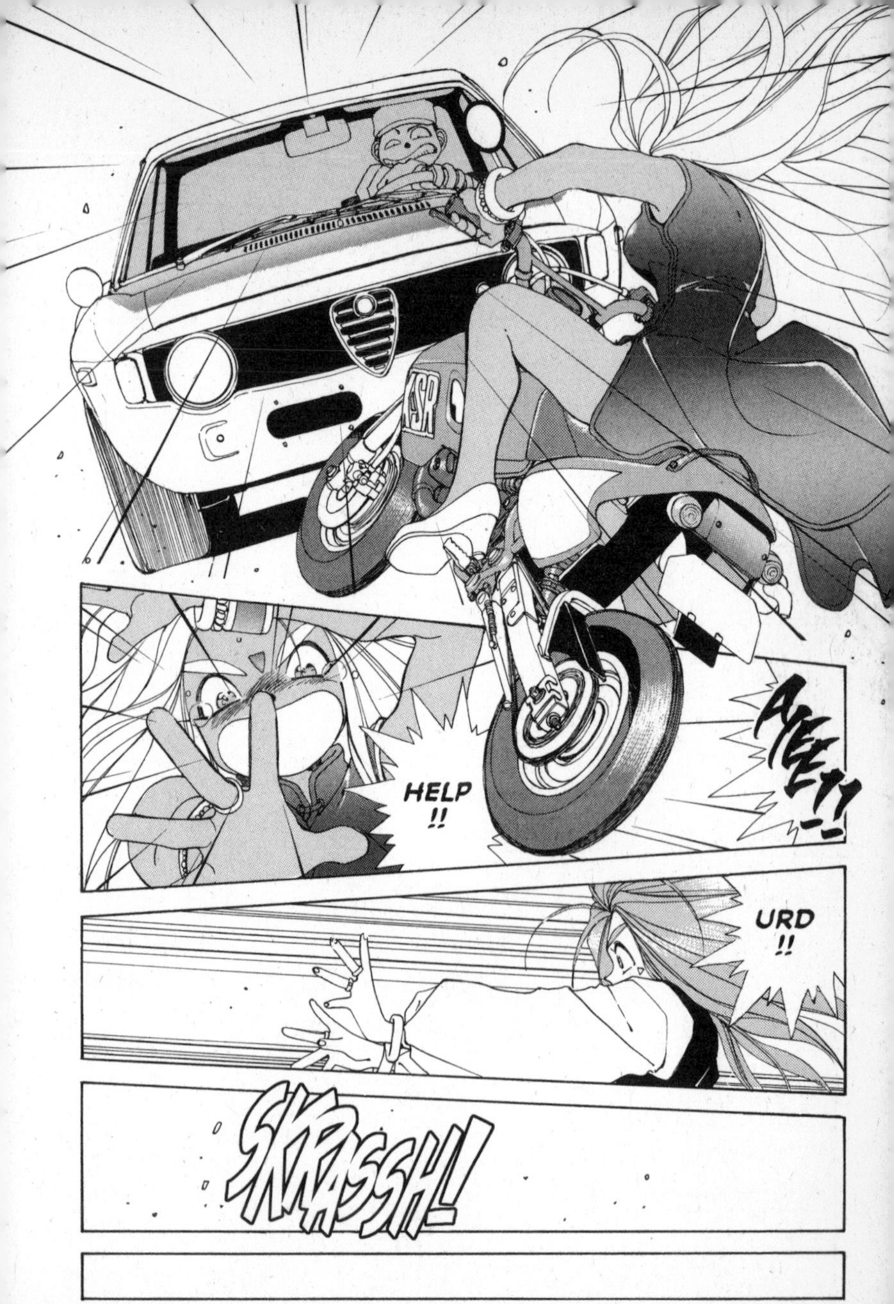
AIEEE!!
HELP !!
URD !!
SKRASSH!

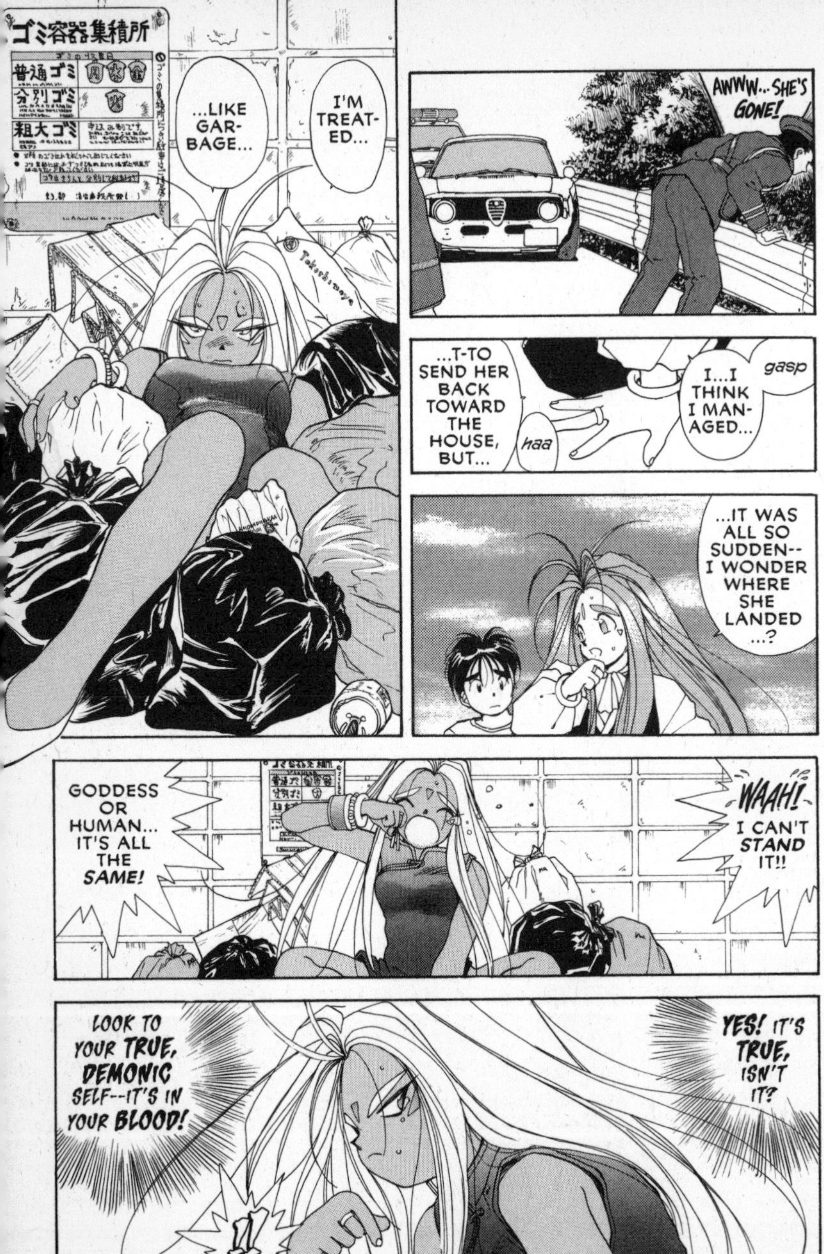
AWWW... SHE'S GONE!
gasp
I...I THINK I MANAGED...
haa
...T-TO SEND HER BACK TOWARD THE HOUSE, BUT...
...IT WAS ALL SO SUDDEN-- I WONDER WHERE SHE LANDED ...?
ゴミ容器集積所
普通ゴミ
分別ゴミ
粗大ゴミ
I'M TREATED...
...LIKE GARBAGE...
WAAH! I CAN'T STAND IT!!
GODDESS OR HUMAN... IT'S ALL THE SAME!
YES! IT'S TRUE, ISN'T IT?
LOOK TO YOUR TRUE, DEMONIC SELF--IT'S IN YOUR BLOOD!

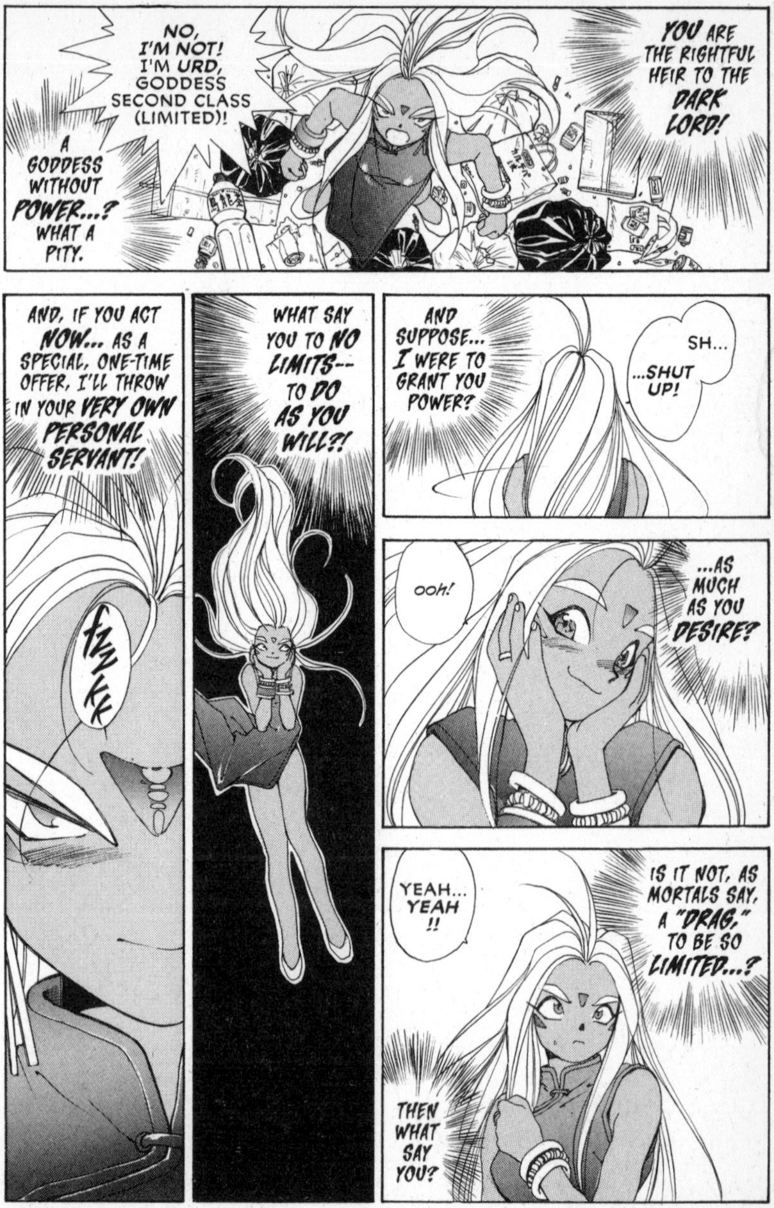
YOU ARE THE RIGHTFUL HEIR TO THE DARK LORD!
NO, I'M NOT! I'M URD, GODDESS SECOND CLASS (LIMITED)!
A GODDESS WITHOUT POWER...? WHAT A PITY.
SH... ...SHUT UP!
AND SUPPOSE... I WERE TO GRANT YOU POWER?
...AS MUCH AS YOU DESIRE?
ooh!
IS IT NOT, AS MORTALS SAY, A "DRAG," TO BE SO LIMITED...?
YEAH... YEAH !!
THEN WHAT SAY YOU?
WHAT SAY YOU TO NO LIMITS-- TO DO AS YOU WILL?!
AND, IF YOU ACT NOW... AS A SPECIAL, ONE-TIME OFFER, I'LL THROW IN YOUR VERY OWN PERSONAL SERVANT!
FZZKK

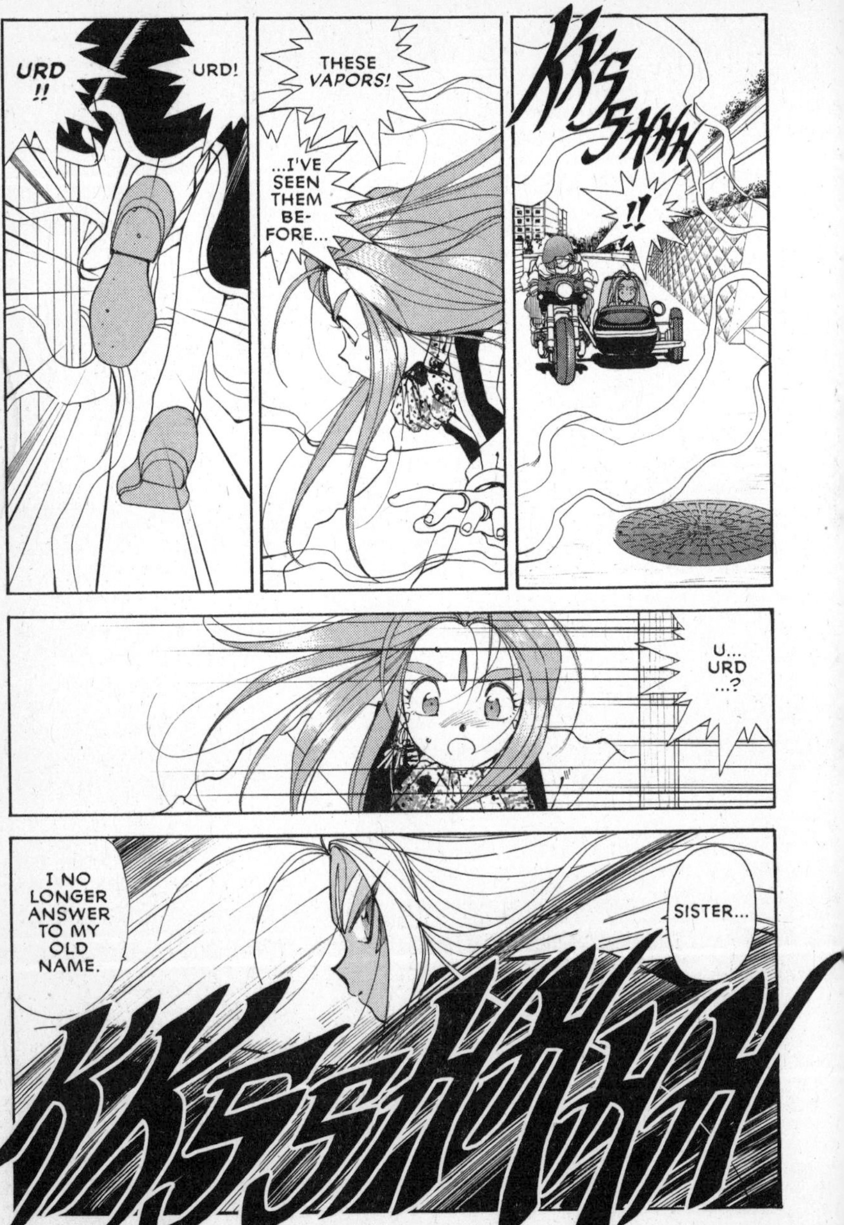
KKSHHH
!!
THESE VAPORS!
...I'VE SEEN THEM BE-FORE...
URD!
URD !!
U... URD ...?
SISTER...
I NO LONGER ANSWER TO MY OLD NAME.

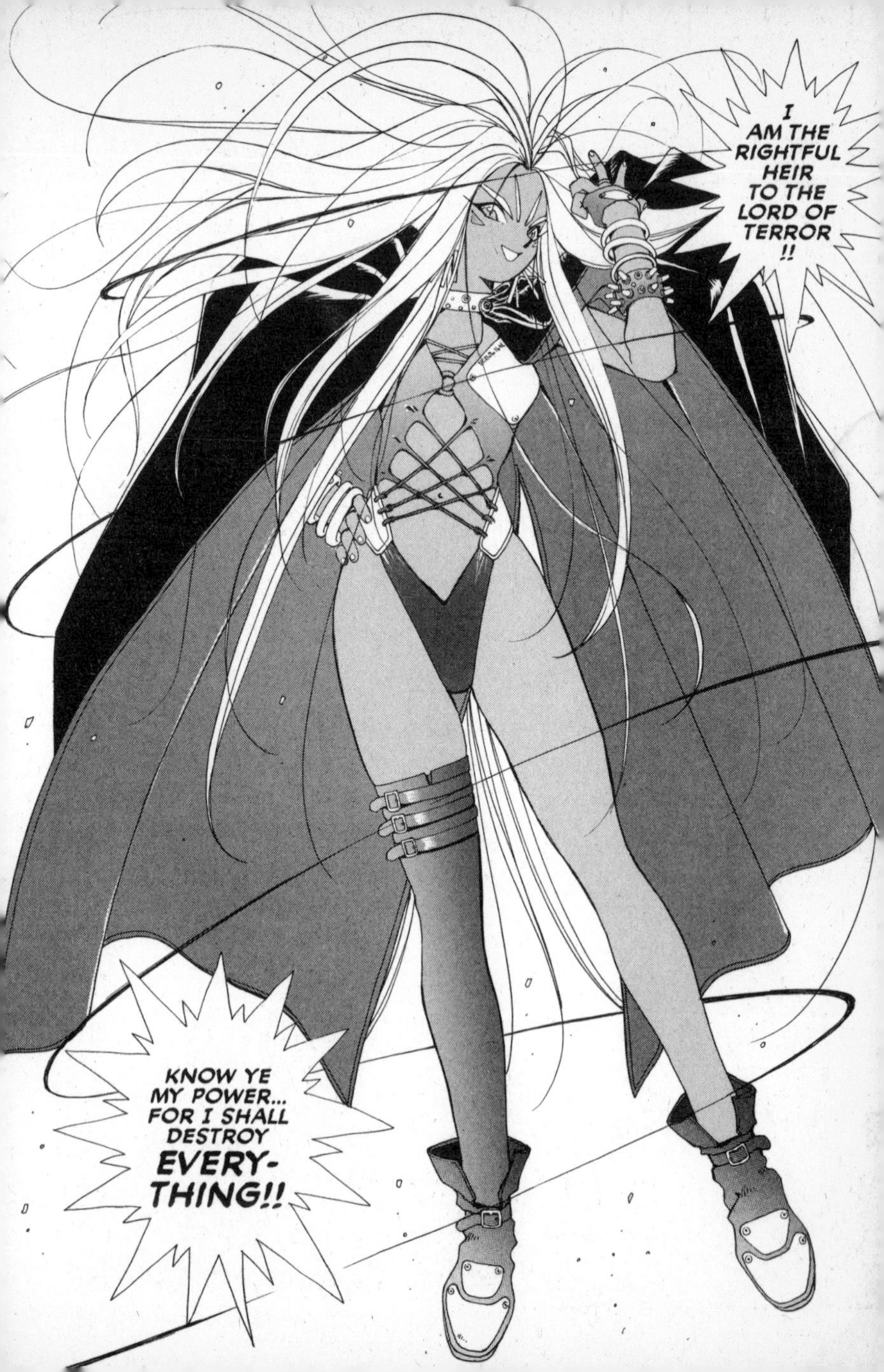
I AM THE RIGHTFUL HEIR TO THE LORD OF TERROR !!
KNOW YE MY POWER... FOR I SHALL DESTROY EVERY-THING!!

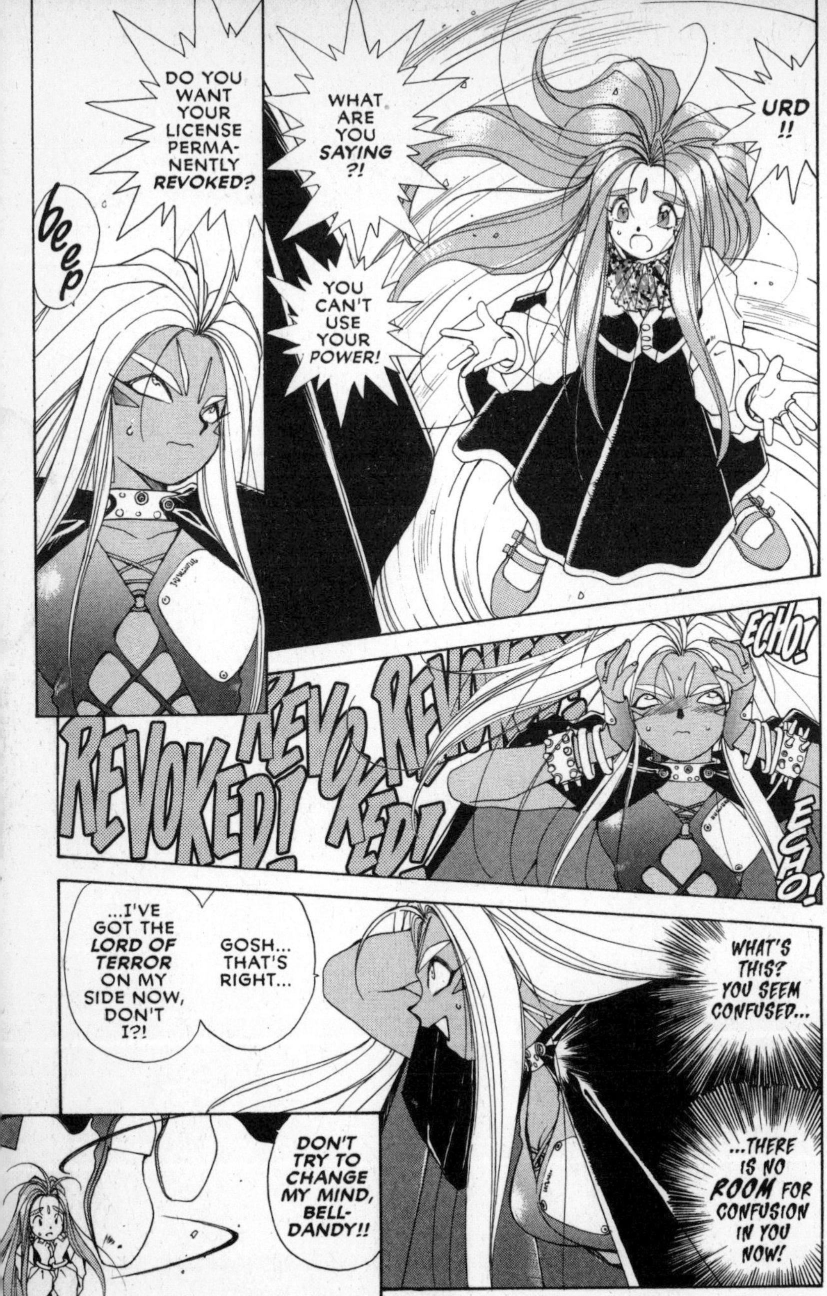
URD!!
WHAT ARE YOU *SAYING*?!
YOU CAN'T USE YOUR *POWER*!
DO YOU WANT YOUR LICENSE PERMANENTLY *REVOKED*?
beep
ECHO!
REVOKED!
REVOKED!
ECHO!
WHAT'S THIS? YOU SEEM CONFUSED...
GOSH... THAT'S RIGHT...
...I'VE GOT THE ***LORD OF TERROR*** ON MY SIDE NOW, DON'T I?!
...THERE IS NO ***ROOM*** FOR CONFUSION IN YOU NOW!
DON'T TRY TO CHANGE MY MIND, BELL-DANDY!!

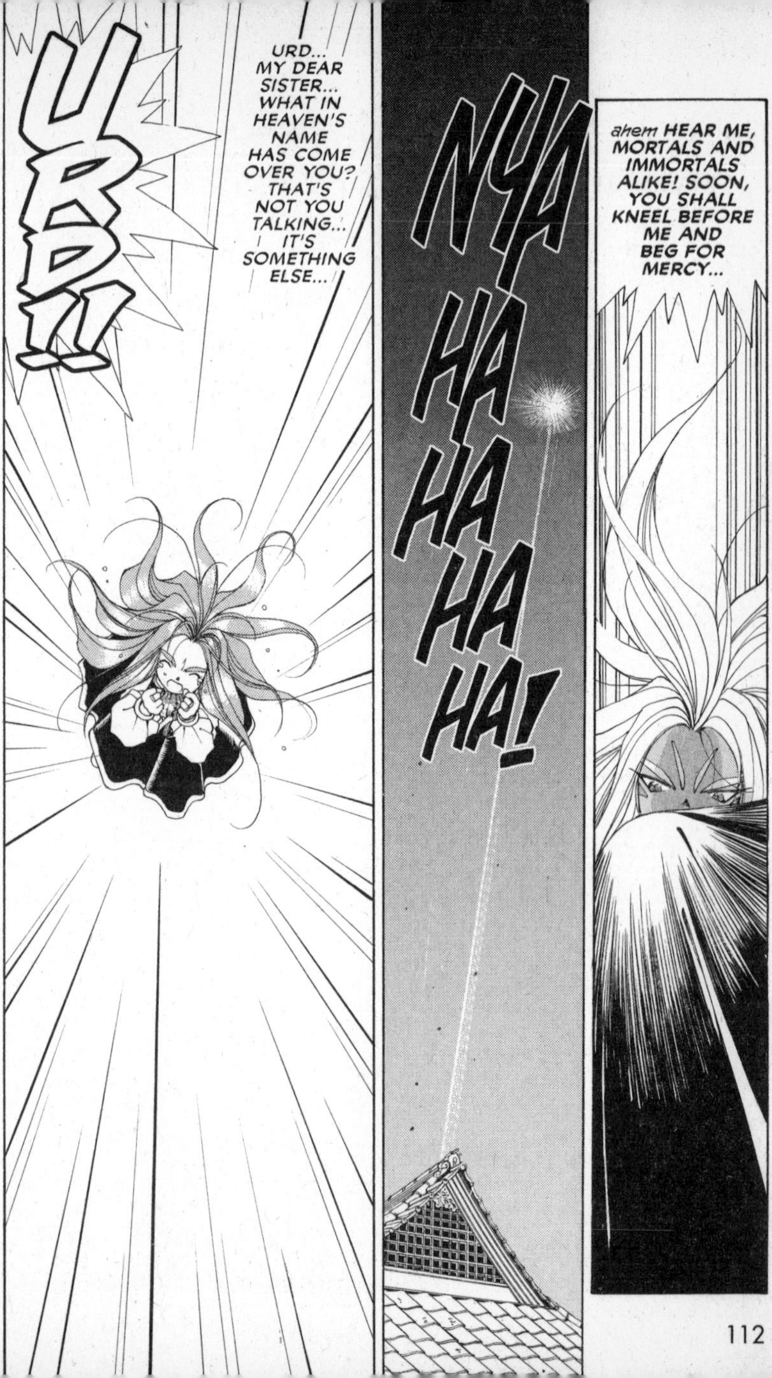
ahem HEAR ME, MORTALS AND IMMORTALS ALIKE! SOON, YOU SHALL KNEEL BEFORE ME AND BEG FOR MERCY...
NYA HA HA HA HA HA!
URD... MY DEAR SISTER... WHAT IN HEAVEN'S NAME HAS COME OVER YOU? THAT'S NOT YOU TALKING... IT'S SOMETHING ELSE...
URD!!

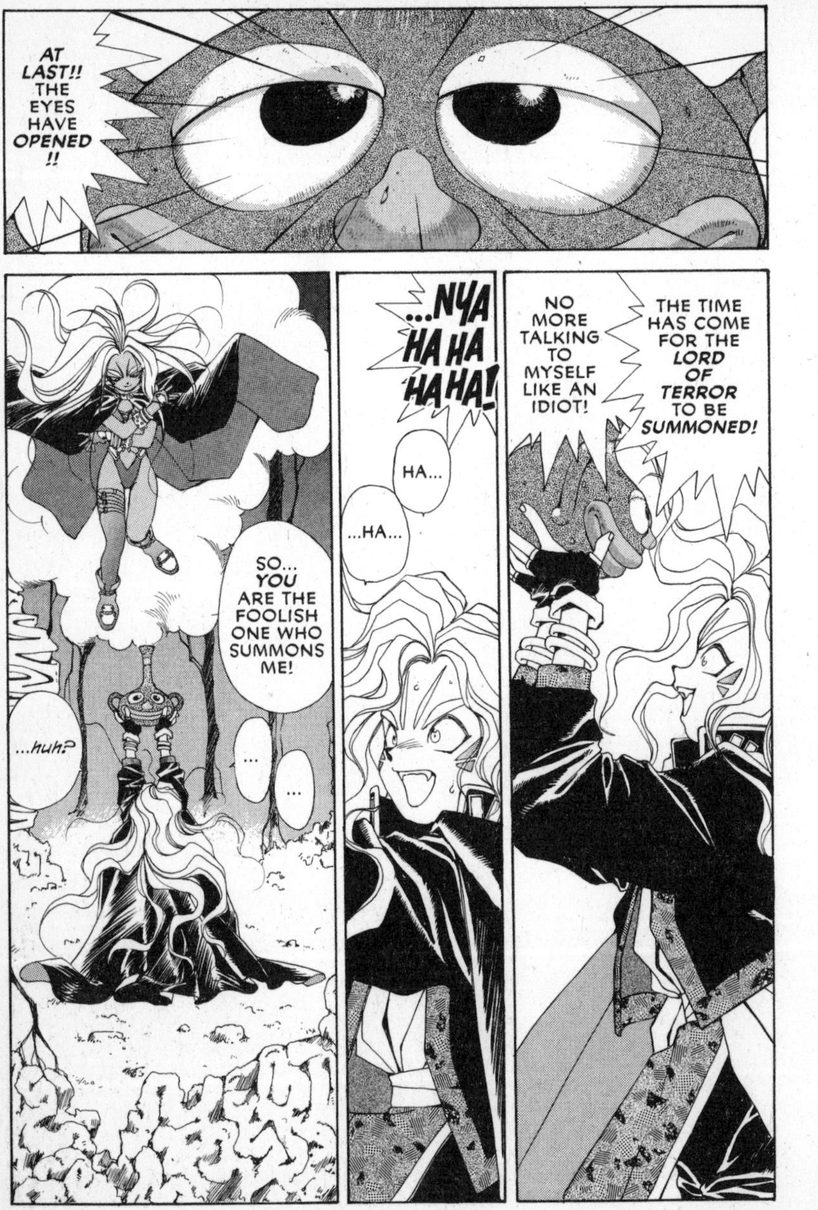
AT LAST!! THE EYES HAVE OPENED!!
THE TIME HAS COME FOR THE LORD OF TERROR TO BE SUMMONED!
NO MORE TALKING TO MYSELF LIKE AN IDIOT!
...NYA HA HA HA HA!
HA...
...HA...
SO... YOU ARE THE FOOLISH ONE WHO SUMMONS ME!
...
...
...huh?

# THE ADVENTURES OF MINI-URD

## WAKE-UP CALL

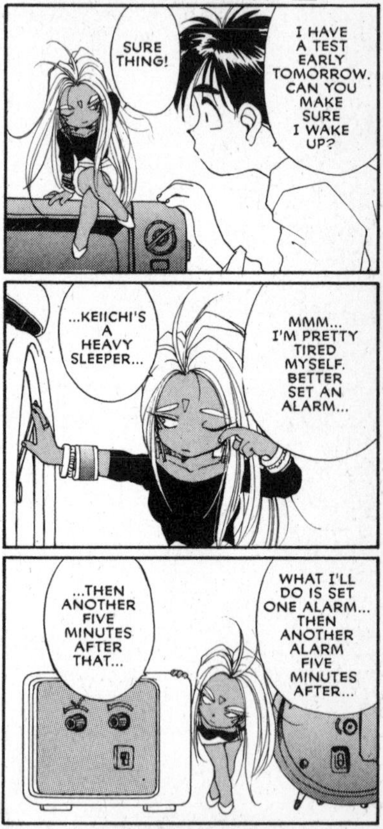
I HAVE A TEST EARLY TOMORROW. CAN YOU MAKE SURE I WAKE UP?
SURE THING!
MMM... I'M PRETTY TIRED MYSELF. BETTER SET AN ALARM...
...KEIICHI'S A HEAVY SLEEPER...
WHAT I'LL DO IS SET ONE ALARM... THEN ANOTHER ALARM FIVE MINUTES AFTER...
...THEN ANOTHER FIVE MINUTES AFTER THAT...
I'LL...
BRI NNGG
BING-BONG
BEEP BEEP
...I'LL NEVER FIND THEM ALL.

## JUST ONE OF THOSE DAYS

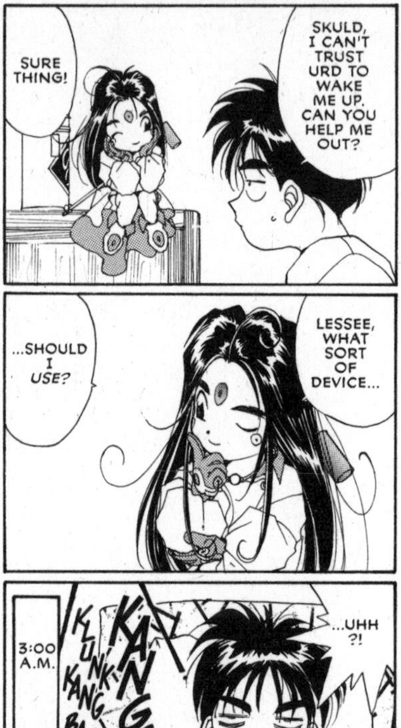
SKULD, I CAN'T TRUST URD TO WAKE ME UP. CAN YOU HELP ME OUT?
SURE THING!
LESSEE, WHAT SORT OF DEVICE...
...SHOULD I *USE?*
...UHH ?!
KANNGG
KLUNK KANG BANG
3:00 A.M.
SORRY... I'M STILL WORKING ON IT.
tik
tok

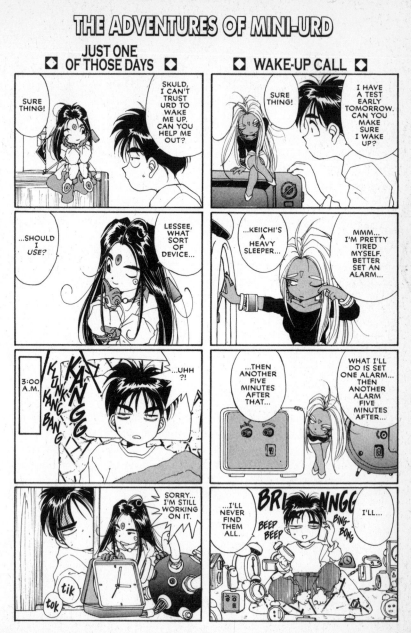

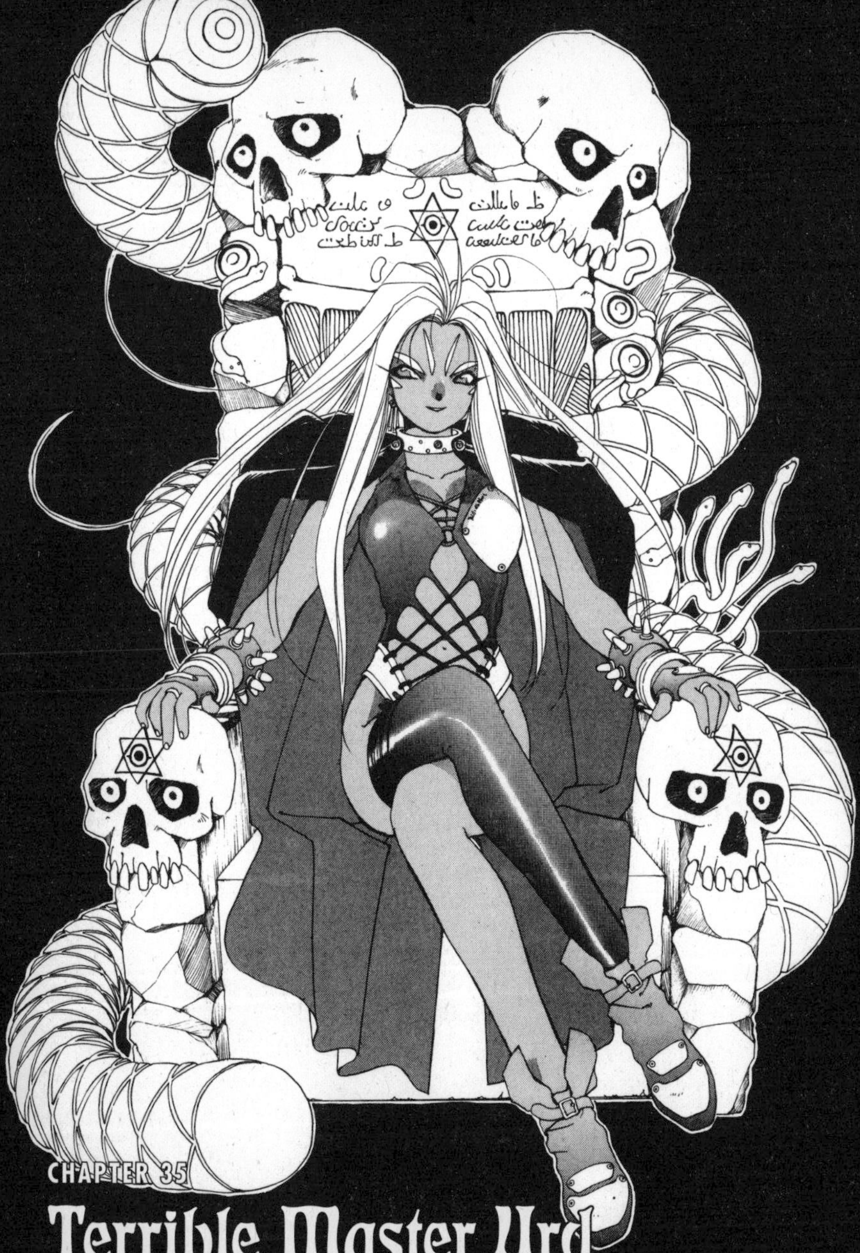

CHAPTER 35

# Terrible Master Urd

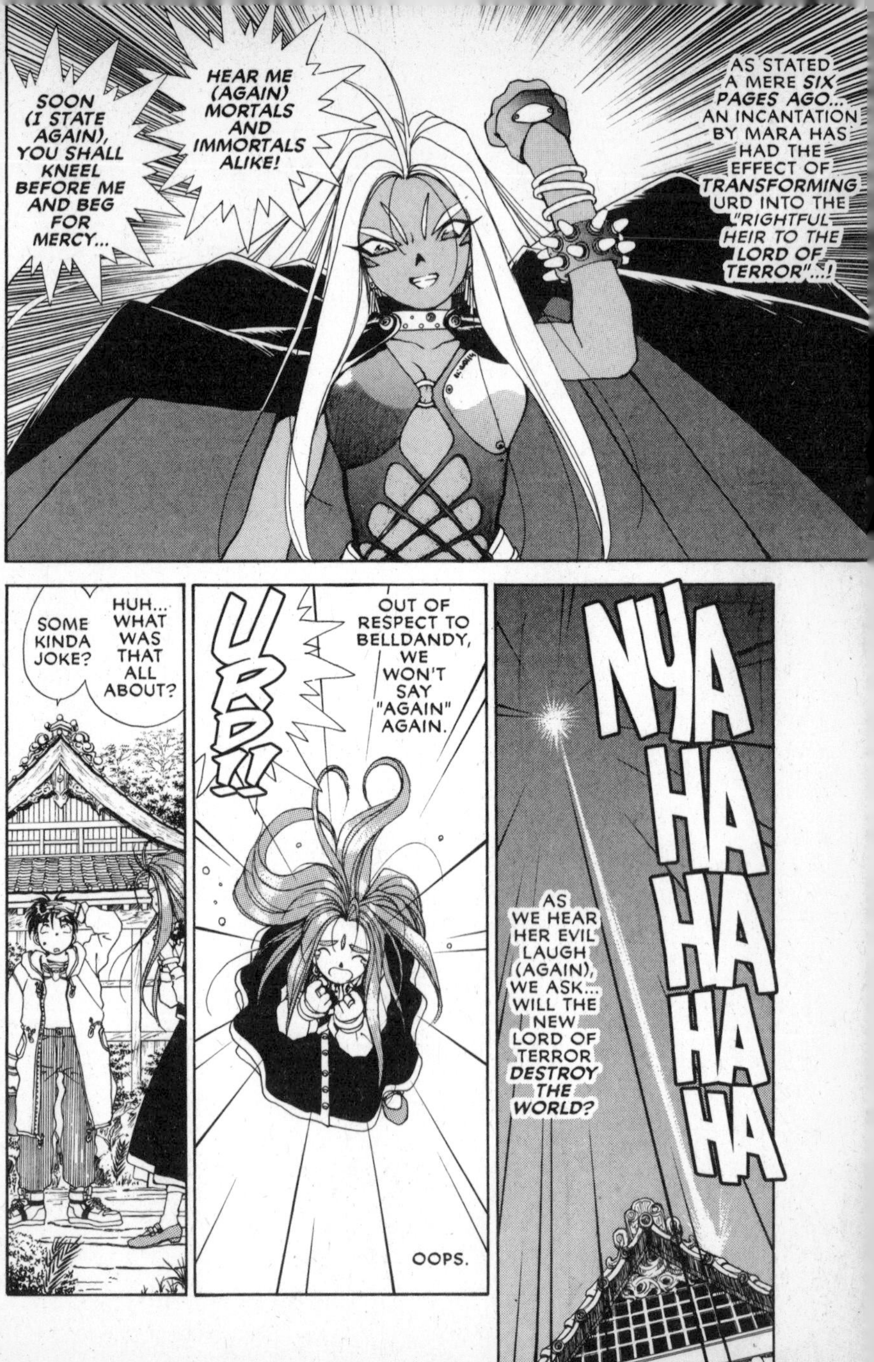
AS STATED A MERE *SIX PAGES AGO*... AN INCANTATION BY MARA HAS HAD THE EFFECT OF *TRANSFORMING* URD INTO THE "RIGHTFUL HEIR TO THE *LORD OF TERROR*"...!
HEAR ME (AGAIN) MORTALS AND IMMORTALS ALIKE!
SOON (I STATE AGAIN), YOU SHALL KNEEL BEFORE ME AND BEG FOR MERCY...
NYA HA HA HA HA HA HA HA
AS WE HEAR HER EVIL LAUGH (AGAIN), WE ASK... WILL THE NEW LORD OF TERROR *DESTROY THE WORLD?*
OUT OF RESPECT TO BELLDANDY, WE WON'T SAY "AGAIN" AGAIN.
URD!!
OOPS.
HUH... WHAT WAS THAT ALL ABOUT?
SOME KINDA JOKE?

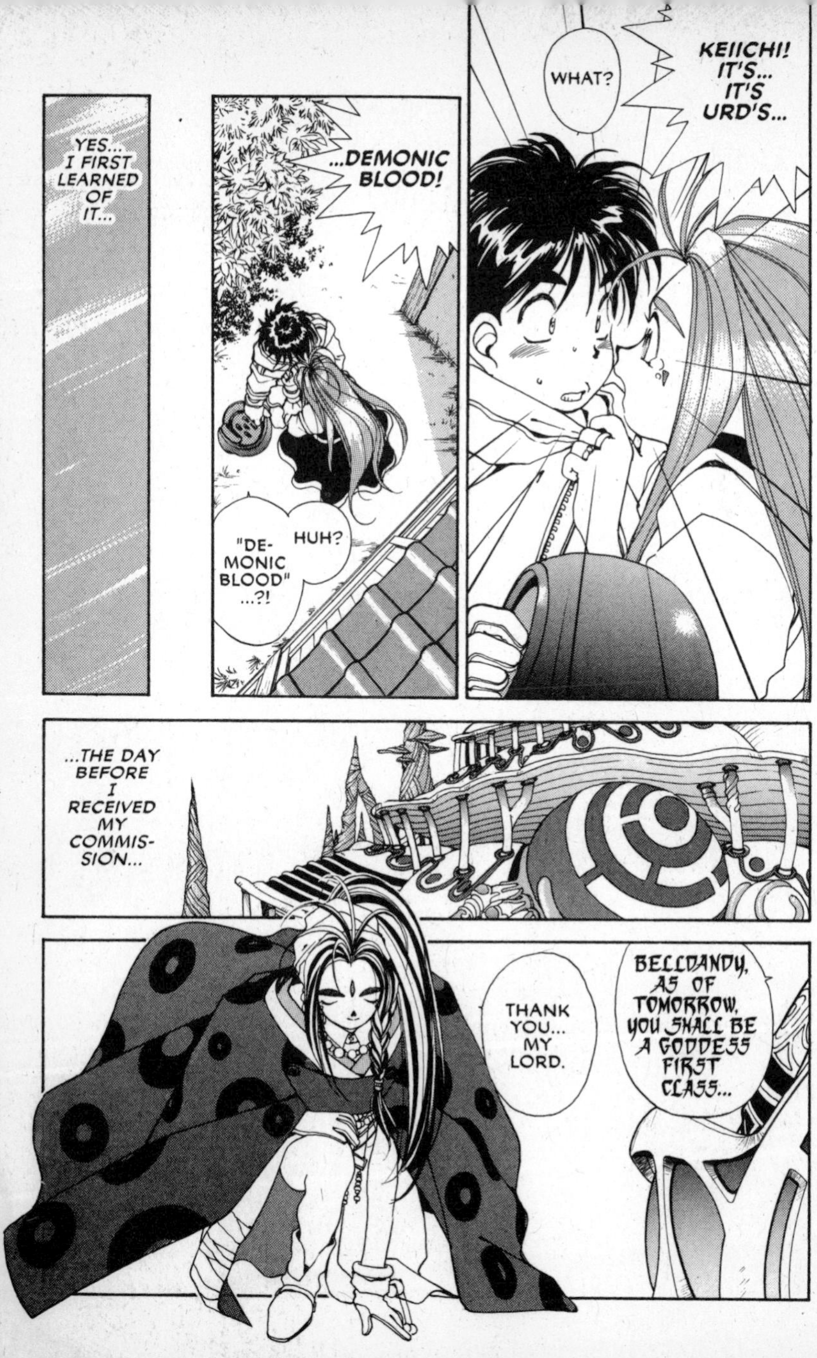
KEIICHI! IT'S... IT'S URD'S...
WHAT?
...DEMONIC BLOOD!
HUH?
"DE-MONIC BLOOD" ...?!
YES... I FIRST LEARNED OF IT...
...THE DAY BEFORE I RECEIVED MY COMMIS-SION...
BELLDANDY, AS OF TOMORROW, YOU SHALL BE A GODDESS FIRST CLASS...
THANK YOU... MY LORD.

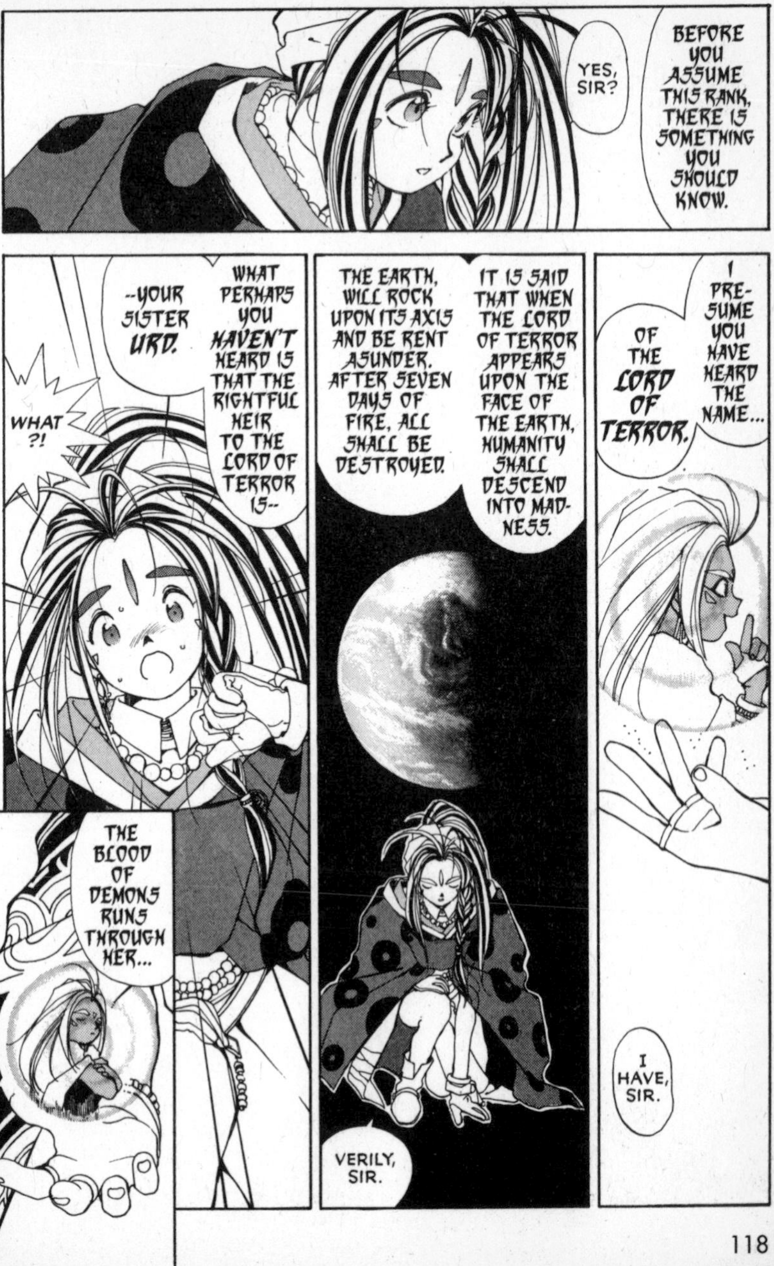
BEFORE YOU ASSUME THIS RANK, THERE IS SOMETHING YOU SHOULD KNOW.
YES, SIR?
I PRESUME YOU HAVE HEARD THE NAME...
OF THE LORD OF TERROR.
I HAVE, SIR.
IT IS SAID THAT WHEN THE LORD OF TERROR APPEARS UPON THE FACE OF THE EARTH, HUMANITY SHALL DESCEND INTO MADNESS.
THE EARTH, WILL ROCK UPON ITS AXIS AND BE RENT ASUNDER. AFTER SEVEN DAYS OF FIRE, ALL SHALL BE DESTROYED.
VERILY, SIR.
WHAT PERHAPS YOU HAVEN'T HEARD IS THAT THE RIGHTFUL HEIR TO THE LORD OF TERROR IS--
--YOUR SISTER URD.
WHAT ?!
THE BLOOD OF DEMONS RUNS THROUGH HER...

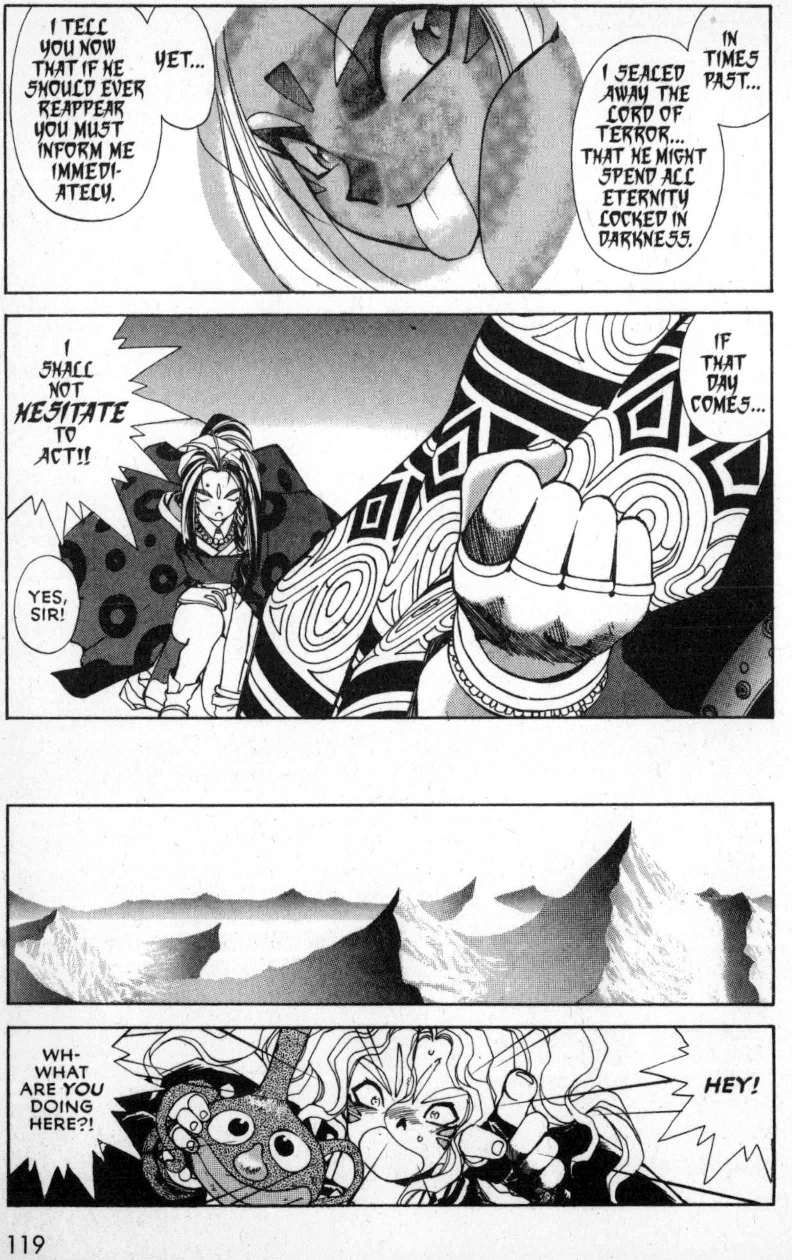
IN TIMES PAST...
I SEALED AWAY THE LORD OF TERROR... THAT HE MIGHT SPEND ALL ETERNITY LOCKED IN DARKNESS.
YET...
I TELL YOU NOW THAT IF HE SHOULD EVER REAPPEAR YOU MUST INFORM ME IMMEDI-ATELY.
IF THAT DAY COMES...
I SHALL NOT HESITATE TO ACT!!
YES, SIR!
HEY!
WH-WHAT ARE YOU DOING HERE?!

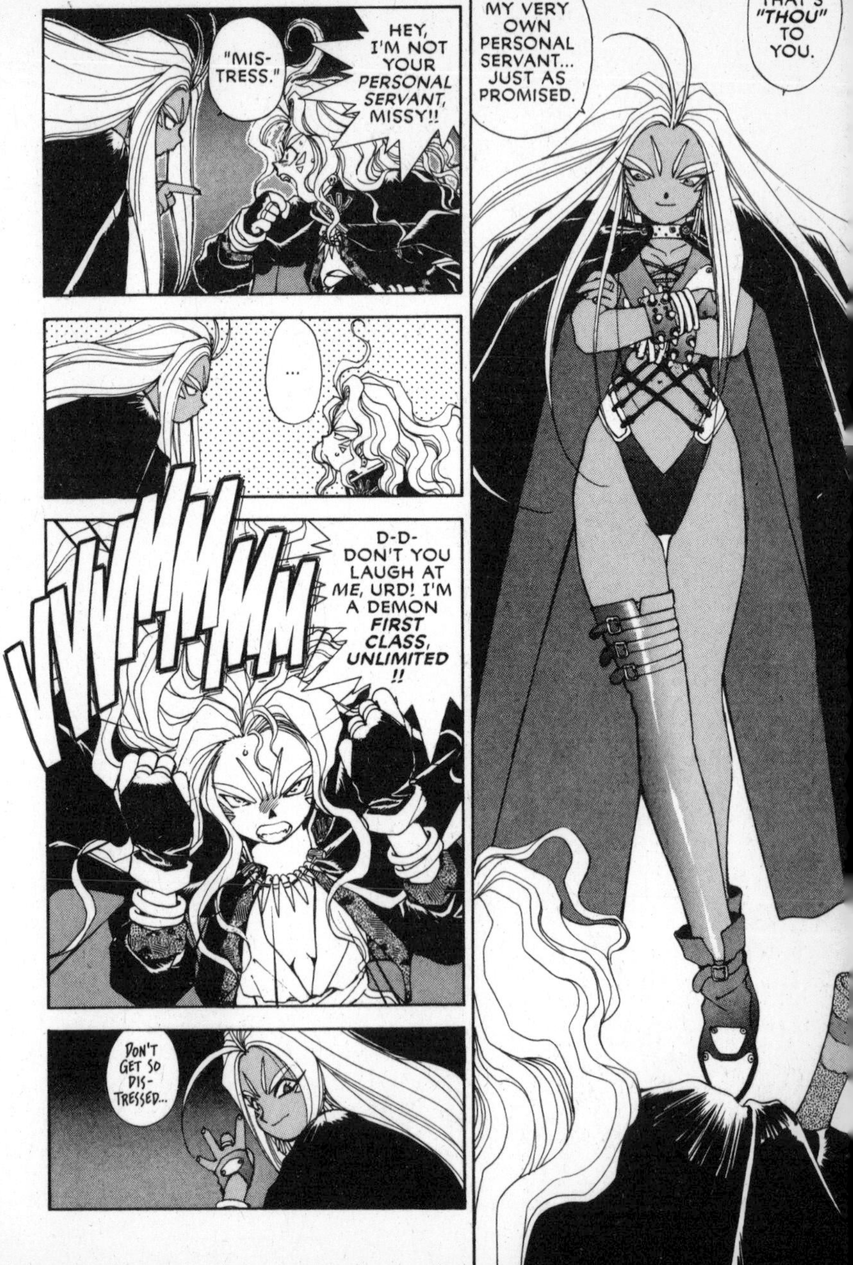
THAT'S *"THOU"* TO YOU.
HMM... MY VERY OWN PERSONAL SERVANT... JUST AS PROMISED.
HEY, I'M NOT YOUR *PERSONAL SERVANT,* MISSY!!
"MIS-TRESS."
...
D-D-DON'T YOU LAUGH AT *ME,* URD! I'M A DEMON ***FIRST CLASS, UNLIMITED*** !!
VVVMMMMMM
DON'T GET SO DIS-TRESSED...

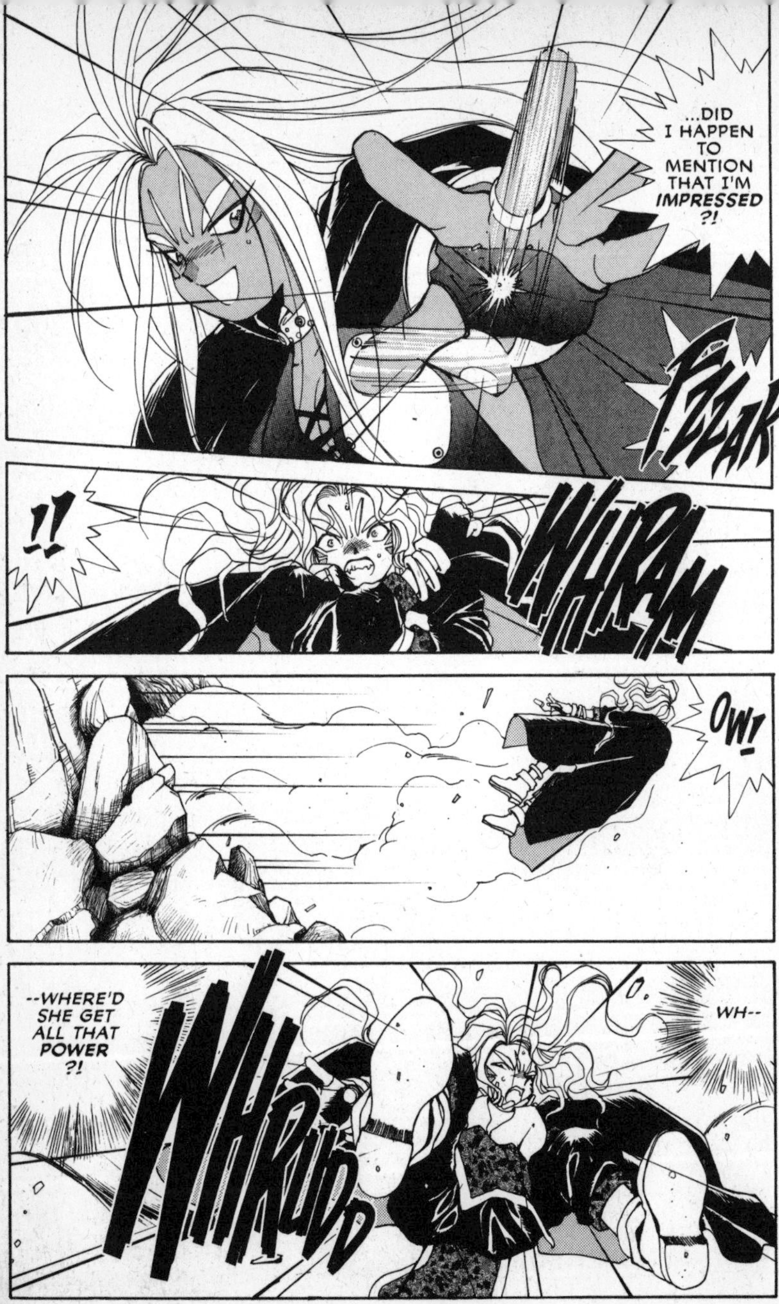
...DID I HAPPEN TO MENTION THAT I'M *IMPRESSED* ?!
FZZAK
WHRAM
!!
OW!
WH--
WHUDDD
--WHERE'D SHE GET ALL THAT POWER ?!

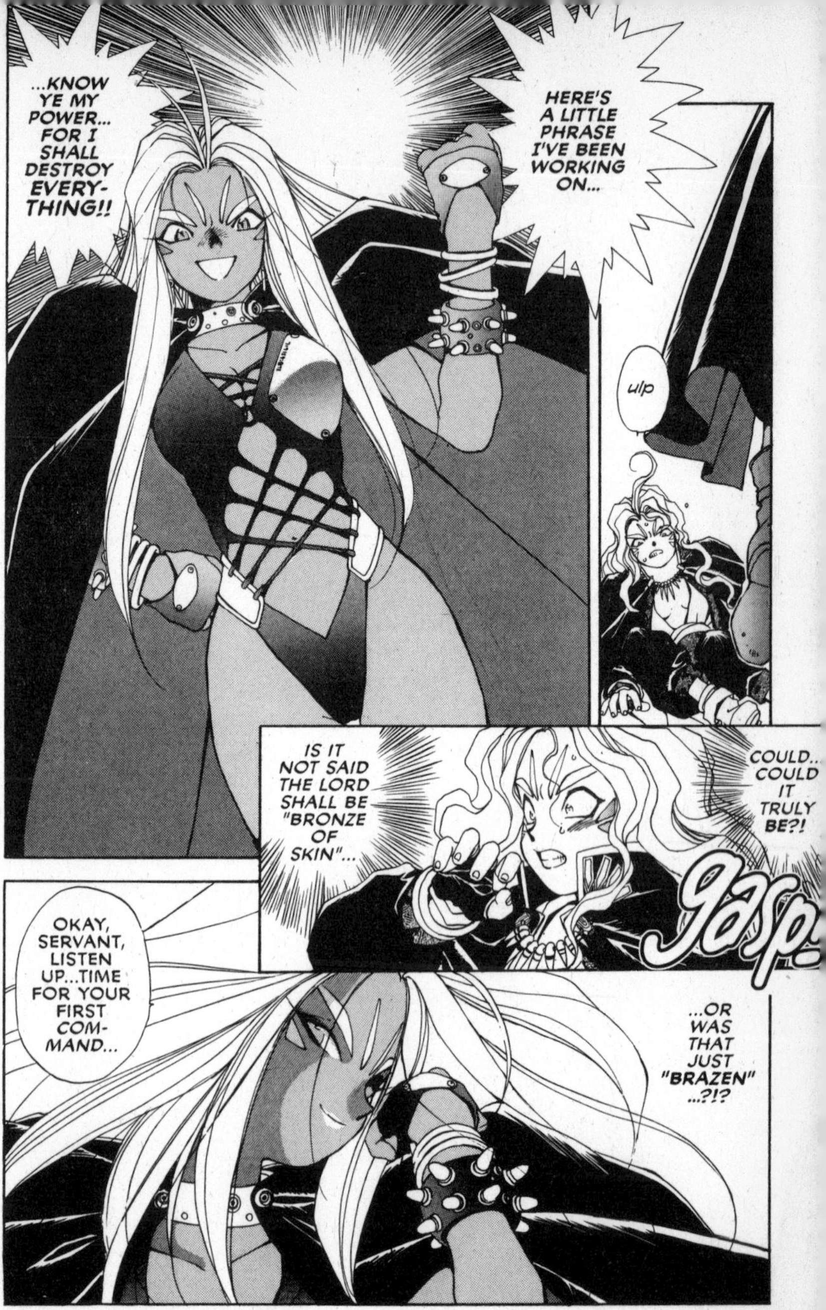
HERE'S A LITTLE PHRASE I'VE BEEN WORKING ON...
...KNOW YE MY POWER... FOR I SHALL DESTROY EVERY-THING!!
ulp
COULD.. COULD IT TRULY BE?!
GASP!
IS IT NOT SAID THE LORD SHALL BE "BRONZE OF SKIN"...
...OR WAS THAT JUST "BRAZEN" ...?!?
OKAY, SERVANT, LISTEN UP...TIME FOR YOUR FIRST COM-MAND...

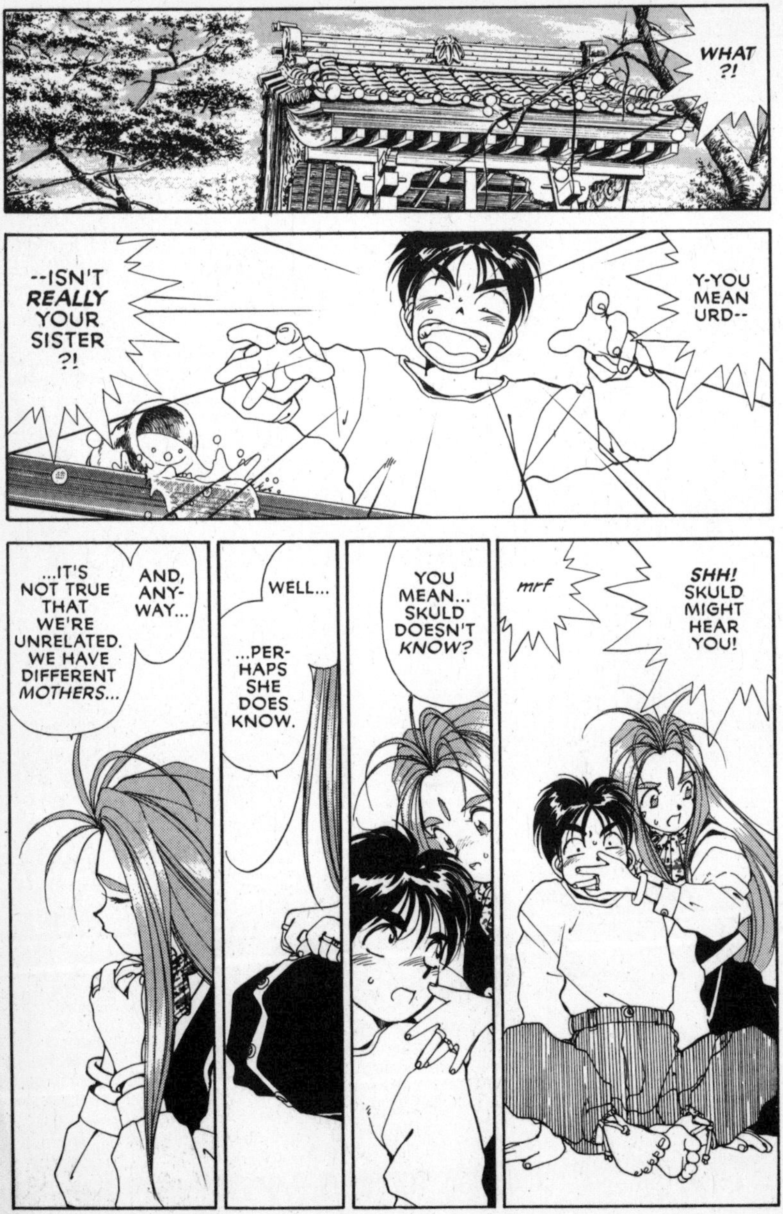
WHAT ?!
Y-YOU MEAN URD--
--ISN'T *REALLY* YOUR SISTER ?!
*SHH!* SKULD MIGHT HEAR YOU!
*mrf*
YOU MEAN... SKULD DOESN'T *KNOW?*
WELL...
...PER-HAPS SHE DOES KNOW.
AND, ANY-WAY...
...IT'S NOT TRUE THAT WE'RE UNRELATED. WE HAVE DIFFERENT *MOTHERS...*

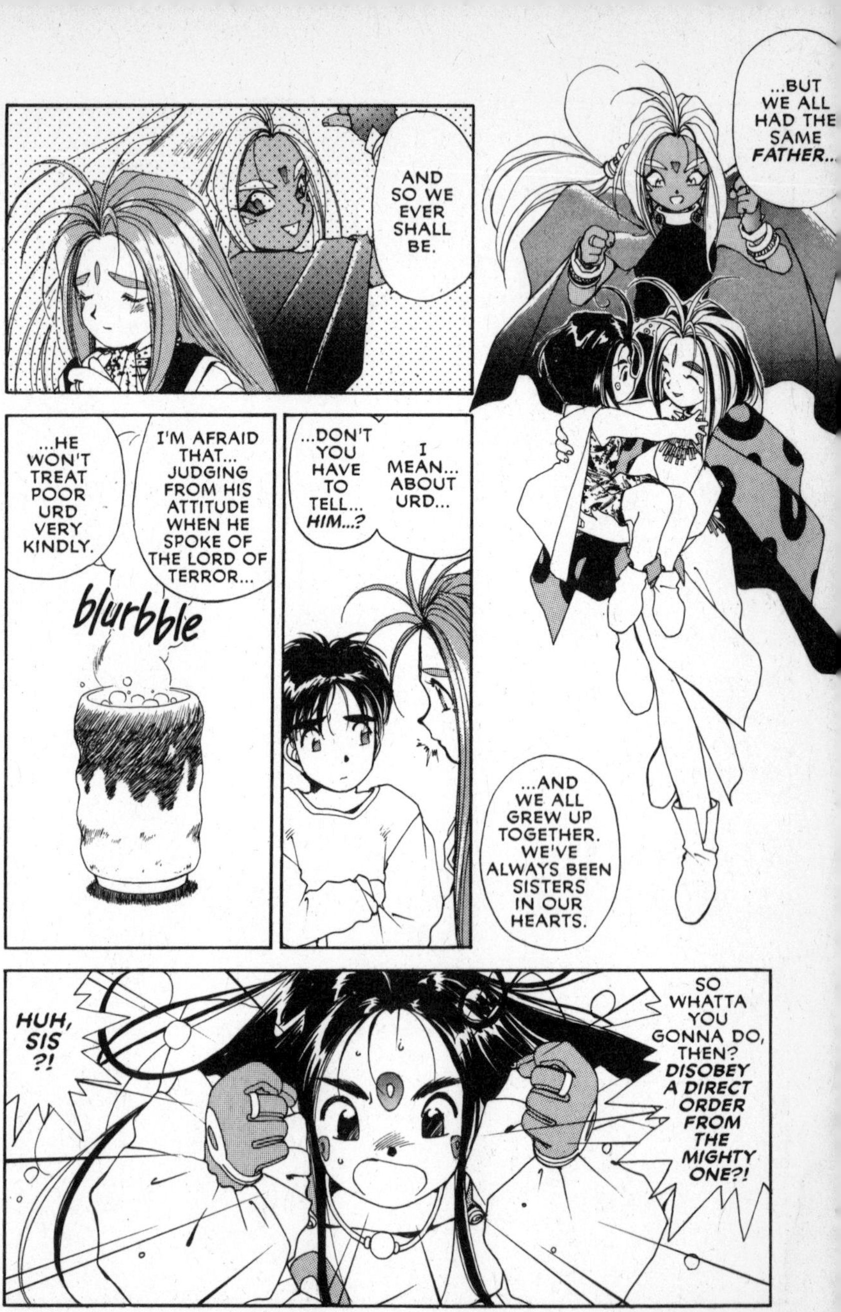
...BUT WE ALL HAD THE SAME FATHER...
...AND WE ALL GREW UP TOGETHER. WE'VE ALWAYS BEEN SISTERS IN OUR HEARTS.
AND SO WE EVER SHALL BE.
...DON'T YOU HAVE TO TELL... HIM...?
I MEAN... ABOUT URD...
I'M AFRAID THAT... JUDGING FROM HIS ATTITUDE WHEN HE SPOKE OF THE LORD OF TERROR...
...HE WON'T TREAT POOR URD VERY KINDLY.
blurbble
SO WHATTA YOU GONNA DO, THEN? DISOBEY A DIRECT ORDER FROM THE MIGHTY ONE?!
HUH, SIS?!

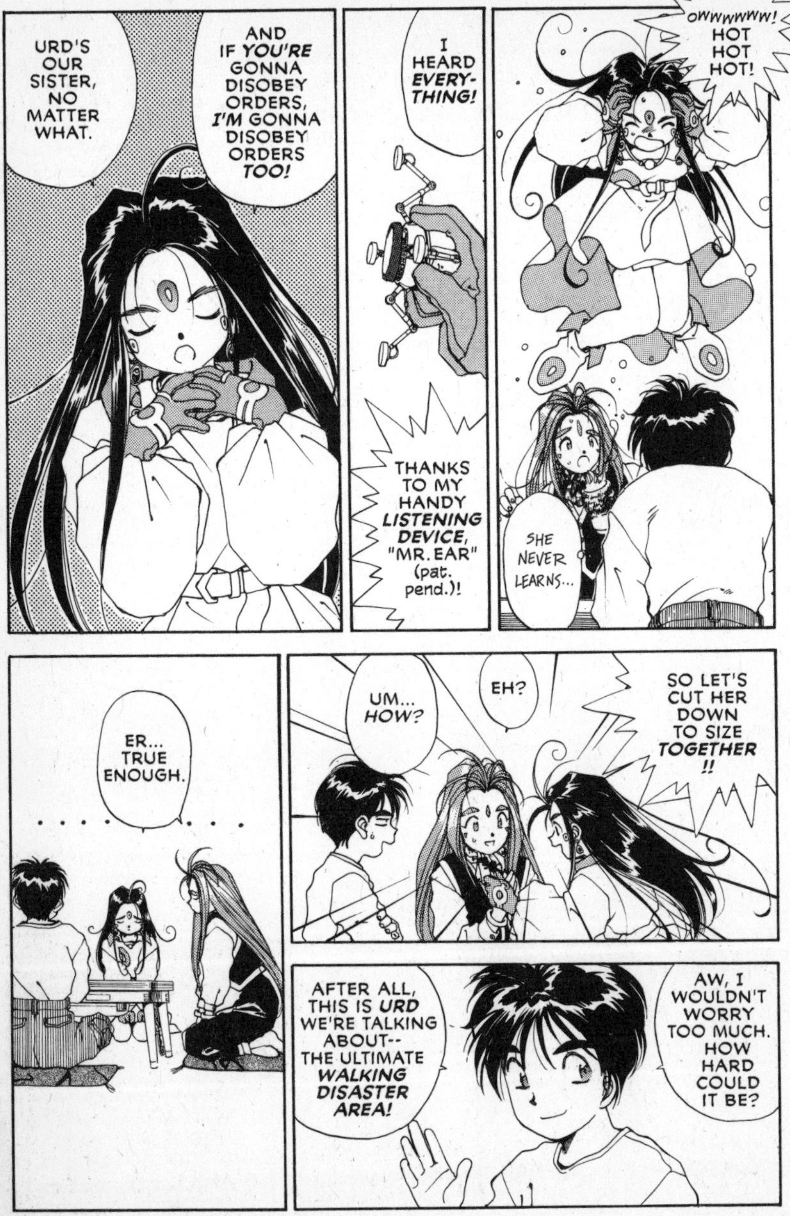
OWWWWWW! HOT HOT HOT!
SHE NEVER LEARNS...
I HEARD EVERYTHING!
THANKS TO MY HANDY LISTENING DEVICE, "MR. EAR" (pat. pend.)!
URD'S OUR SISTER, NO MATTER WHAT.
AND IF YOU'RE GONNA DISOBEY ORDERS, I'M GONNA DISOBEY ORDERS TOO!
SO LET'S CUT HER DOWN TO SIZE TOGETHER !!
EH?
UM... HOW?
AW, I WOULDN'T WORRY TOO MUCH. HOW HARD COULD IT BE?
AFTER ALL, THIS IS URD WE'RE TALKING ABOUT-- THE ULTIMATE WALKING DISASTER AREA!
ER... TRUE ENOUGH.
. . . . . . . .

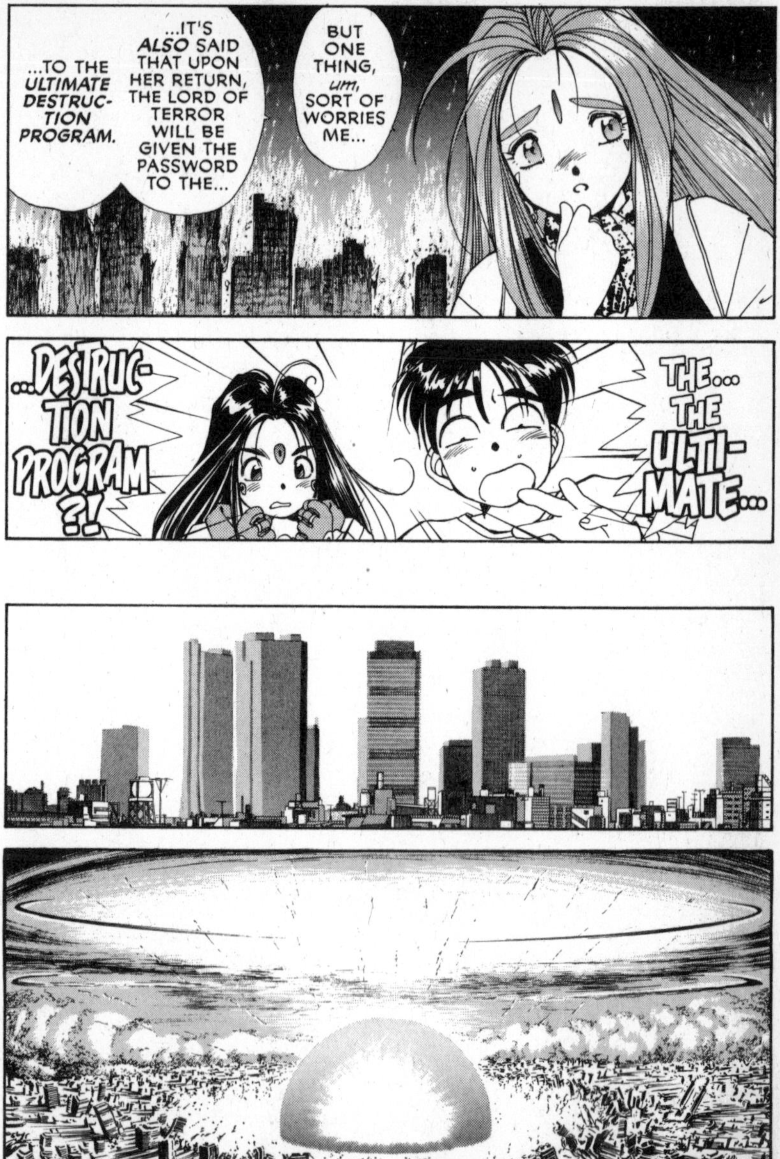
BUT ONE THING, *um,* SORT OF WORRIES ME...
...IT'S *ALSO* SAID THAT UPON HER RETURN, THE LORD OF TERROR WILL BE GIVEN THE PASSWORD TO THE...
...TO THE *ULTIMATE DESTRUC- TION PROGRAM.*
THE... THE ULTI- MATE...
...DESTRUC- TION PROGRAM ?!

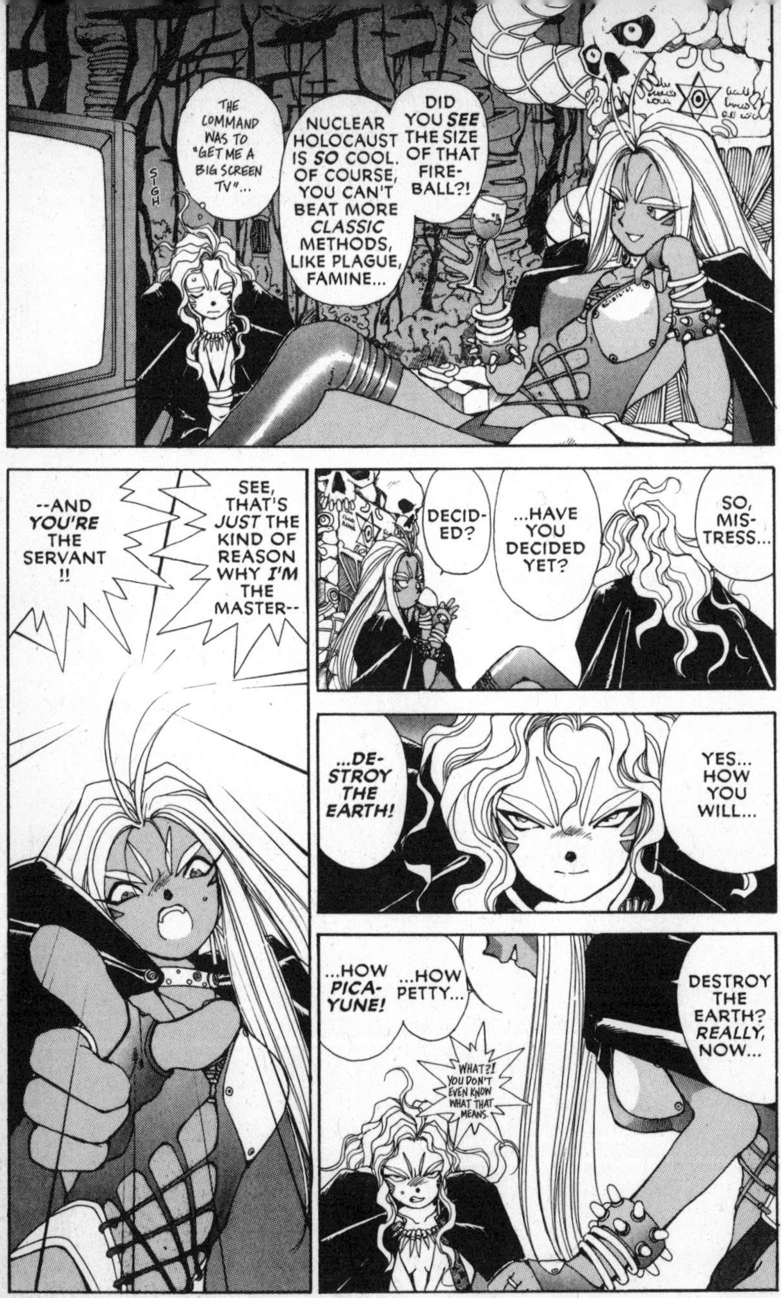
DID YOU SEE THE SIZE OF THAT FIRE-BALL?!
NUCLEAR HOLOCAUST IS SO COOL. OF COURSE, YOU CAN'T BEAT MORE CLASSIC METHODS, LIKE PLAGUE, FAMINE...
THE COMMAND WAS TO "GET ME A BIG SCREEN TV"...
SIGH
SO, MIS-TRESS...
...HAVE YOU DECIDED YET?
DECID-ED?
YES... HOW YOU WILL...
...DE-STROY THE EARTH!
DESTROY THE EARTH? REALLY, NOW...
...HOW PETTY...
...HOW PICA-YUNE!
WHAT?! YOU DON'T EVEN KNOW WHAT THAT MEANS.
SEE, THAT'S JUST THE KIND OF REASON WHY I'M THE MASTER--
--AND YOU'RE THE SERVANT !!

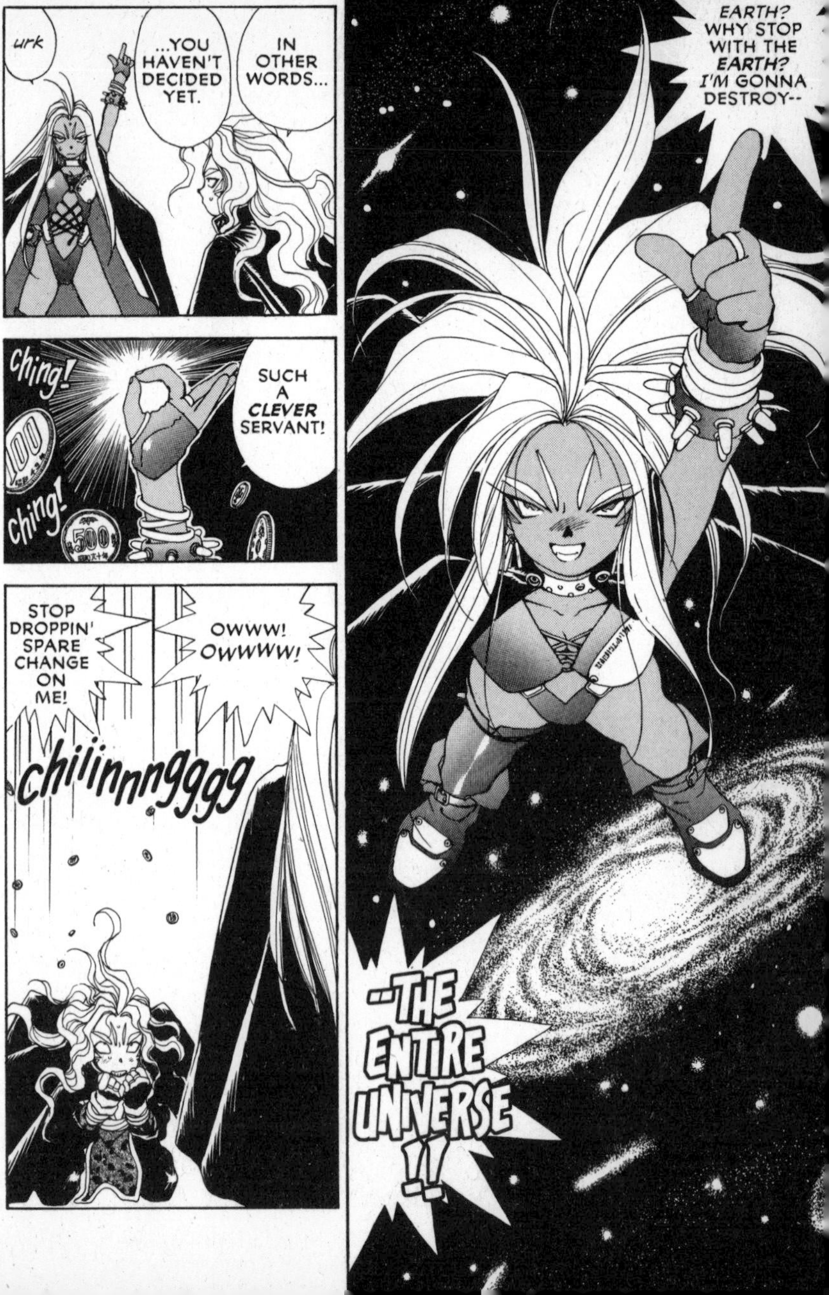
EARTH? WHY STOP WITH THE EARTH? I'M GONNA DESTROY--
--THE ENTIRE UNIVERSE!!
IN OTHER WORDS...
...YOU HAVEN'T DECIDED YET.
urk
SUCH A CLEVER SERVANT!
ching!
ching!
OWWW! OWWWW!
STOP DROPPIN' SPARE CHANGE ON ME!
chiiinnnggggg

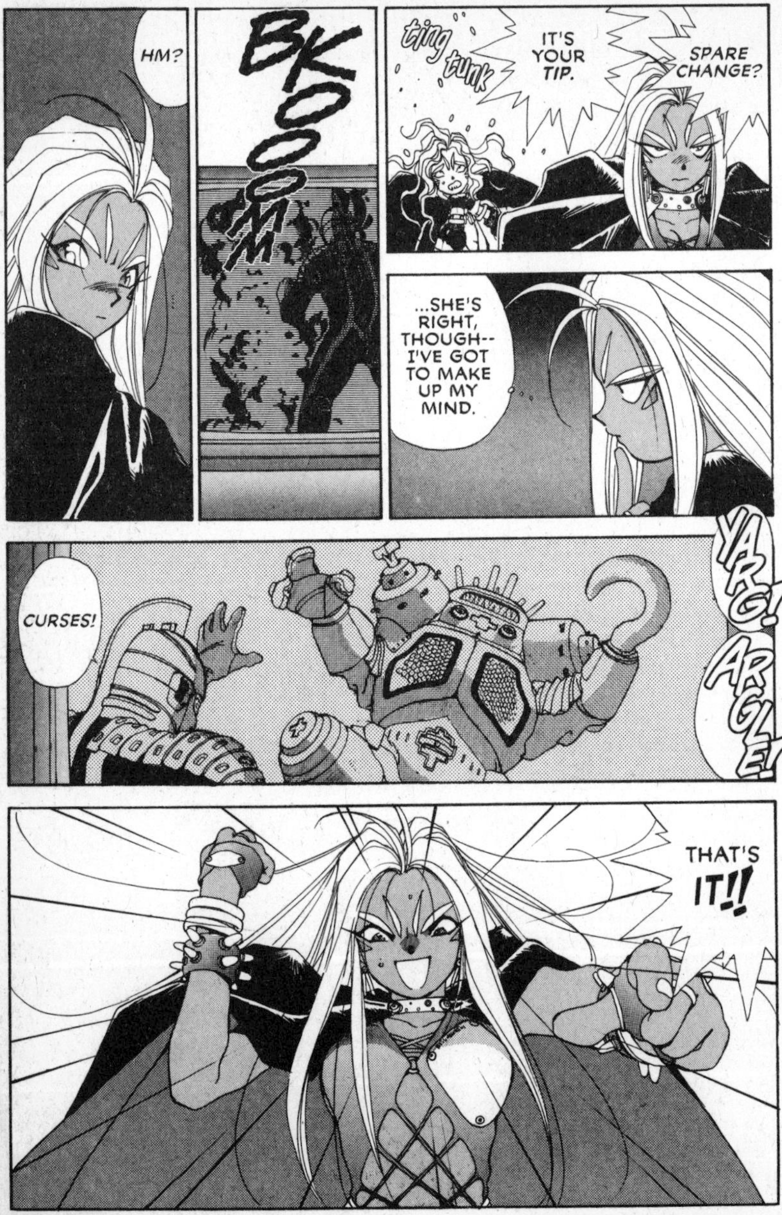
SPARE CHANGE?
IT'S YOUR TIP.
ting tunk
...SHE'S RIGHT, THOUGH-- I'VE GOT TO MAKE UP MY MIND.
BKOOOOMM
HM?
YARG! ARGLE!
CURSES!
THAT'S IT!!

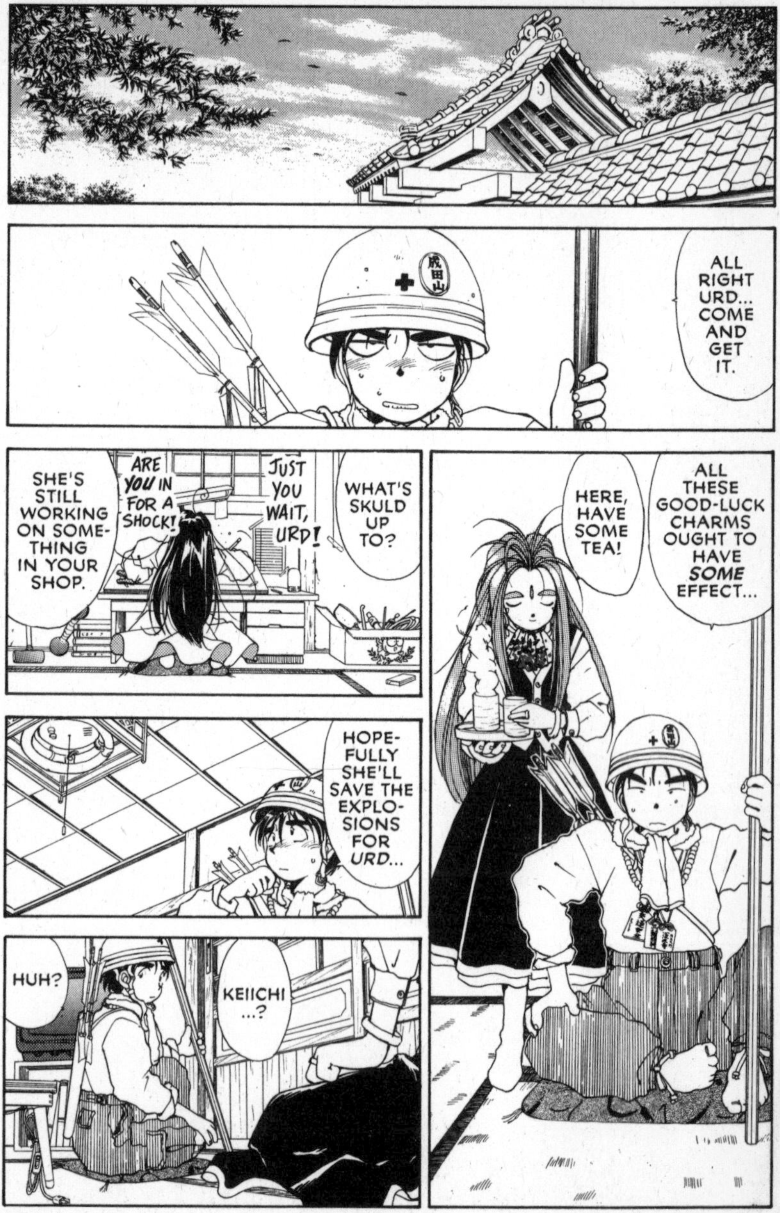
成田山
ALL RIGHT URD... COME AND GET IT.
ALL THESE GOOD-LUCK CHARMS OUGHT TO HAVE *SOME* EFFECT...
HERE, HAVE SOME TEA!
WHAT'S SKULD UP TO?
JUST YOU WAIT, URD!
ARE *YOU* IN FOR A SHOCK!
SHE'S STILL WORKING ON SOME-THING IN YOUR SHOP.
HOPE-FULLY SHE'LL SAVE THE EXPLO-SIONS FOR *URD*...
KEIICHI ...?
HUH?

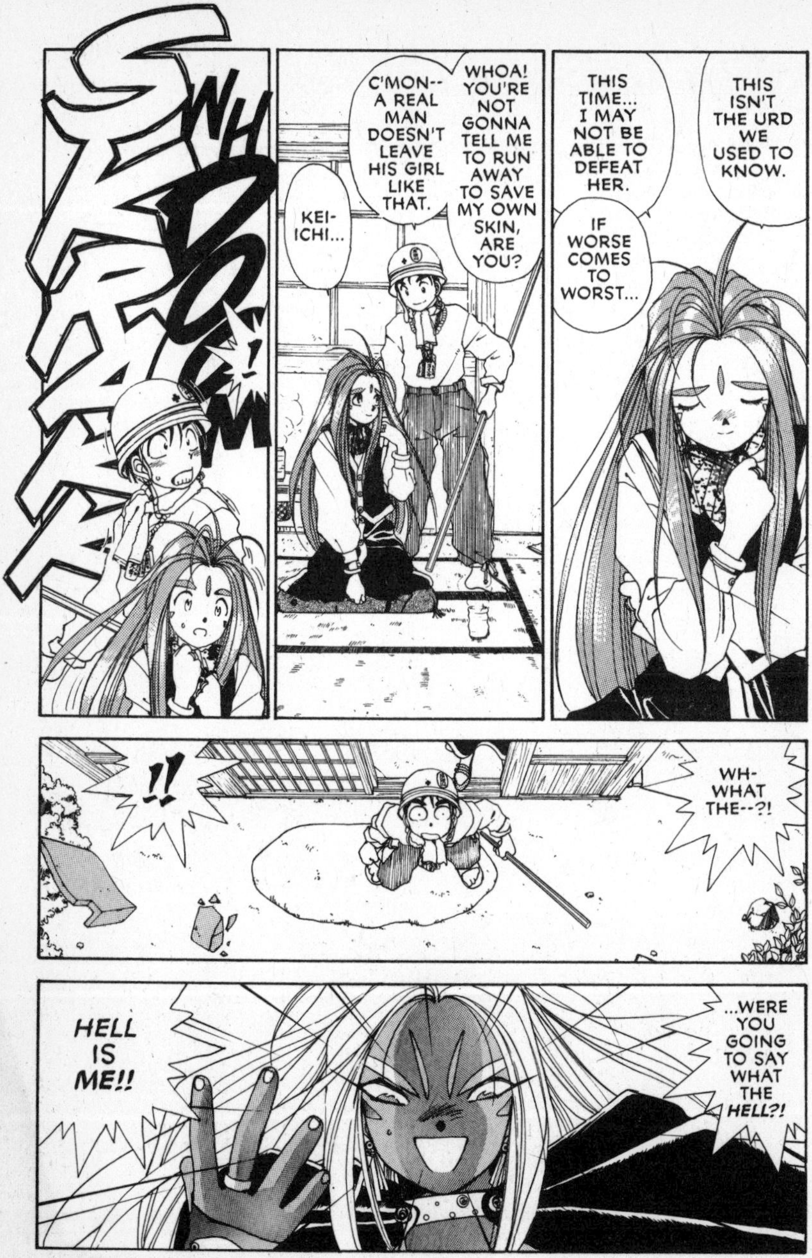
THIS ISN'T THE URD WE USED TO KNOW.
THIS TIME... I MAY NOT BE ABLE TO DEFEAT HER.
IF WORSE COMES TO WORST...
WHOA! YOU'RE NOT GONNA TELL ME TO RUN AWAY TO SAVE MY OWN SKIN, ARE YOU?
C'MON-- A REAL MAN DOESN'T LEAVE HIS GIRL LIKE THAT.
KEI-ICHI...
!
WH-WHAT THE--?!
!!
...WERE YOU GOING TO SAY WHAT THE *HELL?!*
*HELL IS ME!!*

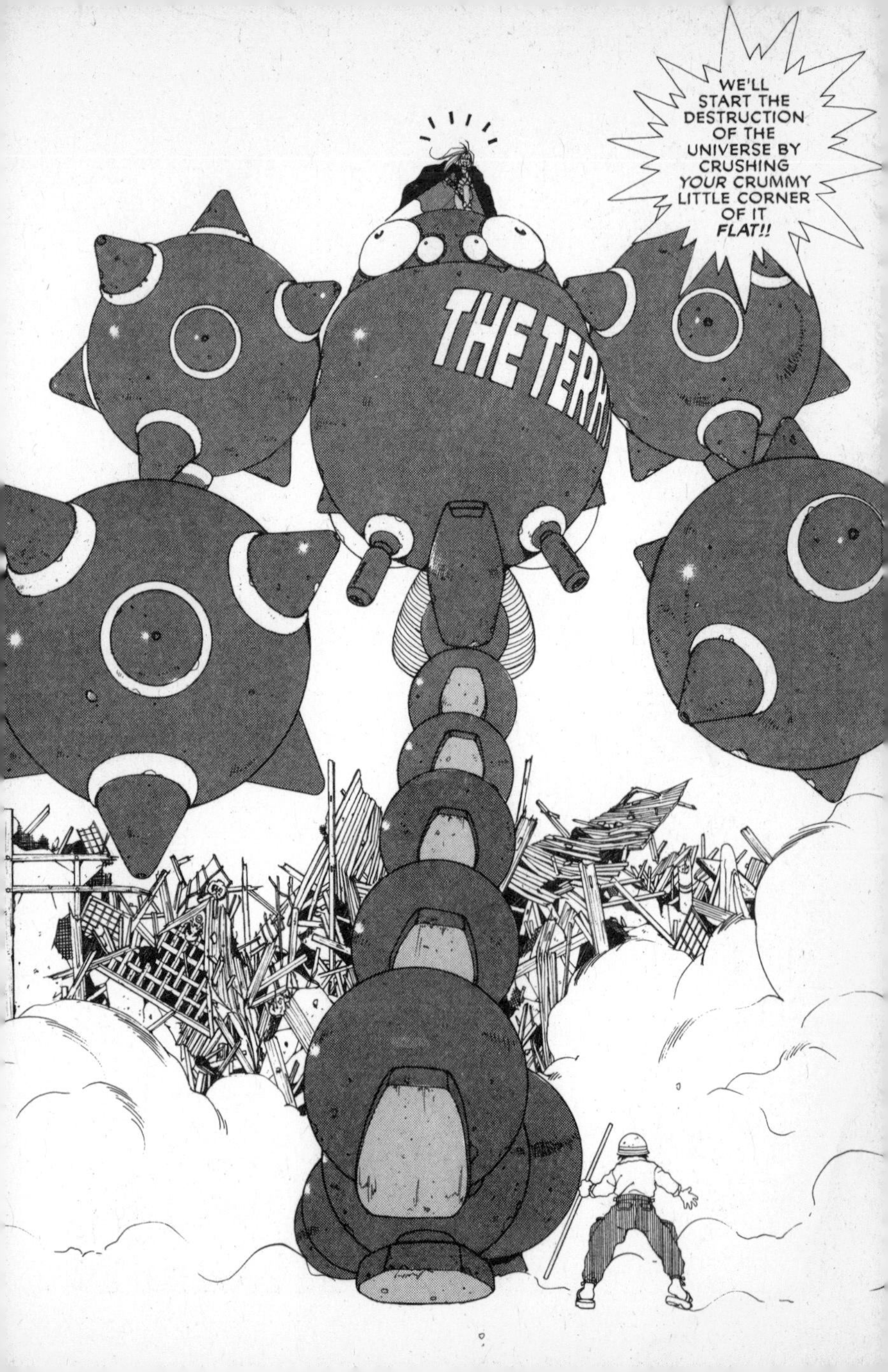
WE'LL START THE DESTRUCTION OF THE UNIVERSE BY CRUSHING *YOUR* CRUMMY LITTLE CORNER OF IT *FLAT!!*
THE TERR

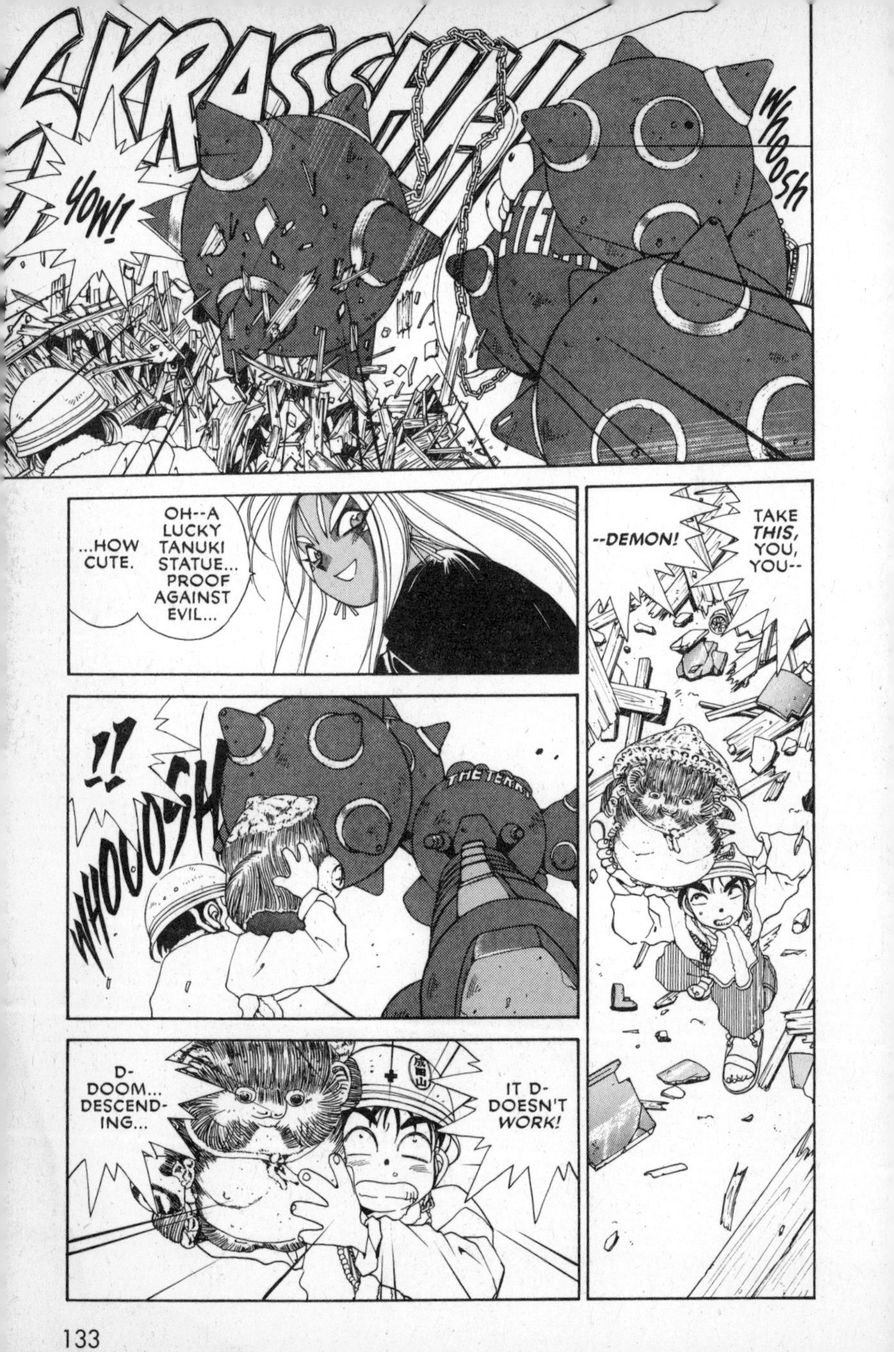
CKRASSHH
whoosh
YOW!
TAKE *THIS*, YOU, YOU--
--DEMON!
OH--A LUCKY TANUKI STATUE... PROOF AGAINST EVIL...
...HOW CUTE.
!!
WHOOOSH
IT D-DOESN'T *WORK!*
D-DOOM... DESCEND-ING...

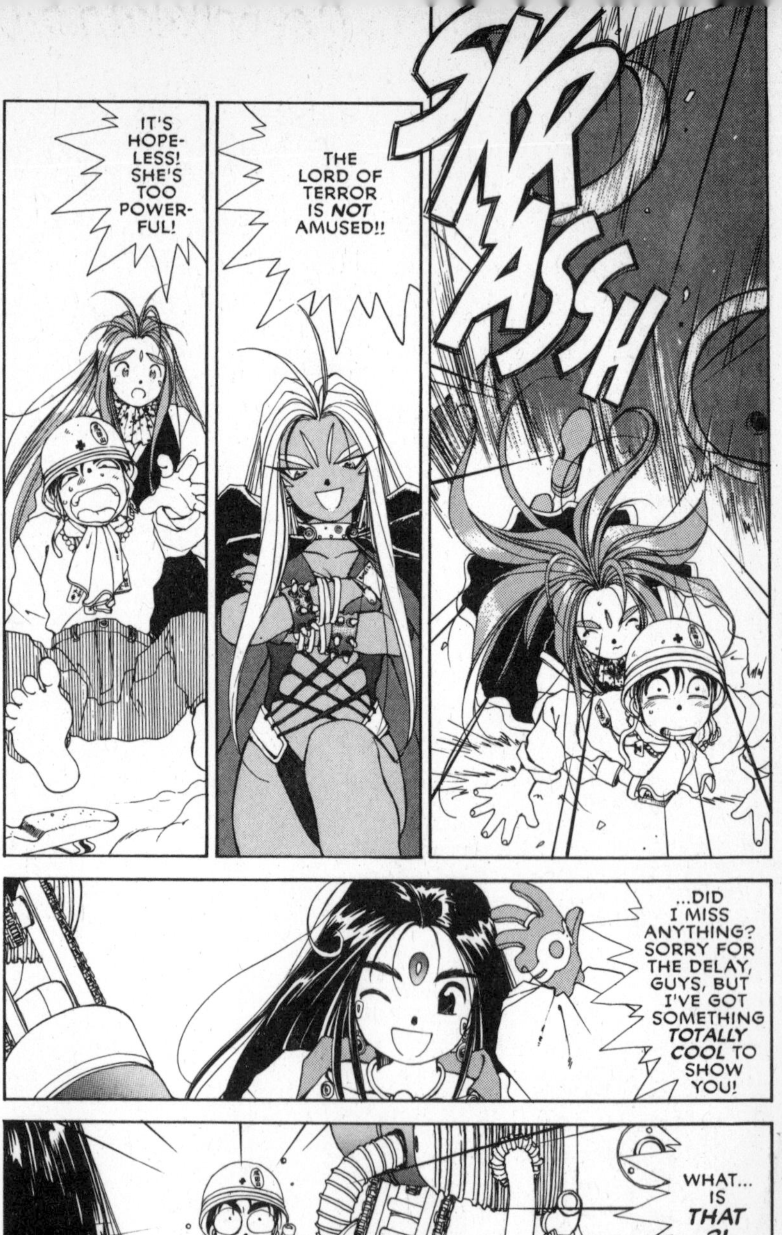
SKRASH
THE LORD OF TERROR IS *NOT* AMUSED!!
IT'S HOPE-LESS! SHE'S TOO POWER-FUL!
...DID I MISS ANYTHING? SORRY FOR THE DELAY, GUYS, BUT I'VE GOT SOMETHING ***TOTALLY COOL*** TO SHOW YOU!
WHAT... IS ***THAT*** ?!

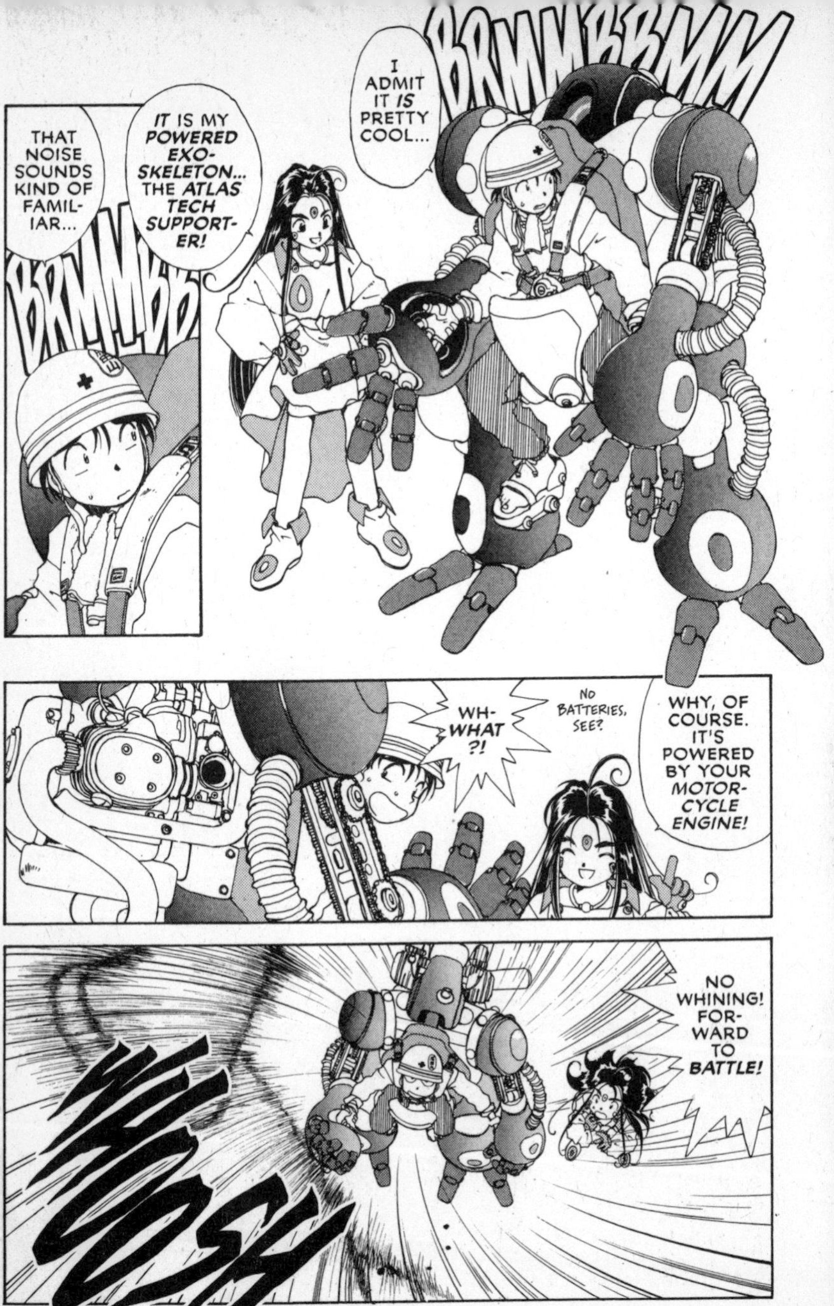
BRMMBRMM
I ADMIT IT IS PRETTY COOL...
IT IS MY POWERED EXO-SKELETON... THE ATLAS TECH SUPPORTER!
THAT NOISE SOUNDS KIND OF FAMILIAR...
BRMMBB
WHY, OF COURSE. IT'S POWERED BY YOUR MOTORCYCLE ENGINE!
NO BATTERIES, SEE?
WH- WHAT?!
NO WHINING! FORWARD TO BATTLE!
WHOOSH

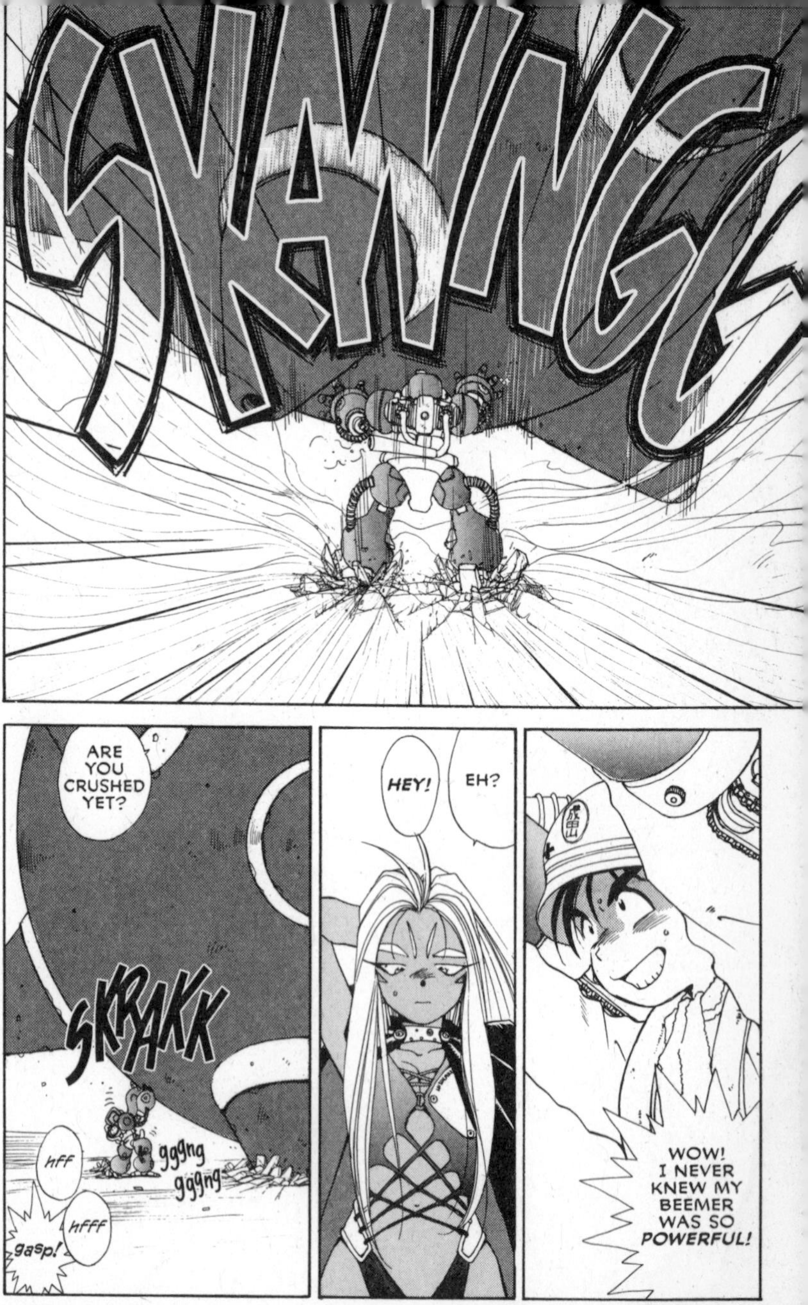
SKWANGK
WOW! I NEVER KNEW MY BEEMER WAS SO POWERFUL!
EH?
HEY!
ARE YOU CRUSHED YET?
SKRAKK
gggng gggng
hff
hfff
gasp!

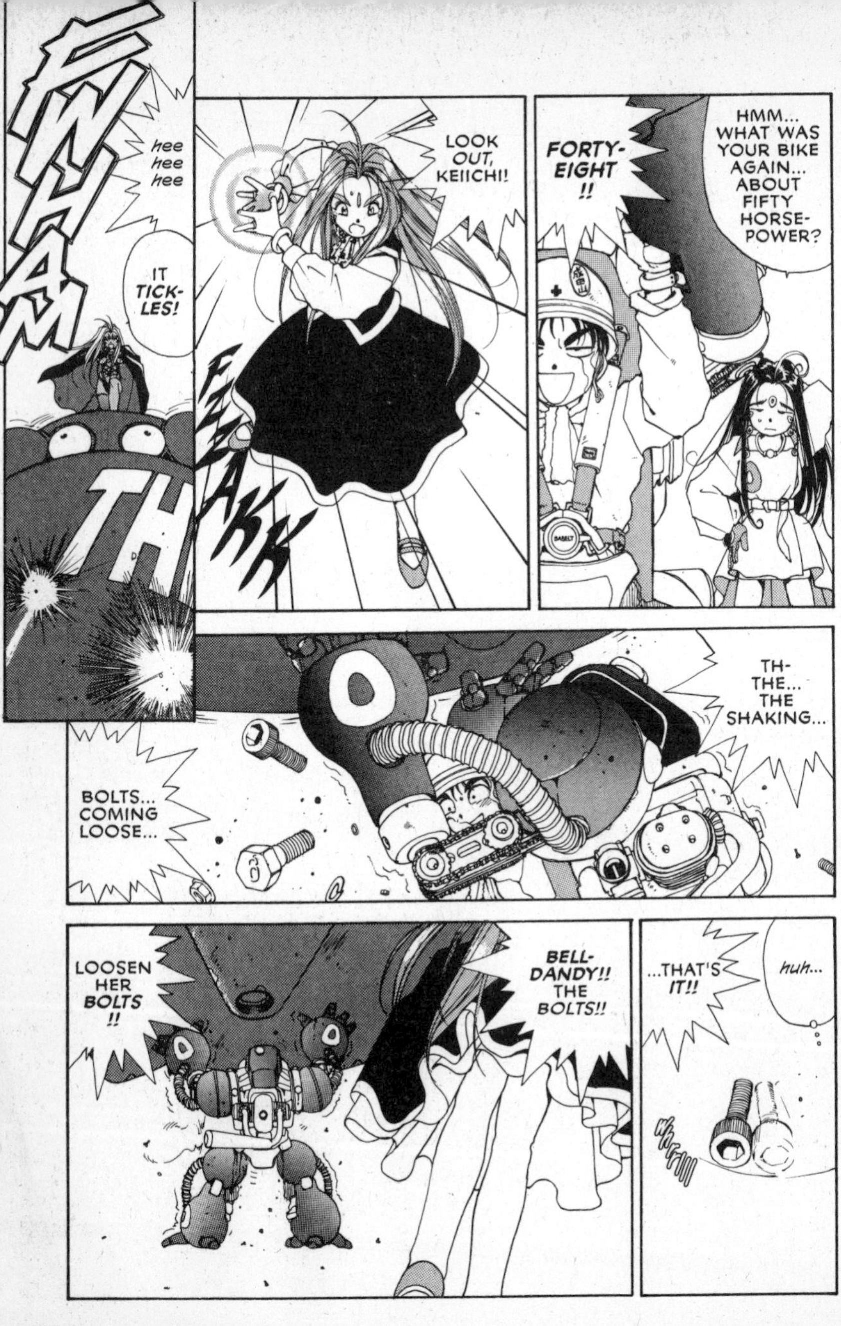
HMM... WHAT WAS YOUR BIKE AGAIN... ABOUT FIFTY HORSE-POWER?
FORTY-EIGHT !!
LOOK OUT, KEIICHI!
WHAM
hee hee hee
IT TICKLES!
TH- THE... THE SHAKING...
BOLTS... COMING LOOSE...
huh...
...THAT'S IT!!
BELL-DANDY!! THE BOLTS!!
LOOSEN HER BOLTS !!

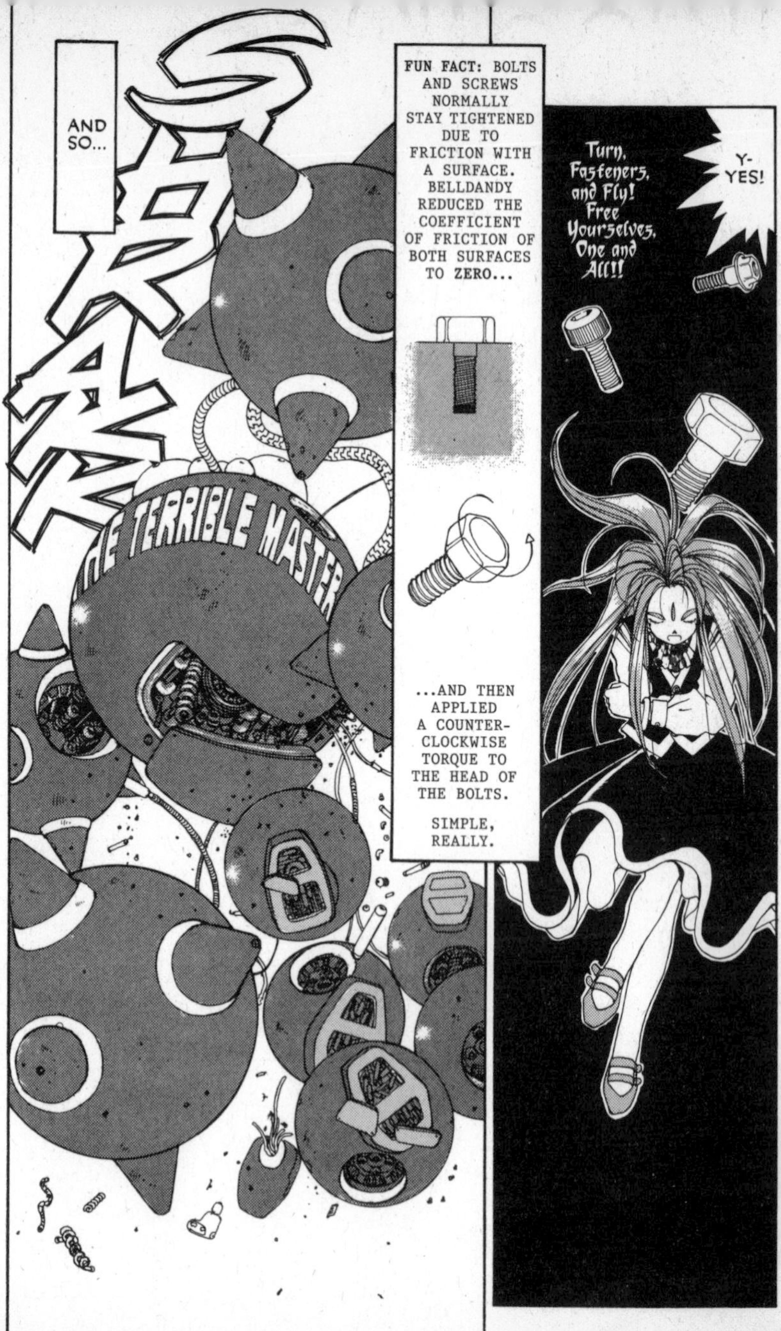
Y-YES!
Turn, Fasteners, and Fly! Free Yourselves, One and All!!
FUN FACT: BOLTS AND SCREWS NORMALLY STAY TIGHTENED DUE TO FRICTION WITH A SURFACE. BELLDANDY REDUCED THE COEFFICIENT OF FRICTION OF BOTH SURFACES TO ZERO...
...AND THEN APPLIED A COUNTER-CLOCKWISE TORQUE TO THE HEAD OF THE BOLTS.
SIMPLE, REALLY.
AND SO...
TERRIBLE MASTER

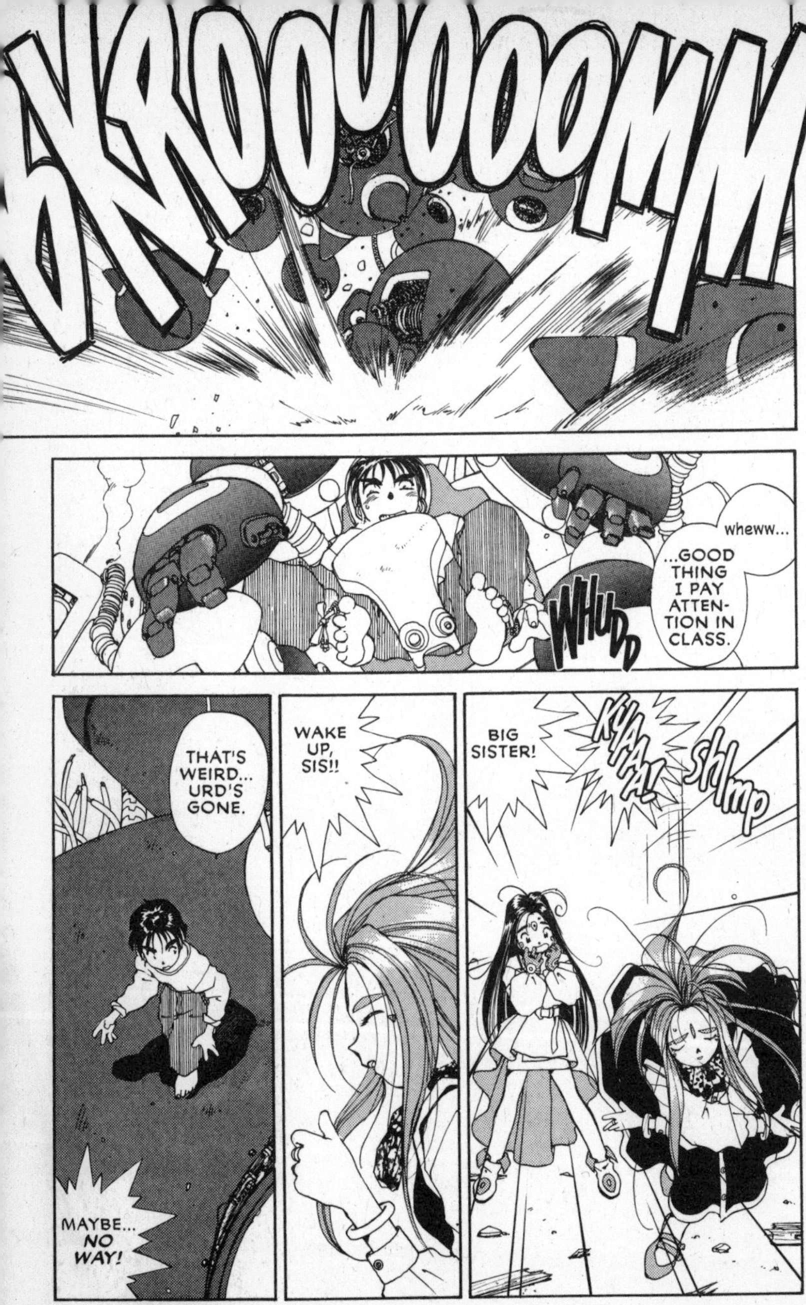

SKROOOOOOMM
wheww...
...GOOD THING I PAY ATTENTION IN CLASS.
WHUDD
KYAAA!
shlmp
BIG SISTER!
WAKE UP, SIS!!
THAT'S WEIRD... URD'S GONE.
MAYBE... NO WAY!

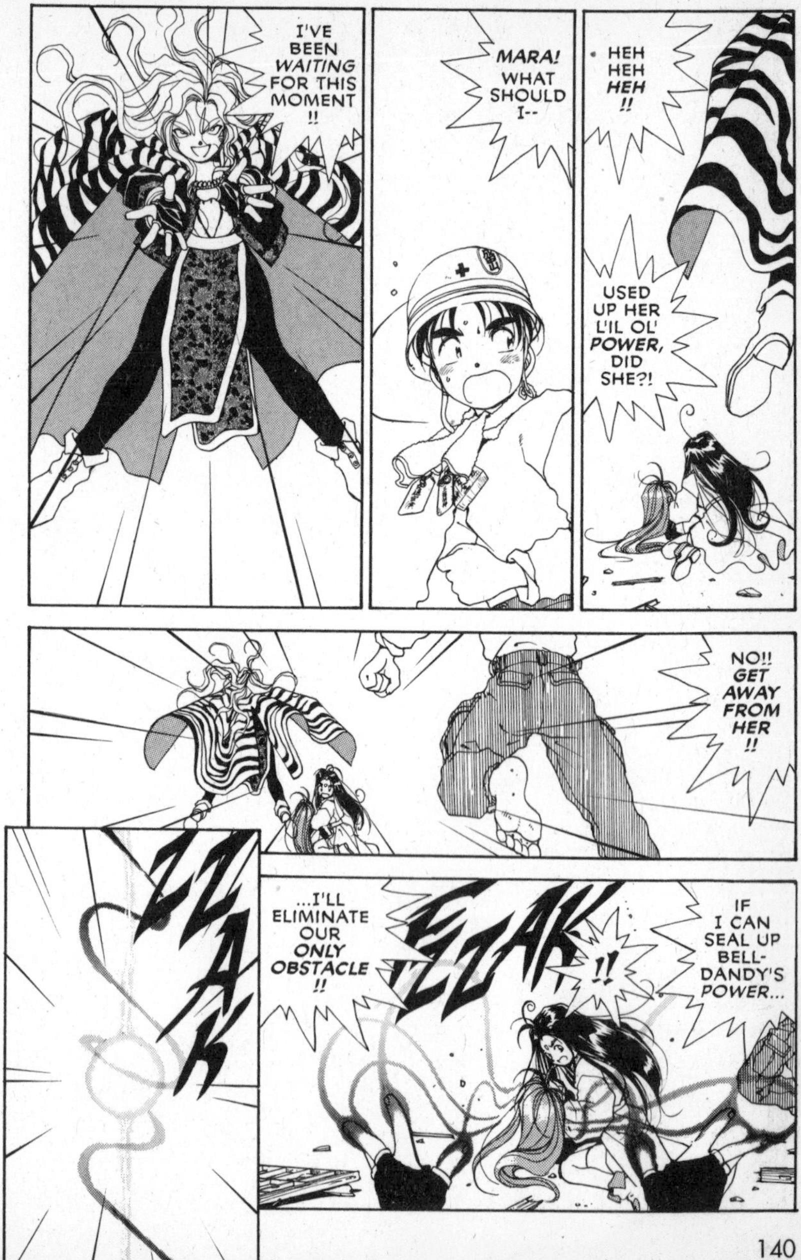
HEH HEH HEH !!
USED UP HER L'IL OL' POWER, DID SHE?!
MARA! WHAT SHOULD I--
I'VE BEEN WAITING FOR THIS MOMENT !!
NO!! GET AWAY FROM HER !!
IF I CAN SEAL UP BELL-DANDY'S POWER...
ZZAK
!!
...I'LL ELIMINATE OUR ONLY OBSTACLE !!
ZZAK

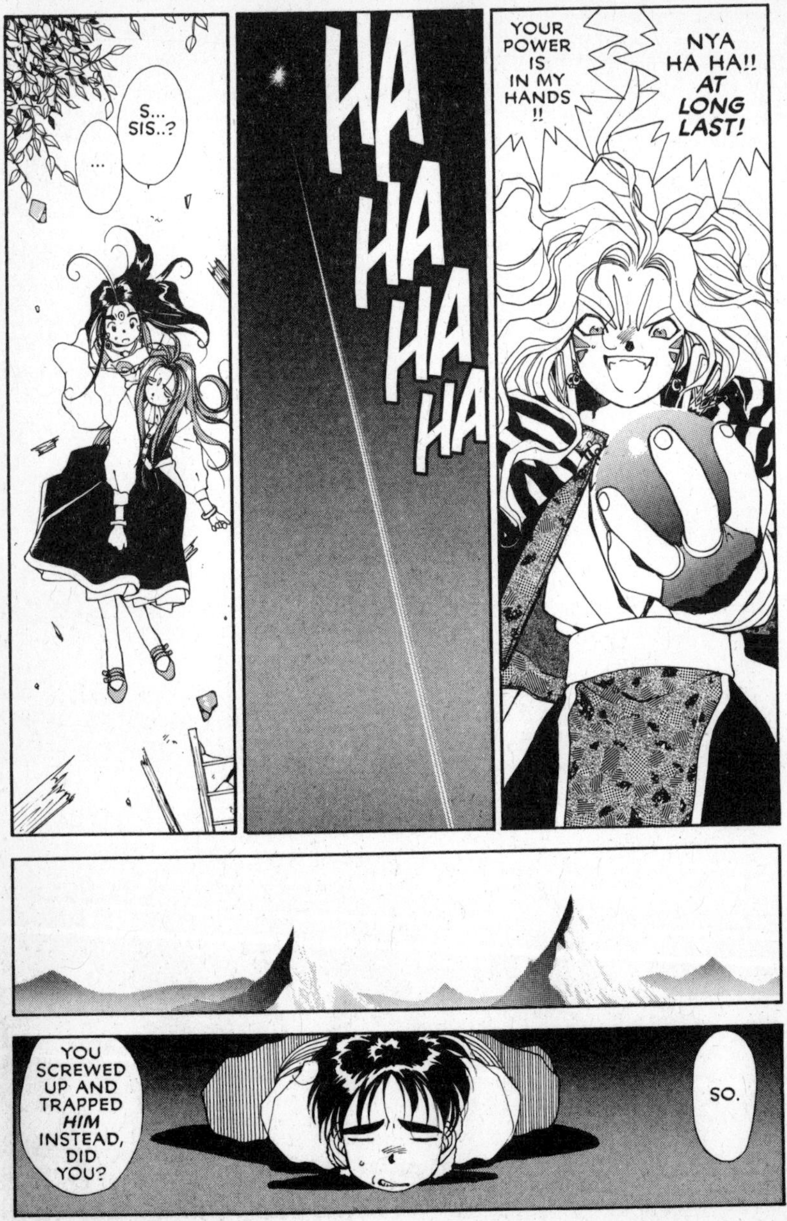
NYA HA HA!! AT LONG LAST!
YOUR POWER IS IN MY HANDS!!
HA HA HA HA HA
S... SIS..?
...
SO.
YOU SCREWED UP AND TRAPPED HIM INSTEAD, DID YOU?

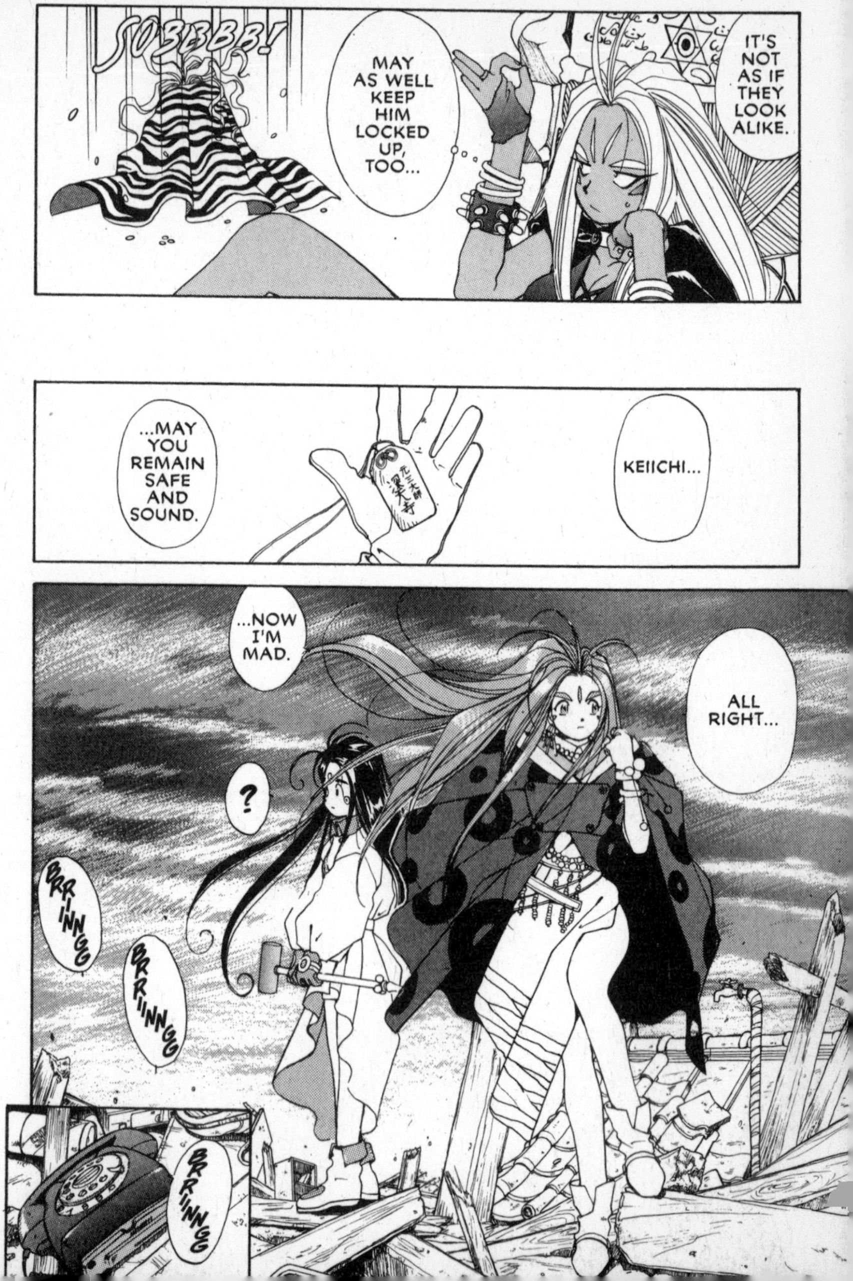
IT'S NOT AS IF THEY LOOK ALIKE.
MAY AS WELL KEEP HIM LOCKED UP, TOO...
SOBBBB!
KEIICHI...
...MAY YOU REMAIN SAFE AND SOUND.
ALL RIGHT...
...NOW I'M MAD.
?
BRRIINNGG
BRRIINNGG
BRRIINNGG

## CHAPTER 36

# The Ultimate Destruction Program

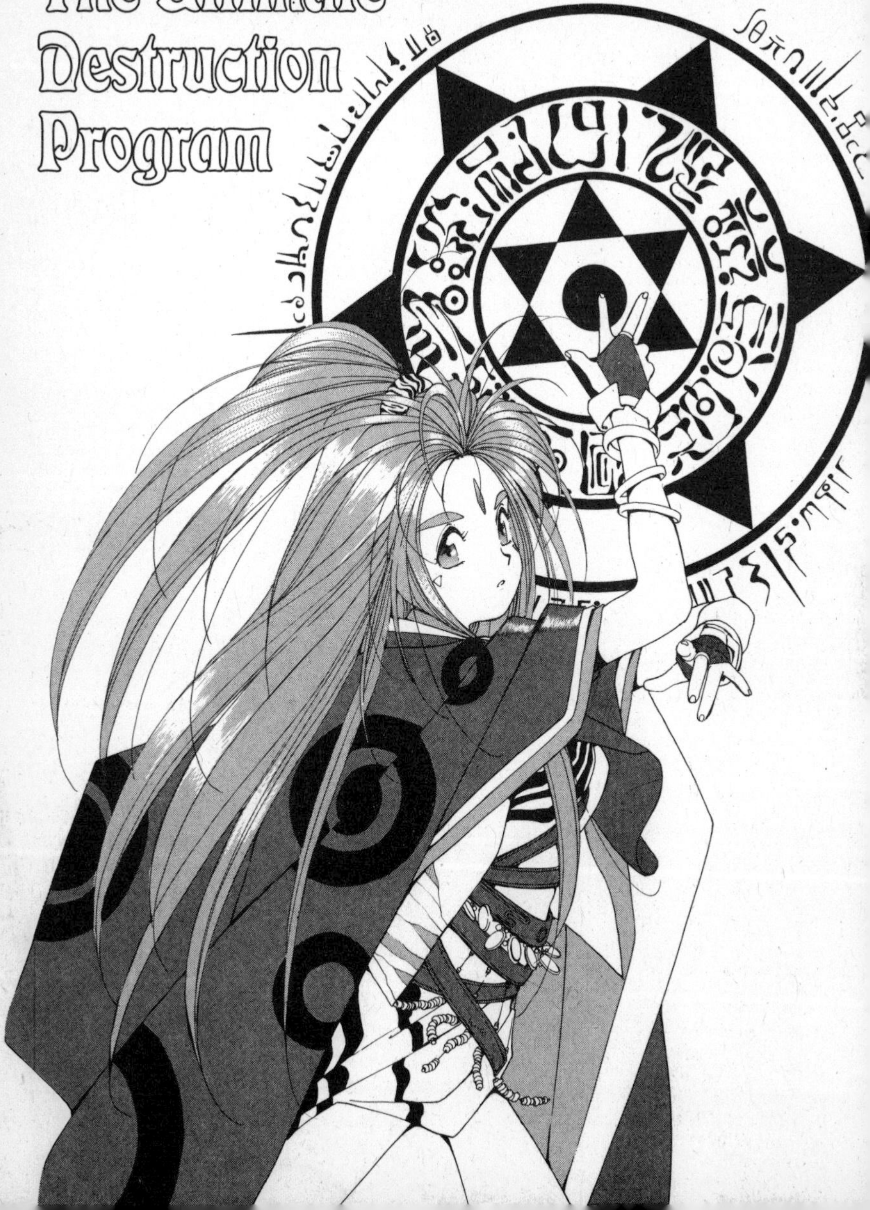

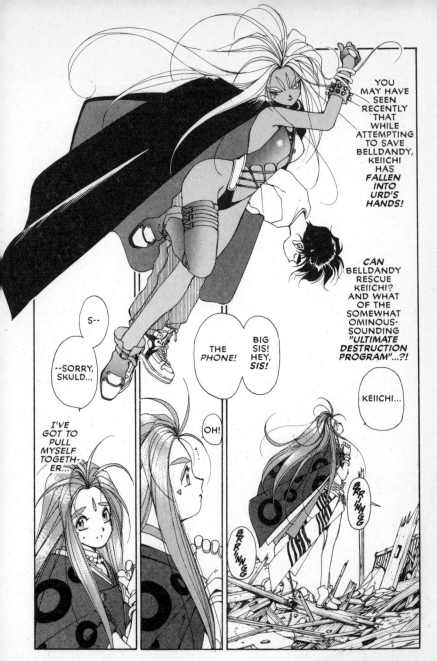

YOU MAY HAVE SEEN RECENTLY THAT WHILE ATTEMPTING TO SAVE BELLDANDY, KEIICHI HAS *FALLEN INTO URD'S HANDS!*

*CAN BELLDANDY RESCUE KEIICHI? AND WHAT OF THE SOMEWHAT OMINOUS-SOUNDING "ULTIMATE DESTRUCTION PROGRAM"...?!*

S--

--SORRY, SKULD...

THE *PHONE!*

BIG SIS! HEY, *SIS!*

KEIICHI...

*I'VE GOT TO PULL MYSELF TOGETH-ER...*

OH!

BRRRIINNGG

BRRRIINNGG

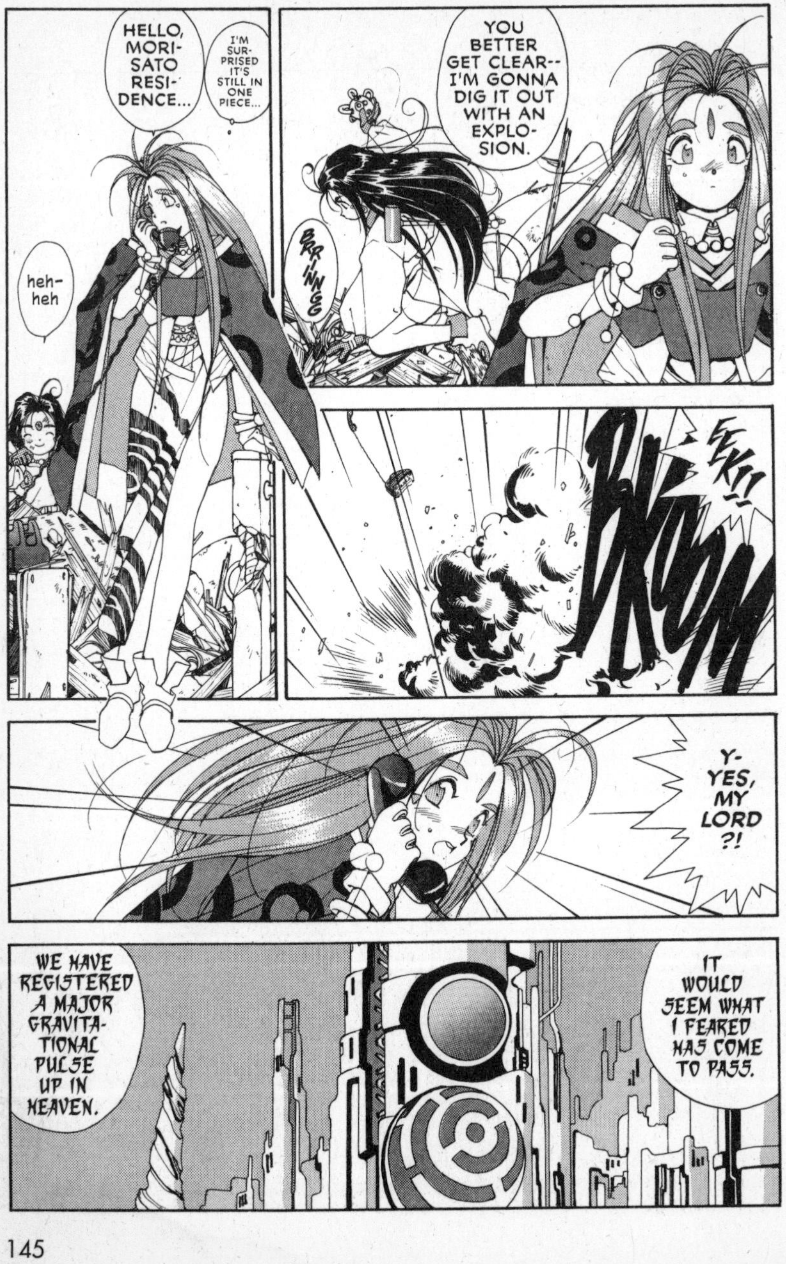
YOU BETTER GET CLEAR-- I'M GONNA DIG IT OUT WITH AN EXPLOSION.
BRRINNGG
EEK!!
BKOOM
HELLO, MORI-SATO RESI-DENCE...
I'M SUR-PRISED IT'S STILL IN ONE PIECE...
heh-heh
Y-YES, MY LORD?!
IT WOULD SEEM WHAT I FEARED HAS COME TO PASS.
WE HAVE REGISTERED A MAJOR GRAVITA-TIONAL PULSE UP IN HEAVEN.

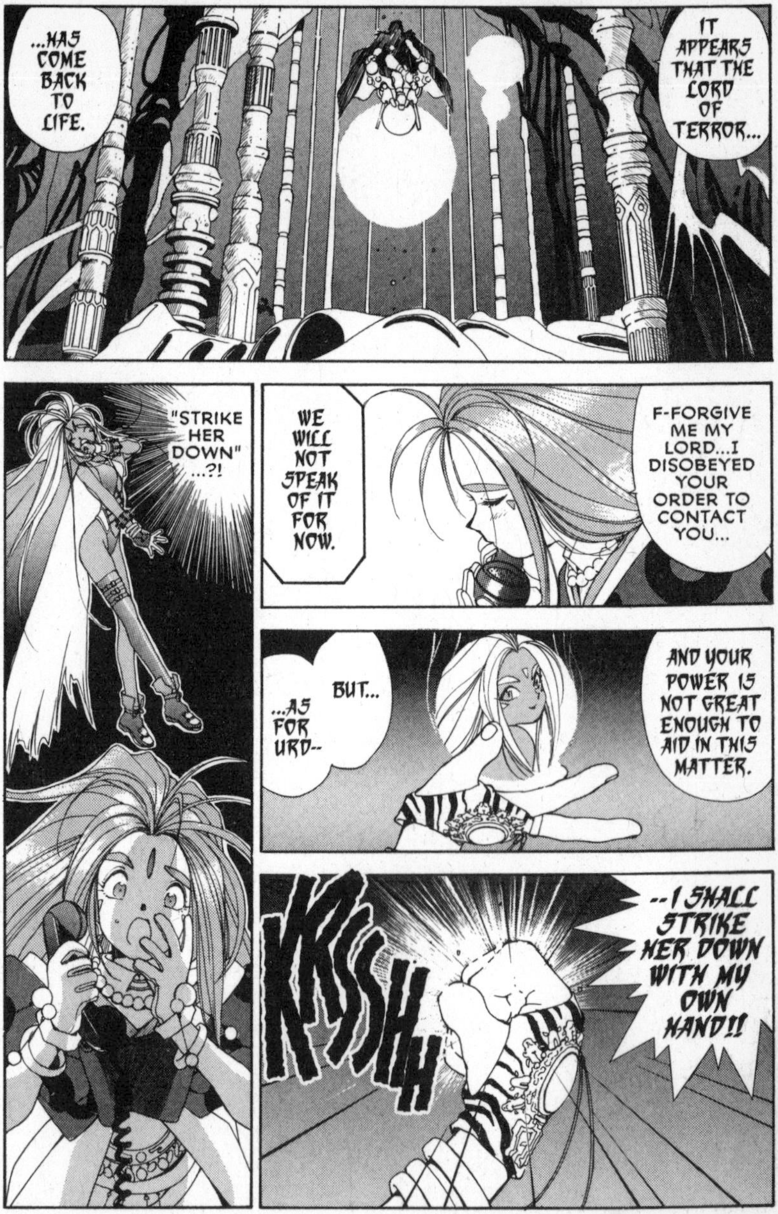
IT APPEARS THAT THE LORD OF TERROR...
...HAS COME BACK TO LIFE.
F-FORGIVE ME MY LORD...I DISOBEYED YOUR ORDER TO CONTACT YOU...
WE WILL NOT SPEAK OF IT FOR NOW.
AND YOUR POWER IS NOT GREAT ENOUGH TO AID IN THIS MATTER.
BUT...
...AS FOR URD--
--I SHALL STRIKE HER DOWN WITH MY OWN HAND!!
KRSSHH
"STRIKE HER DOWN" ...?!

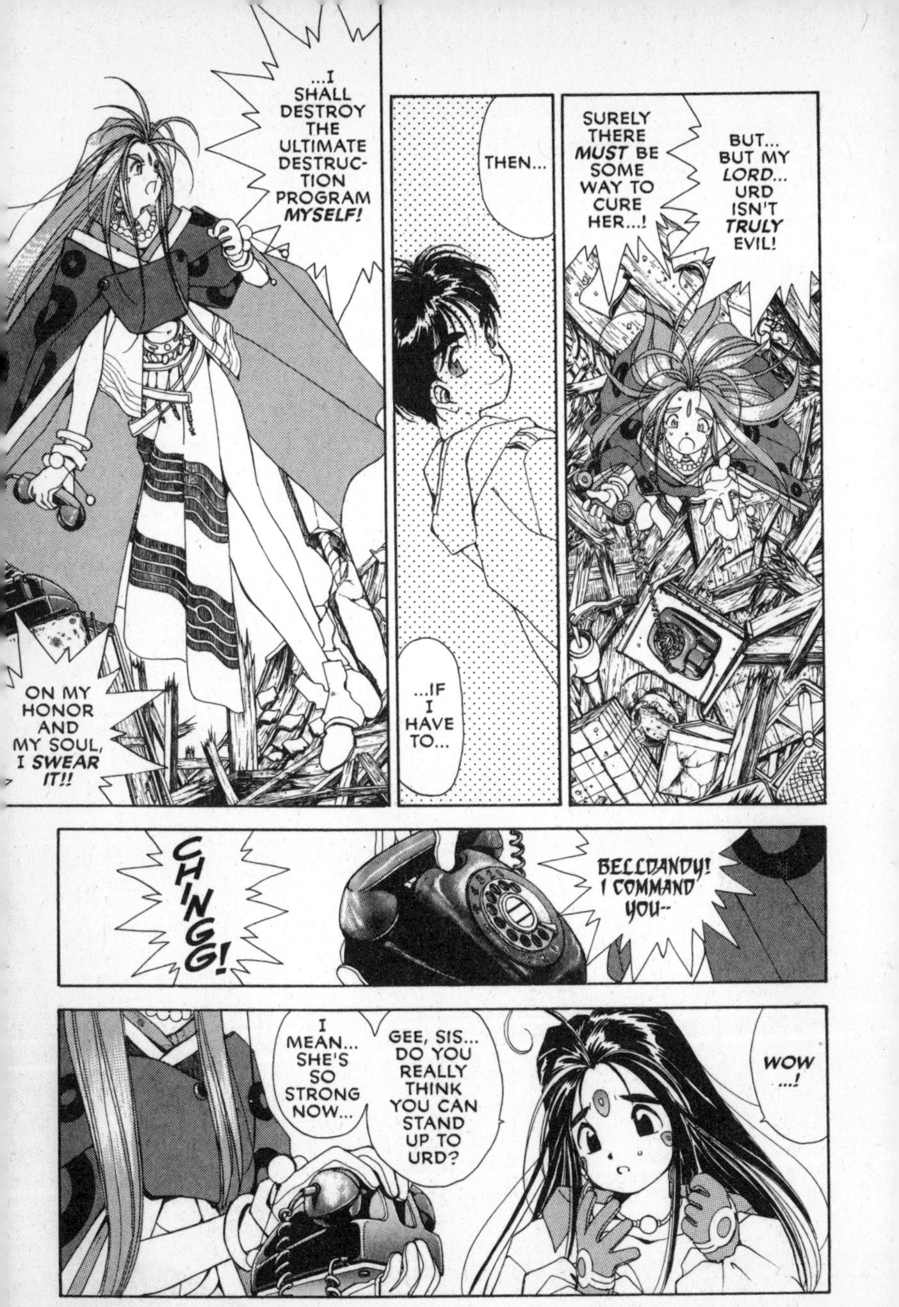
BUT... BUT MY LORD... URD ISN'T TRULY EVIL!
SURELY THERE MUST BE SOME WAY TO CURE HER...!
THEN...
...IF I HAVE TO...
...I SHALL DESTROY THE ULTIMATE DESTRUCTION PROGRAM MYSELF!
ON MY HONOR AND MY SOUL, I SWEAR IT!!
BELLDANDY! I COMMAND YOU--
CHINGG!
WOW ...!
GEE, SIS... DO YOU REALLY THINK YOU CAN STAND UP TO URD?
I MEAN... SHE'S SO STRONG NOW...

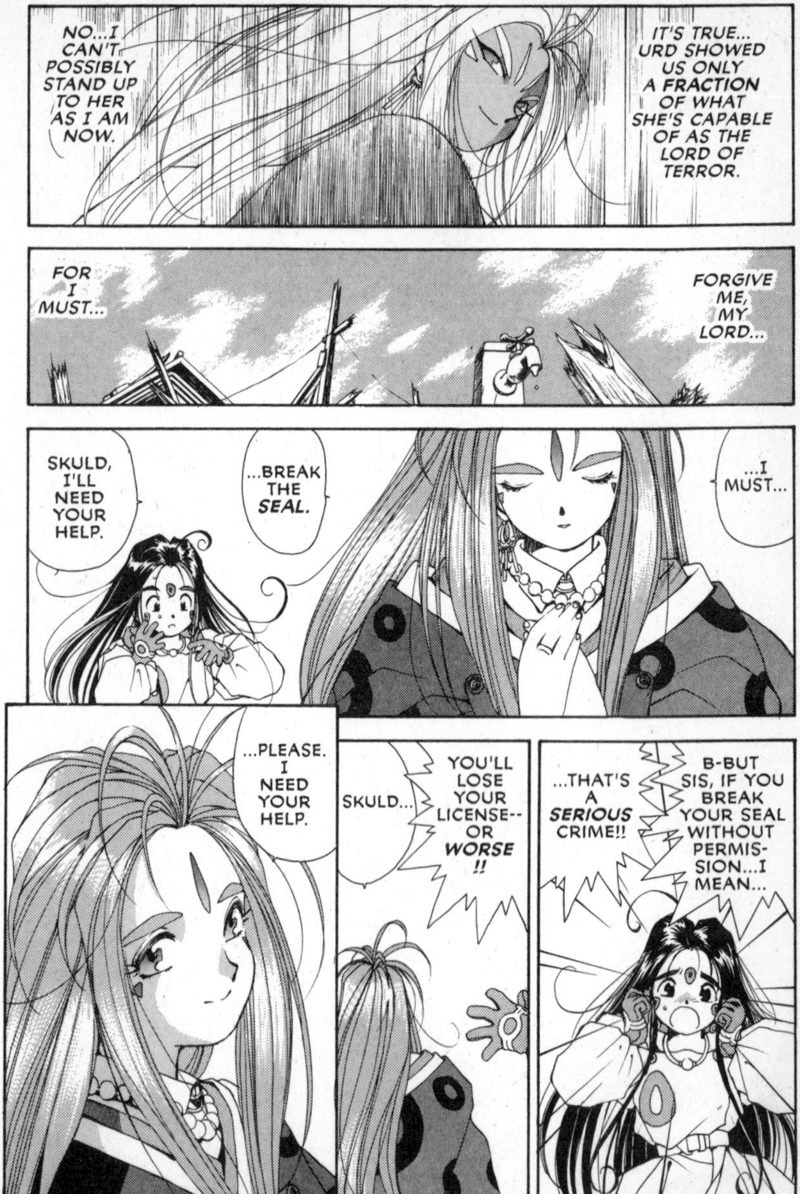
IT'S TRUE... URD SHOWED US ONLY A **FRACTION** OF WHAT SHE'S CAPABLE OF AS THE LORD OF TERROR.
NO...I CAN'T POSSIBLY STAND UP TO HER AS I AM NOW.
FORGIVE ME, MY LORD...
FOR I MUST...
...I MUST...
...BREAK THE *SEAL.*
SKULD, I'LL NEED YOUR HELP.
B-BUT SIS, IF YOU BREAK YOUR SEAL WITHOUT PERMISSION...I MEAN...
...THAT'S A *SERIOUS* CRIME!!
YOU'LL LOSE YOUR LICENSE--OR ***WORSE*** !!
SKULD...
...PLEASE. I NEED YOUR HELP.

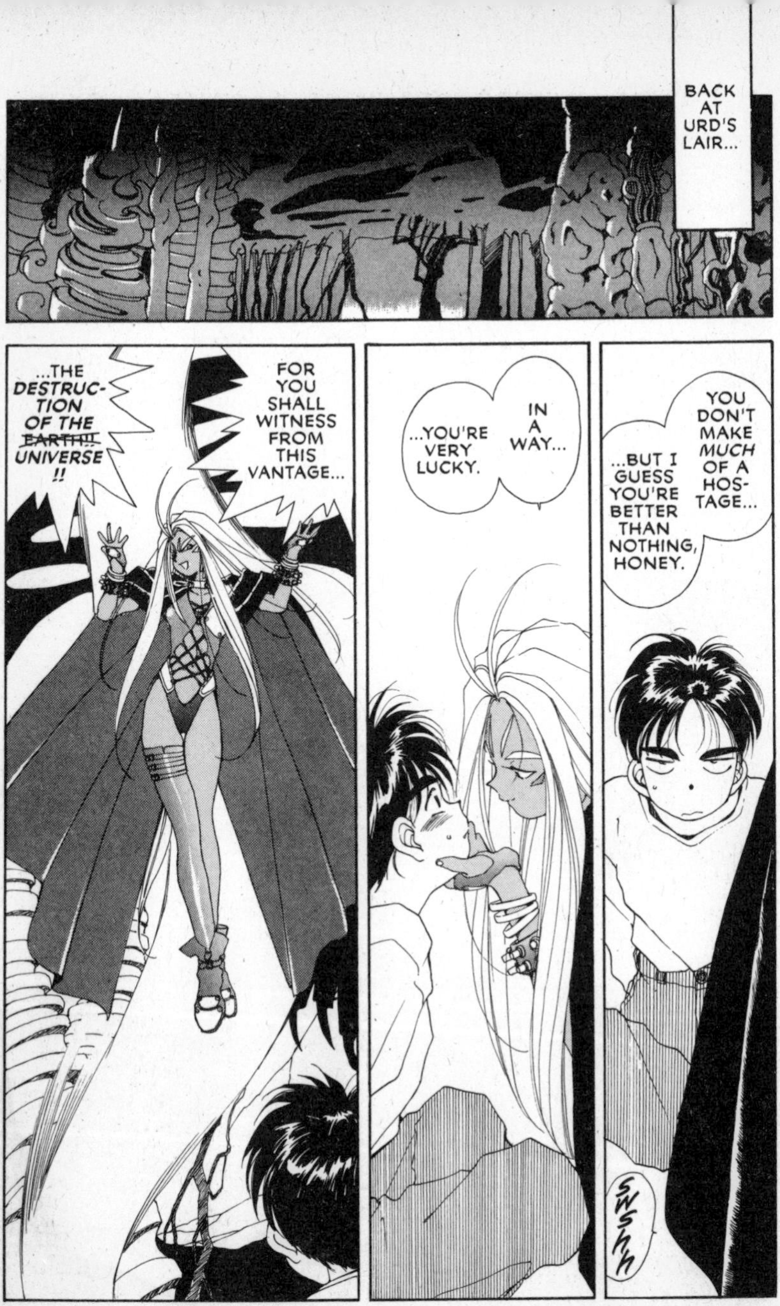

BACK AT URD'S LAIR...
YOU DON'T MAKE *MUCH* OF A HOS-TAGE...
...BUT I GUESS YOU'RE BETTER THAN NOTHING, HONEY.
SWSHH
IN A WAY...
...YOU'RE VERY LUCKY.
FOR YOU SHALL WITNESS FROM THIS VANTAGE...
...THE *DESTRUC-TION OF THE* EARTH!! *UNIVERSE !!*

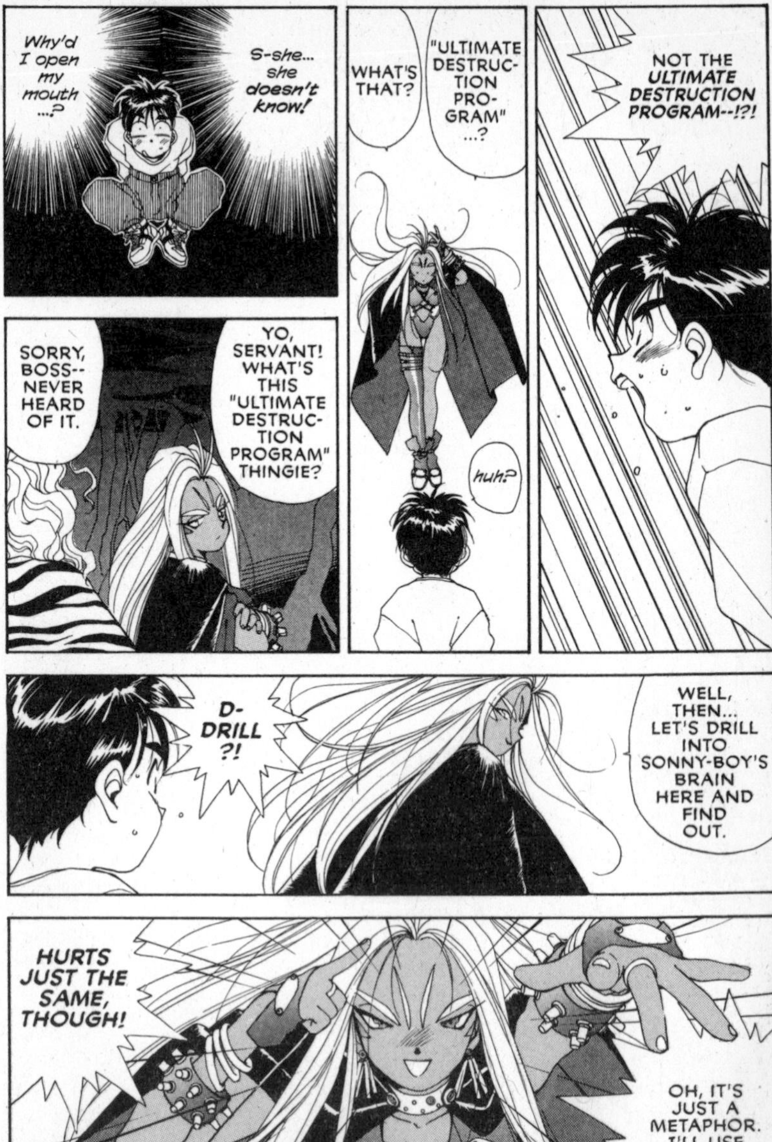
NOT THE *ULTIMATE DESTRUCTION PROGRAM*--!?!
"ULTIMATE DESTRUCTION PROGRAM" ...?
WHAT'S THAT?
huh?
S-she... she doesn't know!
Why'd I open my mouth ...?
YO, SERVANT! WHAT'S THIS "ULTIMATE DESTRUCTION PROGRAM" THINGIE?
SORRY, BOSS-- NEVER HEARD OF IT.
WELL, THEN... LET'S DRILL INTO SONNY-BOY'S BRAIN HERE AND FIND OUT.
D-DRILL ?!
OH, IT'S JUST A METAPHOR. I'LL USE MAGIC.
HURTS JUST THE SAME, THOUGH!

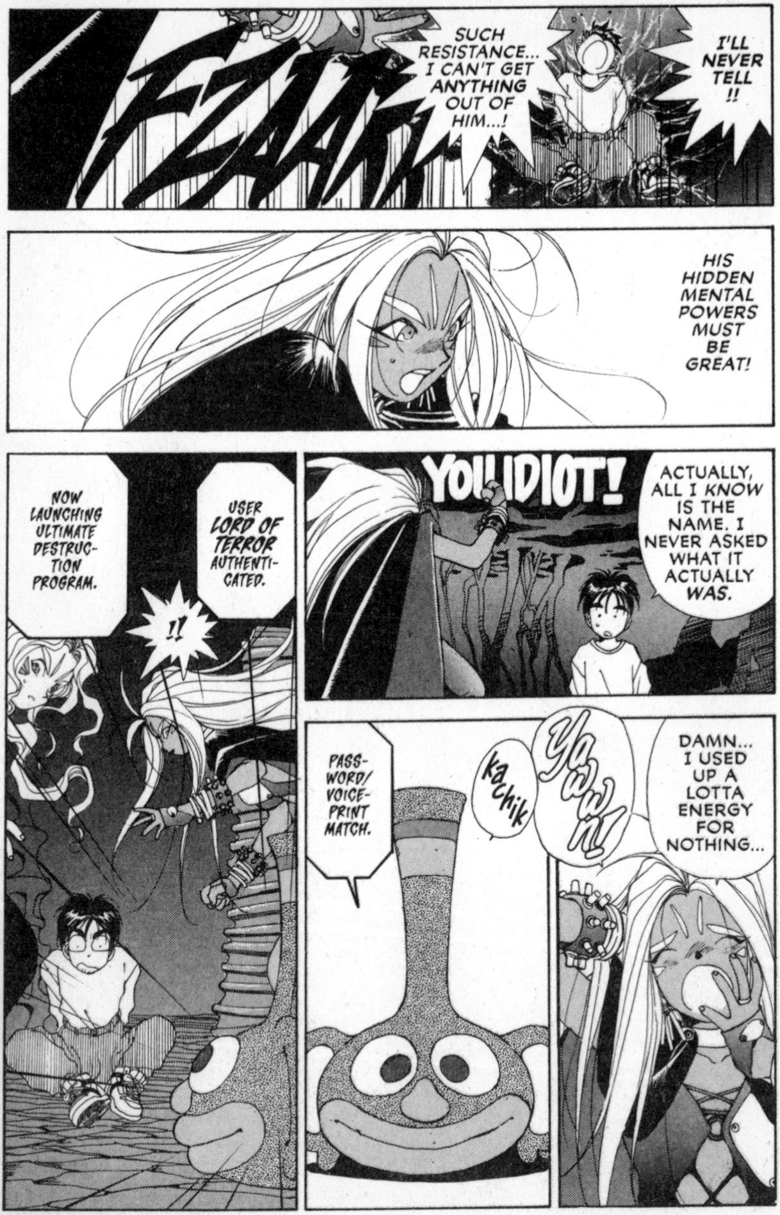
I'LL NEVER TELL !!
SUCH RESISTANCE... I CAN'T GET ANYTHING OUT OF HIM...!
FZAAK
HIS HIDDEN MENTAL POWERS MUST BE GREAT!
ACTUALLY, ALL I KNOW IS THE NAME. I NEVER ASKED WHAT IT ACTUALLY WAS.
YOU IDIOT!
DAMN... I USED UP A LOTTA ENERGY FOR NOTHING...
Yawwn!
kachik
PASS-WORD/VOICE-PRINT MATCH.
USER LORD OF TERROR AUTHENTI-CATED.
NOW LAUNCHING ULTIMATE DESTRUC-TION PROGRAM.
!!

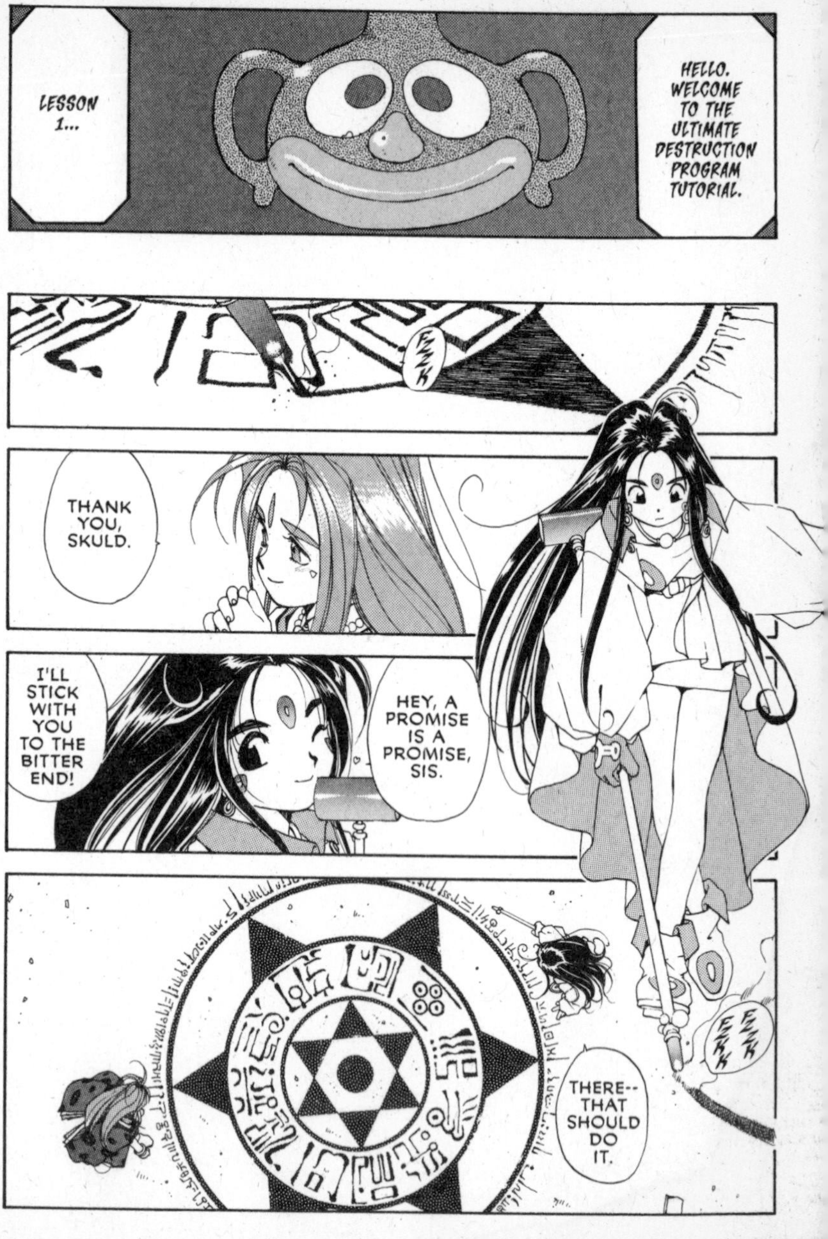
HELLO. WELCOME TO THE ULTIMATE DESTRUCTION PROGRAM TUTORIAL.
LESSON 1...
FZZK
THANK YOU, SKULD.
HEY, A PROMISE IS A PROMISE, SIS.
I'LL STICK WITH YOU TO THE BITTER END!
FZZK
FZKK
THERE--THAT SHOULD DO IT.

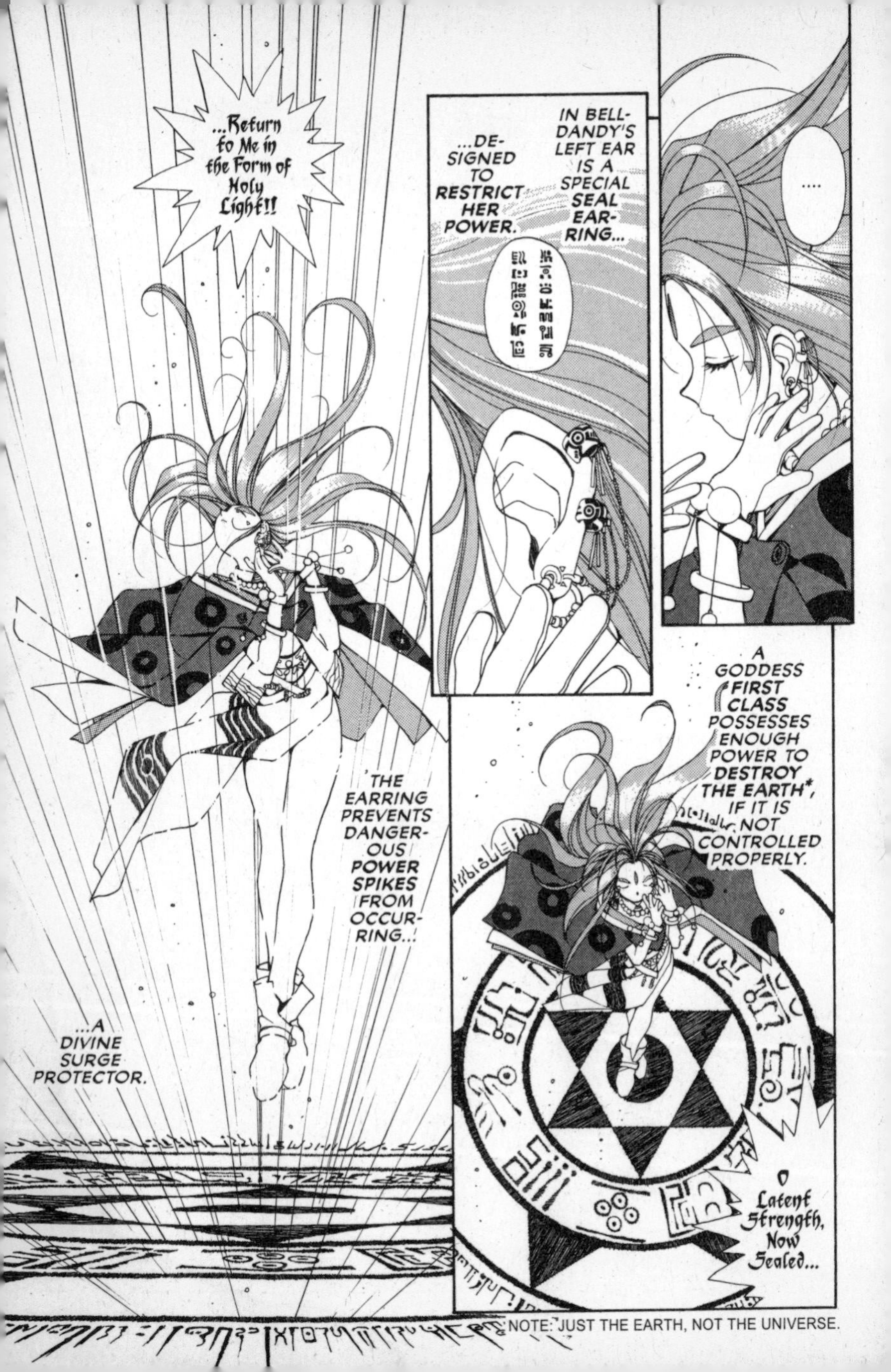
....
IN BELL-DANDY'S LEFT EAR IS A SPECIAL SEAL EAR-RING...
...DE-SIGNED TO RESTRICT HER POWER.
A GODDESS FIRST CLASS POSSESSES ENOUGH POWER TO DESTROY THE EARTH*, IF IT IS NOT CONTROLLED PROPERLY.
Latent Strength, Now Sealed...
...Return to Me in the Form of Holy Light!!
THE EARRING PREVENTS DANGER-OUS POWER SPIKES FROM OCCUR-RING...
...A DIVINE SURGE PROTECTOR.
NOTE: JUST THE EARTH, NOT THE UNIVERSE.

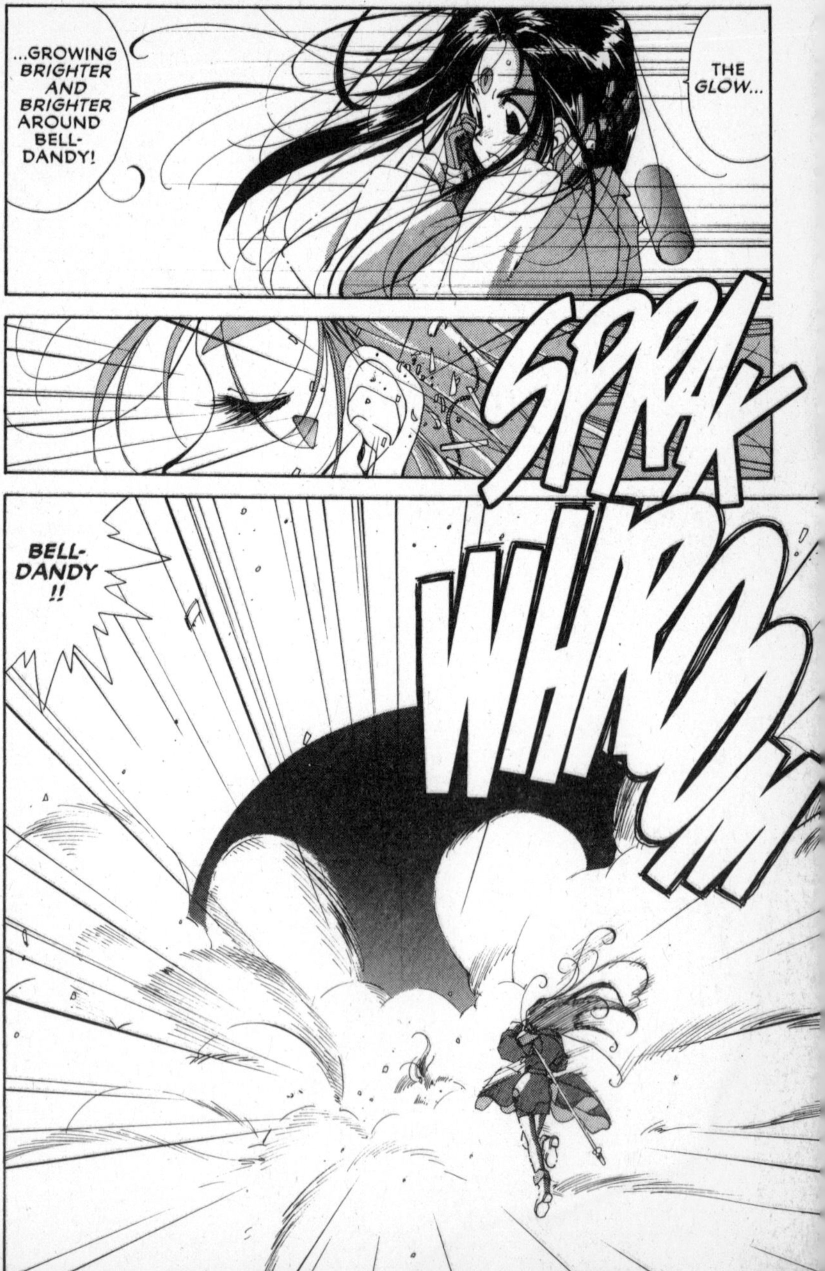
THE GLOW...
...GROWING BRIGHTER AND BRIGHTER AROUND BELL-DANDY!
SPRAK
WHROOM
BELL-DANDY !!

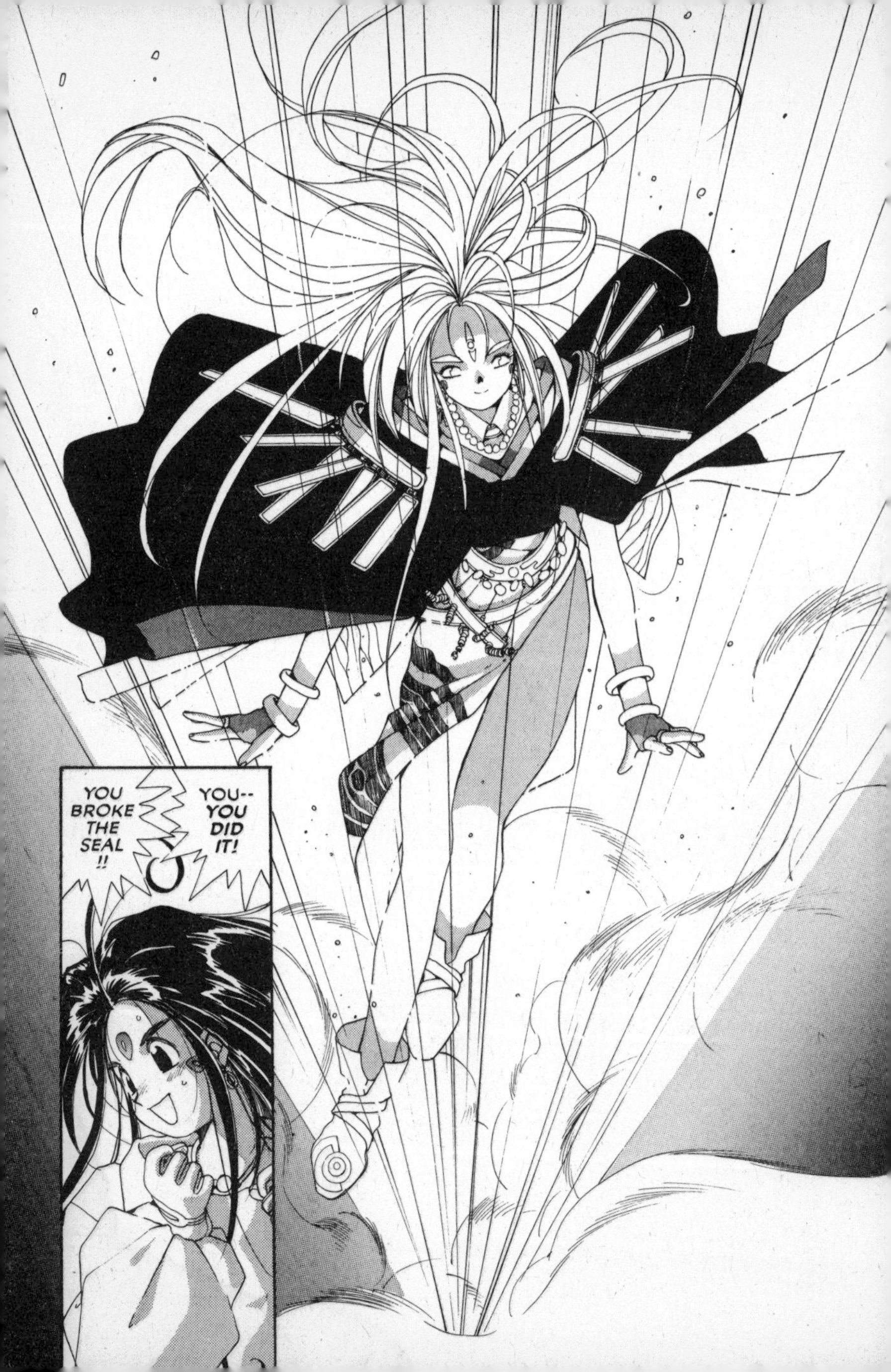
YOU-- YOU DID IT!
YOU BROKE THE SEAL !!

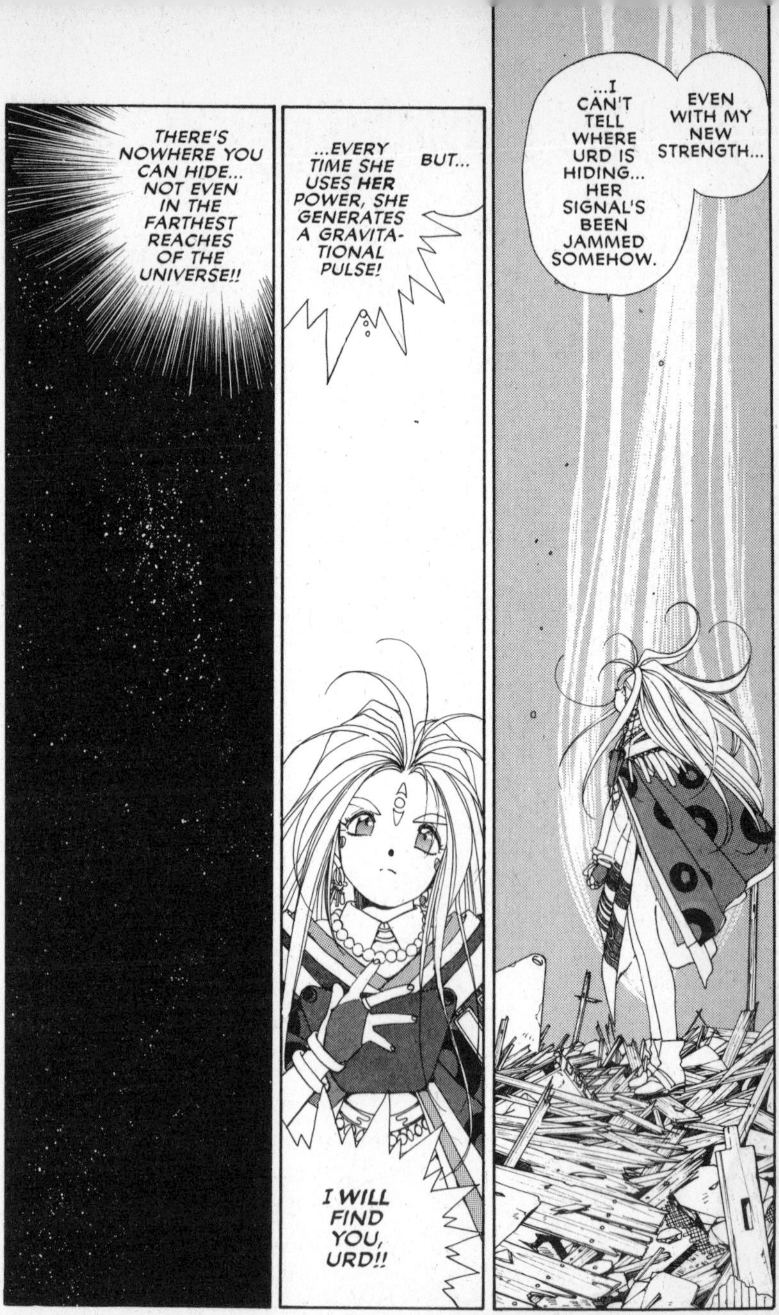
EVEN WITH MY NEW STRENGTH...
...I CAN'T TELL WHERE URD IS HIDING... HER SIGNAL'S BEEN JAMMED SOMEHOW.
BUT...
...EVERY TIME SHE USES **HER** POWER, SHE GENERATES A GRAVITATIONAL PULSE!
I WILL FIND YOU, URD!!
THERE'S NOWHERE YOU CAN HIDE... NOT EVEN IN THE FARTHEST REACHES OF THE UNIVERSE!!

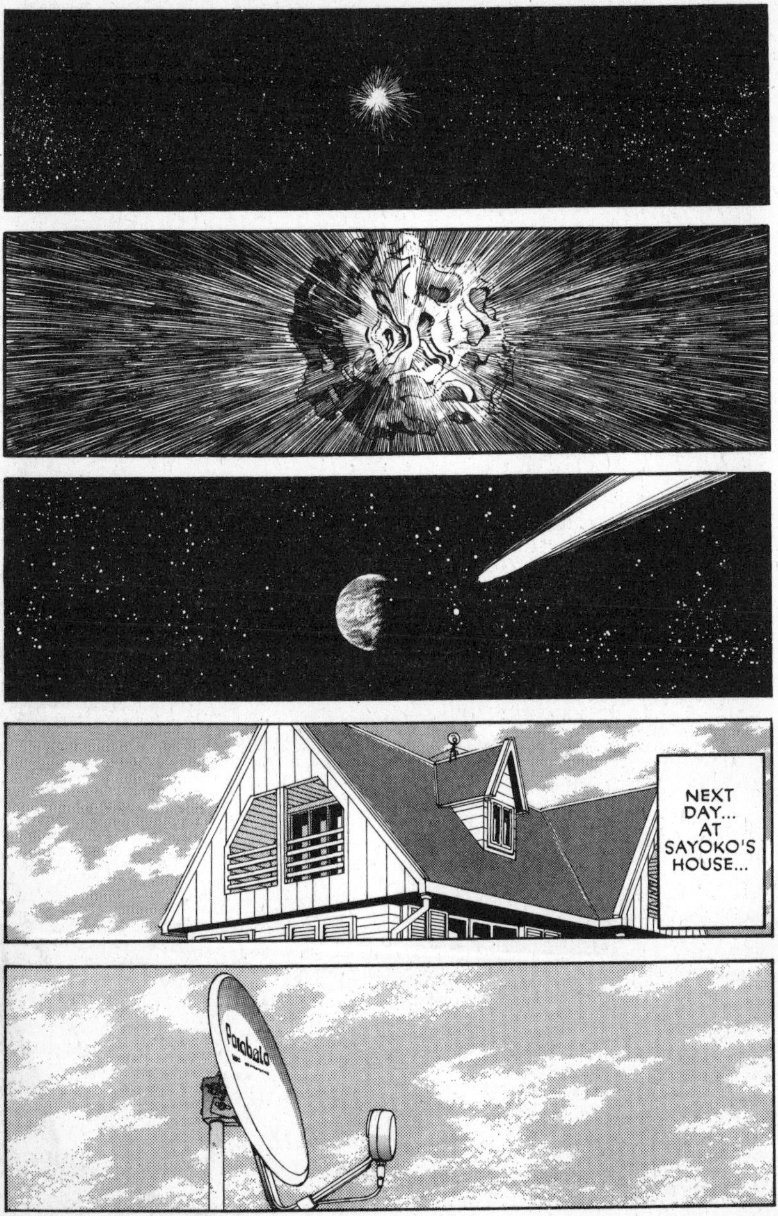
NEXT DAY... AT SAYOKO'S HOUSE...

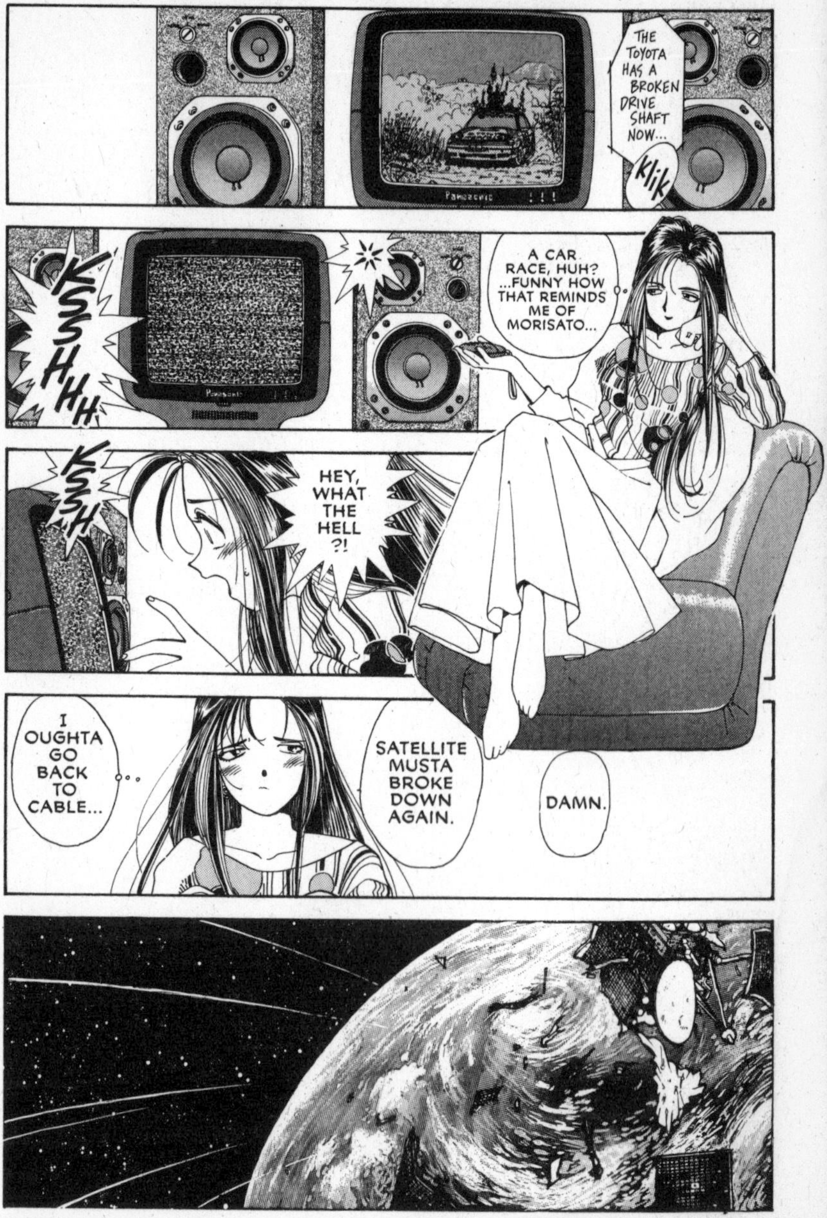
THE TOYOTA HAS A BROKEN DRIVE SHAFT NOW...
Klik
A CAR RACE, HUH? ...FUNNY HOW THAT REMINDS ME OF MORISATO...
KSSHHH
HEY, WHAT THE HELL ?!
KSSH
DAMN.
SATELLITE MUSTA BROKE DOWN AGAIN.
I OUGHTA GO BACK TO CABLE...

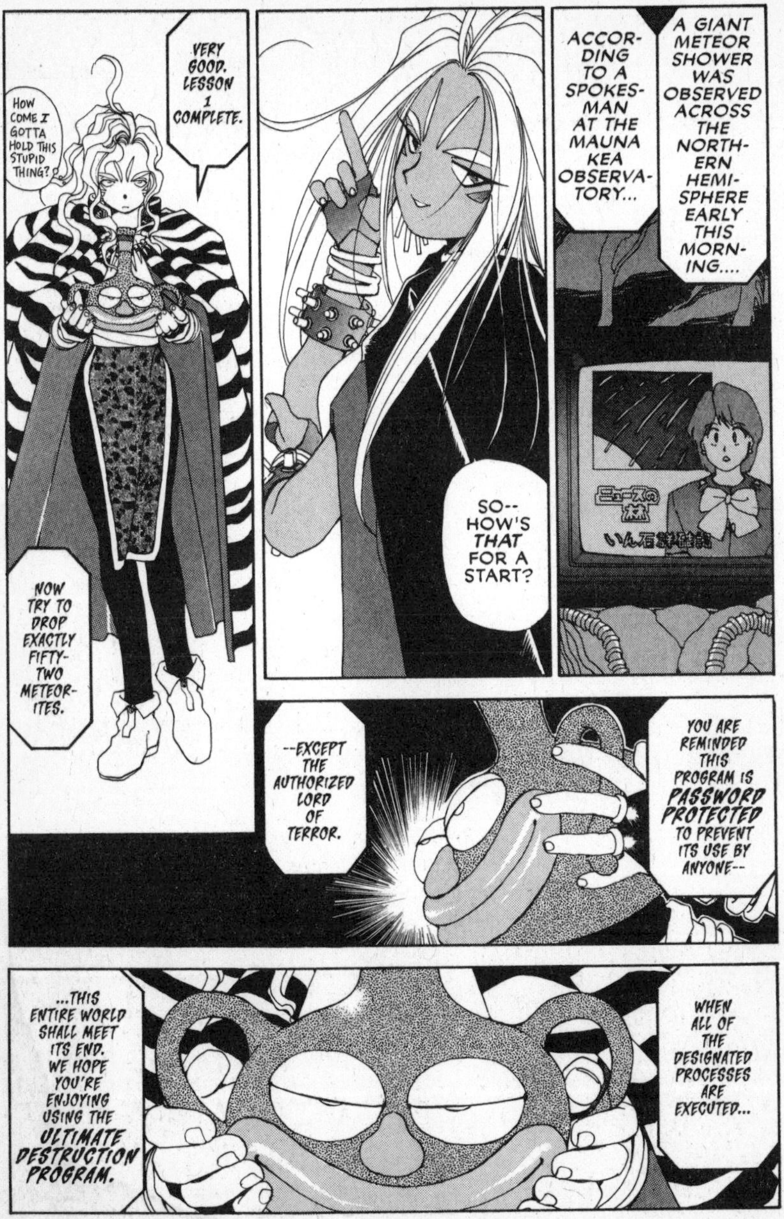

A GIANT METEOR SHOWER WAS OBSERVED ACROSS THE NORTHERN HEMISPHERE EARLY THIS MORNING....
ACCORDING TO A SPOKESMAN AT THE MAUNA KEA OBSERVATORY...
ニュースの森
SO--HOW'S *THAT* FOR A START?
YOU ARE REMINDED THIS PROGRAM IS **PASSWORD PROTECTED** TO PREVENT ITS USE BY ANYONE--
--EXCEPT THE AUTHORIZED LORD OF TERROR.
VERY GOOD. LESSON 1 COMPLETE.
HOW COME *I* GOTTA HOLD THIS STUPID THING?
NOW TRY TO DROP EXACTLY FIFTY-TWO METEORITES.
WHEN ALL OF THE DESIGNATED PROCESSES ARE EXECUTED...
...THIS ENTIRE WORLD SHALL MEET ITS END. WE HOPE YOU'RE ENJOYING USING THE **ULTIMATE DESTRUCTION PROGRAM.**

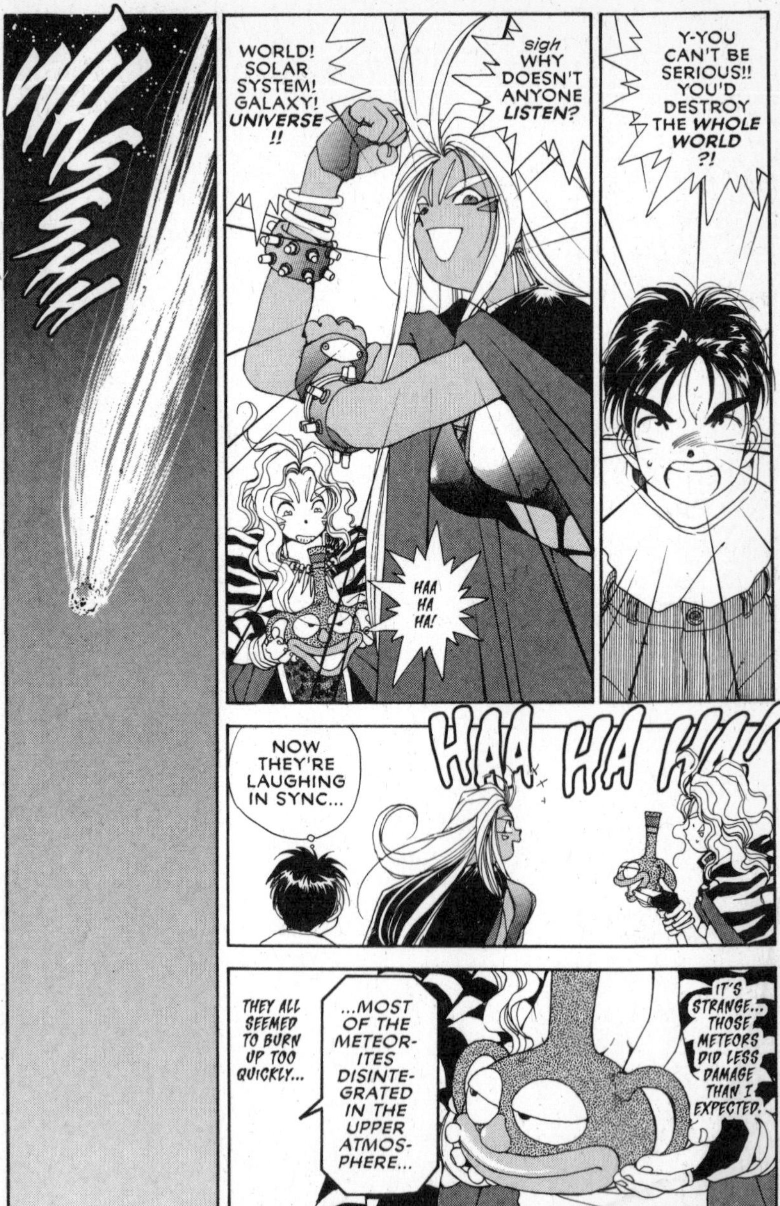
Y-YOU CAN'T BE SERIOUS!! YOU'D DESTROY THE WHOLE WORLD ?!
sigh WHY DOESN'T ANYONE LISTEN?
WORLD! SOLAR SYSTEM! GALAXY! UNIVERSE !!
HAA HA HA!
HAA HA HA!
NOW THEY'RE LAUGHING IN SYNC...
IT'S STRANGE... THOSE METEORS DID LESS DAMAGE THAN I EXPECTED.
...MOST OF THE METEOR-ITES DISINTE-GRATED IN THE UPPER ATMOS-PHERE...
THEY ALL SEEMED TO BURN UP TOO QUICKLY...
WHASHHH

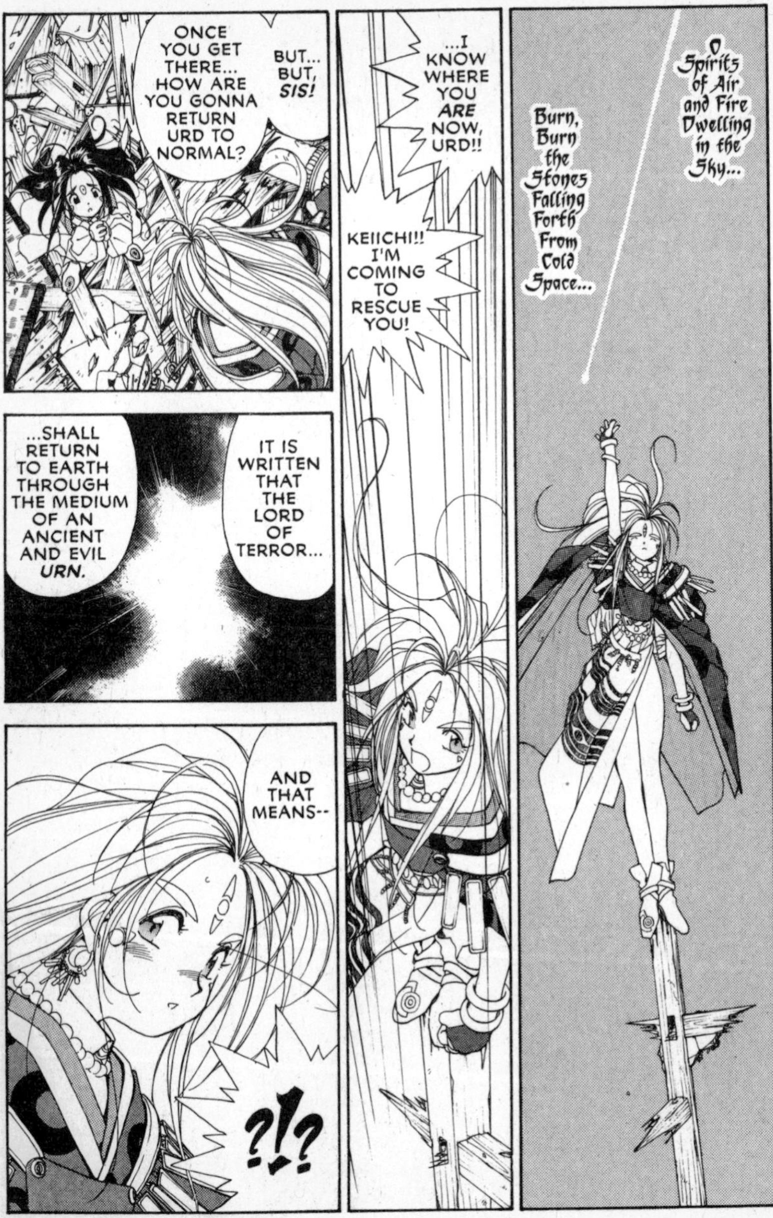
O Spirits of Air and Fire Dwelling in the Sky...
Burn, Burn the Stones Falling Forth From Cold Space...
...I KNOW WHERE YOU *ARE* NOW, URD!!
KEIICHI!! I'M COMING TO RESCUE YOU!
BUT... BUT, *SIS!*
ONCE YOU GET THERE... HOW ARE YOU GONNA RETURN URD TO NORMAL?
IT IS WRITTEN THAT THE LORD OF TERROR...
...SHALL RETURN TO EARTH THROUGH THE MEDIUM OF AN ANCIENT AND EVIL *URN.*
AND THAT MEANS--
?!?

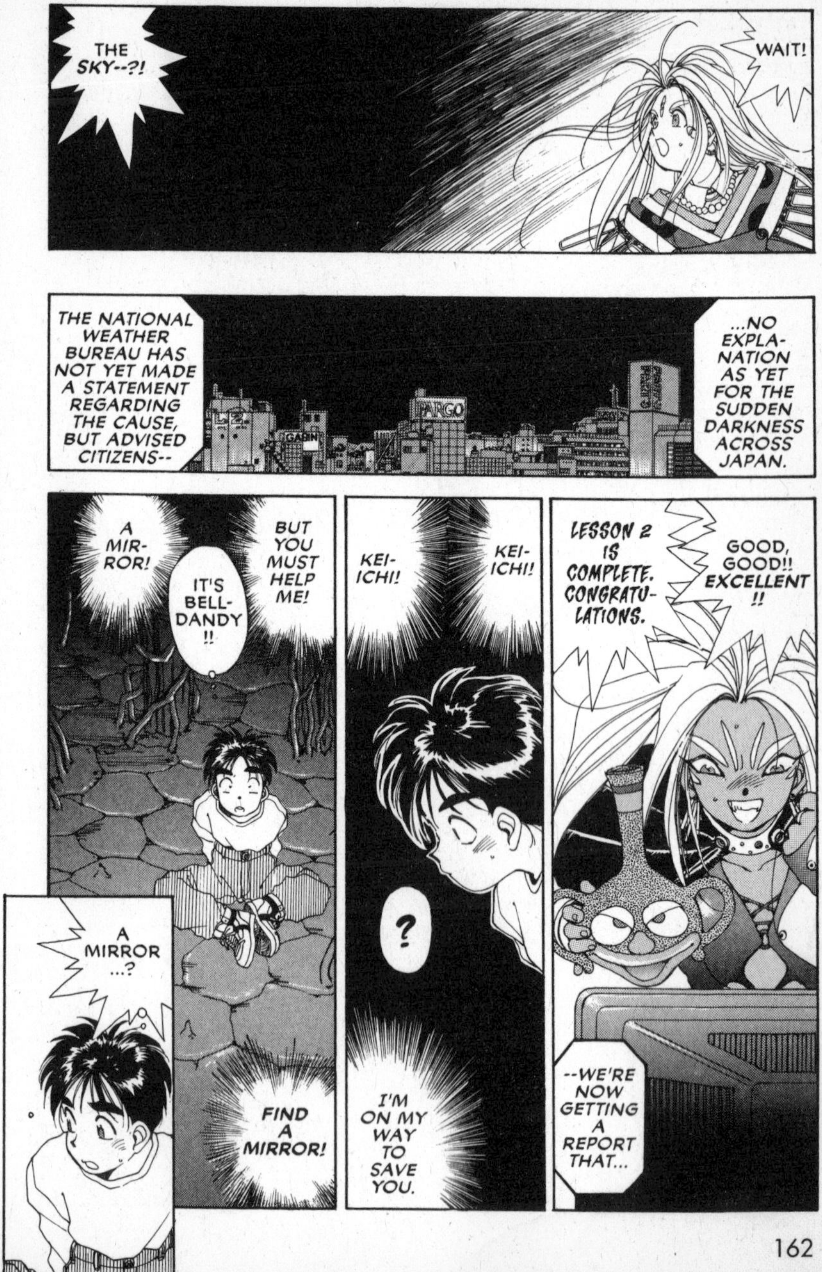
WAIT!
THE SKY--?!
...NO EXPLANATION AS YET FOR THE SUDDEN DARKNESS ACROSS JAPAN.
THE NATIONAL WEATHER BUREAU HAS NOT YET MADE A STATEMENT REGARDING THE CAUSE, BUT ADVISED CITIZENS--
GOOD, GOOD!! EXCELLENT!!
LESSON 2 IS COMPLETE. CONGRATULATIONS.
--WE'RE NOW GETTING A REPORT THAT...
KEI-ICHI!
KEI-ICHI!
?
I'M ON MY WAY TO SAVE YOU.
BUT YOU MUST HELP ME!
IT'S BELL-DANDY!!
A MIRROR!
FIND A MIRROR!
A MIRROR...?

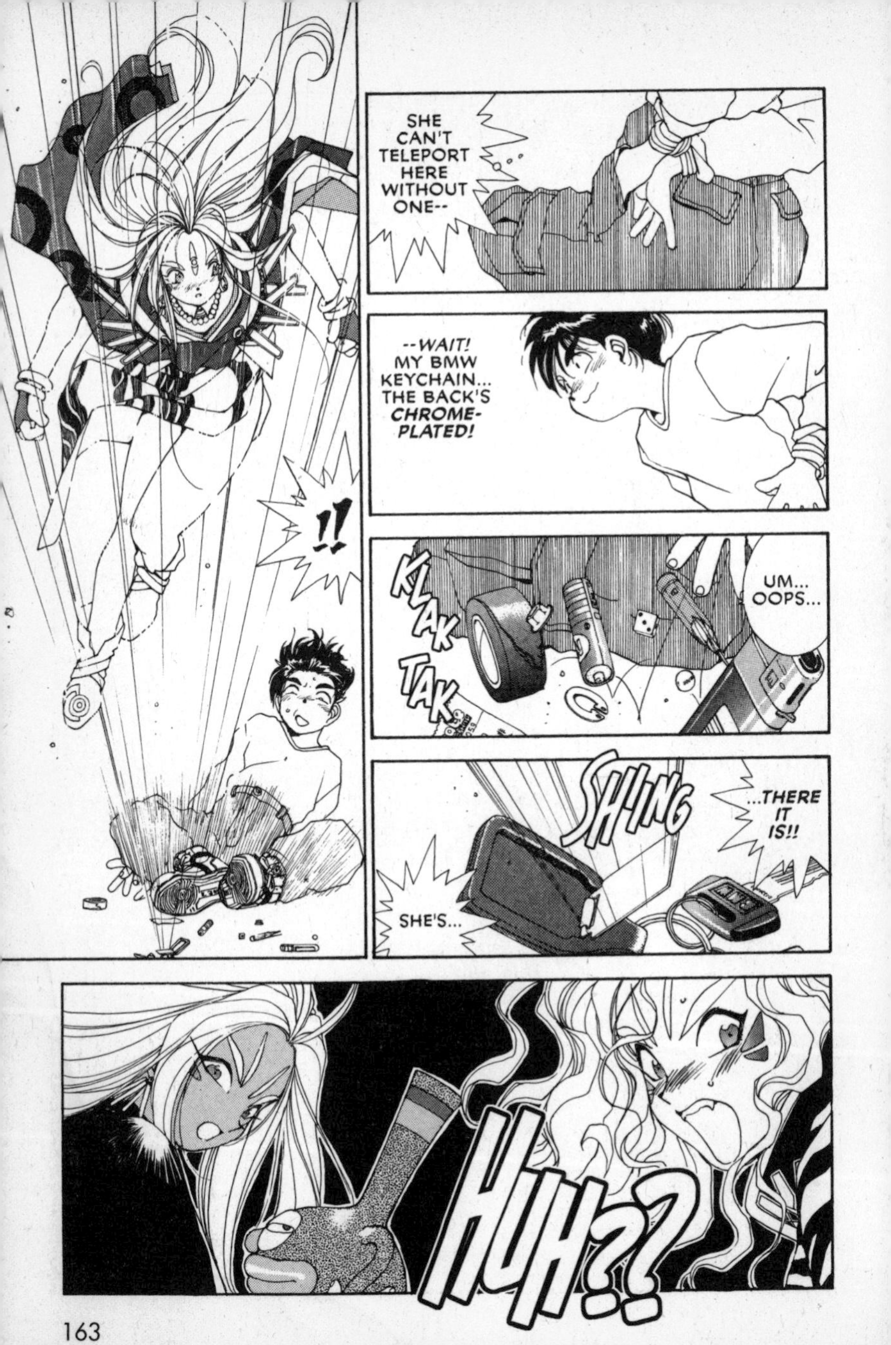

SHE CAN'T TELEPORT HERE WITHOUT ONE--
--WAIT! MY BMW KEYCHAIN... THE BACK'S CHROME-PLATED!
UM... OOPS...
KLAK
TAK
...THERE IT IS!!
SHING
SHE'S...
!!
HUH??

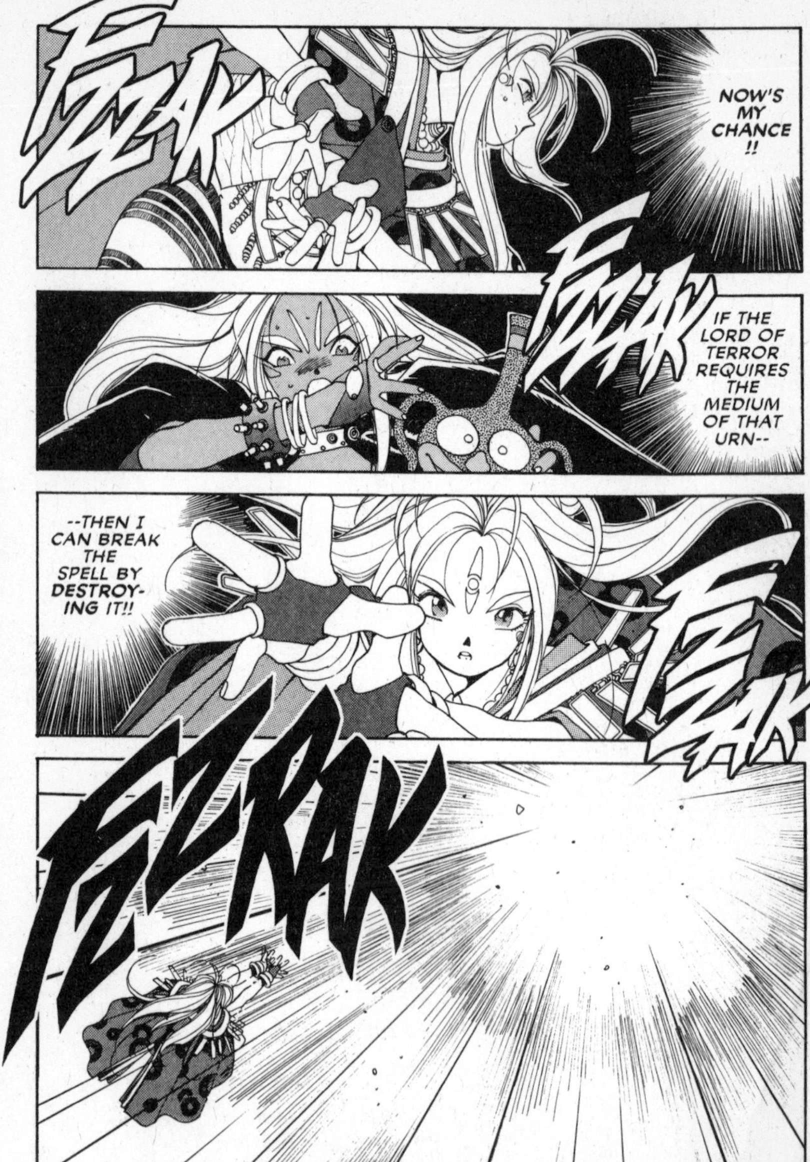
NOW'S MY CHANCE !!
FZZAK
FZZAK
IF THE LORD OF TERROR REQUIRES THE MEDIUM OF THAT URN--
FZZAK
--THEN I CAN BREAK THE SPELL BY DESTROY-ING IT!!
FZZRAK

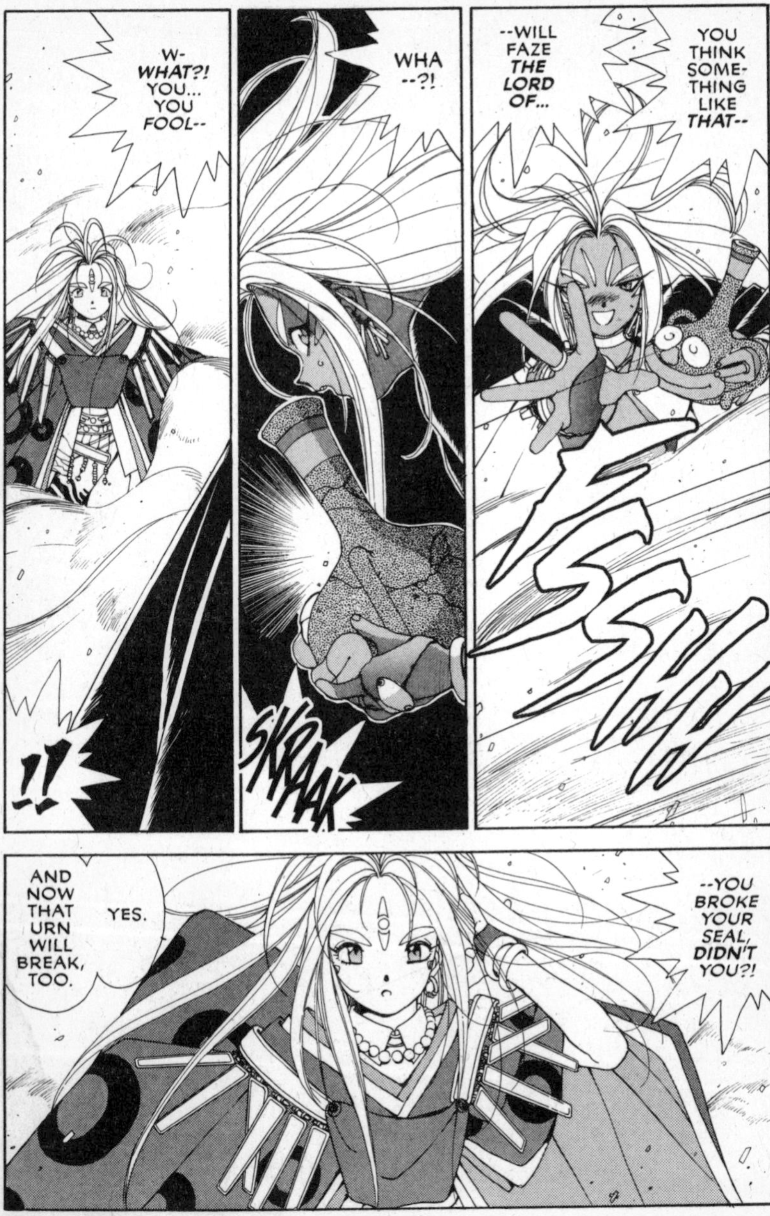
YOU THINK SOMETHING LIKE THAT--
--WILL FAZE THE LORD OF...
VSSHH
WHA --?!
SKRAAK
W-WHAT?! YOU... YOU FOOL--
!!
--YOU BROKE YOUR SEAL, DIDN'T YOU?!
YES.
AND NOW THAT URN WILL BREAK, TOO.

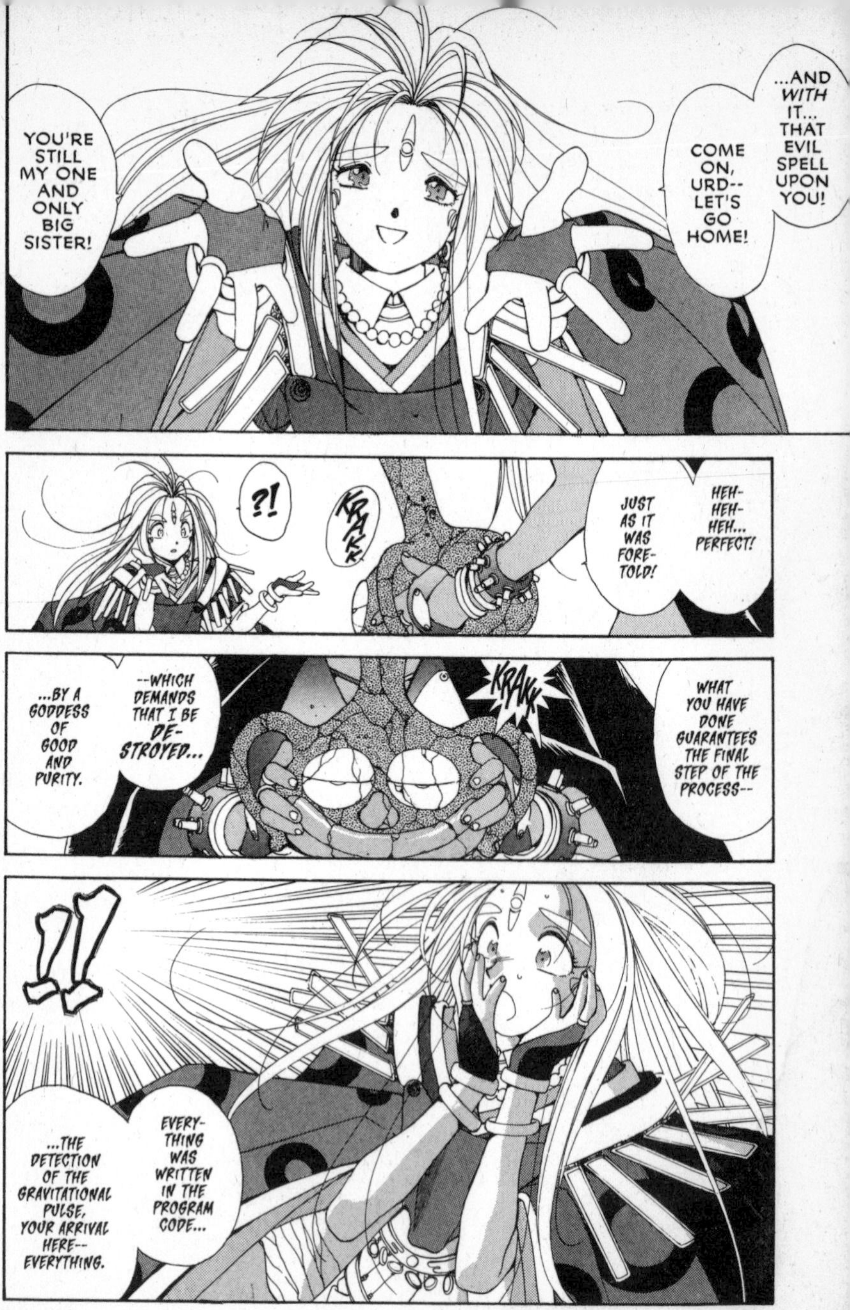
...AND WITH IT... THAT EVIL SPELL UPON YOU!
COME ON, URD-- LET'S GO HOME!
YOU'RE STILL MY ONE AND ONLY BIG SISTER!
HEH-HEH-HEH... PERFECT!
JUST AS IT WAS FORETOLD!
KRAKK
?!
WHAT YOU HAVE DONE GUARANTEES THE FINAL STEP OF THE PROCESS--
KRAKK
--WHICH DEMANDS THAT I BE DESTROYED...
...BY A GODDESS OF GOOD AND PURITY.
!!
EVERYTHING WAS WRITTEN IN THE PROGRAM CODE...
...THE DETECTION OF THE GRAVITATIONAL PULSE, YOUR ARRIVAL HERE-- EVERYTHING.

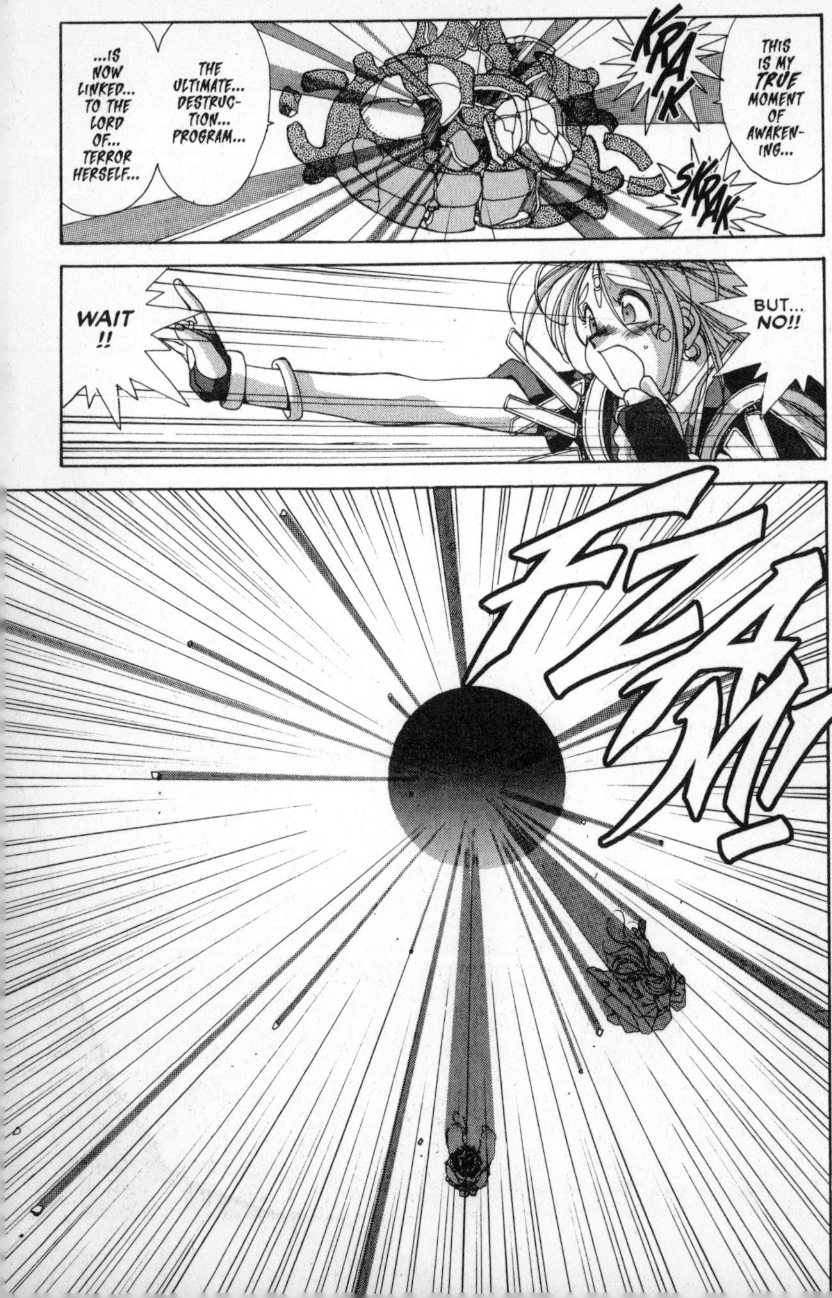
THIS IS MY TRUE MOMENT OF AWAKENING...
KRAK
SKRAK
THE ULTIMATE... DESTRUCTION... PROGRAM...
...IS NOW LINKED... TO THE LORD OF... TERROR HERSELF...
BUT... NO!!
WAIT !!
FZAM!

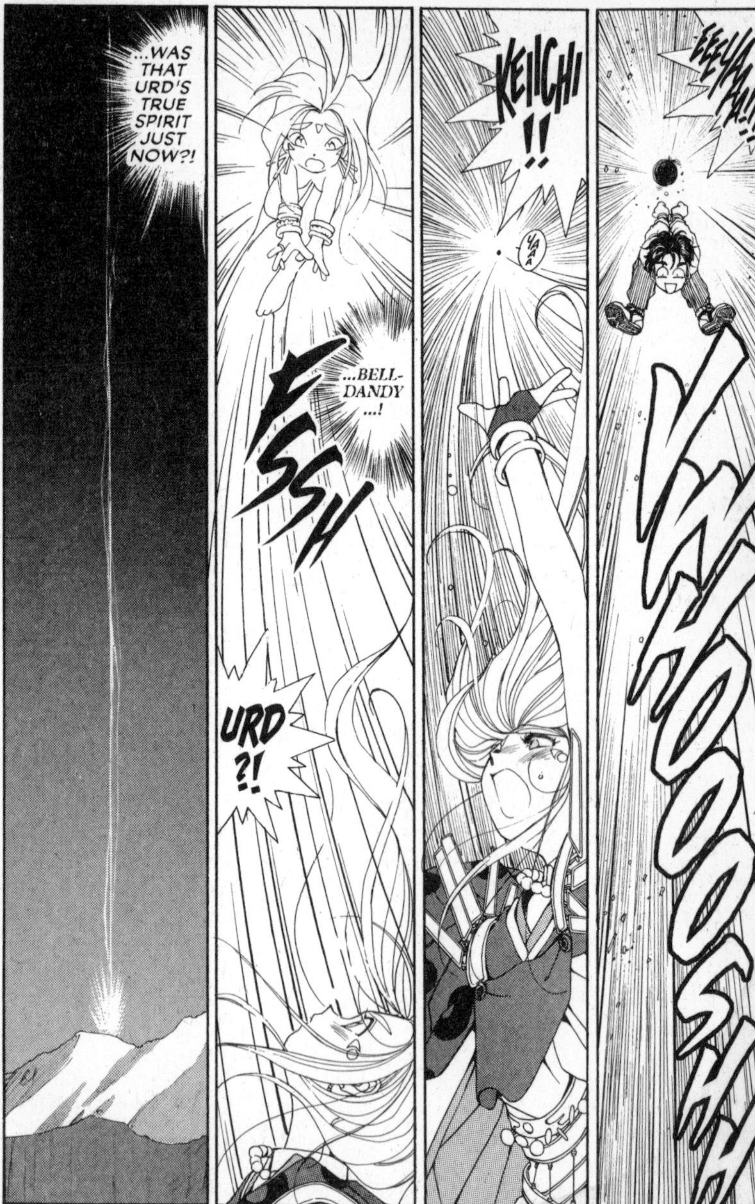
VWHOOOOSHHH
EEEYAHA--!!!
KEIICHI!!
YAAA
...BELL-DANDY...!
FSSH
URD?!
...WAS THAT URD'S TRUE SPIRIT JUST NOW?!

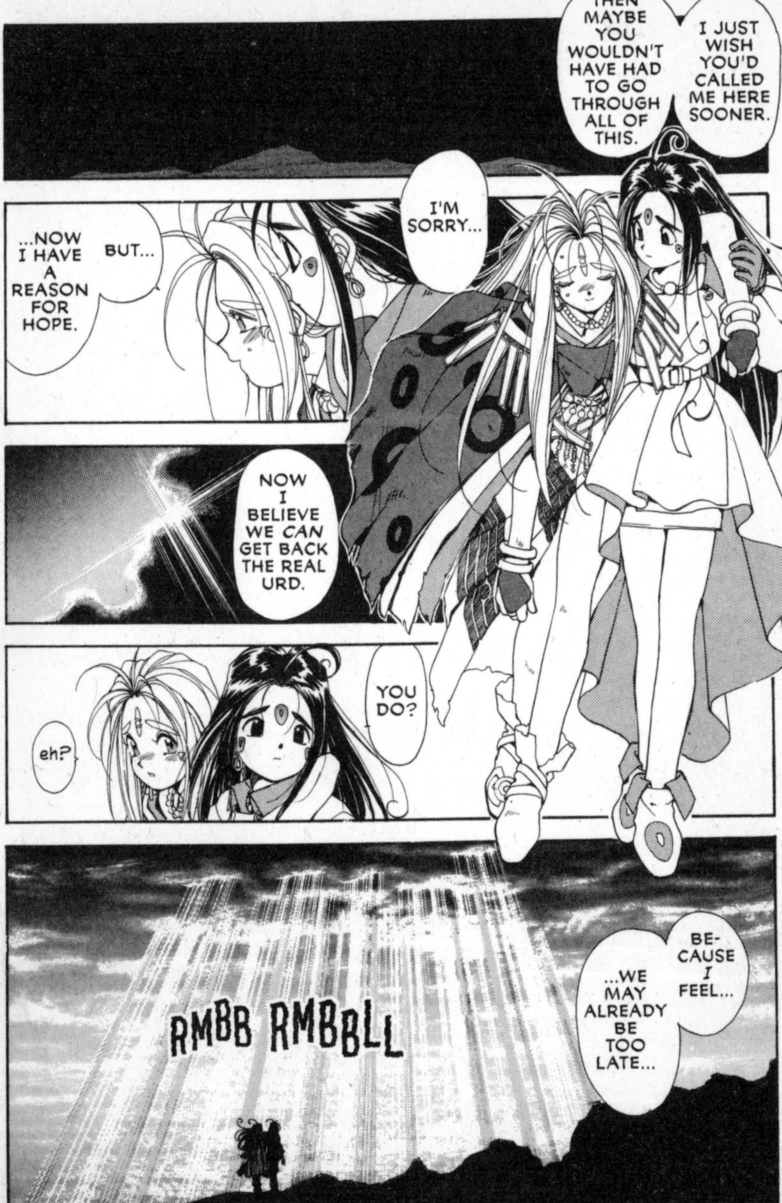
I JUST WISH YOU'D CALLED ME HERE SOONER.
THEN MAYBE YOU WOULDN'T HAVE HAD TO GO THROUGH ALL OF THIS.
I'M SORRY...
BUT...
...NOW I HAVE A REASON FOR HOPE.
NOW I BELIEVE WE *CAN* GET BACK THE REAL URD.
YOU DO?
eh?
BE-CAUSE *I* FEEL...
...WE MAY ALREADY BE TOO LATE...
RMBB RMBBLL

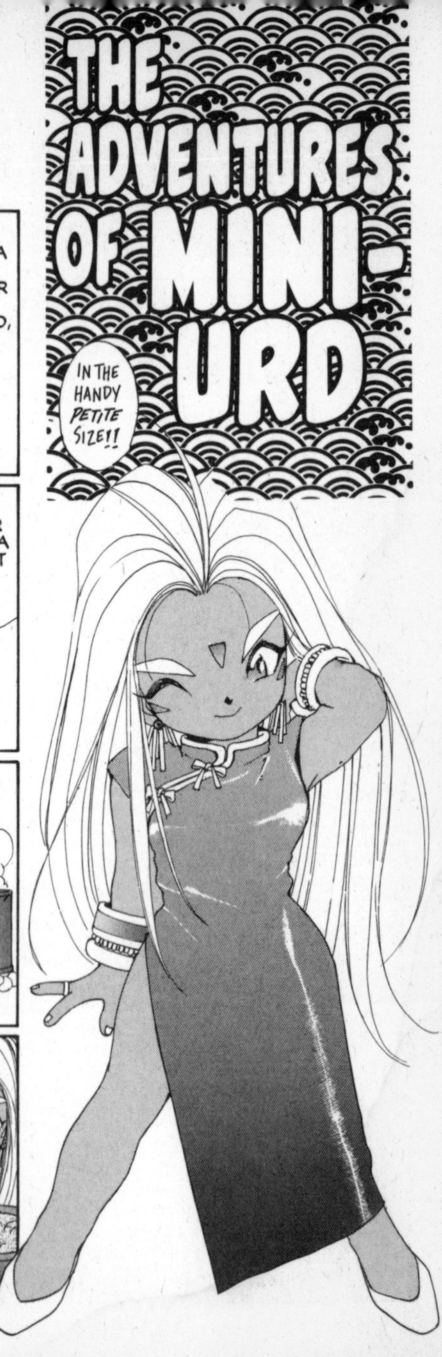
THE ADVENTURES OF MINI-URD
IN THE HANDY PETITE SIZE!!

◆ HEALTH CARE ◆

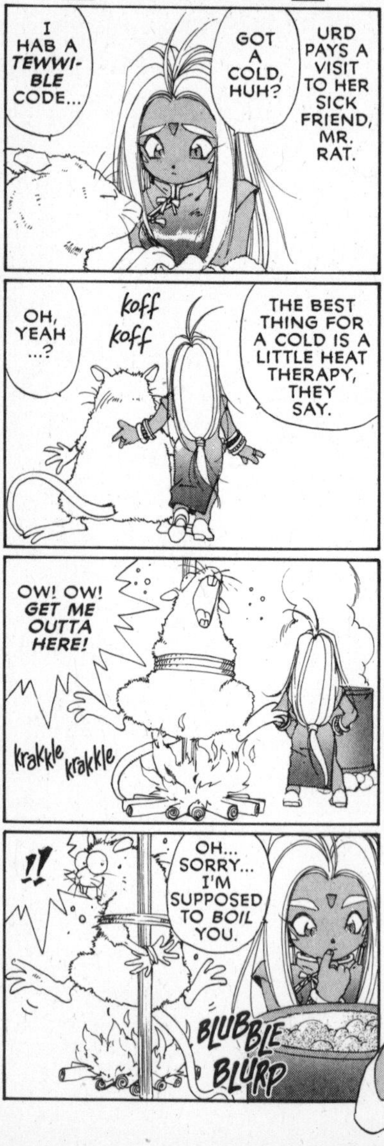
URD PAYS A VISIT TO HER SICK FRIEND, MR. RAT.
GOT A COLD, HUH?
I HAB A TEWWIBLE CODE...
THE BEST THING FOR A COLD IS A LITTLE HEAT THERAPY, THEY SAY.
koff koff
OH, YEAH ...?
OW! OW! GET ME OUTTA HERE!
krakkle krakkle
OH... SORRY... I'M SUPPOSED TO BOIL YOU.
!!
BLUBBLE BLURP

## COLD MEDICINE

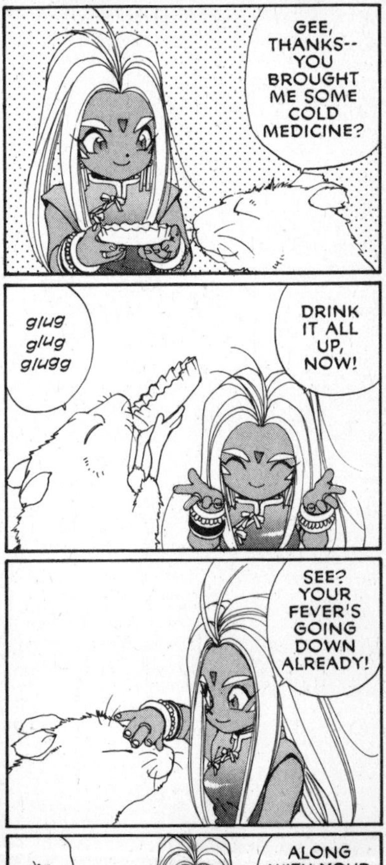
GEE, THANKS-- YOU BROUGHT ME SOME COLD MEDICINE?
DRINK IT ALL UP, NOW!
glug glug glugg
SEE? YOUR FEVER'S GOING DOWN ALREADY!
ALONG WITH YOUR HEART RATE, BLOOD PRESSURE, RESPIRATION...
h-help me...

## STOMACH MEDICINE

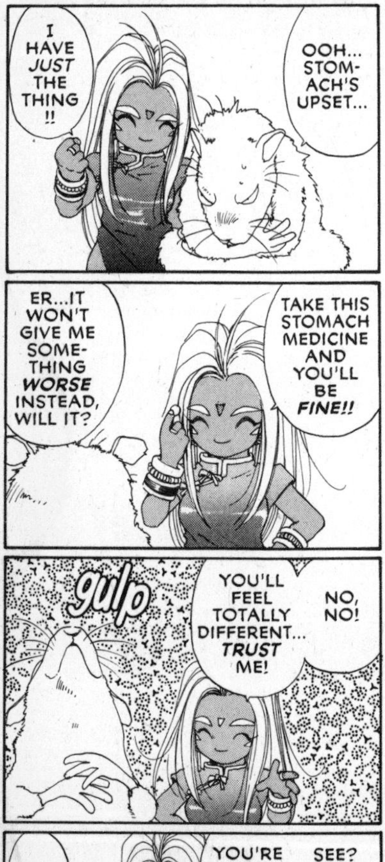
OOH... STOMACH'S UPSET...
I HAVE *JUST* THE THING!!
TAKE THIS STOMACH MEDICINE AND YOU'LL BE ***FINE!!***
ER...IT WON'T GIVE ME SOMETHING ***WORSE*** INSTEAD, WILL IT?
NO, NO!
YOU'LL FEEL TOTALLY DIFFERENT... ***TRUST*** ME!
gulp
SEE? NOW YOU *ARE* A STOMACH!
YOU'RE NOT STILL UPSET, ARE YOU?
...!

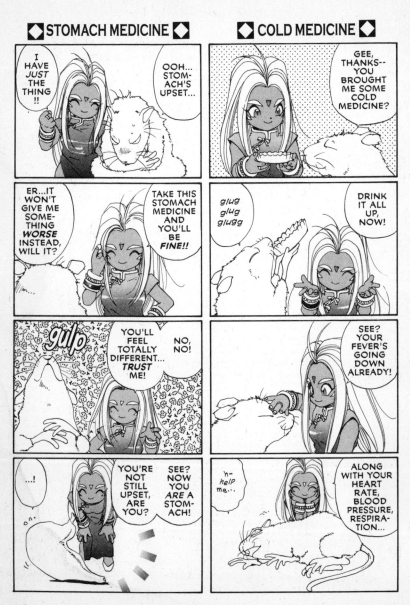

## THE GREAT SLUG RACE

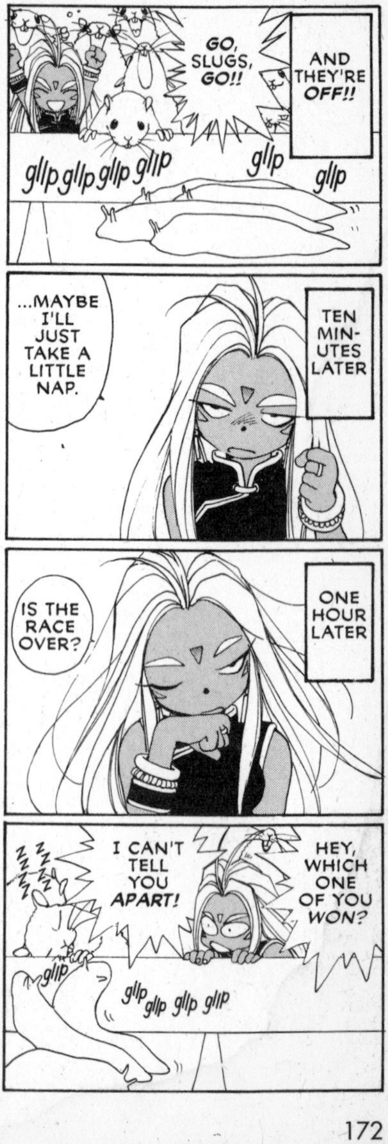
AND THEY'RE *OFF!!*
GO, SLUGS, *GO!!*
glip glip glip glip glip glip
TEN MIN-UTES LATER
...MAYBE I'LL JUST TAKE A LITTLE NAP.
ONE HOUR LATER
IS THE RACE OVER?
HEY, WHICH ONE OF YOU *WON?*
I CAN'T TELL YOU *APART!*
Z Z Z
glip
glip glip glip glip

## THE GREAT CRICKET RACE

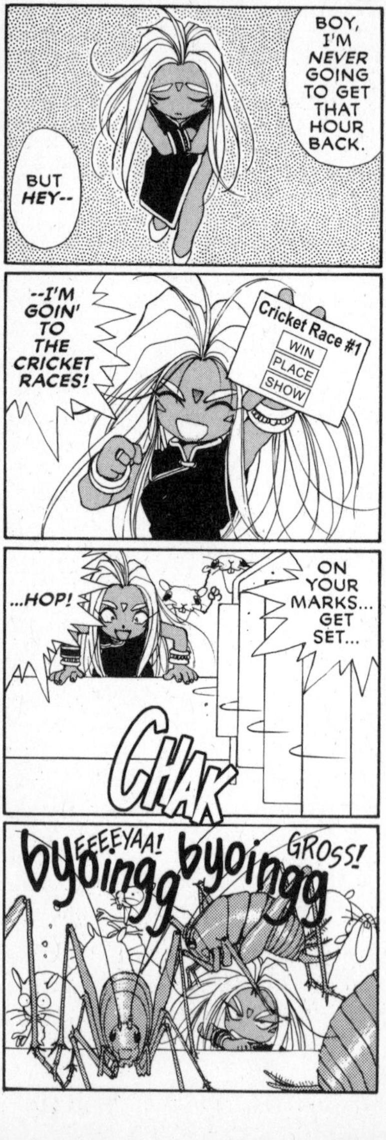
BOY, I'M *NEVER* GOING TO GET THAT HOUR BACK.
BUT *HEY--*
Cricket Race #1
WIN
PLACE
SHOW
*--I'M GOIN' TO THE CRICKET RACES!*
ON YOUR MARKS... GET SET...
...HOP!
CHAK
GROSS!
byoingg byoingg
EEEEYAA!

# COMING SOON!

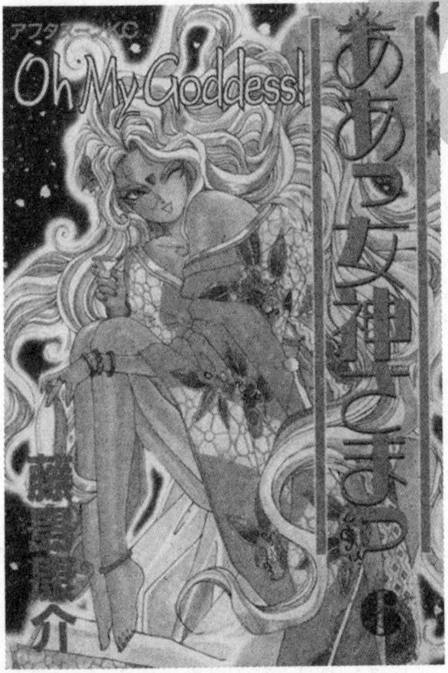
Oh My Goddess!

VOLUME 6
ISBN: 1-84576-509-5
ISBN-13: 978-1-84576-509-5

# ALSO AVAILABLE

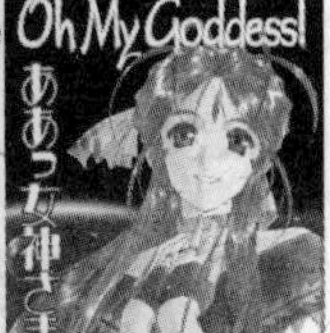
Oh My Goddess!
ああっ女神さまっ
藤島康介

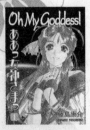

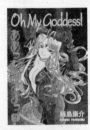

VOLUME 1
ISBN: 1-84576-485-4
ISBN-13: 978-1-84576-485-2

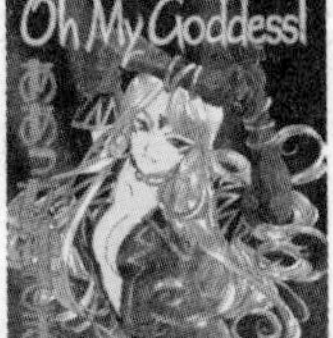
Oh My Goddess!
藤島康介

VOLUME 2
ISBN: 1-84576-486-2
ISBN-13: 978-1-84576-486-9

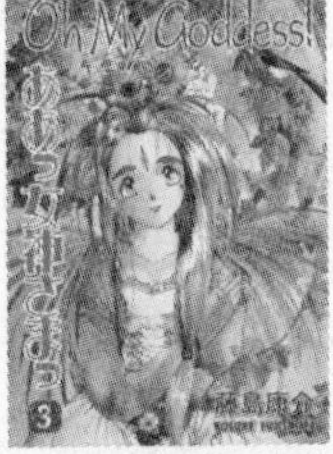
Oh My Goddess!
藤島康介

VOLUME 3
ISBN: 1-84576-504-4
ISBN-13: 978-1-84576-504-0

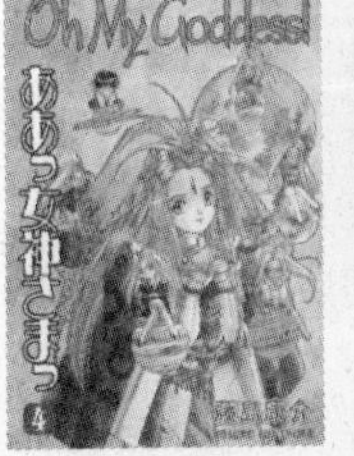
Oh My Goddess!
藤島康介

VOLUME 4
ISBN: 1-84576-505-2
ISBN-13: 978-1-84576-505-7

## Creator Kosuke Fujishima in 1991!

### His message to fans in the original Japanese *Oh My Goddess!* Vol. 5:

*"Mwa-ha-ha! I am Doctor F. Jesheema!! In order to realize my plans of taking of the world (the world), I will modify this rabbit, and all will witness the unstoppable beast, Kaiju 7700i!! You should be afraid—shaking in your boots . . . Which is what I had originally conceptualized right here and got dressed up for it, but the cameraman basically threw in the towel on this scheme. To be honest, though, I had basically resigned this gimmick even earlier than he did (but guess what? I'm gonna give this same gimmick a crack the next time around!!)."*

original series editor
# CARL GUSTAV HORN

us collection designer
# SCOTT COOK

us art director
# LIA RIBACCHI

us publisher
# MIKE RICHARDSON

This edition published by TITAN BOOKS

English-language version produced by
DARK HORSE COMICS

OH MY GODDESS!
VOLUME FIVE

ISBN-10: 1-84576-506-0
ISBN-13: 978-1-84576-506-4

First published October 2007
1 3 5 7 9 10 8 6 4 2

www.titanbooks.com

Please email us at: *readerfeedback@titanemail.com*

A CIP catalogue record for this title is
available at the British Library

Printed in Lithuania

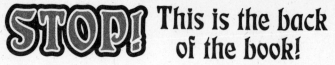

# STOP! This is the back of the book!

This manga collection is translated into English, but arranged in right-to-left reading format to maintain the artwork's visual orientation as originally drawn and published in Japan. If you've never read comics this way before, take a look at the diagram below to give yourself an idea of how to go about it. Basically, you'll be starting in the upper right-hand corner, and will read each word balloon and panel moving right-to-left. It may take a little getting used to, but you should get the hang of it very quickly. Have fun! If this is the millionth manga you've read this way, never mind. ^_^

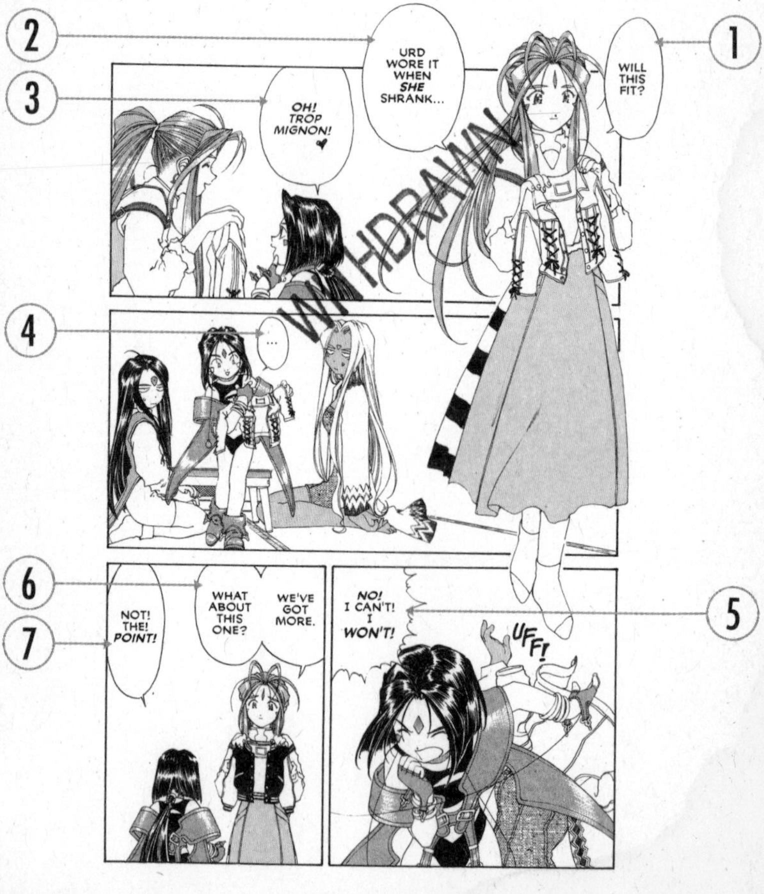
1
WILL THIS FIT?
2
URD WORE IT WHEN SHE SHRANK...
3
OH! TROP MIGNON!
4
...
5
NO! I CAN'T! I WON'T!
UFF!
6
WE'VE GOT MORE.
WHAT ABOUT THIS ONE?
7
NOT! THE! POINT!